Bess of Hardwick's Letters

Bess of Hardwick's Letters is the first book-length study of the c. 250 letters to and from the remarkable Elizabethan dynast, matriarch and builder of houses Bess of Hardwick (c. 1527–1608). By surveying the complete correspondence, author Alison Wiggins uncovers the wide range of uses to which Bess put letters: they were vital to her engagement in the overlapping realms of politics, patronage, business, legal negotiation, news-gathering and domestic life. Much more than a case study of Bess's letters, the discussions of language, handwriting and materiality found here have fundamental implications for the way we approach and read Renaissance letters. Wiggins offers readings which show how Renaissance letters communicated meaning through the interweaving linguistic, palaeographic and material forms, according to socio-historical context and function. The study goes beyond the letters themselves and incorporates a range of historical sources to situate circumstances of production and reception, which include Account Books, inventories, needlework and textile art and architecture. The study is therefore essential reading for scholars in historical linguistics, historical pragmatics, palaeography and manuscript studies, material culture, English literature and social history.

Alison Wiggins is Senior Lecturer in English Language at the University of Glasgow, UK.

Material Readings in Early Modern Culture

Series editor

James Daybell
Plymouth University, UK

and

Adam Smyth
Balliol College, University of Oxford, UK

The series provides a forum for studies that consider the material forms of texts as part of an investigation into the culture of early modern England. The editors invite proposals of a multi- or interdisciplinary nature, and particularly welcome proposals that combine archival research with an attention to theoretical models that might illuminate the reading, writing and making of texts, as well as projects that take innovative approaches to the study of material texts, both in terms of the kinds of primary materials under investigation and in terms of methodologies. What are the questions that have yet to be asked about writing in its various possible embodied forms? Are there varieties of materiality that are critically neglected? How does form mediate and negotiate content? In what ways do the physical features of texts inform how they are read, interpreted and situated?

Recent in this series:

The Age of Thomas Nashe
Text, Bodies and Trespasses of Authorship in Early Modern England
Edited by Stephen Guy-Bray, Joan Pong Linton, and Steve Mentz

Ovidian Bibliofictions and the Tudor Book
Metamorphosing Classical Heroines in Late Medieval and
Renaissance England
Lindsay Ann Reid

Manuscript Miscellanies in Early Modern England
Edited by Joshua Eckhardt and Daniel Starza Smith

Tottel's *Songes and Sonettes* in Context
Edited by Stephen Hamrick

The Elizabethan Top Ten
Defining Print Popularity in Early Modern England
Edited by Andy Kesson and Emma Smith

Bess of Hardwick's Letters
Language, Materiality and
Early Modern Epistolary Culture

Alison Wiggins

LONDON AND NEW YORK

Arts & Humanities
Research Council

First published 2017
by Routledge
2 Park Square, Milton Park, Abingdon, Oxon OX14 4RN

and by Routledge
711 Third Avenue, New York, NY 10017

Routledge is an imprint of the Taylor & Francis Group,
an informa business

© 2017 Alison Wiggins

The right of Alison Wiggins to be identified as author of this work
has been asserted by her in accordance with sections 77 and 78 of the
Copyright, Designs and Patents Act 1988.

All rights reserved. No part of this book may be reprinted or
reproduced or utilised in any form or by any electronic, mechanical,
or other means, now known or hereafter invented, including
photocopying and recording, or in any information storage or
retrieval system, without permission in writing from the publishers.

Trademark notice: Product or corporate names may be trademarks
or registered trademarks, and are used only for identification and
explanation without intent to infringe.

British Library Cataloguing in Publication Data
A catalogue record for this book is available from the British Library

Library of Congress Cataloging in Publication Data
Names: Wiggins, Alison, 1974– author.
Title: Bess of Hardwick's letters : language, materiality, and early
    modern epistolary culture / by Alison Wiggins.
Description: New York : Routledge, 2017. | Series: Material readings
    in early modern culture | Includes bibliographical references and index.
Identifiers: LCCN 2016026062 | ISBN 9781409461296 (alk. paper) |
    ISBN 9781315569079 (ebk)
Subjects: LCSH: English letters—History and criticism. | Letter
    writing—England—History—16th century. | Shrewsbury, Elizabeth
    Hardwick Talbot, Countess of, 1527?–1608—Correspondence. |
    Women and literature—England—History—16th century. |
    England—Social life and customs—16th century.
Classification: LCC PR913 .W54 2017 | DDC 826/.3—dc23
LC record available at https://lccn.loc.gov/2016026062

ISBN: 978-1-409-46129-6 (hbk)
ISBN: 978-1-315-56907-9 (ebk)

Typeset in Sabon
by Apex CoVantage, LLC

Contents

List of plates	vii
Acknowledgements	x
Conventions	xiv
Abbreviations	xvi

Introduction	1

1 Composing and scripting letters — 27

1.1 *'Sett downe the matter plainly': situating epistolary composition within the genre of early modern letter-writing* 27

1.2 *'As yf she were my owne and only chyld': a letter of petition to Sir Francis Walsingham written on behalf of her granddaughter Arbella Stuart, 1582* 62

1.3 *'I am the furst innosent wyffe, that euar was so very extremly vsed in thys realme, god make me the last': a letter to her estranged husband the earl of Shrewsbury written during their marital discord, 1585* 68

1.4 *'My good sweete daughter . . . blesse you deare harte': a letter to her daughter Mary, countess of Shrewsbury, 1607* 80

2 Reading and writing letters — 89

2.1 *'A little deske to write on guilded': situating epistolary production within textual cultures at Hardwick Hall, c. 1601* 89

2.2 *'Your honour's hand': autograph writing and Bess of Hardwick's idiolect* 106

vi   *Contents*

2.3 *'I am not able nowe to write . . . with my owne
hande': scribal writing and idiolects   120*

2.4 *Letters from 'the palace of the sky': Bess of
Hardwick's signature   137*

3   Sending and receiving letters   142

3.1 *'Geven to one that brought a letter': situating
epistolary reception within early modern postal
and delivery networks   142*

3.2 *'Delyver therwith vnto him, so great thankes & good
wordes as yow can devyse': letters with bearers   161*

3.3 *'A note that came with the stuff': letters with
enclosures   173*

3.4 *'Hauinge no betar menes to manifast mi thanckefolnes':
letters with floss and accordion folds   186*

Conclusions   194

Bibliography   199
Index   219

Plates

1   Bess of Hardwick (Lady Cavendish), by an unknown artist, c. 1555–57, oil on panel, at Hardwick Hall, Derbyshire. The painting was later incorrectly inscribed 'Mary Tudor'. © National Trust Images/Angelo Hornak.

2   Bess of Hardwick (dowager countess of Shrewsbury), c. 1590, oil on canvas, unknown artist. © National Portrait Gallery, London.

3   Hardwick New Hall, Derbyshire, seen from the East Court part of the garden. © National Trust Images/Andrew Butler.

4   Hardwick New Hall, rooftop pavilions, 1590–97, which feature the 'ES' initials of Elizabeth, countess of Shrewsbury, surmounted by a countess's coronet. Author's own image.

5   Embroidered red velvet panel bearing the 'ES' monogram of Elizabeth, countess of Shrewsbury. © National Trust Images/John Hammond.

6   Velvet panel with padded applique of cloth of gold and silver showing the Hardwick crest, which features the Cavendish stag and 'ES' monogram. © National Trust Images/John Hammond.

7   Detail from Bess of Hardwick's tomb designed by Robert Smythson in 1603, All Saints Parish church, Derby, now Derby Cathedral, featuring the Hardwick Cross: an heraldic symbol with a saltire engrailed, in chief three eglantines, surmounted by a countess's coronet. Author's own image.

8   Detail of Penelope in the wall hanging of Penelope flanked by Perseverance and Paciens in the Museum Rooms at Hardwick Hall, Derbyshire. © National Trust Images/Andreas von Einsiedel.

9   Letter from Bess (Lady Cavendish) to her servant Francis Whitfield, 14 November [1552], sent, in her own hand, slit-and-band letter packet. Folger CT, X.d.428 (82), ID 99. By permission of the Folger Shakespeare Library.

10   Letter from Bess (countess of Shrewsbury) to Robert Dudley, earl of Leicester, 21 January 1569, sent, in her own hand, slit-and band letter packet. Magdalene College Library, Pepys, MS 2503, pp. 203–6 (image of p. 203), ID 107. By permission of the Pepys Library, Magdalene College Cambridge.

viii *Plates*

11 Letter from George Talbot, sixth earl of Shrewsbury, to his wife Bess (countess of Shrewsbury) [c. 1571], sent, in his own hand, tuck-and-fold letter packet. Folger CT, X.d.428 (92), ID 70. By permission of the Folger Shakespeare Library.

12 Letter from Elizabeth (Cavendish) Stuart, countess of Lennox, to her mother, Bess (countess of Shrewsbury) [1574?], sent, in her own hand. The letter packet (shown) was accordion folded and locked with a red wax seal embossed with the Lennox Stuart arms over goldish-ochre coloured silk floss. Folger CT, X.d.428 (50), ID 41. By permission of the Folger Shakespeare Library.

13 Letter from Bess (countess of Shrewsbury) to her husband George Talbot, sixth earl of Shrewsbury [1577], sent, in her own hand, tuck-and-fold letter packet. The letter covers three sides of paper and the image shows the final page with the postscript. LPL, Talbot Papers, MS 3205, fols 66r–67v (image of fol. 67r), ID 182. By permission of Lambeth Palace Library.

14 Letter from George Talbot, sixth earl of Shrewsbury, with a postscript by his wife Bess (countess of Shrewsbury), to William Cecil, Lord Burghley, 14 May 1578, sent, in their own hands, slit-and-band letter packet. LPL, Talbot Papers, MS 3206, fol. 885, ID 188. By permission of Lambeth Palace Library.

15 Letter from Bess (countess of Shrewsbury) to Sir Francis Walsingham, 6 May 1582, sent, letter in the hand of Scribe A, signed in her own hand. TNA, SP 12/153, fol. 84r-84v (item 39) (image of fol. 84vr), ID 145. By permission of The National Archives.

16 Letter from Bess (dowager countess of Shrewsbury) to Walter Bagot, 14 April [1600?], sent, letter and subscription in the hand of a secretary, signature and postscript in her own hand, tuck-and-fold letter packet. Folger Bagot, L.a.844, ID 2. By permission of the Folger Shakespeare Library.

17 Letter from Bess (dowager countess of Shrewsbury) to Elizabeth I, 29 January 1603, sent, letter in the hand of Timothy Pusey, split subscription in the hand of Scribe B, signed in her own hand. The tuck-and-fold letter packet was locked with a red wax seal embossed with Bess's arms that feature the Hardwick cross (Plate 7). CP 135/127, fols 165–6 (image of fol. 165r), ID 129. By permission of the Marquess of Salisbury.

18 Letter from Bess (dowager countess of Shrewsbury) to Sir Julius Caesar, 31 January 1604, sent, letter in the hand of Scribe D, subscription in the hand of Scribe B, signed in her own hand, tuck-and-fold letter packet. Cover image. BL, Add. 12506, fols 209r-10v (image of fol. 209r), ID 161. © The British Library Board Add. 12506, f209.

19 Letter from Henry Cavendish to his mother, Bess (dowager countess of Shrewsbury), 31 December 1605, sent, in his own hand. The tuck-and-fold letter packet was locked with a red wax seal embossed

Plates ix

with the Cavendish arms that feature three bucks heads cabossed. Folger CT, X.d.428 (11), ID 11. By permission of the Folger Shakespeare Library.

20 Letter from Thomas Howard, earl of Arundel, to his grandmother-in-law Bess (dowager countess of Shrewsbury), 25 May [1607], sent, in his own hand. The letter packet (shown) was accordion folded, locked with two red wax seals, with arms embossed over pinkish-plum coloured ribbon. Folger CT, X.d.428 (1), ID 3. By permission of the Folger Shakespeare Library.

21 Letter from Bess (dowager countess of Shrewsbury) to her son-in-law and stepson Gilbert Talbot and her daughter Mary (Cavendish) Talbot, seventh earl and countess of Shrewsbury, 15 January [1606], sent, the letter and postscript are in the hand of Scribe A, the signature and initials after the postscript in her own hand, tuck-and-fold letter packet. LPL, Talbot Papers, MS 3205, fols 62r-63v (image of fol. 62r), ID 180. By permission of Lambeth Palace Library.

22 Letter from Bess (dowager countess of Shrewsbury) to her daughter Mary (Cavendish) Talbot, seventh countess of Shrewsbury, 30 November 1607, sent, hand of Scribe A, signed in her own hand, tuck-and-fold letter packet. LPL, Talbot Papers, MS 3205, fols 59r-60v (image of fol. 59r), ID 179. By permission of Lambeth Palace Library.

Acknowledgements

The ideas and arguments presented in this book have been tested out and developed at conferences, research seminars and workshops. I am grateful to have had these opportunities to engage in discussion with colleagues at: the Research Unit for Variation, Contacts and Change in English, University of Helsinki, Finland, August 2007; AHRC *Centre for Editing Lives and Letters* Director's Seminar, Queen Mary University of London, November 2008; AHRC *Scriptorium* project Sustaining Digital Resources in the Humanities Symposium, University of Cambridge, July 2009; Mellon *Summer Institute in Vernacular Palaeography*, and the *Teaching Palaeography Workshop*, Folger Shakespeare Library, Washington DC, July and December 2009; HATII Research Seminar, University of Glasgow, 2009–11; RSA annual meeting SHARP *Letters of the Rich and/or Famous* panel, Venice, Italy, April 2010; MEMS Research Seminar, University of Newcastle, April 2010; *Cultures of Correspondence in Early Modern Britain, 1550–1640* Colloquium, University of Aberdeen, July 2010; Edinburgh Book History Seminar, Centre for the History of the Book, University of Edinburgh, November 2010; School of English Research Seminar, Queen's University Belfast, December 2010; RSA annual meeting AHRC *Editing and Unediting Bess of Hardwick's Letters* panel, Montreal, Canada, March 2011; *Cultures of Correspondence in Early Modern Britain, 1550–1640* Conference, Plymouth University, April 2011; Mellon *Cultures of Knowledge* Third Seminar Series, University of Oxford, 2012; *Reading Early Modern Studies Conference, Editing Women* panel, University of Reading, July 2012; *Historical Documents in the Digital Age Workshop* for the EU DocExplore Project, University of Rouen, France, October 2012; The National Archives *Public Lecture Series*, Kew, November 2012; *(Re)Presenting the Archive Symposium*, Humanities Research Institute, University of Sheffield, May 2013; *Gender and Political Culture, 1400–1800* Conference, *Women's Early Modern Letters Online Workshop*, Plymouth University, August 2013; *From Correspondence to Corpora* Conference, University of Helsinki, Finland, November 2013; and the *Huntington Library / University of Southern California Early Modern British History Seminar*, Huntington Library, California, February 2014. For invitations to speak and for stimulating questions and discussions, on

Acknowledgements xi

these or other occasions, I am especially grateful to Robyn Adams, Nadine Akkerman, Gavin Alexander, Kenneth Austin, Richard Beadle, Bill Bell, Judith Bennett, Erin Blake, Jan Broadway, James Brown, Christopher Burlinson, James Daybell, Alice Eardley, Mel Evans, Susan Frye, Andrew Gordon, Cynthia Herrup, Jonathan Hope, Howard Hotson, Lisa Jardine, Samuli Kaislaniemi, Lynne Magnusson, Katy Mair, Joseph Marshall, Steven May, Kim McLean-Fiander, Michael Moss, Terttu Nevalainen, Ryan Perry, Mike Pincombe, Anne Lake Prescott, Catherine Richardson, Fred Schurink, Cathy Shrank, Alan Stewart, John Thompson, Michael Ullyot, Angus Vine, Heather Wolfe and Andrew Zurcher.

The research into primary sources for this book has involved spending time at fifteen different libraries, archives and repositories. I am grateful for access to materials at each of these locations and for the guidance provided to me by staff who have been generous with their time and expertise. Over one hundred of the letters, as well as Account Books and other relevant materials, are held at the Folger Shakespeare Library, Washington DC, and a huge debt of gratitude goes to Heather Wolfe and staff there who answered questions and provided support in 2009 when I spent time at the library to undertake and check transcriptions and to record the physical features of the letters. The remaining letters and documents are spread across eighteen different locations (two are at unknown locations in private ownership, accessed as photographs). It is with thanks to the staff at these locations that I was able to undertake and check transcriptions and record the physical features of letters at: Arundel Castle; the British Library; Cambridge University Library; Chatsworth House; Hatfield House; the Huntington Library, California; Keele University Library; Lambeth Palace Library; Longleat House; Magdalene College, Cambridge; National Library of Scotland, Edinburgh; Nottingham University Library Special Collections; Sheffield Archives; The National Archives, Kew. The supply of images or permission to take photographs for personal use, and in some cases permission for publication, has been important to this research and I thank staff at each of these locations and at the NT and NPG for advice and assistance with such matters. In particular, I thank Steph Eeles, Phillipa Granger, Kate Harris, Paul Johnson, Jenny Liddle, Katy Mair, Andrew Peppit, Vicki Perry, Mary Robertson, Catherine Sutherland, Sarah Whale, Vanessa Wilkie and Robin Harcourt Williams. I thank the Marquess of Bath, the Duke and Duchess of Devonshire, the Duke of Norfolk, the Marquess of Salisbury and the master and fellows of Magdalene College Cambridge for permission to view and transcribe manuscripts. I would like to extend thanks to Philip Riden for our conversations when we met at Chatsworth House. I am grateful to David Durant for his kind interest and for allowing me permission to access his personal archive of box-file cards now held at Nottingham University Library. As I was not able to visit the Parker Library at Corpus Christi College, Cambridge, the letter has been accessed via *Parker on the Web*. As I was not able to visit the letters at Belvoir Castle, I am grateful to

xii *Acknowledgements*

Peter Foden and the Duke and Duchess of Rutland for supply of and permission to use high-quality images.

This research was enabled with the financial support of the UK Arts and Humanities Research Council (AHRC). In 2009 I was awarded an AHRC Research Grants Scheme Award for a project to produce an online edition of Bess of Hardwick's letters, on which I was principal investigator at the University of Glasgow. The award enabled me to travel to archives and libraries during 2009–12, to collaborate with Kathy Rogers at the University of Sheffield HRI, and to work with four postdoctoral research associates, employed successively, part-time or full-time, at the University of Glasgow, each for a portion of the 36-month project: Alan Bryson, Daniel Starza Smith, Anke Timmermann and Graham Williams. The project included two doctoral students, Imogen Marcus funded by the AHRC and Felicity Maxwell funded by the Social Sciences and Humanities Research Council of Canada and the University of Glasgow's Overseas Research Scholarship. I am grateful to all six for their enthusiasm, collegiality, corrections to my knowledge, helpful references and varied insights. The outputs from the AHRC award are listed within the web edition at www.bessofhardwick.org and completed publications, projects and doctoral theses are cited ahead in the footnotes and bibliography to this book. The AHRC project held the exhibition *Unsealed: The Letters of Bess of Hardwick* (at NT property Hardwick Hall, 2011–12, led by Anke, which subsequently travelled to the TNA in 2013) and Graham, Felicity and I had the opportunity to run a workshop for NT volunteers, *Reading Bess of Hardwick's Letters*, in September 2011. I thank NT property manager Nigel Wright for his generosity and for sharing his knowledge about the property, and the NT volunteers for their warmth of interest and for organising the Tudor dance lesson in the High Great Chamber. I thank staff at the TNA, in particular the educational team and Katy Mair for her expertise and encouragement.

I am grateful to the editors and production team for their invaluable support while writing this book: Erika Gaffney at Ashgate and Liz Levine and Nicole Eno at Routledge. I thank the two anonymous reviewers of this book for their full, generous, supportive and helpful comments. I thank the series editors, James Daybell and Adam Smyth, for their continued interest and encouragement. I am very fortunate to have been writing this book while at the University of Glasgow. I thank the remarkable group of colleagues and students I have been working alongside day-to-day in the English Language subject area, who have been extremely supportive in numerous practical and intellectual ways. For their encouragement and many helpful conversations I am particularly thankful to Marc Alexander, Wendy Anderson, Kirstie Blair, Julie Gardham, Johanna Green, Geraldine Parsons, Andrew Prescott, Vicky Price, Bryony Randall, Beth Robertson, Andy Saunders, Alex Shepard, Jennifer Smith and Claire Squires. I am especially indebted, for their generous feedback, unfailing enthusiasm and occasional cajoling, to Katie Lowe and Jeremy Smith.

Acknowledgements xiii

As is the custom, the most important thanks come last, for their love and support, to my friends and family. For the inspiration they provide, I thank my oldest friends, Helen, Ruth, Cinnamon and Zoe. For all their fun and good company, I thank the friends I have made in Glasgow in recent years, in particular, Lizzie, Paul and Tim. For his kindness and resourcefulness, and for making me laugh every single day, I thank Alastair. This book is dedicated with gratitude to Cynthia, David, Mum and Dad.

Conventions

Letter ID numbers

Each letter to or from Bess of Hardwick is referred to in this book by its own allocated identification number, which corresponds to the identification number in the web edition of the letters: *Bess of Hardwick's Letters: The Complete Correspondence, c. 1550–1608*, ed. by Alison Wiggins, Alan Bryson, Daniel Starza Smith, Anke Timmermann and Graham Williams, University of Glasgow, web development by Katherine Rogers, University of Sheffield Humanities Research Institute (University of Glasgow, 2013; www.bessofhardwick.org). The first time a letter is cited in this book, its archive or library reference is given in full, followed by its allocated ID number; on subsequent citations only the ID number is given.

Transcription policy

The selection of letters presented in the following chapters has been newly transcribed and edited for this book, in a form suitable for print publication, as semi-diplomatic transcriptions. While allographic distinctions are not captured in the transcripts, many other original features of the language are because these are relevant to the analyses and findings presented here (which involve features such as spelling, punctuation, capitalisation and abbreviations). Therefore, original spelling and punctuation have been retained; contractions are expanded in italics; common abbreviations (e.g., L. for *Lordship*, la: for *ladyship*, w^t for *with* and y^t for *that*) are retained; the forms i/j and u/v are distinguished; fossil thorn (for 'th') is transcribed as 'y'; insertions are marked with ^^ and are in superscript; legible deletions are indicated using strikethrough; illegible deletions are indicated as [*deletion*].

Editorial annotations on the letter transcripts

Each transcript presented in this book has been marginally annotated to indicate the parts of the letter and the identities of scribes and to gloss hard words. Terminology for the various parts of an early modern letter is used as a guide to the reader and follows established conventions: superscription, subscription, signature, endorsement, postscript, annotation.[1] The term 'autograph writing' is used to refer to a part of a letter written in the sender's own hand; the term 'scribal writing' is used to refer to a part of the letter written not in the sender's own hand but by another person, such as a scribe, secretary or family member. The terms 'autograph letter' and 'holograph letter' have not generally been used in this book because these terms are not sufficiently precise in the case of the particular letters here under analysis (where the different parts of a single letter may be in various different hands). Each letter transcript records information about scribes and material features of particular interest, such as the use of ribbon, seals, accordion folding or space on the page. Dates are given in New Style.[2]

Bess of Hardwick's name

For the sake of clarity and coherence, the name 'Bess', or 'Bess of Hardwick', has been used followed by her status in brackets – for example: Bess (Lady Cavendish) or Bess (countess of Shrewsbury). The need to refer to Bess in this way is necessary partly because of the number of times she changed her name through her four marriages and widowhoods, and partly to avoid potential confusion with other women; for example, there is potential for confusion between Elizabeth, Lady Cavendish (i.e., Bess during her marriage to Sir William Cavendish), and her middle daughter Elizabeth Cavendish (later countess of Lennox); or between Elizabeth, sixth countess of Shrewsbury and then, after November 1590, dowager countess of Shrewsbury (i.e., Bess during her marriage to the sixth earl of Shrewsbury, and then her final widowhood, during which time she was also sometimes referred to as countess), and her youngest daughter, Mary, who became seventh countess of Shrewsbury in November 1590. 'Bess' is the name used by her most recent biographers and by which she is known to history; we also know, from her letters, that this was not a name later attributed to her, but one used during her own lifetime.[3]

1 Stewart and Wolfe, *Letterwriting*, pp. 206–9.
2 Cheney, *A Handbook*, pp. 17–20.
3 References to use of the name 'Bess' in her own lifetime are given in the Introduction at p. 14.

Abbreviations

BL	British Library, London
BL, Add.	British Library, Additional MS
BL, Lansd.	British Library, Lansdowne MS
CP	Cecil Papers, Hatfield House, Hertfordshire
CUL	Cambridge University Library
Folger Bagot	Folger Shakespeare Library, Washington DC, Bagot Family Papers
Folger CT	Folger Shakespeare Library, Washington DC, Cavendish-Talbot Papers
HMC	Historical Manuscripts Commission
HTOED	*Historical Thesaurus of the Oxford English Dictionary*
ID	Letter identification number from *Bess of Hardwick's Letters: The Complete Correspondence, c. 1550–1608*, ed. by Alison Wiggins, Alan Bryson, Daniel Starza Smith, Anke Timmermann and Graham Williams, University of Glasgow, with web development by Katherine Rogers, University of Sheffield Humanities Research Institute (University of Glasgow, 2013), www.bessofhardwick.org
LPL	Lambeth Palace Library, London
MM	Mapping Metaphor with the Historical Thesaurus, *Metaphor Map of English*, Glasgow: University of Glasgow, 2015 mappingmetaphor.arts.gla.ac.uk
MS (pl. MSS)	Manuscript
NPG	National Portrait Gallery
NT	National Trust
ODNB	*Oxford Dictionary of National Biography*
OED	*Oxford English Dictionary*
Parker	Corpus Christi College Cambridge, Parker Library
SP	State Papers
SP 12	The National Archives, State Papers Domestic, Elizabeth
SP 53	The National Archives, State Papers Scotland, Mary, Queen of Scots
TNA	The National Archives (formerly the Public Record Office), Kew

Introduction

This book is a study of letter-writing. Its main source is the set of letters to and from Bess of Hardwick that were handwritten between the 1550s and 1608, which are extraordinary for the variety of activities they document, their breadth of social contacts and their range of interpersonal functions. So while the focus chosen illuminates the letter-writing activities of one individual, at the same time, the materials that have been selected give us a remarkably wide-ranging view of letters written in English in this period. The book examines not only the substantive content of the letters but also the modes and methods by which they were composed, written and read. It is concerned with the visual and material features of the letters, and the processes of their production and reception, but also with the services provided by scribes and bearers. It is concerned with the constellation of forms of handwriting across the letters, by an array of scribes, senders and secretaries, and the associated varieties of English that appear. It is concerned with the forms of language, but also with how these formal features functioned to textualise relationships, encode relative status and construct identities, as well as the potentials and the limitations offered for the expression of emotion. It is concerned with situating the letters within their precise historical moments, but also with their archival afterlives and their treatment (sometimes specious) by later editors. As the letters extended across almost sixty years, they offer a view from different vantage points over a lifetime. The focus is sometimes on events that were remarkable and dramatic and that take us into the heart of Elizabethan political culture, but at other times on the ordinary, routine and everyday. As the letters were written from a series of households, they existed alongside other literate cultures and communities and this book is concerned to position epistolary writing on a continuum with these. This book is concerned with the meanings of material culture, the intersection of gender and genre, the negotiation of interpersonal relationships, and the interrelations between scribal cultures and varieties of early modern English. As such, it incorporates insights generated through the deployment of a range of approaches, material, linguistic and palaeographic, which are brought to bear upon the early modern letter.

2 Introduction

Context and overview

Bess of Hardwick's 242 existing letters constitute the largest and most wide-ranging correspondence for a non-royal woman from Tudor England. This book assesses the place of the letters in her life, their language and handwriting, their production and reception, their physical forms and material features. A handful of individual letters – or, at least, certain quotations from them – are well known as they have been repeatedly cited within the biographical tradition, and this 'greatest hits' of the letters has been appropriated to support different biographical portrayals of Bess.[1] Apart from these extracted 'highlights', the remainder of the letters is far less well known and is typically cited from inaccurate eighteenth- and nineteenth-century transcripts, in which we find their voices blended with an editor's voice.[2] That there has been no previous full-length study of the letters, despite their intrinsic interest, is likely due to a number of factors. We could cite here among these factors: the scattered distribution of the letters across nineteen archives, libraries and repositories; the notorious difficulty of decoding the handwriting of certain of Bess's correspondents; or the problems earlier commentators had interpreting the language or finding interest in the letters as anything more than repositories for nuggets of 'factual' information.[3] However, within the past two decades, three developments in particular have made it possible to move beyond these earlier problems and have enabled this current study. First, we have seen the emergence of women's letter-writing as a the field of study within its own right, inaugurated by the publication in 2006 of James Daybell's *Women Letter-Writers in Tudor England* and followed by a series of further studies that have forcefully demarcated the value and interest of women's letters and set out a range of methods for their analysis.[4] Second, we have seen the burgeoning interest in the materiality of epistolary culture superbly displayed, in 2004, by the Folger Shakespeare Library exhibition and catalogue by Alan Stewart and

---

1 Mair, 'Anne, Lady Bacon', makes a similar point about the afterlife and use of the letters of Anne, Lady Bacon.

2 The 'forging' of a hybrid voice is discussed by Trigg, 'Speaking with the Dead', in relation to editions of Middle English texts.

3 The very bad handwriting of Bess's fourth husband the earl of Shrewsbury, Plates 11 and 14, is discussed by Williams, '"My Evil Favoured Writing"'. Bess's most recent biographer describes the difficulties she had reading the primary sources, admitting that she found them 'impossible fully to decipher'; Lovell, *Bess of Hardwick*, p. xviii; the sources for the letters that Lovell quotes from in her biography are the eighteenth- and nineteenth-century selections edited by Lodge, *Illustrations*, and Hunter, *Hallamshire*.

4 Daybell's 2006 monograph was anticipated by his 2001 edited collection, *Early Modern Women's Letter Writing*, that brings together essays by, among others, Sara Jayne Steen, Alison Wall and Susan E. Whyman, whose publications on Arbella Stuart, the Thynne women and the Verney family have a key place in the field.

Heather Wolfe, *Letterwriting in Renaissance England*, but perhaps inaugurated in the 1990s by two seminal articles on the meaning of space and spatial layout in letters by A. R. Braumuller and Jonathan Gibson. This pair of articles was followed by a series of further studies that have altogether transformed our understanding of handwritten letters.[5] Third, we have seen the publication of new scholarly editions of women's letters that, as well as opening up these materials for analysis, have compellingly demonstrated their historical value.[6] Most immediately relevant to this book has been the publication in 2013 of the web edition of *Bess of Hardwick's Letters: The Complete Correspondence, c. 1550–1608*, the result of an AHRC-funded project, that has provided open access to the letters accompanied by scholarly apparatus.[7] Furthermore, and directly associated with each of these three developments, has been the flourishing of several overlapping communities of researchers into early modern letters, for purposes of scholarly exchange across fields and between disciplines. In particular, the *Centre for Editing Lives and Letters*, *Corpus of Early English Correspondence* Project, *Cultures of Correspondence* Project, *Women's Early Modern Letters Online* Project, *Letter-locking* Project and the Folger Shakespeare Library Palaeography Workshops have each served as important focal points during recent years for the development of research into early modern letters, and for the exchange of ideas across disciplinary perspectives, to which this study is indebted.[8]

The argument of this book is that Bess of Hardwick's letters have been repeatedly underestimated in the past and that through their reassessment we can produce more detailed and accurate insights into Bess's life but also into her society and early modern epistolary culture. Furthermore, the argument made here is that the complex form of the early modern letter best rewards interdisciplinary analysis, and the chapters that follow are underpinned by approaches and techniques from historical, linguistic, literary, palaeographic and manuscript studies. Each of these approaches has advantages for particular aspects of the letter and enables precise analyses

---

5 Braumuller, 'Accounting for Absence', Gibson, 'Significant Space'. Especially prominent among other publications are the book-length studies by Daybell, *The Material Letter*, and Stewart, *Shakespeare's Letters*, and the articles by Wolfe, '"Neatly Sealed"' and 'Women's Handwriting'.

6 These include the recent notable editions by Akkerman, *The Correspondence of Elizabeth Stuart, Queen of Bohemia*, Allen, *The Letters of Lady Anne Bacon*, and Wolfe, *Elizabeth Cary Lady Falkland: Life and Letters*.

7 This is the project at the University of Glasgow on which I was PI, and for which full citation is given earlier (in 'Conventions') and ahead (in the bibliography). The edition, which includes information about the project, is available at www.bessofhardwick.org.

8 The information is available at: www.livesandletters.org and @livesandletters, blogs.plym-Touth.ac.uk/wemlo and @WemloTweets, www.helsinki.fi/varieng, www.janadmbrogio.com/letterlock and @letterlocking, and www.folger.edu and @FolgerLibrary.

4   *Introduction*

of different letter elements and levels of language – genre, rhetoric, linguistic structure, personal spelling systems, handwriting, material features and pragmatic (or interpersonal) context. Overall, this study offers a conceptualisation of the early modern letter as a multilayered technology of communication, where the linguistic, material and social intersect. This blended approach allows for more precise and rigorous historicisation of the letters and for more incisive descriptions and analyses. One of the concerns, here, is to shift the focus away from author-based or biographically based interpretations and, instead, to use biography as a context for individual letters. Rather than seeking to present or to discover a particular portrait of Bess, the aim is to understand her life more accurately through assessment of the terms and conditions of the epistolary culture through which she negotiated her social milieu at particular moments. The questions addressed in this study are outlined in the next section. They intersect with current critical themes and concerns in the field that include the following.[9] In what ways did women use letters to participate in early modern politics and navigate the structures of power and elaborate cultures of Court patronage, diplomacy and favour in Elizabethan society? To what extent did early modern letters allow for the expression of emotion, and how did textualised emotion function in letters? In what ways must our interpretations of letters acknowledge they were the products of handwritten culture? Where do the visual and material features of letters carry meaning, and how do they intersect or overlap with linguistic features? Each chapter focuses upon a particular aspect of the letters in order to address specified research questions, interrogate concepts and define methodologies for analysis. Each chapter begins with a section that situates the letters within their broader historical and social context, and then moves on to a series of case studies drawn from the letters and deployed to address the wider research questions. The chapters are outlined in the next section, along with clarification, at the outset, of the premises (the definitions of terms and concepts) that underpin this study.

Definitions and research questions

Scripting and composing letters

Early modern letters in general, and Bess's letters in particular, require that we historicise our definitions of authorship and genre. This was a culture within which notions of literary originality were not the same as our own

---

9 Other summaries of research questions of interest to the field of early modern epistolary culture and women's writing are suggested by Steen, 'The Cavendish-Talbot Women', p. 146, and Daybell, *Women Letter-Writers*, pp. 10–11.

Introduction 5

and where letters were highly formalised rhetorical constructions (not out-pourings of one's innermost feelings or transparent reflections on one's inner self).[10] Furthermore, it was a culture within which composition and author-ship were more often collaborative and communal than singular or indi-vidualistic, and where Bess had available to her a spectrum of compositional scenarios that involved her own input in different ways and to different degrees. To such considerations of genre and authorship we must take into account that early modern constructions of gender were not fixed or sta-ble and where, within the social discourse of letter-writing, gender did not necessarily or automatically correlate with the sex of the letter-writer. To explore these factors is to ask what we mean by women's writing and how we should define the category of early modern 'women's letters'. More spe-cifically, it is to ask what were the options for expression and for the enact-ment of agency available to Bess as an early modern female letter-writer.

In order to address these questions, Chapter 1, 'Scripting and Composing Letters', examines the range of epistolary styles, rhetorical forms and modes of composition found across the one hundred letters sent from Bess. The forms of her letters are identified and then mapped onto their wide range of functions. The arguments made here are that her letter-writing was stra-tegic and goal-orientated, that she was of her time in this respect, and that her letter-writing involved activities well beyond the domestic or 'personal' realms and was often political. This chapter gains much from feminist lit-erary theory, where questions of authorship, genre and gender have been thoroughly interrogated, in particular within the context of early modern literary studies but also from within medieval studies, where such questions have long concerned scholars.[11] In addition, this chapter has gained from

---

10 Seminal studies of the models, forms and conventions of letter-writing have considered the rules of classical rhetoric and the *ars dictaminis* and their importance during the Renais-sance. The achievement of these studies has been to challenge the anachronistic and mis-leading stereotype of the simple and transparent letter. Key studies include: Henderson, 'Humanism', 'Defining the Genre of the Letter', 'Erasmus on the Art of Letter Writing', 'On Reading the Rhetoric of the Renaissance Letter'; Jardine, *Erasmus*; Mack, *Elizabethan Rhetoric*; Murphy, *Renaissance Eloquence*; Poster and Mitchell, *Letter-Writing Manuals*; Randall, 'Epistolary Rhetoric'. Discussion that summarises the situation in early mod-ern England is offered by Daybell, *Women Letter-Writers*, pp. 17–22, and Gibson, 'Let-ters'. Among the studies that should be mentioned that engage with the genre's rhetorical assumptions and suggest new and nuanced methods for interpretation (and from which this book has particularly benefited) are Magnusson's *Shakespeare and Social Dialogue* and Stewart's *Shakespeare's Letters*.

11 A thorough consideration and discussion is provided by Clarke, *The Politics*, pp. 1–48, and 'This Double Voice', pp. 1–5. A collection of key essays is provided by Hutson, *Feminism and Renaissance Studies*. Orgel, *Impersonations*, pp. 133–38, reviews Bess of Hardwick's life in the context of Renaissance gender roles. Scholars of Middle English writers and texts, such as Margery Kempe and the Wife of Bath's *Prologue*, have offered insights into what it meant to write in the voice of a woman and whether it was even possible to do so

6   *Introduction*

recent research into the history of emotions that has shown that the ways emotions were textualised was culturally specific. These literary and historical approaches have allowed for a far more rigorous historicisation of Bess's letters than has previously been possible. The argument made here is that the relationship between Bess (as letter-sender) and the letters she sent was not a stable or a simple one. Rather, each letter she sent represented her words, views and emotions according to a range of culturally defined models and gendered subject positions. Moreover, her role in the creation of each letter she sent varied very markedly, according to factors that included mode of composition, the presence of collaborators, use of scribes, her relationship with her correspondent and the type and content of the letter itself. Vital to the fine-grained readings presented here has been deployment of analytic methods from linguistics, in particular from historical pragmatics.[12] As a field of study, pragmatics is especially known for its concern with precise context-based analysis of language use, tracking of cohesive features (e.g., speech-act verbs, address terms and pronouns) and deployment of politeness theory (that includes the concepts of negative and positive politeness, and the framework of PDR – power, distance and ranked extremity – as determining politeness levels).[13] The argument of this chapter is that these methods from linguistics offer us a precise set of analytic terms and methods

---

in the context of a patriarchal culture, and a scribal culture, that was predominantly male, which are well known and are usefully summarised and reviewed by Dinshaw, Wallace and Summit for *The Cambridge Companion to Medieval Women's Writing*, pp. 1–12, 91–108 and 222–39.

12   The seminal study, which provides a theoretical discussion of the approach of historical pragmatics and its advantages in relation to early modern letters, is by Magnusson, *Shakespeare and Social Dialogue*, pp. 1–16. A more recent study that applies the approach to a collection of early modern letters, and which includes a review of the current state of scholarship, is by Williams, *Women's Epistolary Utterance*, pp. 1–17. An accessible recent overview and guide to the field of historical pragmatics is provided by Jucker and Taavitsainen, *English Historical Pragmatics*.

13   Discussions and applications of these methods are provided by Taavitsainen and Jucker, 'Speech Act Verbs', Minna Navala, *Address in Early English Correspondence*, and Nevalainen and Raumolin-Brunberg, 'Constraints on Politeness'. The seminal study of politeness theory is by Brown and Levinson, *Politeness*, from which are derived the concepts of 'negative politeness' (i.e., the use of deferential language to acknowledge social distance and power, and therefore to register the perceived social superiority of a correspondent) and 'positive politeness' (i.e., the use of familiar or intimate language to acknowledge acceptance, and therefore used to register that a correspondent is a social equal or social inferior). The framework of PDR is also proposed by politeness theory, whereby power, distance and ranked extremity determine politeness levels. While it is a framework that has been shown to be partially applicable to drama (Brown and Gilman, 'Politeness Theory'), the argument made here is that it is highly applicable to early modern letters, where not only the relative social status (power) of correspondents but also the intimacy or familiarity (distance) of their relationship and the magnitude (ranked extremity) of the request being made in the letter determined the choice of language and linguistic scripts.

Introduction 7

that make it possible to generate more incisive and articulate discussions of women's language and to describe more accurately the discourses of early modern letters.

Reading and writing letters

Early modern letters in general, and Bess's letters in particular, require that we historicise our definitions of language and text production. This was a culture within which the physical realities of text production were very different to our own and where to produce a handwritten letter often involved the employment of scribes or amanuenses at one or more stages of production. Such a production environment presents us with the challenge of how we might discern the handwriting of different individuals and the possible methods for making this important distinction. It is a situation that also raises the question of whether we can consider the notion of a 'personal correspondence' to have existed at all – that is, if textual production was always communal and collaborative to at least some extent. Furthermore, and in order to address such questions, we must remain aware of the status of early modern English as a non-standard language, where the forms of the language were not yet fixed nor stable and decisions over which were 'correct', 'incorrect', 'better' or 'worse' forms of the language had not yet been made. As a result (and while printed texts tended to be more conventionalised), within handwritten culture throughout and well beyond the sixteenth century we still find a great deal of variation in language use between individuals. Letters, in particular, are a good source to illustrate the many varieties of early modern English. It is a situation that requires us to ask questions about how different varieties of early modern English were produced and received at the time, the attitudes involved and how these different varieties of English were perceived by contemporaries writing or reading a letter. While our own attitudes to language tend to be very strongly influenced by present-day English (i.e., by our own linguistic knowledge and usage of a standardised language), the argument made here is that we must detach ourselves from the ideology of standardisation before making any assessments or judgements about the language of early modern letter-writers.[14]

In order to address these questions, Chapter 2, 'Reading and Writing Letters', examines the forms and functions of handwriting across the one hundred letters sent from Bess. That is, different forms of handwriting are

---

14 As Smith and Stenroos emphasise, languages are usually described as if they were standardised and scholars have had difficulty accepting the earlier variability of early modern English; 'English Spelling Before 1600', section 5, 'The Functionality of Variation: Learning One's Letters'. I am grateful to the authors for sending me a copy of this article in advance of publication. Further review of and engagement with current scholarship in this area are presented in Chapter 2.

8 *Introduction*

identified and these are then mapped onto their functions, which relate to the letter's type, content, goal and recipients. The discussion outlines as far as possible the identities of the different individuals involved in penning Bess's letters, who included Bess herself as well as scribes, secretaries, attendants and family members who can be located within her (or her husband's) households or secretariats and, in some cases, where biographical information is available. The discussion therefore offers further welcome detail about the nature of scribal and handwritten cultures within the early modern household.[15] The argument is made that Bess's decisions about when to write in her own hand or when to use a scribe, as well as which scribe to use, were strategic, although also depended on location and relied upon access to resources. The observation is made that, as countess of Shrewsbury her letter-writing and access to epistolary resources were intertwined with that of her husband, and she often benefitted from access to his epistolary networks and secretariat. As dowager countess she gained financial independence, and one of her first tasks was self-empowerment through the creation of her own secretariat. The strong implication throughout this chapter is that there were huge advantages to be gained, for early modern letter-writers, by having the opportunity to choose between writing in one's own hand or using a scribe (i.e., rather than being restricted to either one or the other). There were further advantages to be gained by having the opportunity, as required, to deploy scribes with particular qualities (e.g., confidentiality and discretion) or skills (e.g., legal training). As we will see in 2.2 and 2.3, which compare Bess's idiolect with the idiolects of the scribes or family members who penned letters for her, their language differs at every linguistic level (palaeography, spelling, punctuation, lexis, syntax and morphology, rhetorical scripts).

This chapter cites key concepts from historical linguistics, such as the concepts of standard and non-standard languages and of linguistic form and function, as well as precise terms, such as idiolect, stigmatised form, active repertoire and passive repertoire. These terms and concepts provide a frame of reference for the discussion and a systematic approach to historicisation of the language, the benefits of which have been demonstrated by scholars elsewhere.[16] Beyond the use of these terms and concepts, one of the achievements of this chapter is that it combines methods from historical

---

15 These findings add to those in articles by Burlinson and Zurcher, Hammer and North, discussed in Chapter 2.

16 Definitions and discussion of these key concepts in relation to approaches such as historical sociolinguistics and historical pragmatics are presented by Smith, *An Historical Study of English*, pp. 8–11 and pp. 65–78. A discussion that compellingly argues for the advantages of the term 'idiolect' in relation to early modern letters is offered by Evans, *The Language of Queen Elizabeth I*, p. 2. The concepts of active and passive scribal repertoires are explained by Benskin and Laing, 'Translations and Mischsprachen'. The concepts of stigmatised and

Introduction 9

linguistics with those from palaeography and, in so doing, offers fresh insights by bringing together approaches from the two fields. Important here are the methodologies for scribal identification that have been scrupulously developed over many years by philologists and manuscript scholars for medieval texts.[17] While these methods are well known and have been rigorously refined and applied within medieval studies, they have not yet been fully exploited in relation to early modern manuscript texts. This chapter demonstrates the benefits of a methodology that involves systematically recording not only palaeographic but also linguistic data (that includes spellings and punctuation), for purposes of scribal identification, but also for distinguishing collaborative composition and for discerning the interpersonal and symbolic functions of the visual features of handwriting.[18] To interrogate epistolary language from this dual perspective is to acknowledge the blurred lines between linguistic and material features. It is a blurred boundary perhaps most obviously in the case of Bess's iconic signature, considered in this chapter, through which she not only authorised her letters but also self-fashioned her own identity. There are implications here for editors, with regard to the incorporation of graphical features of texts into editions, tracking scribes through language and handwriting in editions, and the value of original-spelling editions.

Sending and receiving letters

Early modern letters in general, and Bess's letters in particular, require that we historicise our definitions of materiality and text reception. The physical realities of epistolary reception were specific to the period, so we should detach ourselves from any preconceptions based on modern ideas about what it is like to read a letter. When we imagine Bess or one of her correspondents receiving a letter we must imagine a reception scenario that could potentially involve silent reading, reading aloud, discussion with a letter-bearer, decoding the page both visually and through haptic perception, and other material and embodied factors. The communicative function

---

    prestige form are from sociolinguistics, discussed by Nevalainen and Raumolin-Brunberg, *Sociolinguistics and Language History*, pp. 12–19, and Mugglestone, *Talking Proper*.

17 The approach is outlined in detail in the introduction to McIntosh, Samuels and Benskin, *A Linguistic Atlas*, and by McIntosh, 'A New Approach to Middle English Dialectology'; applications of the approach are discussed by Horobin, 'The Criteria for Scribal Attribution', and Smith, 'A Linguistic Atlas'.

18 There has been interest recently in evolving more systematic methods of distinguishing scribal language or uncovering the influence of scribes in late medieval and early modern English texts, in particular: Bergs, 'Linguistic Fingerprints', Doty, 'Telling Tales', Cusack, *Everyday English*, Marcus, 'An Investigation', pp. 65–172, Smith, *Older Scots*, Wiggins, 'Are Auchinleck Manuscript Scribes 1 and 6 the Same Scribe?' and Williams, *Women's Epistolary Utterance*, pp. 53–63, and '"Yr Scribe Can Proove"'.

10   *Introduction*

of a letter was intricately intertwined with the precise etiquettes of its material forms, which included its visual appearance, physical dimensions, associated items, such as enclosures or gifts, and accompanying personnel. It is a situation that reminds us that the locus of meaning and authority was not stable or fixed within letters, nor contained solely within the semantics of the text. As such, we are required to consider which of the elements of a letter communicated meaning, which did not and which took priority. Concurrently, we are required to consider the nature of 'epistolary literacy' for the period, as a competency that included a range of skills and knowledge.[19] In recent years progress has been made towards mapping the landscape of material features in letters in a series of studies, from which this book benefits throughout.[20] This book adds details, from the many superb examples in Bess's correspondence, to elaborate upon the broader mosaic that is emerging. But this book, in addition, discusses models and methods for systematic codification and capture of material features, such as could be appropriated, adapted or refined elsewhere by other projects, and there are implications for editors and archivists here, in how we capture information from letters. The techniques set out here are for converting analogue forms (of which we find a spectrum of variants within handwritten texts) into logical and quantifiable formats, so as to be suitable for incorporation into encoded frameworks, such as catalogues, databases and editions.

In order to achieve these aims, Chapter 3, 'Sending and Receiving Letters', examines the material forms of the 242 existing letters that Bess sent and received in relation to their communicative functions. The discussion examines methods of delivery, postal networks, bearers, enclosures, folding patterns, space on the page, size and quality of paper, use of colour, decoration, ribbon and floss. While there were conventional patterns of use and etiquettes of epistolary materiality in the period, there was also much that was spontaneous, casual and inconsistent, such as was typical of the unregulated and uneven nature of handwritten culture. So, whereas in some instances a particular material form may have been carefully chosen for its symbolic meaning, in other instances its use could have been necessitated by practicalities (e.g., cost or the available materials that happened to be at hand) with no extra symbolic meaning intended. At the same time, the communicative function of a particular material form could shift depending on contextual factors. So, while a particular material form in one context might be unremarkable and unsurprising, in another, the same form could

---

19 The term is proposed and discussed by Whyman, *The Pen and the People*, 'Introduction', in relation to eighteenth-century letters.

20 Especially notable here are the studies, which are engaged with in Chapter 3, by: Akkerman, *The Correspondence*; Brayshay, *Land Travel and Communications*; Daybell, *The Material Letter* Stewart and Wolfe, *Letterwriting*; and Wolfe, '"Neatly Sealed, with Silk, and *Spanish* Wax"'.

be perceived to be extraordinary and inflect the message communicated by the letter in important ways. Ultimately, the argument made here is that one must be wary of the hazards inherent in under- or over-interpretation of these forms and features, and remain alert to both the vagaries and idiosyncrasies of handwritten culture and the variety of contextual factors. As with linguistic and rhetorical forms so too with material features: we find that pragmatic (interpersonal) context can determine function. Whereas historical pragmatics provides an interpretative framework for the management of contextual factors when it comes to language communication, this chapter suggests how we might begin to develop a pragmatics of epistolary materiality.

Materials and methods

Life

Bess of Hardwick's life and popular reputation are far better known than her letters. Anyone approaching her letters must first get beyond the layers of repeated opinion that have accumulated, passed down over several centuries. As Sara Jayne Steen has observed, Bess's reputation has been repeatedly cast in terms that are 'negative and sexualised' and as the 'builder of halls and dynasties' she is 'often described as "ambitious" and "redoubtable", with the implication that her authority was unwomanly'.[21] The harsh treatment of Bess has been traced by E.C. Williams in her biography of 1959, in a line that goes back to William Camden in the seventeenth century, through Horace Walpole and Edmund Lodge in the eighteenth century, Joseph Hunter in the nineteenth century, to the accounts of historians A.F. Pollard and J.E. Neale, from the first half of the twentieth century.[22] These drastically simplified accounts pass down the same negative caricature – never adding anything new from the sources from her life – of Bess as a 'termagant', with 'the tongue of an adder', 'very ambitious and withal overbearing' and as 'proud, furious, selfish, unfeeling'.[23] Remarkably, and despite the efforts of

---

21 Steen, 'The Cavendish-Talbot Women', p. 161. The point is made by Goldring in her *ODNB* entry, with the observation that, although now viewed for her many achievements, Bess has had many detractors over the centuries who have 'cast her as a rapacious, social-climbing shrew'.

22 Williams, *Bess of Hardwick*, p. v.

23 Lodge, *Illustrations* (1791), is the originator of these quotations, and further examples are summarised by Williams, *Bess of Hardwick*, p. v. The quotations from Lodge have been repeated many times to describe Bess; to take a couple of examples (although the practice of using these quotations to sum up Bess's character is not at all unusual), Fraser, *Mary, Queen of Scots*, quotes Lodge and refers to Bess as a 'termagant', p. 511, and Guy, *My Heart Is My Own*, echoes and quotes directly from Lodge in his portrayal of Bess, p. 441 and pp. 448–49.

12   *Introduction*

revisionists, these quotations – which reduce Bess's extraordinary and complex life to a series of tabloid headlines – are still regularly quoted in both scholarly and popular accounts.[24] What we find when we move beyond the repeated clichés about Bess's life is a much more nuanced and realistic portrait both of Bess herself and of the society within which she lived. It is worth mentioning three notable contributions here, from which this study has benefitted, each of which revises one of the gender stereotypes that have haunted Bess's historical reputation.

First, popular portrayals have repeatedly cast Bess as the 'terror of her husbands', a depiction that plays off the age-old stereotype of the shrewish, nagging wife.[25] The achievement of Bess's twentieth-century biographers has been to undermine this stereotype, which is replaced with much more equitable portrayals; in particular, David N. Durant's biography has shown, through meticulous examination of her Account Books and inventories, Bess's extraordinary abilities as a household manager that saw her develop into a talented business leader with a gift for financial acuity. Second, James Daybell has taken on the popular portrayal that plays off the well-known stereotype that women like to gossip about trivia among their female friends; as he acknowledges in the opening of his study, as well as 'the ambitious dynast who made a career out of marriage' Bess is 'well known to the "romance, sex and violence" school of history as the indiscrete gossiper to Mary, Queen of Scots about Elizabeth I'.[26] Through reassessment of the news reports Bess received, Daybell has revealed Bess to be 'a serious political operator' and he has interrogated gendered uses of the terms 'gossip' and 'intelligence' (which are typically used to describe the same activities, only performed by women or by men) as well as how we define the political sphere. Third, another tendency among popular portrayals is to brand Bess as the ambitious 'material girl' and to play off the familiar stereotype that women are acquisitive and vain.[27] The re-examinations of Bess's creations in needlework and embroideries, which acknowledge their status as textile art, serve to counteract the negative sides of this stereotype. In particular, Susan Frye has revealed Bess's textile creations to be not only accomplished artworks remarkable for their high aesthetic quality and fine execution, but also sites for self-fashioning and political expression.[28] In summary: Bess's reputation has been persistently trivialised and defamed in portrayals that

---

24 For example, as observed in the previous note, the descriptions given by Fraser and Guy, p. 511, and p. 441 and pp. 448–49, are almost entirely derived from Lodge and quote directly from his 1791 biography.

25 Lodge, *Illustrations*, is the originator of the phrase 'terror of her husband'.

26 Daybell, '"Suche newes"', p. 117.

27 For example, as we find in the popular biography by Hubbard, *A Material Girl*.

28 Frye, *Pens and Needles*, especially Chapter 1, 'Political Designs: Elizabeth Tudor, Mary Stuart and Bess of Hardwick', pp. 30–74. Also relevant here are the studies of Bess's

play off well-worn and clichéd gender stereotypes; however, through scrupulous scholarly attention to sources in recent years, our view of Bess's life has been transformed. The argument made here is that examination of Bess's language and letters adds substantively to these views and opens up further questions for analysis. Yet, while this book offers fresh insights into Bess's life, the focus here is not primarily biographical and the uneven coverage of her letters means that not every aspect of her life or activities is discussed or represented in the following chapters. For this reason, and as her biography provides an important context for reading the letters, it is worth giving an overview of current knowledge about Bess's life here. The following summary has been focused around points especially relevant to her letter-writing.

The year of Bess's birth is usually given as 1527 (although arguments have also been made for 1521 or 1522).[29] Born Elizabeth Hardwick, she was one of four daughters and a son of John Hardwick of Hardwick and his wife Elizabeth (Leake). The Hardwicks could be described as of modest social standing, parish rather than county gentry. There was nothing auspicious about Bess's start in life as the daughter of a minor landowner whose social horizons were limited almost entirely to north-east Derbyshire. Moreover, when her father, John Hardwick, died leaving debts in 1528, the young Bess experienced considerable hardship and a very uncertain future. Little more is known of Bess's upbringing and early years. She was married to Robert Barlow (or Barley), of Barlow, Derbyshire, a young man of social equivalence to Bess herself. The wedding took place on or before 28 May 1543 and the short marriage (Barlow died on 24 December 1544), said to be unconsummated, left Bess with a small inheritance (of around £24 per year). What happened next has been called 'the greatest unexplained mystery of her life'.[30] We do not know how Bess met her second husband, twice-widowed Sir William Cavendish (1508–57), treasurer of Henry VIII's chamber, who was some fifteen years older than Bess. Biographers have speculated that Bess may somehow have secured a position as lady-in-waiting to Frances Grey, marchioness of Dorset, which would explain why, on 20 August 1547, her wedding to Cavendish took place in the Grey family chapel. Whatever the explanation, marriage to Cavendish was, for Bess, a prodigious step up the social and economic ladder and the point at which the course of her life changed. To use Durant's words, Bess's marriage to Cavendish was 'the foundation stone of a remarkable and fantastic future'.[31]

---

achievements as a builder by French, 'A Widow Building in Elizabethan England', and Friedman, 'Architecture, Authority, and the Female Gaze'.

29 The debate over Bess's date of birth is summarised by Lovell, *Bess of Hardwick*, pp. 481–82, and the evidence in favour of 1521/2 is presented by Riden, 'Bess of Hardwick'.

30 Riden and Fowkes, *Hardwick*, p. 19.

31 Durant, *Bess of Hardwick*, p. 1.

14 *Introduction*

It is as Lady Cavendish that we first encounter Bess as a letter-writer. Penned in her own hand, her letters from this era give us our earliest samples of the distinctive handwriting and personal spelling system that Bess was to use throughout her life. We have only one letter between Bess and her second husband, Cavendish: written from Chatsworth House on 13 April, some time during the period of their marriage, between 20 August 1547 and Cavendish's death in 1557, it is nothing more than a brief note from Cavendish asking his wife to pay a London man for 'otys' (i.e., oats).[32] While we might feel disappointed by the limited nature of this short letter, it does nevertheless provide one of the few examples we have, within her own lifetime, of the name 'Bess' being used: Cavendish superscribed his letter to 'Besse Cavendyssh my wyff' and opened with an address to 'Good Besse'.[33] That none of their other letters survive is undeniably frustrating: it leaves us with little to go on from the letters when it comes to Bess's relationship with Cavendish. Other sources give an impression of the vibrancy of their marriage. We know Cavendish was the man with whom Bess purchased Chatsworth House and surrounding estates and, in ten years, had all eight of her children, Temperance and Lucretia (who died in childhood) and the six who survived to adulthood: her three sons, Henry, William and Charles, and three daughters Frances, Elizabeth and Mary. From the couple's selection of godparents, who included Princess Elizabeth and Lady Jane Grey, we see their Protestant preferences and position in the upper echelons of Elizabethan society. From their account books we glimpse their pleasurable life: there were regular purchases of fine clothes, trips to London and money for games and gambling. From the commissions for deluxe decorative objects we find the marriage to have been a union that was celebrated and glorified: such as their magnificent Pearl Bed, which was carved and gilded with the Cavendish coat of arms; and the book set with portraits of the couple and adorned with gold and jewels.

We do not know how Bess responded when Cavendish died, suddenly, on 25 October 1557, but we do know that he left her with debts of over £5,000 owing to the Crown. Within two years, by 1559, Bess had married her third husband, wealthy widower Sir William St Loe (c. 1520–65?), captain of the guard to the new queen Elizabeth I. It was a match that improved Bess's financial situation as well as her social capital and as Lady St Loe she

---

32 We know that Cavendish wrote other (longer) letters to Bess as he said that this brief note was an afterthought, something, he added, 'I had forgotten to wryt in my letters'; Folger CT, X.d.428 (13), ID 13.

33 The only other uses of 'Bess' in the letters were by her third husband, Sir William St Loe, who closed one of his letters 'farewell my owne swete besse', and by St Loe's mother (Bess's third mother-in-law, Margaret), who wrote regarding rumours of a plot to poison her son and his wife 'besse sayntloo'; 12 October and 13 June [c. 1560], Folger CT, X.d.428 (76 and 74), IDs 60 and 58.

Introduction   15

became a gentlewoman of the queen's Privy Chamber. At the same time, the couple's letters tell a story of genuine marital affection and compatibility. St Loe's very charming letters to his wife leave us with the impression that he must have been a most attentive, pleasant and good-humoured man to have as a husband, and that he adored Bess. As well as letters he sent choice gifts, rarities and delicacies, which included lemons, olives, cucumbers, frankincense, virginal wire, canvas and the latest fashion in ladies' headwear, a bongrace. This was the stuff of harmonious marital discourse and his presents accompanied the kind words of his letters. He is the only correspondent we know to refer to Bess with the pronoun 'thou', which was a marked form (by comparison to the more usual and unmarked 'you') that he employed in his letters to her to show special intimacy and affection. Perhaps most memorable among St Loe's good-humoured and affectionate teasing is the pet name he gave his wife: 'my honest swete chatesworth'. It was a shared joke that made reference to Bess's fierce preoccupation with Chatsworth, and was a playful reminder of the dominant status the ongoing building works had in her mind and in her life. In another letter St Loe used a similar playful pet name for Bess: he wished farewell to his wife who was 'my owne good sarvantte and cheyff oversear off my worcks'.[34] The building of Chatsworth House spanned three of Bess's marriages and to some extent defined them all. Purchased with Cavendish in June 1549 along with hundreds of acres of surroundings lands, from the 1550s Bess led the management of the renovation of the house, which was extensively rebuilt and luxuriously furnished. In 1564 an unidentified correspondent wrote to Bess to report on the good progress with the building works at Chatsworth, which he anticipated would mean a great deal to her: 'I am glad you are in healthe, and I trust the sight of your nere fynyshyd building will contyneue yt'.[35] These building activities continued, ever-present for many more years. They reappeared in the letters more than two decades later in comments from Bess's fourth husband, the earl of Shrewsbury, who was far less genial than St Loe on the topic.

When St Loe died, probably early in 1565, Bess returned again to Court. As a wealthy widow and one of Elizabeth I's inner circle of women, Bess was a very eligible prospect. Within three years she had married her fourth husband, George Talbot, sixth earl of Shrewsbury (c. 1522–90), a man she had known for many years and who inhabited the very highest realms of the Elizabethan social and economic stratosphere. As well as vast lands, Shrewsbury owned eight main properties (Sheffield Castle and Manor, Pontefract Castle, Rufford Abbey, Welbeck Abbey, Wingfield Manor, Worksop Manor and Buxton Hall), plus two houses in the city of London and a house

---

34   24 October and 4 September [c. 1560], Folger CT, X.d.428 (77 and 75), IDs 61 and 59.
35   Unknown correspondent, 22 October 1564, Folger CT, X.d.428 (78), ID 62.

16   *Introduction*

at Chelsea, as well as Tutbury Castle, which he rented from the Crown. Shrewsbury was, as Durant puts it, 'a Prince whose princedom was north of the Trent'.[36] On paper, this was an unbeatable match for Bess, and Shrewsbury's doting letters to his 'dere none' in the early years of their marriage attest to a genuine affection. The couple were married before 27 August 1567, the date of the earliest known letter that Bess signs 'EShrouesbury'.[37] The next letter we have was from two months later, 21 October 1567, a report from Court from Elizabeth (Leach) Wingfield, Bess's half-sister, to announce that the queen was looking forward to seeing Bess in her new position as countess of Shrewsbury: 'I haue bene glade to se my lady sayntloa but now more dyssirous to se my lady shrewsbury'. Elizabeth Wingfield took particular care to quote the queen's exact words about Bess: 'I hope sayd she' (the queen) that 'my lady' (Bess) 'hath knowne my good openon of her'. The letter continued by quoting the queen, who said that, when it came to Bess, 'there ys no lady y[n] thys land that I beter loue and lyke', and we are left in no doubt as to the bond between the two women, sovereign and subject. So while Bess's marriage to Shrewsbury certainly expanded her social horizons, Elizabeth Wingfield's letter reminds us not to overlook Bess's pre-existing connections, established good regard in the queen's eyes and knowledge of the intricacies of Elizabethan Court life. Bess may have been a financially well-resourced widow, but she had much more than money to attract the (already amply wealthy) earl of Shrewsbury.

The honeymoon period did not last long. In 1568, Queen Elizabeth I entrusted the newlywed earl of Shrewsbury and his countess, Bess, with the onerous task of keeping Mary, Queen of Scots. From this point on, there were three people in the marriage and it was a relationship dominated by the woman who was to stay in their custody for sixteen years, until November 1584. As a Catholic and blood relative of Queen Elizabeth, and therefore a claimant to the throne, the Scottish Queen represented a serious national security threat and was the focus of endless treacherous plots and intrigues. Bess and Shrewsbury were forever required to move her, along with her extensive royal retinue, between their numerous properties, trailing for miles along muddy roads. External circumstances had thrust the couple onto the political centre stage and into a situation more physically and psychologically demanding, not to mention financially draining, beyond which either of them could possibly have imagined. In later years, Mary attempted to implicate Bess in treasonable plots and rumours and, while Bess managed to survive these, the situation certainly contributed to the subsequent breakdown of her marriage to Shrewsbury. Rumblings of problems between the Shrewsburys were audible as early as c. 1577 in a letter from Gilbert Talbot

---

36 Durant, *Bess of Hardwick*, p. 54.
37 Longleat, Thynne Papers, TH/VOL/III/170, ID 114.

Introduction 17

to his mother-in-law and stepmother, Bess, where he described how he had tried to defend her against his father's anger and he reported Shrewsbury lamenting 'how often I have curced the buylding at Chatsworthe for want of her [i.e., Bess's] companye'.[38] By 1582 the marriage had severely deteriorated: servants were complaining, saying of Sheffield Castle that the 'house is a hell', and by June 1583 Bess had left her husband's seat at Sheffield for her own property, Chatsworth. The earl of Leicester made repeated attempts to mediate, but Shrewsbury was having none of it. By this point in 1584, we find Shrewsbury's regretful tone had turned to spitting venom when it came to 'Chatsworth house that dovowringe gulf of myne and other your [i.e., Bess's] husbandes goodes'.[39] In July 1584, he mustered a force of forty men on horseback, rode over to Chatsworth, armed with a halberd and pistol, and claimed the property as his own. Bess was forced to leave and, soon after, Shrewsbury had her son William Cavendish thrown into the Fleet for his attempts at resistance. In retrospect, had Shrewsbury not evicted his wife from Chatsworth in 1584, she may never have gone on to embark on her most magnificent building project of all. As we shall see, while Bess originally intended Chatsworth to be her legacy, it became her blueprint.

Shrewsbury's claim to Chatsworth in 1584, as well as his subsequent protracted hostilities and lawsuits brought against his wife, had implications not only for Bess but also for her children and for her role as guardian to her granddaughter Arbella Stuart. It is worth recalling that the clandestine marriage of Arbella's parents – Bess's daughter Elizabeth Cavendish and Charles Stuart, first earl of Lennox – was orchestrated by their mothers without the knowledge of Queen Elizabeth, who was angry not to have been informed, given that any child of the marriage would be a royal claimant through the Stuart line. The queen forgave Bess even after Arbella was born, but it was only the start of the troubles Arbella would cause for her grandmother. When only an infant of under a year old, in 1576, her father, the earl of Lennox, died suddenly and unexpectedly. In the following months, Bess used her influence to pursue her inheritance claims and to petition the queen to ensure 'my poore Arbella' was permitted to live with her mother, Bess's daughter, Elizabeth, countess of Lennox.[40] Only a few years later, in January 1582, tragedy struck again when Arbella's mother, Elizabeth Lennox, died as suddenly as her husband, and the seven-year-old Arbella was left an orphan and ward of Lord Burghley. At this point, it was Bess (as requested in her daughter's will) who took over custody of the child and immediately began to fight for Arbella's financial entitlements, petitioning the queen. As Arbella grew older, there were regular fears of 'wicked and

---

38 [July 1577?], Folger CT, X.d.428 (111), ID 84.
39 4 August 1584, LPL, Misc. Papers, MS 3152, fol. 58r-v, ID 119.
40 23 September 1578, CP 10/42, fols 72–3, ID 121.

18   *Introduction*

mischeuous' kidnap plots surrounding her, as a claimant to the throne, and, as a result, the queen required Bess keep her teenage granddaughter under virtual house arrest.[41] The queen watched Burghley watching Bess watching Arbella. It was a situation that continued for many years and which mirrored Bess's earlier role as co-keeper of the Scottish Queen: in both cases, Bess was under royal command to watch over a woman who was a claimant to the crown (and therefore a potential security threat to Queen Elizabeth) and who was involuntarily kept within the confines of Bess's household. In the case of Arbella Stuart, tensions within the household were inflamed by a clash of generations and personalities.

Shrewsbury died at 7 a.m. on 18 November 1590 and one month later, on 19 December, Bess wrote from Sheffield to William Cecil, Lord Burghley, to express her hope that all quarrel in her family had died with him: 'I hope my good Lord that all disagreement (in this famely) died with him'.[42] Shrewsbury's death marked a new era for Bess and with her final widowhood came greater independence and financial freedom. Bess was now staggeringly wealthy in her own right: a widow for the fourth and final time, she commanded an enormous annual income of up to £10,000. At this point in her life, aged in the sixties, we may have expected a lesser woman to step back and allow one of her sons to take over the reins of the estates and businesses. Indeed, as Bess herself reflected, in a letter to Burghley, her main desire now was for a quiet and peaceful life: 'quiett ys my prencipall desire; and I shall rather suffer then enter into controuersy'.[43] Perhaps peace and quiet were, as Bess said here, her ultimate aim. But first, however, she had legal issues to settle and business matters to take care of. One of Bess's earliest undertakings as dowager countess was to arrange what was to be her final trip to London, where she spent eight months accompanied by all the key members of her upper household, who included her granddaughter Arbella and her sons William and Charles. With her trademark competency, the purpose of the visit was threefold. First, determined to consolidate her children's inheritances, while in London Bess had her solicitors and secretaries carefully close all legal loopholes to Shrewsbury's heir, Gilbert Talbot, the incoming seventh earl of Shrewsbury, who had disputed the terms of her marriage settlement in Shrewsbury's will. Second, she reconnected with her social network, made contact with old

---

41 Details about the strictures under which Arbella was kept at Hardwick are outlined in Bess's letter to Burghley of 21 September 1592. Bess responded to Burghley's fears about 'wicked and mischeuous' plots to kidnap herself and the now seventeen-year old Arbella, and tried to offer reassurance about security measures in the household: Arbella was not allowed to leave the house late or unattended, or to walk far from the house, or to go to anybody else's house; BL, Lansd. 71, ff. 3r-4v, ID 163.
42 19 December 1590, Arundel Castle, Autograph Letters 1585–1617, No. 123, ID 231.
43 ID 231.

Introduction 19

friends, wined and dined her most influential and powerful acquaintances and discussed Arbella's marriage prospects with the queen. Third, Bess made a series of extravagant purchases that included investments in gold and silver plate, fine clothes and jewels for herself and Arbella, swathes of black velvet lace and taffeta, yards of brightly coloured satins, luxurious gold fringes and trimmings for her new litter, bulk purchases of tapestries and wall-hangings, as well as two new seal rings and multiple quires of fine imported paper. Bess was gearing up for a new reign and a new household. Moreover, it was not just a new household that Bess was equipping, but a new house. By the time she had left for London in November 1591, work on the new house was already well underway. It is worth backtracking for a moment to recall how her building projects had reached this point. On 2 June 1584, having been ousted from Chatsworth by Shrewsbury, Bess purchased outright (in her son William's name – Bess was married at this point and therefore, as a woman, unable to hold property in her own name) the family manor house at Hardwick from her brother James for £9,500. Leaking, squalid and barely habitable, the manor house at Hardwick nevertheless provided a roof for herself and her son William and his family. Once the legal battle with her husband Shrewsbury was settled in Bess's favour in 1587, the income enabled her to expand dramatically and renovate the modest manor house at Hardwick into the impressive property known today as Hardwick Old Hall.

By 1591, when the development of Hardwick Old Hall was complete, and her income had substantially increased following the death of Shrewsbury, Bess's vision for her building works had further expanded in her mind. As a result, two more building projects were commissioned with famous architect Robert Smythson. The first was Hardwick New Hall, begun in 1590, located next to Hardwick Old Hall and designed for Bess to live in herself. The second was Oldcotes (or Owlcotes), begun in 1593, located a few miles from Hardwick and intended as a home for her son William and his family. No trace of Oldcotes survives today and it never fulfilled its intended function of providing William with a home during his life. The year it was completed, in 1598, William's wife Anne died and William and his young children never left his mother's home at Hardwick New Hall, into which Bess had moved on 4 October 1597 and which came to combine their two households. As a cumulative result of Bess's activities she had become an extraordinary builder, perhaps, 'the greatest woman builder ever known'.[44] Bess's activities as a builder permeate her letters as they defined and pervaded her life. Her letters are shot through with glimpses

---

44 Handover, *Arbella Stuart*, p. 77; Girouard describes Hardwick New Hall as 'the supreme triumph of Elizabethan architecture'; *Robert Smythson*, p. 146, both quoted by Steen, *The Letters*, p. 12.

20 Introduction

of these ongoing activities and her commitment to a vision that was at times all-consuming.[45]

When Burghley wrote to Bess again a couple of years later, on 9 August 1593, his comments were indicative of the reputation Bess had developed. He expressed his concern that she had left London to isolate herself in what seemed like (from his perspective at Court) the wilds of Derbyshire, a solitary figure at Chatsworth amid the hills, rocks and stones: 'I wishe to your Ladyship to take more Comfort by stirringe abroade to visit your frendes and children, and not to lyue so solitary as yt semeth yow doe there in Chattesworthe amongest hills and Rockes of Stones'.[46] Burghley's portrayal of Bess here acknowledges that she had taken a step back from the public life of Court. However, the image of her as windswept and isolated relates very little to the realities of life at Chatsworth and Hardwick in the 1590s; certainly, Bess's Account Books tell a story of a rather plush and convivial household. Far more, Burghley's comments tell us about how Bess had, in her own lifetime, become synonymously associated with the great houses she created, first Chatsworth and, later, Hardwick and Oldcotes. For Bess, the activity of building was part of the fabric of her world. Each building was the material realisation, the nexus point, of networks of trade, industry, social contact, reported fashions, cultural aspiration and dynastic ambition. In 1603 she supervised one final design project with Robert Smythson, her own marble tomb effigy, where she is famously memorialised as the 'aedificatrix' of Chatsworth, Hardwick and Oldcotes.

We know that in the final decade of her life Bess was concerned with spiritual matters. There were regular payments to the poor but, characteristically, Bess's spirituality found clearest expression in architectural form: she built and endowed alms houses in Derby for twelve elderly people, a project started in 1598 and complete by March 1600. It is worth

---

45 We have seen some of the ways in which Chatsworth features in Bess's letters, but there are numerous other small insights into her building activities. For example, Bess wrote to give orders for payment for weathervanes for Chatsworth and to send herb, flower and mallow seeds for the garden, accompanied by instructions 'yn euery pynt' (*point*); to borrow a plasterer from Sir John Thynne of Longleat House; to tell her husband to send a plumber and iron; to donate black stone to William Cobham and to send lead to Lord Burghley. The letters written to Bess include those which reported on the progress of the garden paving at Chatsworth; the getting of timber and marl and plants for the orchard; and to respond to her requests for iron. Whatever needed to be done, Bess ensured it was done; or, in her own words to her servant James Crompe: 'yn any other thyngs that well be a helpe to my byldeynge Let yt be done'. Folger CT, X.d.428 (83, 17, 57 and 4); Longleat, Thynne Papers, Thynne Book 57 pp. 129–30; LPL, Talbot Papers, MS 3205, fol. 58 and MS 3206, fol. 885; IDs 100, 113, 178, 16, 188, 17, 47, 5.

46 9 August 1593, Belvoir Castle, Rutland MSS, Letters & Papers XII, folios 131–132, ID 108.

Introduction 21

recalling that there had been, for many years, a ritual of daily prayer in Bess's household, attested in letters sent from family members throughout her life which end asking Bess for her daily blessing. Bess herself referred to this routine of daily prayer in a letter to Sir Francis Walsingham, 6 May 1582, where she said that, for the Queen, 'I dayly with most zealous mynd pray'.[47] Bess's wording here hints at a degree of zeal in her Protestant agenda, although biographers have always supposed her to have been conservative in her Protestantism and we know that Bess's daughter Mary and her daughter (i.e., Mary's, Bess's granddaughter) Aletheia were themselves devout Roman Catholics. An indication of a devote Protestantism is signalled by the letters Bess received in her final years from James Montague, dean of that Royal Chapel: he sent news of the persecution of priests, recusants and 'papistes', of parliamentary decisions over compulsory communion and of the Gunpowder Plot.[48] Something more of the tenor of Bess's piety can be gauged from the books prominently displayed on her dressing table in her bedchamber in 1601, which set out a weighty programme of Protestant reading.

It is here in her bedchamber that we should picture Bess when we imagine her final days. The bedchamber overlooked her estates for miles around. Bess sat up in her bed or in her rich russet- and silver-striped chair, insulated from the cold by numerous Spanish woollen blankets, quilts and fine scarlet coverings. Bess's women Mistresses Digby and Cartwright were ever in attendance to stack up the fire and read to Bess, meditations or recently received letters. Bess's favourite son, William Cavendish, was a regular presence, and conferred with his mother over her concerns for his future. Surrounded by her trusted circle, Bess received letters to enquire after her own health and send news of various sorts, from her children, grandchildren, friends at Court, kin and neighbours. It is here in her bedchamber that Bess died on 13 February 1608, and her funeral took place in great state on 4 May. She was buried at All Saints' parish church (now Cathedral) in Derby beneath the monument designed by Robert Smythson. At this point in time, in 1608, the letters Bess had sent to numerous correspondents during the course of her life lay scattered in various locations around the country. Her own Papers (which contained the letters she received) were stored together in the purpose-built muniments room at Hardwick New Hall. As is described in the next section, her Papers passed through the hands of various private owners, and were thoroughly picked over, from the seventeenth until the twentieth century. It was only in 1961 that the largest part of her extant Papers, as we have them, were purchased and became publically available at their current location at the Folger Shakespeare Library,

---

47 6 May 1582, TNA, SP 12/153, fol. 84r-84v (items 39), ID 145.
48 10 February and 7 March 1606, Folger CT, X.d.428 (59 and 60), IDs 48 and 49.

22   Introduction

Washington DC. Located on Capitol Hill, within walking distance of the Senate and the White House, amid a cityscape of supreme architectural grandeur, it somehow seems a fitting final home, one which Bess may well have fully approved.

Letters

The 242 letters we have to and from Bess of Hardwick are a remarkable number for an English woman born before 1550, and are even more unusual being from one born into the lesser gentry. There are very few other non-royal women for whom we have anywhere near so many letters from such an early date. Perhaps the best comparison, although she was far better educated than Bess, was Bess's friend and contemporary Lady Anne (Cooke) Bacon (c. 1528–1610), for whom we have 197 letters.[49] However, whereas the majority of Anne Bacon's letters were to and from one correspondent over a relatively short period (to and from her son Anthony in the 1590s), Bess's correspondence is, by contrast, wide-ranging and thinly spread. In fact, among Tudor women, with the notable exception of Elizabeth I, Bess's correspondence is unrivalled for its extensive scope and for the variety of activities that are recorded and can justifiably be cited as the best-documented letter-writing of any of her non-royal female contemporaries.[50] The letters span over six decades, from the 1550s to her death in 1608, and reflect the diverse range of her contacts and the wide reach of her social networks. Her eighty-eight known correspondents ranged from across the social scale, from her servants, mother and brother in Derbyshire, to the most powerful, rich and famous in the land, among whom were numbered Elizabeth I, Mary, Queen of Scots, Robert Dudley, earl of Leicester and William Cecil, Lord Burghley.

Today, Bess's letters are scattered across nineteen different archives and repositories, the reason for which is that most of the letters we have to and from Bess are 'sent' letters – that is, actually sent and delivered rather than being unsent drafts or administrative 'file' copies.[51] The letters Bess sent were distributed far and wide at the time of delivery, and their current locations can be partially mapped onto Bess's own epistolary networks. So, her letters sent to Sir John Thynne at Longleat House in the 1550s and 1560s are still in the Thynne Papers at Longleat today, and those to Queen Elizabeth and Lord Burghley now reside today in the State Papers in The

---

49 Allen, *The Letters*.

50 Daybell, *Women Letter-Writers*, describes her letters as 'the best documented of any sixteenth-century aristocratic English woman', p. 117.

51 Methods of the storing, copying and filing of early modern letters are described in Daybell, *The Material Letter*, pp. 175–216.

Introduction 23

National Archives and the Cecil Papers at Hatfield House. The letters sent to Bess, on the other hand, were incorporated into Bess's own Papers, which passed down through her own family in the seventeenth century, via her sister Jane Boswell or Bosville (née Hardwick), and were eventually purchased by the Folger Shakespeare Library, where they are held today.[52] We do not know how many of Bess's letters disintegrated or went missing before they reached these secure locations, where they are today conserved and stored in humidified environments. However, we can speculate upon the shape and content of what is not there. The number of letters lost is suggested by the numerous internal references within the existing letters, combined with Account Book payments to bearers and messengers for particular periods, which suggest a regular flow of letters to and from Bess, into and out of her households, that is only partially reflected in the actual survivals. The Account Book payments also specify deliveries (that may or may not have included letters) from correspondents for whom we no longer have letters, but which remind us that Bess's surviving letters do not reflect the full extent of her social network.[53] There is no doubt, then, that many letters have been lost over the years. The reason for these losses may sometimes have been simply neglect, and we know that there were still parcels of papers that included letters to Bess in the abandoned library at Hardwick Old Hall in the late eighteenth century.[54] But we must also take into account the 'politics of the archive' and the greater likelihood that women's letters were less likely be regarded as worthy of keeping.[55] To take one example, among Bess's correspondence are thirty-two letters held in the Shrewsbury-Talbot Papers at LPL.[56] These letters were originally located at Sheffield Manor, the administrative centre of the earls

52 The provenance of Bess's Papers has been traced in the *Folger Shakespeare Library Finding Aid* for the Cavendish-Talbot MSS.
53 These include records of deliveries to the follow persons, for whom we have no existing letters to or from Bess: Anne (Russell) Dudley, countess of Warwick (1549–1604), Bishop of London John Aylmer (1521–94), Mary (Browne) Wriothesley, second countess of Southampton (b. c. 1552, d. 1607), Douglas (Howard) Sheffield, Lady Sheffield (1542–1608), Thomas Butler, tenth earl of Ormond and third earl of Ossory (1531–1614), Anne, Lady Bacon (c. 1528–1610), Isabel, Lady Bowes (d. 1622).
54 In 1789 tourist John Byng visited the Old Hall and, after being given a tour by the housekeeper of the New Hall, Elizabeth Brailsford, he reported how he had rooted about in the abandoned library 'amidst a large parcel of pamphlets, letters and accounts . . . some letters directed to the old Countess . . . which wou'd bear a hearty rummage'; Worsley, *Hardwick Old Hall*, p. 34.
55 The 'politics of archival survival' as an issue for researching women's lives is discussed by Daybell, 'Social Negotiations', p. 2.
56 We know that Bess was corresponding with the earls and countesses of Shrewsbury (who included her fourth husband George Talbot, sixth earl of Shrewsbury, her son-in-law and stepson Gilbert Talbot, later seventh earl of Shrewsbury, and her daughter Mary [Cavendish] Talbot, wife of Gilbert and later seventh countess of Shrewsbury). Their letters bring a

24 Introduction

of Shrewsbury's great estates. In the 1670s they were put into their current order and given a thorough sorting by antiquary Nathaniel Johnston (1628–1705), whose annotations appear all over them. Johnston describes how, at Sheffield Manor, he rescued the letters 'from amids multitudes of waste papers, and the havock that mice, ratts, and wett, had made'.[57] He oversaw the binding of the letters into multiple volumes and divided what he regarded as being 'political' and 'public' letters from the 'domestic' and 'private' (his own artificial separation into separate spheres). Many of the latter were siphoned into one single volume, a filleted selection Johnston labelled in his own hand as 'only the letters from the Old Countesse of Shrewsbury [and] diverse other great Ladyes & gentlewomen' (Shrewsbury Papers, Vol. O). Johnston's bundling of many of the women's letters into one volume (the final one) suggests these were the letters of least concern or interest to him and we can only imagine what he discarded, left to rot in some damp corner of Sheffield Manor.

Whereas for Johnston these letters were of the least interest, their content has been of great value to scholars in recent years in illustrating many aspects of women's lives. As Daybell has put it, Bess's letters are 'emblematic of' and illustrate 'in microcosm' the wide variety of forms that Renaissance women's letters could take and many functions they could perform in this period.[58] Bess's correspondence extended into many areas as letters enabled her to conduct business, participate in politics, petition for entitlements, gather information about trade and legislation, extend her geographical networks, maintain relationships at Court and fashion her own identity. In particular scholars have emphasised the importance of the letters for showing Tudor women's participation in business and politics; to paraphrase Daybell, Bess's correspondence counters traditional understanding of women's letters as domestic, parochial and non-political.[59] Her letters have been used to show that Bess was a hub for intelligence, news and information; the driving force behind the building of Chatsworth and Hardwick; and a political operator involved in delicate negotiations. This book extends and augments these views and goes further in demonstrating the value of these letters and how we can extract their meanings. Furthermore, the argument here is that we cannot read these letters out of context of the sequences of which they were part – we cannot fillet out Bess's letters, as Nathaniel Johnston did, and set them aside as specimens of a category of women's letters that Johnston imagined was somehow separate from the main discourses

---

range of news, greetings and well wishes, as well as being the forum where family disputes were played out.

57 14 May 1677; quoted by Lodge, *Illustrations*, I, p. viii.

58 Daybell, *Women Letter-Writers*, p. 1.

59 Daybell, *Women Letter-Writers*, pp. 1–5.

of the surrounding letters to which they react or respond. The argument here is that we must read these letters within the contexts of the sequences of exchange of which they were part, and which were intertwined with and embedded within the epistolary exchanges with the women and men in Bess's life.

This approach, which involves, as far as possible, reading the letters as part of the sequences of exchange within which they were sent and received, is vital to re-contextualising and historicising the letters. Furthermore, this book argues that we must read the letters alongside other kinds of texts and material items with which they were contiguous, which surrounded them and can illuminate their meanings in a multitude of ways. Therefore, the discussions and analyses presented here move between Bess's letters and the other texts and objects that bring to life the literate cultures of the households within which they existed. We have a wealth of other documents and material survivals that make it possible to illustrate how epistolary writing was part of this broader continuum. Letter-writing manuals, household inventories, wage lists, financial accounts, wills, deeds, architecture, stonework, interior furnishings, embroidery and textile artworks have all been examined for this study. They are deployed to reconstruct scribal and literate cultures within Bess's households; to build a picture of her secretariat and the identities of her scribes; to track bearers and messengers coming in and out of her households; to re-imagine the spaces and locals where reading and writing took place; to describe more fully and precisely her relationships with her correspondents; to deduce the extent and nature of Bess's epistolary literacy; and to contextualise the visual and verbal iconography of her letters. The argument of this study is that we must draw upon these materials that capture the relationships that surrounded the letters if we are to return Bess's letters to the mobile, animate and dynamic environment within which they were produced and received.

Rather than a chronological or thematic approach, the chapters that follow are organised by processes. Chapter 1 is concerned with the process of composition. It considers the rhetorical models and linguistic scripts available to Bess and applied by her in the letters she sent. It includes consideration of letters she composed herself, but also reviews how the process of composition often involved collaboration with scribes and co-senders, and the implication of such collaborations for the rhetorical forms and interpersonal functions of her letters. Chapter 2 is concerned with the process of physically putting pen, ink and wax to paper. It considers Bess's own range of literate skills and competencies, and her practices when it came to sealing and signing letters. It concerns the roles of scribes, secretaries and amanuenses in her service and offers a detailed picture of scribal cultures within her households. It explores the range of factors (practical, interpersonal, rhetorical or to do with security and confidentiality) that were involved in the decision about when and how to use a scribe, and considers the identities of

26 Introduction

the most important scribes of her letters and their relationships with Bess. Chapter 3 considers the process of delivery. It concerns the services provided by bearers and messengers, but also the implications for transmission and reception of the material features of letters, such as enclosures, paper, use of space, ribbon, floss and locking and folding patterns. In these ways, this book is concerned with the multi-stage processes of production and reception, the various interpersonal relationships intertwined with these, and the materiality of early modern letters.

1 Composing and scripting letters

1.1 'Sett downe the matter plainly': situating epistolary composition within the genre of early modern letter-writing

> I coulde not by any possible meanes prevayle with hir to sett downe the matter plainly, as I desired she woulde in fewe lynes / Theise strange courses ar wonderfull to me.[1]

When Bess discussed the best way to write a letter, she used the everyday metaphor of 'plain language'. Here she described the advice she had given to her wayward granddaughter, Arbella Stuart, in an attempt to encourage Arbella to make her point 'plainly', a term she also used elsewhere to refer to her own language and to instruct others.[2] Plainness in this context meant language that avoided elaborate literary embellishments or ornamentation and that followed the precept of 'brevity and aptness' by getting to the point

---

1 2 February 1603, Bess (dowager countess of Shrewsbury) writes from Hardwick Hall to Sir Robert Cecil and Sir John Stanhope, sent, hand of Timothy Pusey. Glosses: hir: *her*, strange: *unaccountable*, courses: *proceedings, ways of behaviour*, wonderfull: *astonishing*. CP 135/129, fols 169–70, ID 130.

2 For example, in another letter where Bess gave letter-writing advice, discussed ahead at p. 59, she instructed her correspondent that 'The more ernyst and playn yt ys the more good yt wyll doe'. Other examples where Bess used the term 'playne' to refer to her own language include: 'playnely & truly' and 'made all thinges playne' (to her husband Shrewsbury, 9 June 1586, LPL, Talbot Papers, MS 3198, fol. 331r-v, ID 176; and to Sir Robert Cecil and Sir John Stanhope, 3 March 1604, CP 92/1, ID 134). 'Plainness' was a term used in contemporary epistolary theory: Angel Day's letter-writing manual *The English Secretary* (1586) was subtitled the *Plaine and Direct* method for enditing letters, and he opened by advising correspondents to use words that are 'plain for the matter', which, he explained, meant appropriate to the context and natural-sounding (not improper, obscure, new coined or archaic). The everyday metaphor LANGUAGE IS PLAIN in early modern English, with the associations of being clear, lucid, straightforward, frank, not styled, guileless, innocent, manifest and open, can be tracked through the *HTOED* using the *MM* project's *Metaphor Map of English* (categories: E18, E28, H18, H23, H25, K1, K4, W1, Z6).

28   Composing and scripting letters

'in fewe lynes'.[3] It is language that avoided copiousness or prolixities of the kind found in Arbella's 'wonderfull' and 'strange courses' of which Bess here thoroughly disapproved. In this way, Bess's own comments revealed her awareness of contemporary theories about letter-writing, as advised by epistolary manuals or observed in practice. Declarations of 'plainness' themselves had a rhetorical function as they served to frame language as being sincere and 'earnest' while drawing on contemporary Protestant discourses of manifest truthfulness.[4] As Bess's chosen *modus operandi*, when we read Bess's letters we can observe that for her 'plainness' was associated with finding the most effective way to present a case or request according to available epistolary models and conventions. Her letter-writing involved a disciplined approach to matters of decorum and attended to matching the letter's form to its intended purpose and function. Her letter-writing was precisely orientated towards a goal or desired outcome.[5] Where textualised emotion was included, it had a strategic purpose and was mindful of its anticipated reception. This goal-orientated attitude to letter-writing was quite the opposite of any notion of letters as vehicles for uncontrolled emotional catharsis or psychological release whereby the desire for an outpouring of expression took precedence over concerns with outcomes and reception.

What the concept of 'plain' language did not mean was that there was only one way to write and compose a letter, or only one epistolary style for each person. On the contrary, Bess, like many of her contemporaries, deployed an array of epistolary styles according to context and purpose. The concern of this chapter is to explore these distinctive epistolary styles deployed in the letters Bess sent. The aim is to show how the rhetorical forms of Bess's letters matched their pragmatic and socio-historical functions: how different epistolary styles were shaped in relation to the anticipated reception of the letter, its purpose and goal, as well as in relation to the relative social status of her correspondents, their familiarity with Bess and the topics covered in the letter. As Lynne Magnusson, James Daybell and others have shown, early modern letters encoded social and power relations; as Daybell puts it specifically in relation to Bess's letters, they 'textualise family and other relationships, mirroring the social and gender hierarchies of their social worlds, through modes of address, language, style and tone'.[6] The concern here is

---

3 The recommendation to follow precepts of 'brevity and aptness' was from epistolary manuals such as Fulwood's *The Enimie of Idleness* and Day's *The English Secretorie*, reviewed by Stewart and Wolfe, *Letterwriting*, pp. 21–33.

4 An overview of how the everyday language of sincerity was influenced by Reformation and Protestant discourses is provided by Williams, 'The Language of Early Modern Letters: Sincerity' in Wiggins, Bryson, Smith, Timmermann and Williams, *Bess of Hardwick's Letters*.

5 Bess's deployment of expected epistolary forms and structures meets expectations for a letter-writer from this period, as observed by Mack in his study of the influence of rhetorical theory and norms upon the practices of letter-writing, *Elizabethan Rhetoric*, pp. 114–16.

6 Daybell, *Women Letter-Writers*, p. 3; Magnusson, 'A Rhetoric of Requests' and *Shakespeare and Society Dialogue*.

to track these social relations through identification and analysis of particular epistolary styles and linguistic scripts. The argument made is that these distinct epistolary styles can be associated not only with sets of available linguistic scripts but also with particular compositional scenarios, which were often collaborative. That is to say: it was through diverse methods of composition – autonomous composition, dictation to a scribe, collaborative composition, co-sending or instructions to a scribe – that Bess's range of epistolary styles were forged. As such, Bess's letters provide us with an opportunity to interrogate early modern processes of composition, which incorporated fluctuating modes of collaborative and individual composition, and which show that Bess was alert to the suppleness and flexibility of the epistolary genre.

We are immediately struck, when we read the letters from Bess, by their range of different types of confident, assured and authoritative styles of writing.[7] We know of other Tudor women who generated bold, forceful and authoritative letters. Some of these women, such as Anne Lady Bacon (née Cooke), created linguistic capital through mastery of classical languages and engagement with intellectual debates, whereas this was not an option available to Bess, who had nothing like Anne Bacon's level of education.[8] While lacking in humanist educational resources, due to her more modest social background and educational start in life, the argument here is that Bess was nonetheless able to generate symbolic and linguistic capital and to use letters for expression and to enact her agency. Letters allowed her to achieve a series of empowered roles through which she was able to persuade, defend, assuage, cajole, reprimand, command or enhance emotional bonds. Letters allowed her to respond by changing the emotional tone or temperature of a situation or by redirecting another person's projected disrespect, indifference or anger. To do so, Bess, in her letters, skilfully combined techniques that included deployment of contemporary epistolary scripts and cultural models, collaboration with scribes and co-senders, precisely situated textualised emotion and projected confidence in her self-perception of her own power.[9]

---

7 Magnusson, 'Widowhood and Linguistic Capital', p. 3, observes that 'The most usual note struck in the existing letters of sixteenth-century English gentlewomen is of deference, often signaled by apology and self-deprecation', although it has been shown that its use was often strategic. Daybell, *Women Letter-Writers*, p. 3, observes that 'the codes of female deference (whether real of feigned) that marked some women's writing in the sixteenth century' are rarely found in Bess's letters. It is an observation that relates to the wider findings of his study that show how closer attention to Tudor women's letters reveals 'greater levels of female confidence, tenacity and forcefulness in writing to men than might previously have been suspected'; pp. 187–88.

8 Anne Bacon has been discussed in detail by Magnusson, 'Widowhood and Linguistic Capital', Mair, 'Anne, Lady Bacon', Stewart, 'The Voices', and Gemma Allen, *The Letters*.

9 Magnusson has argued for the correlation between choice of linguistic scripts and a woman's 'self-perception of her own power' in 'A Rhetoric of Requests', p. 55 and p. 63; a point which is explored further by Daybell, 'Scripting a Female Voice'.

30 *Composing and scripting letters*

Social historians over the past two decades have succeeded in mapping out early modern women's participation in a range of social roles, in particular as mothers, wives and mistresses of households. As Bess's letters so richly document her activities, they illustrate how one woman could move between different roles during her lifetime and deploy epistolary styles to be appropriate and advantageous to herself as, variously, mistress of the household, estate manager, spousal partner, business negotiator, political friend, grandmother, petitioner, estranged wife, female friend or affectionate mother.[10] Because we have a range of letters from Bess from across her lifespan that involved different correspondents, topics and collaborators, we are able to build a detailed and dynamic picture that shows how epistolary styles came in and out of use, or were called into service at particular moments. Over time, we can observe Bess's increased confidence, which grew as she gathered experience in negotiations, acquired expertise in legal matters and achieved financial independence.[11] These epistolary styles were available to Bess throughout her life, and as her circumstances fluctuated we see different levels of self-assurance or, conversely, insecurity emerge and recede. While the styles and tones deployed vary dramatically, underlying her letters we can detect a force of personality, which is apparent in the stances she chose to take, the subject positions from which she argued and her control of epistolary forms. At times she remained within the boundaries of expected convention; at other moments she tested the limits of acceptable behaviour and, when required, she was not afraid to offer direct challenges to authority through her letters.[12]

We have a total of one hundred letters existing from Bess and, of these, eighteen are entirely autographed by her; that is, eighteen letters exist where the whole letter, including the main body of the letter, was penned by Bess herself.[13] There has been a tendency, among editors and biographers seeking to find letters to represent Bess, to prioritise these entirely autograph letters. It is perhaps not surprising that commentators have so often cited from among this cluster of letters when seeking to represent Bess: it is a reflection of

---

10 The point is made by Daybell, *Women Letter-Writers*, pp. 168–69, specifically with reference to Bess, and has been made by Stewart in relation to Bacon, 'The Voices'.

11 We can make a comparison in this respect with Anne Bacon, who unleashed a stronger 'voice' when newly empowered as a widow; Magnusson, 'Widowhood and Linguistic Capital', Stewart, 'The Voices', Allen, *The Letters*. Daybell, *Women Letter-Writers*, p. 203, observes among women letter-writers more generally in the period a tendency towards increased confidence over time as they gained experience or achieved a higher status in later marriages.

12 The observation is also made by Steen in relation to Bess's daughter Mary (Cavendish) Talbot and granddaughter Arbella Stuart; 'The Cavendish-Talbot Women', p. 161.

13 These letters in Bess's own hand date from the early 1550s to 1587, are all sent letters, and the total word count of autograph writing (in letter texts and postscripts) from Bess is around 5,200 words. Section 2.2 considers the question of the reasons for the decision to write in her own hand or not. Most of the remaining letters from Bess include some element of writing in her own hand, such as her signature, initials, a subscription, a postscript, a forwarding note or a combination of these: 73 include some text in Bess's own hand and only 9 are entirely scribal including the signature.

Composing and scripting letters 31

the strong general tendency to associate autograph writing with a somehow more authentic voice of the sender. However, there have been two problems here. On the one hand, there have been some drastic misreadings by earlier editors and biographers of these autograph letters, which have reverberated throughout the biographical tradition and resulted in various distortions or misrepresentations. In particular, we find that, in early edited versions, Bess's voice was blended with and supplemented by editorial voices to create a forged hybrid voice.[14] On the other hand, and apart from problems with the unreliability of earlier editions, the argument made here is that we need to be careful of prioritising autograph writing based on the assumption that it is automatically closer to, or a better reflection of, the signer's personality or interior life. There are a number of reasons for caution and in favour of extending the category of a person's letters to include letters penned in the hands of scribes.[15] First, autograph writing was not hermetically sealed off from scribal writing or scribal influence; rather, letters penned in Bess's own hand can be shown in some cases to have involved direct input from scribes or collaborators. Second, letters penned in the hands of scribes or collaborators were, likewise, not hermetically sealed off from Bess's authorial influence; rather, letters written in the hands of scribes involved a range of types and levels of input from Bess and, in all cases, there is good evidence that Bess retained a high level of control and a final say over each letter that was sent out. Third, both the autograph letters and the scribal letters that Bess sent deployed well-established epistolary styles and linguistic scripts, selected to match their interpersonal function. Therefore, while we can detect Bess's own distinct personality throughout her letters, we do not find, neither in her autograph nor in her scribal writing, unique or highly innovative styles. Rather, all her letters are deeply implicated in contemporary cultural scripts and generic forms, which are deployed and shaped to purpose. To put it another way: letters do not themselves constitute the sender's language; they are always representations of the sender's language, whether scribal or autograph.

In order to illustrate these points, the remainder of this section discusses a selection of the letters Bess sent, which have been chosen to represent the main epistolary styles she deployed during her life and to allow for examination of her methods of composition. There are inevitably blurred lines between these different epistolary styles, and some letters switch between different styles. However, for the purpose of providing an overview, four distinct epistolary styles are identified here and letters that deploy these styles are grouped as follows: letters of household and estate management to her servants; letters of spousal partnership to her fourth husband, the earl of Shrewsbury; letters of petition and political friendship;

---

14 The concept of editing as 'forging' is proposed by Trigg, 'Speaking with the Dead', in relation to Middle English texts.

15 The view that we must extend the definition of authorship to include collaborative and scribal letters is also repeatedly made, specifically in relation to Tudor women's letter-writing, by Daybell, *Women Letter-Writers*, pp. 76, 84, 89–90.

32 Composing and scripting letters

letters in curial prose concerned with business and legal matters. For each, the discussion presents example letters, points out formal features of the style and then assesses the compositional scenarios and involvement, or not, of collaborators. While the focus here is upon questions of genre and authorship, at the same time the letters selected serve to portray vividly Bess's active involvement in political life and in spheres traditionally considered to be male realms of activity. We know that Tudor women were far more actively involved in these areas than depicted in contemporary prescriptive literature or given credit for in earlier historical accounts of the period, and the letters Bess sent strongly confirm this view.[16] We see Bess as estate manager and builder, responsible for directing male servants and workmen. We see her as a partner and advisor to her husband during the period of the keeping of Mary, Queen of Scots, when the management of their households was a matter of state security. We see her directly involved in political life as a petitioner with an interest in bills going through parliament and who was required to navigate Court power relations. And we see her hands-on involvement in business and legal matters, resolving issues with kin and neighbours and developing her own financial interests.

Letters of household and estate management to her servants

To reiterate, the purpose of the following discussion is to give an overview of the four main epistolary styles that featured in the letters Bess sent: household management, spousal partnership, political friendship and curial prose. The first of these styles (household management) was deployed in her letters to servants written in her own hand. While these letters have been discussed elsewhere, the interest here, in addition to providing an overview, is historiographical, as these letters have been regularly cited within the biographical tradition. Perhaps the letter most often cited by editors and biographers has been the one penned by Bess in her own hand to her servant Francis Whitfield around 1552.[17] It is one of the earliest letters we have from Bess (Lady Cavendish) and it presents her to us in full flow as the confident and authoritative householder, sending instructions to her servant back at Chatsworth while she was away in London (Plate 9):

---

16 The range of women's roles and the disparities between prescriptive literature and social realities have been discussed by, among others, Sommerville, *Sex and Subjection*, Houlbrooke, *The English Family*, Wall, 'Elizabethan Precept' and Peters, *Women in Early Modern Britain*.

17 Accurate transcriptions are provided in the editions by Daybell in Ostovich and Sauer's anthology, *Reading Early Modern Women*, pp. 192–95, which includes an image, and by Maxwell, 'Enacting Mistress and Steward Roles', pp. 77–80; both provide commentaries on the letter. A discussion of all the letters to and from Bess and her servants is presented by Maxwell, 'Household Words'. There is one other autograph letter from Bess to Francis Whitfield, written in her own hand, sent, 20 October [c. 1560], Folger CT, X.d.428 (84), ID 101.

Superscription, autograph:	To my sa[rvant] francys wytfelde [delive]r thys at chattysw[orth]e
Annotations, by Whitfield:	for the myller / for taking shepe / for taking Coll woodes / for Capons to be fatt / for swyne/ for the hard Cornefeldes / for a pyndr
Letter, autograph:	francys I haue spoken w^t your mayste for the clyltes or bordes that you wrete to me of and he ys contente that you shall take some for your nesecyte in the aponntemente of neusante. so that you take seche as y wyll do hyme no saruese aboute hys byldynge at chattysworthe. I pray you loke well to all thynges at chattysworthe tyll my auntes comynge whome whyche I hope shalbe shortely and yn the meane tyme cause bronshawe to loke to the smethes and all other thynges at penteryge lete the brewar make bere for me fourthew^t fore my owne drynkyng and your mayster and se that I haue good store of yet for yf I lacke ether good bere, or charcole or wode I wyll blame nobody so meche as I wyll do you. cause the flore yn my bede chambe to be made euen ether w^t plaster claye or lyme and al the wyndoyes were the glase ys broken to be mended and al the chambers to be made as close and ~~war~~ warme as you cane. I here that my syster Iane cane not haue ~~thyne~~ thynges that ys nedefoulle for hare to haue amowngste you yf yet be trewe you lacke agreat of honyste as well as dyscrescyon to deny hare any thynge that she hathe amynde to beynge yn case as she hathe bene. I wolde be lothe to haue any stranger so youshed yn my howse and then assure your selfe I cane not lyke yet to haue my syster so yousede. lyke as I wolde not ~~hau~~ haue any superfleuete or waste of any thynge. so lyke wysse wolde I haue hare to haue that whyche ys nedefoulle ~~for~~ and nesesary. at my comynge whome I shal knowe more. and then I wyll thynke as I shall haue cause. I wolde haue you to geue ~~to~~ to my mydwyffe frome me and frome my boye wylle. and to ^my^ syster norse frome me and my boye as hereafter folowyet fyrste to the mydwyfe frome me tene shyllynges. and frome wylle fyue shyllynges. to the norse frome me fyue shyllynges. and frome my boye iij fore pence. f so that yn the wolle you mouste geue to them twenty thre shyllynges and fore pence make my syster Iane preuye of yet and then paye yet to them fow[th]w^t yf you haue noother money take so meche of the rente at penteryge tyll my syster Iane that I wyll geue my dowter somethynge at my comyng whome and prayinge you not to fayle to se all thynges done accordyngely I bede you fare well frome london the xiiij of nouember
Subscription, autograph:	your mystrys
Signature, autograph:	Elyzabethe Cauendyssh
Postscript, autograph:	tyll Iames crompe that I haue resauyed the fyue ponde and ix^s that he sente me by heue alsope

(*Continued*)

34 Composing and scripting letters

(Continued)

14 November [1552], Bess of Hardwick (Lady Cavendish) writes from London to Francis Whitfield at Chatsworth House.[18] Gloss: mayste: *master*, whome: *home*, yet: *it*, Iane: *Jane*, hare: *her*, amowngste: *amongst*, hathe: *has*, yousede: *used*, wysse: *wise*, folowyet: *follows*, wolle: *whole*, dowter: *daughter*, tyll: *tell*.

Here we see Bess in command of the training she would have received as a young woman in how to manage a household and give orders with confidence and authority. The style of writing is characterised by terms of address that were direct to the point of abruptness ('Francis', 'your mistress'); matter-of-fact content and an absence of hedging or politeness tropes; commands that structure the letter and take the imperative form ('look well', 'cause', 'look to', 'let', 'see that', 'cause', 'give to them', 'make', 'pay', 'take', 'tell', 'tell'); and speech-like features.[19] It is a style appropriate to household business, and we are reminded that the letter dealt with practical matters by the list of notes on the outside in Whitfield's hand regarding sheep, capons, swine and cornfields. We might notice the level of energy Bess evidently put into personally managing the estates and we are left in no doubt as to her role as the 'driving force' behind the building of Chatsworth House.[20] While enacted here with some vigour, it was a style recognisable from other contemporary letters by women in charge of managing households and estates.[21] It was not a style restricted to women but applicable to authority figures

---

18 Folger CT, X.d.428 (82), ID 99, Plate 9.

19 An analysis of speech-like features across Bess's letters, which applies methodologies from discourse analysis, is presented by Marcus, 'An Investigation', the results of which show a markedly higher density of speech-like features in letters written in Bess's own hand compared to letters written in the hands of her scribes (the results summarised at pp. 208–9, 222–25, 233–36, 245–46, 268). Where the following discussion, here in this section of the chapter, mentions the higher density of speech-like features in Bess's autograph writing it is with reference to the results of Marcus's study. A summary list of speech-like features of language is given by Hughes, *English in Speech and Writing*, pp. 31–34; a more detailed and recent account of the relationship between speech and writing is by Culpeper and Kytö, *Early Modern English Dialogues*.

20 Bess's achievements as a builder and 'the driving force behind Hardwick' (p. 168) are reviewed by French, 'A Widow Building'. An overview of Bess's building activities that includes Chatsworth is provided by Durant, *The Smythson Circle*.

21 Daybell, *Women Letter-Writers*, pp. 184–85, describes such letters as typically 'curt and formal' in tone. Sommerville, *Sex and Subjection*, Chapter 8, discusses the roles of women in estate management in this period and the difference between 'precept and practice', summarised by Daybell, pp. 24–25.

Composing and scripting letters 35

for giving instructions to servants whether male or female, as we can see in the letters of Bess's fourth husband, the earl of Shrewsbury, when he wrote to his servant Baldwin.[22] Such comparisons remind us that we must read these letters within the context of the wider social discourse in which each correspondent took a well-established social role as part of a mistress/master–servant duologue.

To contextualise this letter further we can add information from the household records that shows the high status of upper servants such as Francis Whitfield, reflected in their payment and long service.[23] We can also add letters in the other direction, from Whitfield to Bess. When read as part of a long-standing relationship and wider pattern of epistolary exchange, not in isolation, we see that Bess's words here reflected her robust relationships with Whitfield and the high levels of mutual regard that were evidently in place and that allowed for uncompromising exchanges and directness on both sides.[24] Overall, Bess's letters to servants give us glimpses of how she utilised a particular social role and epistolary style – that of a mistress to her servant – to run an effective and efficient household from a distance. It is another question whether the cultural scripts implicated within this epistolary style had been internalised by Bess to the extent that they shaped her interactions with Whitfield in other everyday contexts and in person. Certainly, the two letters we have from Bess to Whitfield were part of a long-standing relationship and to a greater or lesser extent must have been contiguous with their other interactions.

While use of this epistolary style was conventional, it is here executed with a force and sharpness that are heightened by Bess's reprimands dispensed in an angry-sounding tone. The most severe reprimand was removed by Bess's first female biographers, who both presented bowdlerised versions of this letter and a toned-down, airbrushed version of Bess's words. Their attempts to excise what were evidently regarded as embarrassing displays of emotion, or a style of authority that sounded unwomanly, were well meaning: as feminist, revisionist biographers they were responding to a tradition in which Bess had been cast as a one-dimensional, stereotypical

---

22 There are numerous examples of Shrewsbury's letters to Baldwin in the Shrewsbury Papers at LPL, such as MS 697, fol. 181, MS 699, fol. 25 and MS 704, fol. 151 (IDs 193, 194 and 195), which open 'Baldwen', close 'Your Lord & Master' and share other features of style of Bess's letters to her servants.

23 For example, James Crompe, another upper servant at Chatsworth House to whom Bess wrote in a similar epistolary style, had his own room at Chatsworth House, 'Crumps Chamber'; Levey and Thornton, *Of Houshold Stuff*, p. 27.

24 Maxwell, 'Enacting Mistress and Steward Roles' and 'Household Words', provides a thorough analysis of both sides of the correspondence exchange, along with full details of the biographical and contextual information, from which this discussion benefits.

36   Composing and scripting letters

shrew and their accounts represented attempts to erase this depiction.[25] The way they monitored her letters can be seen by citing the extract as it was published:

Original letter

I here that my syster Iane cane not haue ~~thyne~~ thynges that ys nedefoulle for hare to haue amowngste you yf yet be trewe you lacke agreat of honyste as well as dyscrescyon to deny hare any thynge that she hathe amynde to beynge yn case as she hathe bene. I wolde be lothe to haue any stranger so yoused yn my howse

Maud Stepney Rawson, *Bess of Hardwick and Her Circle* (1900), pp. 9–10

I hear that my sister Jane cannot have things that is needful for her to have amongst you: If it be true, you lack a great of honesty as well as discretion to deny her anything that she hath a mind to, being in my house; and then assure yourself I cannot like it to have my sister so used.

Ethel Carleton Williams, *Bess of Hardwick* (1959), p. 24

I hear that my sister Jane can not have things that it is needful for her to have amongst you. If it be true you lack a great honesty as well as discretion to deny her anything that she hath a mind to, being in my house, . . . and then assure yourself I can not like to have my sister so used.

Rawson (silently) and Williams (with an ellipsis) removed Bess's strongest outburst of feeling, expressed in relation to her displeasure over the poor treatment of half-sister Jane (Leache) Kniveton: 'I wolde be lothe to haue any stranger so yoused yn my howse'.[26] The omission seems intended to

---

25 Bess's reputation and negative portrayals of her authority as 'unwomanly' are discussed by Steen, 'The Cavendish-Talbot Women', p. 161. The inaccuracies in the earlier editions of this letter (and also in Hunter's edition, *Hallamshire*, p. 107) are pointed out by Daybell and Maxwell, in their editions, already given earlier, and by Lovell, *Bess of Hardwick*, pp. 80–81. The biographical information relating to 'Jane' named in the letter is presented by all three.

26 There has been some confusion over which of Bess's sisters called 'Jane' she is, but Maxwell has confirmed her identity: 'Bess had two sisters named Jane: her elder, full sister Jane Boswell or Bosville (née Hardwick) and her younger, maternal half-sister Jane Kniveton (née Leche). "My syster" first appears in account book entries in March 1549, the same month as Whitfield . . . and a "Mistress Jane" appears in the Cavendishes' London accounts for 1552–53 . . . From the 1560s onwards, there are scattered references to "Mistress Kniveton" in the Chatsworth and Hardwick accounts, reaching a high concentration in the Hardwick accounts of the 1590s. Since Jane Kniveton demonstrably lived with Bess for much of their adult lives, the early sources, including this letter, more likely refer to her than to Bess's full sister Jane'; 'Enacting Mistress and Steward Roles', p. 78.

remove the severity of the reprimand, but by allaying the emotional force of the letter, Rawson and Williams deny Bess some of her anger and diminish her authority. In addition, they revise Bess's precise point of argument, 'beynge yn case as she hathe bene', a reference to Jane Kniveton having recently given birth, apparent from the payments to her midwife. Their sanitising of the letter by removing the reference to childbirth, instead giving the rather vague 'being in my house', also removes the precise reason Bess gives for her displeasure. The expurgation is important because Bess's point of argument shows us that her use of anger was justified and motivated by a specified target and rationale.

Such tampering by biographers is anachronistic and must be reassessed in the light of more recent, historically rigorous understandings of the history of the household and of emotions. As Linda Pollock has shown, 'situated' anger – that which was specific and appropriate to a particular set of circumstances – was deemed a socially acceptable, even necessary, negotiating technique for relationships in the early modern household.[27] To deliver a reprimand charged with anger was to display the limits of tolerance. Bess's textualised anger functions here to redefine and open up negotiations over what she saw as an unsatisfactory household dynamic. As was true of Bess's textualised emotion elsewhere in her letters, her display of anger was specifically situated and harnessed to purpose. We have no letters from Bess that descend into uncontrolled tirades or lengthy diatribes, or the kind of 'poison pen' letters that exist for some of her contemporaries, who included women such as her own daughter Mary (Cavendish) Talbot.[28] By contrast, Bess's expression of anger here is directed towards a particular point, a tactic she used to establish authority in her letters and as a strategy of negotiation. The textualising of emotion according to more recent developments in the field of the history of emotions, then, goes well beyond the readings of these letters by earlier biographers. We see elsewhere that textualised emotion was a feature of Bess's letters as a means of social negotiation as well as individual expression, and such examples allow us to go beyond seeing letters primarily as functioning to inscribe power relations and social status. This is not to suggest that her emotion, here, was not real or felt: an emotion can be experienced physiologically and, at the same time, textualised as an epistolary strategy. We cannot recreate the experience of the emotions that she felt – or determine if and how they were felt – but we can observe that her letters present us

27 Pollock, 'Anger and the Negotiation of Relationships', is the key study here, from which this discussion has benefitted.
28 Daybell, *Women Letter-Writers*, pp. 185–86, describes one such 'malicious' letter from Mary, countess of Shrewsbury, to Thomas Stanhope in 1593 (BL Lansd. 99, f. 274). The letter is here and elsewhere misattributed to Bess, as with others of Mary's letters once she became countess of Shrewsbury.

38   Composing and scripting letters

with a wide palette of emotions that were aligned with the intended goals of her letters.[29]

There is no reason to suggest that this letter, and the other existing autograph letter to her servant Whitfield, were anything other than Bess's own compositions. That is, on the spectrum of possible compositional scenarios, her two letters to Whitfield are at one extreme pole: they were both penned in her own hand and composed autonomously based on social scripts in which she had been trained. When we imagine their composition, we should perhaps envisage Bess drawing from her knowledge of verbal discourse and extemporising in writing with minimal self-censure or revision (not reworking or revising written drafts).[30] Further support for this envisaged compositional scenario is suggested by one more letter to a servant in the same epistolary style: to her servant James Crompe written in 1560, sent from Bess (Lady St Loe) and penned in the hand of a scribe. In this case, it is most likely that Bess was dictating directly to a scribe who wrote down her words virtually verbatim. It is a method of composition that we do not see elsewhere in the letters she sent but which it seems, based on this letter, she would utilise at times. There are three reasons for deducing that this letter to Crompe was copied down verbatim from dictation.[31] First, the letter is written in the same style and argued with as much frankness and force of personality as her letters to Whitfield written in her own hand.[32] Second, the letter is copied by a scribe writing in an italic hand that is so inexpert we might suspect this was an individual with a lower level of literacy (e.g., a child or lower servant), not the kind of highly trained individuals seen

29 The case of Bess adds detail to Daybell's broad survey of Tudor women letter-writers, which has tracked women's use of letters for purposes of unburdening themselves of anxieties, fears and worries or unloading emotional distress, with the observation that 'the sixteenth century is thus marked by women's growing familiarity and inventiveness with letters and letter-writing practice'; *Women Letter-Writers*, p. 174. The arguments here further coincide with Daybell's claims for the potential further value and interest of early modern letters within the field of history of emotions; 'Social Negotiations'.

30 One of the overall conclusions by Marcus, 'An Investigation', pp. 268–69, specifically with reference to Bess, is that early modern female education meant women were often less familiar with written texts than their male contemporaries, which resulted in, as Truelove, 'Commanding Communications', p. 54, has put it, 'a greater reliance on verbal discourse to formulate written sentences'.

31 These reasons can be compared to assessments of other early modern women's writings, such as the duchess of Suffolk and Lady Lisle's letters, that have been shown to be dictated verbatim to scribes, as summarised by Daybell, *Women Letter-Writers*, pp. 81–82.

32 We can contrast this letter to the one other letter we have from Bess to a servant in the hand of a scribe: to her husband Shrewsbury's servant Thomas Baldwin, with additions by Shrewsbury himself, 17 January 1580 (LPL, Talbot Papers, MS 3206, pp. 1017–18, ID 190). The style of the letter is completely different to those of her other letters to servants, which are either in her own hand or dictated verbatim. It is in a secretary script by a hired scribe and includes many features of curial prose suggestive of the role that scribes could play in shaping the language of a letter, discussed in section 2.3.

Composing and scripting letters **39**

elsewhere in her letters who could be involved in shaping form and content.[33] Third, we can observe that the letter contains rhetorical punctuation; colloquial and informal language (e.g., telling Crompe that if her mason will not apply himself to his work then 'you know he ys no mete mane for me'); speech-like features; and impoliteness forms similar to those reported in her speech elsewhere that therefore seem especially distinctive of her. To give an example of the latter: Bess told Crompe that if her workman Worth claimed to be behind in payment then he 'doth lye lyke a false knaue'. It was an insult in recognisably the same forthright tone and turn of phrase as that quoted in a letter a few years later by her husband the earl of Shrewsbury, who told Bess that the rent receiver's man had been and that he (the rent receiver's man) told him (Shrewsbury) that she (Bess) 'called him a knave' and so he had 'payd the knave your Rent'.[34] Shrewsbury's wry comment acknowledged his wife's formidable and uncompromising directness applied to the management of her workmen. Again, we see situated anger in the form of a reprimand as a strategy in Bess's negotiations with employees, dispensed with a force that Shrewsbury clearly regarded as noteworthy even if par for the course in his wife's robust mistress–servant interactions.

Letters of spousal partnership to her husband the earl of Shrewsbury

The second epistolary style under consideration here is that which Bess deployed within letters of spousal partnership. The letters that feature this epistolary style are also among those most often cited by editors and biographers: they are the four letters written in Bess's own hand to her fourth husband, the earl of Shrewsbury, between 1570 and 1577.[35] Marital correspondence from the sixteenth century provides, as social historians in recent years have shown, a 'useful corrective to prescriptive texts', such as conduct books and sermons, and offers us more realistic portrayals of married life.[36] The 'less unequal' partnership that has been depicted between spouses – which involved women taking active roles beyond the narrowly domestic realm, taking charge of cattle, managing men, giving advice to

---

33 Details of the palaeography and spelling of this letter, and their distinctiveness from Bess's autograph writing and personal spelling system, are discussed in section 2.3.

34 The letter is from Shrewsbury to Bess in his own hand, sent, [1574?], Folger CT, X.d.428 (94), ID 72.

35 The letters, which were all sent between 1570 and 1577, are LPL Talbot Papers, MS 3205, fol. 58–69, IDs 178, 184, 182, 183. There is one other existing letter from Bess to Shrewsbury in her own hand (at fol. 73, ID 186), written in 1587 during a period of reconciliation in their marital dispute. There are four other letters written from Bess to Shrewsbury, all of which are scribal, and their marked contrast in style and tone to the four in her autograph hand from the 1570s is discussed in section 1.3.

36 Daybell, *Women Letter-Writers*, p. 200, and Chapter 8 on marital correspondence.

40 *Composing and scripting letters*

husbands and resolving disputes – was frowned upon in conduct books but, in reality, and as social historians have repeatedly shown over recent years, many wives took these roles and were valued by their husbands for their practical capabilities. This sense of a 'less unequal' partnership is certainly evident in the letters between Bess and her fourth husband, the earl of Shrewsbury, during the first decade of their marriage, and the following letter gives us a vignette of Bess as the competent and capable wife. As with her two letters to Whitfield (discussed in the last section), there is no reason to think that this letter (along with the other letters in her own hand to Shrewsbury) is anything other than an autonomous composition, by Bess herself (Plate 13):

Superscription, autograph: To my lorde my hosbande the erle of Shrouesbury

Letter, autograph: my deare harte I haue sende your latter agene and thanke you for them they requyre no ansore, but when you wryte remember to thanke hym for them, yf you cane not gett my tembur caryed I moste be w^t out yt tho I greuly wante yt, but yf yt wolde plese you to comand heberte ^or any other^ to moue your tenanter to brynge yt I knowe the wyll not denyue to do yt, I prey you lette me knowe yf I shall haue the tone of Irone, yf you cane not spare yt I moste make ^heste^ to gette yt else were, for I may not now wante yt, you promysed to sende me money afore thys tyme to by oxxen, but I se out of syght ^out^ of mynde w^t your onkende none, my sone gelberte hathe bene vary yll yn hys hede euer sence he came frome Shefelde, ~~but~~ I thynke yt ys hys oulde dyseasse. he ys now I thanke god some what better and she vary well, I wyll sende you the byll of my wode stoff I prey you lett yt be sente to fore that he may be sure to reseaue all. I thanke you for takynge order for the caryage ~~l~~ of yt to hardwycke, yf you wolde comande your wagene myght bryng yt thether I thinke yt wolde be saffeleste caryed, her ys nether malte nor hopes, the malte come laste ys so vary yll and stynkenge as hankes thynkes none of my workemene wyll drynke yt, showe thys latter to my frende and then retorne yt, I thynke you wyll take no dyscharge at sowches handes nor the reste, you may worke stylle yn dysspyte of them, the laue is one your syde, yt cane not be but that you shall haue the quenes consente to remoue hether therfor ^yf^ you wolde haue thynges yn redynes for your prouysyon you myght the soner com*m*e. com*m*e ether afore medsomer or not thys yere, for any prouysyon you haue yet, you myg[h]t haue come as well at ester as at thys day, here ys yt no maner of ^prouysyon^ more then a letyl drenke, whyche makes me to thynke you mynde not to come god sende my Iuwell helthe. ~~thys f~~ saterday mornynge

Subscription, autograph: your faythefoul wyffe

Signature, autograph: EShrouesbury

Postscripts, autograph:	I haue sente you letyss for that you loue them, and euer seconde day some ys sente to your charge and you. I haue nothynge else to sende lette me here how you dyour charge and loue dothe and comende me I prey you, yt were well you sente fore or fyue pecus of the great hungeng that the myght be pott oup and some carpetes, I wysshe you wollde [*in the margin:*] ~~thynkes yn~~ haue thynkes yt that redynes tha[t] you myght come w'yn iij or fore dayes after you here frome corte wryte to balwene to call one my lorde tresorare for ansore of you [*sic*] leters [1577], Bess of Hardwick (countess of Shrewsbury) to her husband George Talbot, sixth earl of Shrewsbury, sent.[37] Gloss: onkende: *unkind*, none: *from 'myn own'*, wode stoff: *wood stores*, saffeleste: *safeliest*, laue is one: *law is on*, yt cane not be: *it cannot be*, soner: *sooner*, ester: *Easter*, here ys yt: *here is yet*, Iuwell: *jewel*, letyss: *lettuce*, pecus: *pieces*, pott oup: *put up*, wollde: *would*, ~~thynkes yn~~ haue thynkes yt: *have things in*, here frome corte: *hear from court*, call one: *call on*.

This letter was written during the period when the couple were the keepers of Mary, Queen of Scots, and finds Bess in the midst of making arrangements for the preparation of her household, in expectation that her husband may soon bring the Scottish Queen along with her vast retinue to Chatsworth.[38] The enormous logistical, financial and psychological demands involved as the Scottish Queen's custodians cannot be underestimated, and it was a role that eventually took its toll on Shrewsbury's health and on the couple's marriage. Yet, we must not to project forward when reading letters from this earlier period of their sixteen-year custodianship, when interactions between the couple were harmonious. For many years the couple dealt with the challenges of their duty amicably and with high levels of mutual support, based on their shared social and political responsibilities, and Shrewsbury evidently had great trust in his wife's abilities and judgement, as reflected in this letter. So, we see a high level of trust apparent in the references to the couple's dual epistolary activities: Bess returned to her husband letters written to him, which he had forwarded to her, and advised him how to answer them ('remember to thanke hym'); then advised him to 'wryte to balwene' (i.e., write to his servant in London Thomas Baldwin) to tell Baldwin to speak to Lord Burghley for an answer to his (Shrewsbury's) letters about moving the Scottish Queen to Chatsworth ('to call one

---

37 ID 182 (Plate 13).

38 Guy, *My Heart Is My Own*, p. 518, records the frequent movement of the Scottish Queen and her entourage between Chatsworth and other households.

42 Composing and scripting letters

my lorde tresorare for ansore of your leters').[39] We see that Shrewsbury had sought and received other kinds of advice from Bess and that she gave her opinion on issues that included a dispute (saying 'the laue is one your syde') and the likelihood that Queen Elizabeth would give permission for Shrewsbury to bring Mary, Queen of Scots, to Chatsworth ('yt cane not be but that you shall haue the quenes consente to remoue hether').[40] We see ongoing discussions of practical matters to do with estate management, building works and, above all, Bess's concerns over the drastic lack of provisions at Chatsworth for receiving the household of the Scottish Queen ('here is y[e]t no maner of ^prouysyon^ more then a letyl drenke'). These arrangements included getting timber, iron, cattle, wood supplies, malt and hops for beer, and carpets and wall-hangings to equip Chatsworth for the imminent arrival of their royal guest. We can also observe the conversational style of this letter, which is not hedged with high levels of politeness or stiff formulae but characterised by speech-like features of syntax, as well as proverbs and interjections ('out of sight out of mind', 'I thanke god'), discourse deixis ('thanke hym', 'she vary well', 'my frende') and interspersed concerns over the health of family members (e.g., the return of their son Gilbert's 'oulde dyseasse' that makes him 'yll yn hys hede'). The corrections, errors, insertions and crossings-out throughout show the letter was not drafted in advance and was subject to only a minimum of revision. Overall, these features indicate Bess's confidence in the kind of reception her letter would receive – that is, confidence that robust and direct exchanges with her husband, with minimal level of self-censure, were appropriate and reflected the tenor of their relationship. These features are found reflected

---

39 There are other examples of Bess's involvement in her husband's letter-writing, which included acting in his place when he was absent, as she described in her letter on the eve of the arrival of the Scottish Queen, to the earl of Leicester on 21 January 1569: 'your lorddshypp latters directed vnto my lord my husband and to me yn hys absence', Magdalene College Library, Pepys, MS 2503, pp. 203–6, ID 107 (Plate 10). We see Shrewsbury's request that his wife write for him due to pain in his hand, in reply to a letter from the earl of Leicester, 10 October 1580: 'I haue returned vnto you my Lord of Leycesters letter and praye you when you write againe let his Lord vnderstand that becasuse I perceived by his last letter vnto me it was doutfull how sone I shulld obteyne graunte of payment I haue staied furder writing vnto him therin having no dout of his Lordship's good remembrance & furderance therof'; Folger CT, X.d.428 (104), ID 79.

40 It is something we know from throughout many years of their correspondence – for example, there is Shrewsbury's reference to 'your Advyse in your lettar you wylled me to burne which I dyd', apparently regarding the difficult issue of managing the Scottish Queen's access to correspondence, and, on another occasion, his request to Bess urging her to send him her advice on the matter of a persuivantship: 'I pray you fale nott but sent me your Advyse consarnyng this mattar'; c. 1570 and c. 1571, Folger CT, X.d.428 (89 and 91), IDs 68 and 69. We see the giving of advice in the letters of other sixteenth-century married couples, where husbands displayed high levels of trust in the competence of their wives, discussed by Daybell, *Women Letter-Writers*, p. 107, and Harris, *English Aristocratic Women*.

Composing and scripting letters   43

back in Shrewsbury's letters to her in this sequence and from this era the letters between the countess and earl mirrored one another in their language, which reflected the nature and quality of their relationship. It reminds us that we should not read the four existing letters from Bess to Shrewsbury during this era in isolation. Rather, they existed as part of a sequence with his letters and were contiguous with a larger and well-established social discourse between husbands and wives.[41]

As well as a depicting a practical partnership, the letter gives us evidence that their relationship included emotional bonds that were affectionate and thoughtful and involved shared humour. So, we see Bess addressed her husband through terms of endearment, such as, here, 'my deare harte', 'none' and 'my Iuwell', which were typical of the affectionate nicknames that appeared throughout their letters to one another and were part of an ongoing exchange of mutual affection between the couple.[42] We see the exchange of thoughtful gifts, such as, here, lettuce, which was a delicacy.[43] Further evidence of their affectionate relationship came in the form of playful teasing and here Bess – in terms reminiscent of the Thynne women's playful subversion of the stereotype of the shrew – mock-berated her husband for not fulfilling one of her requests: 'I se out of syght ^out^ of mynde with your onkende none'. We know that 'none' (from 'myne own') was their favourite pet name for one another, and here Bess joked that she had been forgotten using this shared term of endearment. It was evidently an ongoing joke between the couple as it appeared in two other letters from Bess, both amicable and

41 There are nineteen letters from Shrewsbury to Bess written during the harmonious years of their marriage, from June 1568 to September 1580, all in his own hand and all sent letters that on receipt came into Bess's Papers. In total, seventeen of these letters are held at the Folger CT, X.d.428 (85–89, 91–99 and 102–103), IDs 64–78 and 154, one is at Chatsworth House as part of the Devonshire MSS (ID 203) and one is in private ownership (a copy is available at BL RP 120, ID 245). One more letter from Shrewsbury to Bess, sent on 10 October 1580, is in the hand of a scribe because of pain in his own hand (ID 79).

42 Elsewhere in her four letters to Shrewsbury during this period, Bess refers to Shrewsbury as 'my Iuwell' (i.e., 'my jewel'), 'my none', 'my deare none' and 'my deare swete harte'. These names are reciprocated repeatedly throughout Shrewsbury's affectionate letters to her, with names such as: 'My dere none', 'swete none', 'trew none', 'swete', 'my one swete harte', 'my swete harte', 'my only Ioye', 'My Iuell', 'my swete trew none & fethefull wyfe', 'my one harte' (Ioye: *joy*, Iuell: *jewell*). Such terms of endearment appeared in other letters between wives and husbands in the period, as outlined by Daybell, *Women Letter-Writers*, pp. 216–17, who comments in particular on their usefulness as guides to 'the "quality" of the marriage', p. 204, as well as the tendency for husbands to be more expressive than wives in the earlier period, p. 208 and p. 227. The critique by Daybell of the controversial view derived from Lawrence Stone, that there was an absence of 'conjugal and maternal love and affection' and people were 'emotional cripples' in the early modern period, p. 23, aligns with developments in the burgeoning field of history of emotions, discussed further in section 1.4.

43 The items and food gifts sent between the couple are discussed in section 3.3.

44   *Composing and scripting letters*

congenial letters where Bess asked after Shrewsbury's health, sent lettuce, butter and a news-letter and expressed longing to see him: in one Bess closed 'fare well onkende none' and in the other she again mock-berated him for forgetting his 'none', saying 'you for get your none', before closing her letter saying 'ther moste be better proueysyon made or ells I shall thynge my none meanes not to come here thys somer'.[44]

The playful humour, then, is readily apparent when we read this letter of 1577 in the context of the couple's wider correspondence and by comparison with other husband–wife exchanges of the period. Yet this letter has been the subject of drastic misreadings. The originator of the problem was Edmund Lodge, whose edition of 1791 (which has been one of the main sources for Bess's life and letters used by recent biographers and historians) contained two editorial changes. First, Lodge silently expurgated Bess's playful and affectionate term of endearment, and therefore dramatically changed the letter's overall tone:

Original letter

I se out of syght ^out^ of mynde with your onkende none

Edmund Lodge, *illustrations of British history* (1791), II, pp. 167–68, quoted by Williams, *Bess of Hardwick* (1959), p. 128, and Lovell (2005), *Bess of Hardwick*, p. 262

I see out of sight out of mind with you.

Lodge's editorial revision here transformed a humorous and ironic joke between the couple into a harsh-sounding complaint or reprimand, and Lodge also inserted a paragraph break here (not in the original letter) to drive home the point. Second, Lodge punctuated and italicised Bess's postscript for emphasis and to make the awkward-sounding syntax appear comprehensible:

Original letter (Plate 13)

lette me here how you dyour charge and loue dothe and comende me I prey you

---

44 IDs 184 and 178. We know of several other Tudor women who used humour in a similar way, such as the countess of Southampton, and an overview is given by Daybell, *Women Letter-Writers*, p. 215; he comments in particular on the well-known case of Maria Thynne, whose letters to her husband play with precepts of ideal wifehood, that her epistolary writing 'exposes a private playfulness and compatibility with her husband' and that such a reading 'is one of companionship rather than opposition'; detailed discussions of the Thynne women's letters are given by Williams, *Women's Epistolary Utterance*, and Wall, 'Elizabethan Precept'.

> Edmund Lodge, *illustrations of British history* (1791), vol. 2, pp. 167–68, quoted without italics by Williams, *Bess of Hardwick* (1959), p. 128, and Lovell (2005), *Bess of Hardwick*, p. 262
>
> Lette me here how you, your charge *and love*, dothe, and commend me, I prey you.

Bess's biographers have repeatedly been puzzled by this postscript reference to, as Lodge has it, with his own italics added, 'your charge *and love*'. Lodge, ever keen to spice up his entertaining history, took this to be a sarcastic reference from a jealous wife to Mary, Queen of Scots, and added a footnote to say as much; E. C. Williams suggested that 'charge and love' may refer to a ward of Shrewsbury's, whereas Lovell suggested humour might be possible, although her reading is tentative.[45] Lovell's hesitancy is understandable, especially given that her reading was based on Lodge's expurgated and annotated edition, where the affectionate tone and shared humour of the preceding letter had been removed. By contrast, when we read the postscript in the context of a full and accurate transcription, and in the broader context of the couple's affectionate epistolary exchanges, the postscript could, certainly, plausibly be read as a continuation of the playful and humorous tone. That is, according to such a reading: when Bess asked after the health of Shrewsbury and 'your charge and loue', she was asking after the health of the Scottish Queen, his charge, who was also, as it were, his 'loue', being the woman who kept them apart. In the context of this affectionate letter, it would be another example of playful humour of which Bess was confident of an appreciative reception and which speaks of a level of mutual understanding and compatibility between husband and wife. Bess's revision and the awkward-sounding syntax here perhaps suggest that she hesitated for a moment over how to formulate the phrase, something we might expect from someone trying to select wording that would convey just the right tone and level of irony.[46]

While this reading is possible, there is another interpretation that we must also consider, one that has been invisible to previous commentators reading the letter from (inaccurate) printed editions. That is, it seems that the wording of the postscript here has been garbled as a result of 'eye-skip'

---

45 Williams, *Bess of Hardwick*, p. 128 and footnote 4, notes that the postscript is 'a strange sentence which has puzzled many historians' and suggests that although the 'words "your charge and love" are generally taken to mean Mary Queen of Scots' it is possible 'they may refer to a ward of the Earl's.' Lovell wonders if this was a 'tease'; *Bess of Hardwick*, p. 263. Both use Lodge as their source.

46 Bess's biographers have (silently) adjusted this line in order to try to make it comprehensible: for example, 'Let me hear how you and your charge and love doth', where 'and' is an editorial addition; Williams, *Bess of Hardwick*, p. 128; and 'Let me hear how you, your charge and love, do', where both commas are editorial additions; Lovell, *Bess of Hardwick*, p. 262.

46   *Composing and scripting letters*

(*homoioteleuton*), a well-known type of slip in handwritten texts, even among the most careful of scribes.[47] The correction Bess made (when she converted her second 'y' from a letter that looks like an 'a' but is more likely to be the start of a 'd') suggests she had begun to write: let me hear 'how you dothe . . .', but then, getting as far as 'how you d . . .', remembered to ask after her husband's charge, the Scottish Queen. Bess's intention was then to write, by copying out the same wording that appears in exactly the same position three lines directly above here, 'how your charge and you dothe'. The eye-skip – whereby Bess wrote 'loue' instead of 'you' – resulted from her eye skipping upwards by six lines instead of three, to where the word 'loue' appeared directly below the word 'you', as it did in the line she was currently writing (Plate 13). To summarise: 'loue' instead of the intended 'you' was a visual copying error (known as eye-skip) that resulted from Bess following the phrase 'charge and you' from three lines directly above, but then accidentally skipping up six lines instead. It is a reminder of the importance for interpretation not only of full and accurate transcripts but also of the graphical layout of the handwritten page, which shows the position of words and lines in relation to one another.

Lodge used his expurgated, regularised and annotated transcripts to support his reading of this letter as being in an angry tone, which he perceived to be barbed with bitter, jealous and sarcastic comments. This was the only letter from Bess he included in his three-volume edition and, detached from the context of the sequence of exchanges with Shrewsbury, he appropriated it as the basis for his own misogynistic biographical portrayal of Bess. Famously, in his portrayal, Lodge cast Bess as 'proud, furious, selfish, unfeeling', a quotation that has been used *ad infinitum*, not only in popular contexts but also in scholarly narratives and despite the revisionist accounts there have been of Bess's life.[48] But what Lodge presented as a 'proud and furious' tone of voice in fact represents a drastic misreading of the letter, one designed to enliven his hagiographical narrative of the lives of the earls of Shrewsbury. Lodge's reading also projected forward to the couple's much

---

47 Beal, *A Dictionary*, p. 361.
48 Lodge, *Illustrations*, I, p. xvii. For example, Kiefer, 'Architecture', p. 695, while praising Bess's qualities, cannot resist quoting Lodge's often-repeated biographical sketch of her as 'proud, furious, selfish and unfeeling'; Worsley, *Hardwick Old Hall*, p. 23, summarises Bess's mixed historical reputation using the same quotation; Fraser, *Mary, Queen of Scots*, uses Lodge as her source and, again, uses exactly the same quotation, p. 551; and Guy, *My Heart Is My Own*, uses Lodge's edition (p. 453) as a source for Bess's life and letters in his own biography of Mary, Queen of Scots, and echoes Lodge in his summary description of Bess as 'a woman of lofty pride, quick jealousy, and an almost insatiable ambition', p. 441. The notion that Bess was fuelling salacious 'gossip' about her husband having a sexual relationship with the Scottish Queen is a red herring that goes back to Lodge, but which has been repeatedly cited in historical accounts – for example, Guy, *My Heart*, p. 452. These untrue rumours were generated by the Scottish Queen herself as one of her desperate ploys for survival, as has been shown by Durant, *Bess of Hardwick*, pp. 129–31.

later marital disputes and he included several of Shrewsbury's letters about or to Bess that are highly critical of her, while including none of her letters of response. It is a reminder that letters need to be precisely situated in their historical and linguistic contexts as well as within the contexts of the wider sequences of epistolary exchanges in which they were embedded. In this case, in order to produce a more accurate and fair reading, the letter must be situated in the context of the correspondence exchange with Shrewsbury, in the context of the social roles of husband–wife partnerships and in its original handwritten form. In many respects, the form and style of this letter are predictable and known elsewhere from other successful early modern marriages – although distinctive to Bess were her high levels of energy and drive, her competency, the mutual affection shared with her husband and their evident enjoyment of shared humour.[49] Yet commentators have repeatedly read this letter (from Lodge's inaccurate transcription) in isolation from its social and material contexts and the result has been a crushing portrayal of Bess's character and historical reputation.

Letters of petition and political friendship

The third epistolary style under consideration here is that of political friendship. Among the styles reviewed so far, we have seen seven letters written in Bess's own hand (to her servants and husband). The remaining eleven letters we have in Bess's own hand span the period from 1550 to 1586 and all deploy the language of 'political friendship', an epistolary style well known in the period for letters of request, petition, thanks and social courtesy.[50] While the discourse of political friendship was traditionally associated with men, it also appeared in letters sent to and from women.[51] It is espe-

49 Daybell, *Women Letter-Writers*, p. 76, observes that several Tudor women expressed themselves in 'very distinct and individual styles identifiable through their letters, which argues strongly for the fact they wrote them' and he includes here Anne, Lady Bacon, Elizabeth, Lady Russell, Margaret Clifford, countess of Northumberland, and Katherine, duchess of Suffolk.

50 These eleven letters are all in her own hand and all sent: there are four to Sir John Thynne, Senior, written on 15 March and 31 March [1550s], in February 1558, and on 25 February 1558 (Longeleat, Thynne Papers, MS 4, fols 243–47v, and TH/VOL/III/9 and 11, IDs 200, 198, 111 and 112); three to the earl of Leicester written on 21 Jan 1569 (ID 107, Plate 10), 27 June [1576?] and, with additions by her husband Shrewsbury, 18 May [1577?] (Longleat House Dudley Papers, DU/II/110 and 173, IDs 110 and 109); one to Queen Elizabeth on 17 March 1578 (CP 9/62, fols 101–2, ID 120); two to Lord Burghley on 24 October 1578 and 13 August 1586 (CP 10/70, fols 125–6, and HMC (Salisbury), III, p. 167, IDs 122 and 252); and one to Sir Francis Walsingham (CP 10/77, fols 137–8, ID 123). There exist at least another twenty letters from Bess that also use this epistolary style but are penned by scribes, from throughout her life.

51 An overview of the forms and functions of Tudor women's petitionary letters that includes discussion of 'women's easy familiarity in using a language of patronage, favour and "political friendship" – a language typically seen as predominantly male', is provided by Daybell, 'Scripting a Female Voice', p. 4.

48   *Composing and scripting letters*

cially valuable for tracking social relations and power dynamics because writers adjusted their language, in each letter, to correlate with contextual factors, such as the relative social status of sender and recipient, their familiarity with each other, the magnitude of any request made and the broader context of writing. Across the letters Bess sent we find a range of different power dynamics inscribed: at one end of the spectrum are those where she acknowledged her recipient's perceived social superiority; at the other are the letters she wrote '*en grande dame*'.[52] Her letters thus offer us compelling insights into Bess's self-perception of her own power at particular moments during her life. They also reveal her use of conventional linguistic scripts, which were available to her to encode and inscribe her social relations. These conventional scripts, to express either humility, deference and inferiority or, alternatively, confidence of equality of status, empowerment or superiority, were used in letters throughout her life and were the warp and weft of how her social relations were textualised. It is therefore worth considering two letters from different points along the spectrum and their use of linguistic scripts.

On the one hand, we have a letter from 1558 to Sir John Thynne, written in Bess's own hand but in an epistolary style immediately distinguishable from the letters in her own hand that we have seen so far, such as those to her servants and husband. This letter was written when she was the widow Lady Cavendish, left in debt after her second husband Sir William Cavendish's sudden death. In addition to the letter being in Bess's own hand, there are various linguistic features that argue in favour of it being Bess's own composition (e.g., the use of straightforward syntax, rhetorical rather than grammatical punctuation and her distinctive spellings), which indicates to us that she was trained in these linguistic scripts herself and had them at her fingertips. As such, the letter shows that, at an early stage, Bess was aware of contemporary conventions available to express relative social power relations between sender and recipient and could compose a letter of this kind herself:

Superscription, autograph:	Too the Ryghte worchoupfulle syre Iohen thynne knyghte w^t spede and all posybell delygence
Endorsement, by Thynne's secretary:	1558̶7 from my lady Cavendysshe
Letter, autograph:	Syr I am now dreuen to craue your helpe I haue defaryed the tyme of my sendynge to you for that I haue welhopyed tyll now of late that I shulde haue hade no ocasyon at thys presente to haue trobellede ^you but now^ so yt ys that ther ys abyll yn the parlamente howse agenste me. yt ys aganarall byll and dothe towche many. and yt passe yt wyll not

---

52 Magnusson, 'A Rhetoric of Requests', p. 63, points out that Bess often wrote her letters of request '*en grande dame*', here quoting Rawson, *Bess of Hardwick*, p. 84.

Composing and scripting letters 49

only ondo me and my poore chyldery[n] but agreat
nomber of hotheres yt hathe bene twyse rede yn the
lordes howse and ~~thy~~ yt shalbe brought yn agayne
of monday or tewyesday. so that yt ys thought yt
wylbe ~~m~~ wedynnesday or ^thourysday^ ~~tewyesday~~ or
yt be brought yn to the lowar howse. ~~so that~~ yf yt
wolde plese you to be here at that tyme I shulde
thynke my selfe mouste bowden to you. and thought
I be nowayes habyll to recompence you yt dewrynge
my lyffe I wyll neuer be forgotfoulle. the tyme
ys so shorte that I wolde not thus bouldely haue
sente for you onles you might haue ^had^ more ~~more~~
tyme, to haue ~~more~~ prepared your selfe yn. but that
mayster marche wylled me yn any wysse to yntrete
you to come. whyche ys more then becomyth me.
allthynges consedered. I trouste I shall haue agreat
sorte of frendes. yt wolde I trouste yf you wyll take
the paynes to come I shall haue many more by your
meanes then. by agreat sorte of hothers. and so I
wyll take my leue praynge you to bare w^t my rewde
later ~~ane yn conn~~ yn consederynge what atrobeled ys
habyll to do

Subscription, autograph: your pore frende for euer as I am bowden

Signature, autograph: E Cauendyssh

Postscript, autograph: yf you be here of fryday you shall stande me yn great
stede

[February 1558], Bess (widow of Sir William
Cavendish) writes to Sir John Thynne at Longleat
House.[53] Gloss: defaryed: *deferred*, hotheres: *others*,
or: *before*, thought: *though*, habyll: *able*, rewde:
rude, later: *letter*.

Here we see many of the characteristic features of the epistolary style of
'humility and entreaty' that was appropriate to code the relationship in a
letter from a social inferior to a social superior.[54] These included use of the
verb 'crave'; framing the letter as one that will 'trouble' him, saying she
does not want to trouble him, praying him to 'bare with' her 'rewde later';
saying her letter was sent in 'boldness' to 'yntrete' him which is 'more then
becomyth' her; asking him to 'take the paynes'; describing a low level of
personal agency, such as saying she is 'driven' to crave his help and that
'Master March willed' her to do so; offering flattery by saying that his help
would be more valued than others' and will stand her 'yn great stede'; and
humbling the self by saying she will be bound to him and is his 'pore frende

---

53 Sent, ID 111.

54 As recorded by Angel Day and described and documented by Magnusson, 'A Rhetoric
of Requests', where she delineates the linguistic scripts associated with two alternative
petitionary strategies, repeatedly used by both men and women, those of: 'humility and
entreaty' and 'supposal and assurance'.

50 *Composing and scripting letters*

for euer'. All of these linguistic scripts were entirely conventional for a letter of 'humility and entreaty'. It is important to emphasise again that these scripts were available both to men as to women and, indeed, were traditionally associated with men's letters.[55] It is therefore important not to project a feminised reading onto these tropes of humility or submission, which were most often used by and associated with letters from men.[56] Furthermore, it is important to remain aware that this letter deployed a set of conventions: it does not reveal to us the particular mental state of the sender; rather, it presents to us the sender performing a role according to the available and well-known linguistic scripts.

On the other hand, and further along the scale of social relations, we can compare this letter of 'humility and entreaty' to a number of later letters of political friendship and social courtesy that are also written in Bess's own hand but in which she took the stance more of a social equal. These are from the period when she had risen to the status of countess of Shrewsbury and was writing to high-status contacts at Court, often on matters of state security or succession, to do with the keeping of the Scottish Queen or the political marriages of her children. For example, in the following letter we can observe the deployment of an alternative set of linguistic scripts when writing to the earl of Leicester in 1577. The letter involved treading a delicate diplomatic path: while Bess wanted to ensure that she and her family would continue to benefit from the powerful earl of Leicester's support, at the same time she wanted to retain some control, herself, in the matter of finding a husband for her daughter the recently widowed Elizabeth (Cavendish) Lennox. Leicester's interest in these matchmaking activities reflected their relevance to Court politics: Elizabeth Lennox was the mother of Arbella Stuart, the child a claimant to the throne, which meant that her second husband would be stepfather to a potential princess-in-waiting. Bess, writing to Leicester, may well have anticipated that her letter would also be seen by Queen Elizabeth. The arrangement of Elizabeth Cavendish's first marriage (to Charles Stuart, earl of Lennox) had, notoriously, been orchestrated by their mothers without the queen's approval and much to her displeasure; this time around, Bess was keeping the queen informed via Leicester. When, as we see in the

---

55 Magnusson, 'A Rhetoric of Requests'. We can see, for example, that Bess's husband Shrewsbury used these scripts, such as in his letters to Lord Burghley, 14 May 1578 and 22 June 1579, written on Bess's behalf: he opened one saying he was 'Alas bold to trobell your Lordship' and the other saying he was 'lothe to trobell your Lordship with Any brablyng mattares' (brablyng: *brabbling*, i.e., quibbling), then going on to 'crave' his help to 'take the penes' (penes: *pains*) to support his wife's cause; LPL, Talbot Papers, MS 3206, fol. 885 and 967, IDs 188 and 189.

56 Magnusson, 'A Rhetoric of Requests', p. 63, theorises such an approach through Bourdieu's notion of linguistic capital and linguistic habitus and argues that we need to read these letters with the context and 'field of engagement' within which they were written.

Composing and scripting letters   51

letter ahead, she offered Chatsworth as 'a place for sondery cau*u*cus' her choice of the word 'caucus' here indicated her awareness that these were political negotiations – ones in which she wanted to have a stake. In order to navigate these sociopolitical relations, Bess combined several epistolary strategies:

Superscription, autograph:	To the Ryght honorabell my [synge]uler good lorde an[d b]rother the erle of lecester
Letter, autograph:	My good lord and brother yt ys wrete to me at lenth by my sone gelberte talbott how honorabley your .L. contenewes your wontyed care to do good styll to me ~~an~~ and myne, and theryn ys expressed your .L. honorabe[ll] prouydence now entended for my dowter len*n*ox yn maryage, I shall euer acknolege besydes ane enfenytte nomber your goodnesses to me and myne, the latte good spede and prefarment my sonne charles hade, brought to passe by your .L. only wysdome. but as your .L. nobell mynde ys euer workenge nobell effectes and of the same frewtes by good fourtune I and all [mi]ne amongst otheres to owre great comfortes do [ta]ste, I beynge of no poure nor abelyte any . . . to make apeare the dewty of thankes/ . . . your .L. the greatter by me and myne ough[t] . . . onde your .L. worthey fam*m*e whyche ys all the [re]compence I cane make and the beste sarues all myne are [*deletion*] abell to do vnto your .L. all the dayes of ther lyues. and for my dowter lennox of whome your ^.L.^ plecythe to haue that esspecyall care, and we most bonde to your .L. for yt, yeldynge humbyll thankes to your .L. she dothe styll fynde har selfe so many wayes bonde to you, as wylbe aduysed by your .L. more then any man [*deletion*] and I hartely desyre your .L. ^to^ contennew that honorabell mynde towardes har ether for the Lord Sandes or any other that shalbe thought metyste, and yf yt plese your .L. to comende eny to Chattysworth as a place for sondery cau*u*cus I desyre fourst to enter ther aquentance, he or whome elce your .L. comendes shalbe as frendly welcome as I am beho*u*ldyng to geue one sent by your .L., wereyn as yn althynges elles I do refare h~~a~~er happy mache, h~~a~~er well bestoynge ys my greatys care, some of my frendes haue heretofore wyched sondery good machus for her, yf I coulde haue fou*n*de yn her the lyste lykenge more to one then another I wolde haue trobeled your .L. herw^t^ w^t^out who*u*se specyall help I knowe yt colde take no good affecte she sayth euer to me she cane nott determyne har selfe to lyke of any for a hosbande whome she neuer saye nor knoywethe [*deletion*] not hys lykenge of har. I defare all to your .L. honorabell good consederacyon of whome as of vary nobelyte hym selfe I take my leue w^t^ my prayer for all hapynes to you and yours shefelde the xviij of maye

(Continued)

52 Composing and scripting letters

(Continued)

Subscription, autograph:	your .L. faythefull Syster
Signature, autograph:	EShrouesbury
Postscript, hand of George Talbot, sixth earl of Shrewsbury:	I cannott contente my celfe my wyfes lettares shall passe. w'oute Rememberenge & commendynge my celfe vnto yo' L my derest frende w' my moste hartyste thankes for the honorabell care of vs & oures whereby if it comlebe you . . . more & more bynde me to be yo'es/ G Yo' L moste fethe[full] G S § 18 May [1577?], Bess of Hardwick and her husband George Talbot, sixth earl of Shrewsbury, co-written in their own hands from Sheffield to Robert Dudley, earl of Leicester, seal embossed with Bess's arms featuring the Hardwick cross.[57] The words missing (indicated by ellipses) are due to damage on one side of the paper from a seal tear. Gloss: .L.: *Lordship* or *Lordship's*, dowter: *daughter*, frewtes: *fruits*, poure: *power*, plecythe: *pleases*, cauucus: caucus, machus: *matches*, lyste: *least*, celfe: *self*.

We can observe, first, that the letter was written in the language of equitable friendship and social courtesy and in a mixed style. Bess acknowledged Leicester's high status by use of the deferential address term 'your Lordship', used nineteen times (by contrast with 'you/your', which appeared only three times). But, at the same time, positive politeness was deployed as he was addressed as her 'good lord and brother' (both in the superscription and in the letter itself), and she subscribed from his 'faythefull Syster', a pattern of address terms that was reciprocated when Leicester wrote to her.[58] At the opening and closing of the letter there are effusive expressions of thanks and gratitude for the help he had given her family. In the middle part of the letter she made her request, and here we find none of the features of 'humility and entreaty' encountered in the letter to Thynne and that encoded a submissive, inferior position. Rather, Bess presented her request as her own particular desire, stating 'I hartely desyre' and 'I desyre' (i.e., she is not 'forced' or 'willed to it' and she does not 'crave, 'beseech' or 'entreat' Leicester). She went on to reverse the 'troublemaking' trope familiar from letters of 'humility and entreaty'. So, rather than signalling deference by saying to Leicester that she was sorry to have troubled him, she stated that she was not able to trouble him, but 'wolde haue trobeled' him if only she had known her daughter's preferences over a match. She emphasised her role as a mother whose daughter's 'well bestoynge' in marriage was her 'greatys care',

---

57 Sent, ID 109.

58 We find Leicester addressing Bess as 'my good lady & systar' (twice), 'systar' and subscribing as 'your ashured loving brother'; 23 November 1586, Arundel Castle, Autograph Letters 1585–1617, No. 114, ID 214.

Composing and scripting letters   53

which was figured through the syntax of a series of I-centred deliberations that placed her own thoughts on the matter at the very centre of the situation.[59] Finally, her husband, the earl of Shrewsbury, added a postscript to her letter in his own hand: a personal endorsement in the form of his own commendations and declarations of loyal friendship to Leicester. The earl's own contribution to the letter functioned to bolster his wife's request, and thus Bess's letter channelled her husband's authority to her own advantage and for strategic political purpose. The epistolary style of this letter, then, diverged from her letter to Thynne some twenty years earlier in such a way as reflected, at this moment in time, not only Bess's actual increase in social status but also her greater self-perception of her own power.

Compellingly, we can further observe here a number of distinctive linguistic forms that suggest this letter to Leicester was likely to have been drafted by a scribe before being copied out by Bess in her own hand. These forms include: grammatical (rather than rhetorical) punctuation; delaying of the main clause and use of embedded subclauses, such as qualifying phrases ('Lord Sandes or any other that shalbe thought metyste', 'he or whome elce', 'wereyn as yn althynges elles', 'of whome as of vary nobelyte hym selfe'); use of compound determiners for anaphoric reference ('theryn', 'wereyn'); and revisions to her usual spelling forms (e.g., the change four times to <her> from her usual <har>: 'hær', 'hær', 'her', 'her'). These features do not appear in Bess's autograph writing, with the exception of her cluster of letters to high-status Court contacts, of which this is one. Elsewhere, these are all features associated with scribal language.[60] This letter, then, is a reminder that we should take care when reading what might appear to be a 'personal' letter from Bess to Leicester, when it was, in fact, communal and political, based on the evidence of the context, composition, language, palaeography and paratexts. There is no doubt that Bess was fully aware of this letter's exact content and wording, attested by the use of her own hand, signature and seal, which show her presence at every stage of the production process. But the letter was nevertheless composed with some level of involvement from a scribe and from her husband. To take counsel from experts or to benefit from the influence of her high-level contacts was a shrewd move and not unusual in Bess's letters. One year later, on 30 June 1578, Bess asked Leicester for his advice about a letter to the queen and Leicester obliged by giving his opinion on exactly the tone and style of letter she should write, as

---

59 For comparison, we can observe that on 1 October 1582, Bridget Russell, countess of Bedford, wrote a letter of 'supposal and assurance' that used some similar strategies, as described by Magnusson, 'A Rhetoric of Requests', p. 60.

60 The linguistic and palaeographic evidence for whether they were copies from scribal drafts is discussed in section 2.2. The four letters in this cluster, and some of the suspected scribal forms are: to the earl of Leicester 21 January 1569 ('thys Instant montthe', 'the sayd letters', 'thervpon', 'reposed', syntax and punctuation, ID 107, Plate 10) and 27 June [1576?] ('albeyt', 'therby', 'yet not withstanding', syntax and punctuation, ID 110); to Lord Burghley 24 October 1578 ('theryn', 'for whych', 'hereby', 'aduertys', 'whereof', ID 122); and to Sir Francis Walsingham on 29 December 1578 ('therby', 'the same', ID 123).

54   Composing and scripting letters

well as offering to deliver the letter himself in person. It is an example that reminds us that Bess sought and received advice on epistolary composition from a range of sources, and that powerful individuals such as the earl of Leicester were themselves very well aware of the importance of selecting just the right words.[61]

Letters in curial prose concerned with business and legal matters

So far we have seen letters composed and copied by Bess herself; a letter composed by Bess herself that was dictated verbatim to a scribe; and a letter composed with advice from a scribe or collaborator, and then copied out in Bess's own hand, with a postscript penned by her husband Shrewsbury. To these types of letter we must add those in the format most common among her existing letters: where the main body of the letter was penned by a scribe before being signed by Bess in her own hand, sometimes also adding a postscript. Letters in this format included those in the hands of academically trained hired scribes that dealt with legal, business or financial matters, of which there are around fifteen existing sent from Bess. Anyone receiving one of these letters would have immediately seen the neat, compact handwriting of the scribe. As well as being visually distinct from letters written in Bess's own hand, these letters also contrasted in their epistolary style. Typically, they were written in a form of 'curial prose' entirely appropriate to their function and which gave to these letters a particular distance and gravitas. As such, they construct authority in a different way to Bess's household letters or letters of political friendship.

Curial prose was a technical style of writing that consisted of a set of formal features concerned with exactness of meaning and precision of reference.[62] One of its essential characteristics was the use of compound adverbs and other anaphoric reference terms that functioned as cohesive devices and included words and phrases such as 'the said', 'the same', 'thereof', 'aforesaid'.[63] Other typical

---

61 The letter is Folger CT, X.d.428 (110), ID 83, and Leicester's offer to act as bearer is discussed in section 3.2. There are many other examples of early modern women letter-writers who asked for or received advice about their letter-writing (apparent from draft letters or from letters that directly ask for or give advice), and they included high-status and educated women, such as Frances, Lady Cobham, Barbara Sidney, Mary, Queen of Scots, Elizabeth I, Lady Burghley, Lady Neville, Dorothy Percy and Elizabeth Willoughby, discussed by Daybell, *Women Letter-Writers*, pp. 75–79.

62 The medieval tradition of the administrative 'curial style' has been defined by Burnley as 'a set of formal features used in legal and diplomatic documents, with the functional purposes of precision in reference and ceremony of tone'; 'Curial Prose in England', p. 595.

63 An analysis of linguistic features typical of curial prose in the scribal letters of Joan Thynne, which shows scribal influence in shaping her letters by comparison with letters in her own hand, provides a comparison to Bess here, and from which this discussion has benefited; Williams, *Women's Epistolary Utterance*, pp. 57–62. Related relevant studies are by Rissanen, 'Standardisation', and Kilpio, 'Participal Adjectives with Anaphoric Reference'.

Composing and scripting letters   55

features included clause connections managed with the present participle 'touching' or with discourse deictics, extensive clausal qualifiers and the use of lexical doublets or lists of near synonyms to clarify an exact meaning.[64] The earliest letter we have existing from Bess penned by a hired scribe in a secretary script and that deployed curial features of style was to Sir John Thynne, 27 August 1567, when Bess was the newly married countess of Shrewsbury and made use of her husband's secretariat at Sheffield Castle.[65] After this date, we have other existing letters in the secretary-script hands of hired scribes written from Sheffield, whom Bess used to write her business correspondence during her marriage to Shrewsbury.[66] Bess continued to employ secretaries throughout her life and we see many examples, not least after 1590 when she assembled her own secretariat at Hardwick Hall as dowager countess of Shrewsbury. It is worth giving an example here, written by 'Scribe D', one of Bess's secretaries at Hardwick Hall:

Superscription, Scribe D:	To the right wor:ll Sr Julius Cecer knight Mer of the requestes to the Kinges most Excellent Ma:ty.
Endorsement, secretary:	Vlt. Ianuarij .1603. Eliz Countesse of Shrewsbury. touching her answer to the inhabitants of the forest of high Peake.
Letter, Scribe D:	Whereas aboute the xxth of Iune last past a petition was preferred to the Kinges most excellent Ma:tie by Robert Allyn Hugh Needham and Iohn Wright in the behalf of themselves and others Inhabitantes in and nere the forest of the Highe Peake wherein they alledge that they ought to haue Common of pasture for theire Cattle wthin his Highnes seuerall demesnes of the Castle of the High Peake Called the Inner

(*Continued*)

Further examples from the letters are: 'the said' (BL, Add. 12506, fols 109r-10v, ID 161; CUL, Hengrave MSS, 88/2/81, ID 236), 'the same' (LPL, Talbot Papers, MS 3198, fol. 331r-v, ID 1; Keele UL, Paget Papers, MSS 4, 7 and 8 ff. 15-, ff. 77- and ff. 55-, IDs 103–105), 'the which' (Belvoir Castle, Rutland MSS, Letters & Papers XIII, folios 27–28, ID 239), 'thereby' (IDs 104 and 161), 'therefore' (IDs 103, 105, 236, 239 and Arundel Castle, Autograph Letters 1585–1617, No. 89, ID 227), 'therein' (IDs 114, 227 and TNA SP 53/10, f 79 item 79, ID 234), 'thereof' (IDs 1, 104, 161, CP 84/75, ID 139 and Belvoir Castle, Rutland MSS, Letters & Papers XIV, folios 54–55, ID 240), 'thereunto' (Parker 114A, p. 153, ID 238), 'wherein' (IDs 1, 103, 104, 139, 161, 238, 239 and CP 86/12, ID 127), 'whereof' (IDs 105, 227), 'whereunto' (ID 105).

64 Examples of clause connections include: 'touching' (IDs 1, 139, 227 and CP 135/127, fols 165–6, ID 129) and 'To conclude' (ID 227). Examples of precise qualifiers include: 'hath and yet doth' (ID 139), 'neyther is not can be' (ID 236), 'is and allwayes hath ben' (Belvoir Castle, Rutland MSS, Letters & Papers XIV, folios 129–129, ID 241), 'I saye and am suer', 'presently, or in short tyme', 'lowar or as lowe as possiblely yow can' (all ID 227), 'in and nere the forest' ID 161 (Plate 18).

65 ID 114.

66 ID 104, 28 November 1581; 'the same' is used repeatedly.

56 Composing and scripting letters

(Continued)

	seuerall of the Champion The sayd petition: is altogether vntrue and thereby they Clayme some of his Highnes Inheritaunce to be theire owne as by a decree vnder the Duchie Seale and by my answere and my sonne William Cauendishe sent you by this bearer you may perceive. The said petitione^rs were presently after the delyvery of theire petition dispatched to Come to me for Answere thereof but they Came not to me vntill w^thin this weeke at wch tyme they desired rather some Composition in ground then any thinge Conteyned in theire petition./ I hartily pray yor lawfull fauour for the speedie receivinge of the answere and dispatch of the matter restinge much beholdinge to you and willinge in parte to requite yor trooble as this bearer vpon the dispatch of the matter will further signifie vnto you to whom I pray you geve Credytt./ And soe wth my very harty Com*m*endacions I Ceasse. ffrom Hardwicke this last day of Ianuary .1603./
Subscription, Scribe B:	your uery louing frend
Signature, autograph:	EShrouesbury
	31 January 1604, Bess (dowager countess of Shrewsbury) writes to Sir Julius Caesar, hand of Scribe D.[67]

We can observe here the density of features of curial prose, characteristic of this type of letter, such as management of the opening of the letter with 'Wheras'; precise referencing of the date and content of the petitions in a series of embedded subclauses up to 'Champion'; the repeated use of anaphoric devices, such as 'wherein', 'The sayd' (twice), 'thereby', 'thereof'; and the use of qualifying phrases, such as 'themselves and other Inhabitantes' and 'Called'. As we can see from this letter, it was a style of language that functioned both for precision of reference and to give the impression of an 'authoritative-sounding statement' and 'an air of importance'.[68] Such letters could also be supplemented with a postscript penned by Bess herself, and it is worth giving an example to show the combined functions of scribal writing and the autograph writing on a single page (Plate 16):

Superscription, unknown scribe:	To my very Loving frend Mr Bagott Sheriff of Staffordshyer
Letter, unknown scribe:	Good Mr Bagott. Wheras one wedow Bagshaw of wetton detaineth contrary to right a farme in the same towne/ and will not by eny resonable meane be avoyded/ I am bould of small aquantancye ernestly to crave yor favor/ that yow will cawse a p^rvy Sessions to be, for the better avoyding of her yt towcheth my very neere frend, whose

---

67 ID 161 (Plate 18 and cover image). A discussion of Bess's Scribe D is presented ahead, pp. 134–36.
68 Burnley, 'Curial Prose in England', p. 613.

Composing and scripting letters 57

case I accomt as my owne/ therfore yo[r] gentle and frendly
dealing shall bynd me to be as redy to shew yow or
eny frend of yo[rs] what pleasure I may as eny frend yow
have. and I pray yow make that accomt. Thus trusting
of yo[r] favor and furtherance, and that yow will creditt
this bearer/ wth most harty commendacions I bid yow
farewell. Sheffield the xiiijth of Aprell

Subscription, Yo[r] very Loving frend.
unknown scribe:

Signature, autograph: EShrouesbury

Postscript, autograph: thys womane hathe yoused har selfe vary dysorderly and
wyll yelde to no resoune as my saruante thys ~~ear~~ barare
cane declare vnto you therfor I ones agene I prey hartely
grante me all your fauorabyll forderance and you shall
fynde me neuer onmyndfall to requyat you

14 April [1600?], Bess (dowager countess of Shrewsbury)
writes from Hardwick to sheriff Walter Bagot, hand of a
scribe, postscript in her own hand.[69]

The main body of this letter was written in a secretary script and, although
we do not know the scribe's name or identity, the language and handwriting leave no doubt that this was a hired male secretary. The curial features
of language are entirely appropriate to the subject of the letter, dealing as
it does with a legal matter, an eviction. We might particularly note features
characteristic of curial prose in the phrasing and vocabulary, such as the
use of anaphoric determiners as cohesive devices ('the same', 'therefore'),
management of a clause connection using a present participle phrase ('for
the better avoyding of'), the series of qualifying subclauses before the main
clause, and the precise qualification of points through near-synonymous lexical doublets ('yow or eny frend of yours', 'favor and furtherance'). Below
the scribally penned body of the letter a signature and postscript were added
by Bess in her own hand, which reiterated the message of the main letter and
remind us of the discrepancy between Bess's autograph and scribal writing.
Bess's postscript was executed in her large angular handwriting and functioned to inscribe her personal presence as dowager countess and therefore
to encourage positive interpersonal relations and ensure the letter was not
overlooked.[70] While the postscript did not add any new information, that
Bess chose to include it is indicative and reveals she was available and
was quite capable of putting pen to paper herself. That is, the decision to
have the body of the letter penned by a secretary was not because Bess was
absent or incapacitated, but was a deliberate choice made for stylistic and

69 Folger Bagot, L.a.844, ID 2 (Plate 16).
70 Daybell reviews the autograph postscripts by a range of Tudor women, their range of functions in 'personalising secretarial letters' and value as exhibiting 'spontaneous and intimate
forms of expression, uninhibited by secretarial constraints'; *Women Letter-Writers*, from
p. 109.

58   Composing and scripting letters

communicative reasons, not least that it would have been *infra dig* for the grand dowager countess to pen her own routine business letters. The postscript also tells us that Bess was fully up to speed with the content of the letter and that it had come into her own hands to be authorised before sending. That is to say, Bess remained very much on the scene after she had delegated copying to this scribe and retained control over what went out by checking (and in this case adding to) the final letter that was sent. That her postscript echoes the exact wording of the main letter (her 'fauorabyll forderance' repeats the letter's 'favor and furtherance') leaves us in absolutely no doubt that Bess was carefully checking these scribal letters word for word.[71] It is an example that recalls Bess's household business and Account Books, which were keep by her servants and secretaries but which every week she would check herself and authorise with her signature, often correcting their mistakes in her own hand.[72] The scrupulous attention she applied to every detail of the business accounts, apparent from her annotations and corrections, we can see from this example was also applied to her scribal letters.

The distinctive and well-established form of language known as curial prose is so marked in these letters that we must conclude they were composed by scribes based on consultation with Bess.[73] That is, we must envisage a compositional scenario whereby the scribe was heavily implicated in shaping the language and selecting the linguistic forms. We do not have any existing examples of written notes or instructions from Bess that corresponded to one of her existing letters, and it is possible that Bess's directions were spoken and remembered rather than written down. But that Bess did on at least one occasion write instructions is apparent from a document of 1573 in which she set out detailed advice for a letter to be written.[74] While the exact context is unclear and the correspondent unknown, her guidelines concerned how to write a persuasive letter to one of her sons and give us a rare insight into the form such instructions could take. Bess's first instruction was that in order to be most effective the letter should be composed by the sender in his or her own words, rather than in words she (Bess) had chosen: 'your selfe wyll vse more effectuall and good words then I can deuyce'. She nevertheless went on

---

71 Bess's garbled 'fauorabyll forderance' echoes the letter's 'favor and furtherance'.
72 Bess's scrupulous account keeping is well known – for example, mentioned by Worsley, *Hardwick Old Hall*, p. 7.
73 Other examples of Tudor women giving instructions to scribes but still retaining control of their letter by checking and signing are given by Daybell, *Women Letter-Writers*, pp. 84–85. As we will see, there were other modes of composition involving scribes; for example, two scribe could be involved, one to draft the letter and another to write out the final copy, discussed in sections 2.2 and 2.3.
74 The document is in the hand of Scribe A and was sent unsigned; it is now in the SP and endorsed: 'The Countesse of Shrewsbury 1573'. The intended recipient is unknown; SP 12/93, f 102r-v (item 19), ID 143.

Composing and scripting letters 59

to give a fairly detailed list of items that should be included. The letter, she said, should begin by expressing grief ('shar your grefe') for her son's loss and should then express the sender's favour, good will and gratitude towards her son. Next, the letter should express 'trust and desyar' her son will be dealt with well following his loss, for both of their sakes, and the sender should promise to be forever 'thankfull to hym and hys and to requyt yt by all good means that shall Ly in your power'. Bess ended her instructions by emphasising that the style and tone of the letter were important: the letter would be most effective if written in a straight-forward and unadorned style that conveyed genuineness and sincerity, 'the more ernyst and playn yt ys the more good yt wyll doe'. She reiter-ated that it must be clearly apparent that the letter came from the sender directly and represented his or her own personal intentions: she said that 'you wyll do yt in such sort' (i.e., you will write the letter in such a way) so that 'he maybe assured yt coms from you to my sonne'. Bess expected the requested letter to come to her the same night ('thys nyght') by return of her bearer, perhaps so that she could check it or make arrangements for it to reach her son. This unique document, then, reveals to us that when Bess directed the writing of a letter she was aware of not only the substantive content but also the structure and ordering of material, the conventions of social courtesy, the style, tone, implied personal presence of the sender and the mode of delivery.

This remarkable document leaves us in no doubt that, when Bess gave directions for writing a letter, or when she checked a scribal letter, she was alert to a number of different linguistic levels. Moreover, it reinforces for us a picture of the essentially communal nature of early modern epistolary cul-ture. The range of collaborative scenarios that could be involved included not only those whereby Bess was involved in directing the composition of her own scribal letters (the ones she signed and sent herself), but also the letters of others. The implication is that we should expand our conception of Bess as a letter-writer to include her authorial influence behind other people's letters, such as those from her husbands and children. These were not letters where she was visible as a signer or named as a sender, but where she had influence in directing, advising or orchestrating behind the scenes. We know of at least one other example where Bess carefully stage-managed the content and delivery of a letter: the letter from her daughter Elizabeth (Cavendish) Stuart, countess of Lennox, in 1577.[75] We might also detect her influence upon other letters, such as those from her husband and network of contacts and 'political friends' written to support her own causes, where we can ascertain Bess's presence lubricating the wheels of diplomacy, enhancing social networks and developing advantageous connections.

---

75 Discussed in section 3.2. That Bess gave advice to her husband on his letter-writing has already been discussed.

60   *Composing and scripting letters*

Epistolary composition and gender dynamics

The discussion so far has emphasised that the four epistolary styles considered (household management, spousal partnership, political friendship and curial prose) were conventional in the period and were not peculiar to women. On the contrary, as we have seen, Bess's letters to her servants and spouse were composed in epistolary styles also deployed by her male contemporaries, including by her husband the earl of Shrewsbury. While found in many husband–wife and mistress–servant exchanges, these were styles more traditionally associated with male realms of activity and that would have been frowned upon by contemporary conduct books and prescriptive literature that took a more limited view of women's roles. Similarly, the language of political friendship and curial prose can likewise be associated with traditionally male realms of activity and these can therefore be gendered as male forms of discourse.[76] However, while none of the letters assessed so far used specifically feminised tropes or forms of language, Bess did also send letters that deployed cultural scripts that can be gendered as female. These feminised constructions all appear in sent letters that were penned in the hand of Scribe A. We do not know the identity or have a name for Scribe A, who could have been male or female by sex. That is to say, although feminised, it is quite possible that these letters involved a collaborating male scribe just as much as the business letters in curial prose by Bess's secretaries Timothy Pusey and Scribe D.[77] The handwriting of Scribe A and available biographical information (such as it is) would not be incompatible with either a female or a male scribe, so the question remains open for now.[78] Most important, when we consider these letters penned by Scribe A, is that we must remember, as literary scholars have shown, that there was no direct or straightforward correspondence between sex and gender when it came to scripting written personae.[79] That is, in the case of early modern letters, the sex of the letter-sender does not automatically map onto the gender of the persona constructed in the letter. So a female sender may construct a persona that can be gendered either male or female, and may do so either individually or through collaborations with scribes or co-writers, who may be male or female.

---

76   Previous scholarship is summarised by Daybell, 'Scripting a Female Voice', p. 4.

77   There is also an unsent draft letter of this sort, in the hand of another scribe, discussed in section 2.3. As Clarke has reminded us in relation to early modern literary texts, 'the sex of the author is neither a reliable nor an authentic indication of the speaker's gender' either for women or for men; *This Double Voice*, p. 12. The female epistolary examples aimed at men are well known, such as Erasmus advising male pupils to practice writing their letters in the manner of Penelope to Ulysses, a wife to a husband who is away; as Daybell points out, such writing exercises were models 'male amanuenses could have appropriated in writing for women in order to script or "ventriloquize" female voice'; *Women Letter-Writers*, p. 21.

78   The possible identity of Scribe A is discussed in section 2.3, based on evidence of language and information from household accounts and wage lists.

79   Daybell, 'Scripting a Female Voice', p. 4, and discussed earlier in the introduction, pp. 5–6.

Composing and scripting letters 61

These feminised epistolary styles are discussed in the remaining three sections of this chapter. In some cases these feminised constructions emphasise forms of submission and a melancholy tone familiar from other women's letters of the period, as well as from men's letters.[80] However, more often, Bess's letters show preference for deployment of cultural scripts of ideal womanhood – such as idealised 'natural' motherhood or 'faithful' and 'dutiful' wifehood – which are typically appropriated within the context of a forceful argument.[81] It is here in the mobilisation of cultural models of idealised motherhood and wifehood that the language of early modern women's letters departed from that of their male contemporaries, and these were images of womanhood that Bess strategically deployed when required.[82] Each of the next three sections takes, as its focus, one letter, and considers the epistolary style of that letter in the context of the larger exchange of correspondence and Bess's relationship with the correspondent, as well as the wider context of rhetorical models that defined early modern social relations. Each of the letters chosen was part of a sequence that captured the dynamics of some of the most important relationships in Bess's life. The argument here is that the individual letters cannot be isolated from the sequences in which they were embedded, nor can they be isolated from the larger epistolary, rhetorical and cultural models that they inscribed and that are implicated within them. To these ends, section 1.2 considers a letter of petition from Bess written in 1582 on behalf of her orphaned granddaughter Arbella Stuart. The discussion considers the deployment of the cultural model of idealised motherhood and how the letter textualises emotion (specifically, the grief of a bereaved mother) as a means of conveying sincerity and credibility for the purpose of persuasion. Section 1.3 considers a letter from Bess to her fourth husband written in 1585 following their estrangement and during the period of their marital discord. The discussion tracks the precise appropriation of the cultural model of idealised wifehood in order to construct for herself a defence against her husband's angry accusations. Section 1.4 takes a letter to her daughter Mary (Cavendish) Talbot, seventh countess of Shrewsbury, from the very end of Bess's life in 1607, which is part of a sequence written in a more relaxed, familiar epistolary style. The discussion considers how these letters encoded family hierarchy while textualising intimacy and emotional bonds within this mother–daughter correspondence. Ultimately, all of these letters drew on the conventional epistolary styles and rhetorical models available to letter-writers, and thus show us how Bess's letter-writing was implicated within the generic forms and structures of her own culture.

---

80 The Ovidian melancholy tones in letters – the 'male scripted' textual voice of female complaint – has been discussed elsewhere, summarised by Daybell, 'Scripting a Female Voice', pp. 13–15.

81 For examples of contemporary women 'styling themselves as "natural" mothers, and "faithful" and "dutiful" wives' see Daybell, *Women Letter-Writers*, pp. 15–16.

82 Daybell, *Women Letter-Writers*, p. 18.

62 *Composing and scripting letters*

1.2 'As yf she were my owne and only chyld': a letter of petition to Sir Francis Walsingham written on behalf of her granddaughter Arbella Stuart, 1582

Superscription,
Scribe A:

To my very frend Syr Frances Walsyingham knyght prencepall secretory to her ma^{ty}

Letter, Scribe A:

good m^r Secretorye wth my ryght harty comendatyons, I pray you take in good parte my Lyke desyar that yt wyll please you to prefare my humble sute vnto the quenes ma:^{ty} in the behaulfe of apore ynfant my Iuyll arbella who ys to depend wholly vpon her ma:^{tys} bounty and goodnes being in her tender age depryued of her parrents. whos Late mother in her extreme sycknes and euen at the approching of her end (wch I cannot wthout great grefe. remembar) dyd most earnestly sundrye tymes recommend to her ma:^{tys} gracyous goodnes and fauor that poore infant her only care wth hartye desyar and confedence that her ma:^{ty} myght inioy a Long and prosperous raigne and be a gracyous patrone and soufarigne to that her innocent chyld as her ma:^{ty} had hetherto ben to them both./ and forasm[uch] as the foure hondryth poundes yerely graunted to my sayde daughter ys by her death at the quenes ma^{ts} dysposytyon; my humble sute ys that her hyghnes whos manyfould gracyous fauors and bountye haue so much bound me as no subyecte can be more to a most worthy souf^r^aigne wyll vouchesaffe to graunt the same foure hondryth poundes yearly wth the other tow hondryth pounds to arbella for her maintenance duaring her mynorytye, wch ys but for a few yeares, whereof I dout not but her ma:^{ty} wyll fauorable accepte as hetherto she hath don of all my sutes, and conseder that her brenging vp euery way as appartayneth, and so as she maybe able the sonnar in seruice to attend vpon her ma:^{ty} (wch I chefly desyar) wyll hardly be parformed wth syxe hondryth pounds yearly in mony and more commodetye ys not to be made of thos Lands being as they are in Lesse. I do not Lyke she should be now here as she was wth her mother in her Lyfe tyme, nether can I be conte[nted] she be in any place wher I may not somtymes se her and dayly here of her well doing, and therfore at great chargs to kepe her in house wth such as are fytt to attend vpon her and be in her company and being neare well towards vij yeares ould she ys of very greate towardnes to Learne anytheng, and I very carefull of her good educatyon as yf she were my owne and only chyld, and agreat deale more for the consanguynitye she ys of ^to^ her ma:^{ty} whos happye raigne ouer vs I dayly wth most zealous mynd pray the allmeghty gouernor of all thenges Long to contenew, and now craueing most hartelye your frendshep in mouing thys sute to her ma:^{ty} I refare the same to your wysdom being better able to conseder therof then I am at this present who can not so sonne enter into any thought of thes clauses but that I am ouercharged wth gryefes, and so make an end of this my vnconsederat Letters trusting her hyghnes wyll accepte of my Loyall dutye and seruice wch I desyar you wyll comend vnto her royall mayestye./ Sheffeld this vjth of may

Composing and scripting letters 63

Subscription, Scribe A:	your very Louing frend
Signature, autograph:	EShrouesbury

6 May 1582, Bess of Hardwick (countess of Shrewsbury) writes from Sheffield to Sir Francis Walsingham[83]

This letter of petition followed the death of Bess's daughter Elizabeth (Cavendish) Stuart, countess of Lennox, who died suddenly, six years after her husband Charles Stuart had died, just as unexpectedly. Both parents gone, their ill-fated daughter, Bess's granddaughter, Arbella Stuart, was left an orphan at seven years old and assigned to the custody of her grandmother Bess, who petitioned for her entitlements. The letter is one of a pair written the same day, both penned by Scribe A and signed by Bess herself, in which she asked Burghley and Walsingham to present her request to Queen Elizabeth that the portion of money previously assigned to her daughter Elizabeth Lennox now go to Arbella. Bess requested that Arbella's financial 'portion' was essential in order to provide the child with a proper education suitable for a future high-ranking courtier and princess-in-waiting. Bess argued the financial case with skill and precision, as Williams has summarised, that, first, 'the allowance must be continued, not as royal charity, but as the income from the English estates of Margaret Countess of Lennox which Queen Elizabeth had seized at her death' and, second, that 'Arbella's kinship to the Queen must be the basis for a liberal grant for her maintenance and education'.[84]

Bess's astute understanding of the finances was accompanied by dexterous handling of petitionary language, and we can observe the letter's mixed style. On the one hand, the letter deployed linguistic scripts of 'supposal and assurance', which involved high modality and positive politeness. She opened the letter not by 'craving' or 'beseeching' Walsingham's help but by stating that her desire was that it would 'please' him to present her suit. She gave an account of her confident and unqualified expectations, saying that she had no doubt ('I dout not') the queen would accept the suit 'as hitherto she hath don of all my sutes' and, furthermore, she anticipated that the queen would consider £600 a year to be hardly enough for Arbella's upbringing, given the costs. Her account of Arbella's requirements was centred on her own opinions and deliberations, being syntactically structured around a series of I-centred phrases, such as: 'which I chefly desyar', 'I do not lyke', 'nether can I be contented', 'I may not', 'and I very carefull of'. An added air of importance and authority, as well as precision of reference, was

---

83 ID 145 (Plate 15).

84 Williams, *Bess of Hardwick*, p. 152. Ultimately, the £400 to Elizabeth Lennox was cancelled and only the £200 to Arbella continued, although Bess did ensure that Arbella continued to live with her.

64   *Composing and scripting letters*

achieved by the interspersed curial forms with anaphoric reference, such as: 'my sayde daughter', 'the same' (twice), 'whereof', 'therfor', 'therof'. Overall, the selection of these linguistic scripts projected estimated power relations through her assessment of the likely success of her request. On the other hand, the letter signalled respect and used negative politeness with some features of 'humility and entreaty': she twice referred to her 'humble' suit and ended by 'craueing most hartelye' Walsingham's friendship. That is, while the letter was underpinned by a confident stance and strong argument, it was interspersed with some more submissive scripts. It might be tempting to suggest that this mixed style may have been the result of collaborative composition, whereby the forceful stance reflected Bess's line of argument, while the selection of a mixture of linguistic scripts, to achieve what was perceived to be the right tone, was on the advice of Scribe A or another collaborator during the drafting process.

In addition to the use of these linguistic scripts to textualise power relations, we can observe that Bess mobilised the cultural model of 'natural' motherhood for two specific rhetorical functions. First, Bess framed the letter with reference to her own emotional state as a grieving mother. The letter began with a depiction of her daughter's deathbed scene, which, she said she could not 'without great grefe. Remember'. The dying words of her daughter Lennox were quoted – said to have been spoken 'most earnestly . . . sundrye tymes' in her 'extreme sycknes' just as she approached 'her end' – and which expressed her daughter's hope that the queen would continue to be a patron to Arbella. Bess returned again to the scene at the close of the letter when she stated that she now gave the matter over to Walsingham's greater 'wysdom' because she was too 'ouercharged with gryefes' to think about it herself. She specifically stated that grief had so incapacitated her that she was not able to think: she said that she could not 'enter into any thought of thes causes but that I am ouercharged with gryefes'. She cast her letter as one that was ill considered ('vnconsederat'), dashed off as best she could in her emotional state. That is, her words were cast as written from a mind incapable of any calculated thought, and therefore 'earnest', genuine and sincere. This emphasis on her emotional state, resulting from the bereavement, had a rhetorical function: to present the petition as the request of a mother fulfilling her daughter's dying wish and to signal sincerity. Second, Bess emphasised that she, herself, now had the role of being a mother to the orphan Arbella, which she would fulfil 'as yf she were my owne and only chyle', and the letter was, as Daybell has put it 'couched in a language of natural grandmotherly affection': she referred to Arbella as her 'pore ynfant' (twice), 'my Iuyll', being of 'tender age' an 'innocent chyld' and mentioned her 'towardnes to Learne anytheng'.[85] While demonstrating her grandmotherly affection for Arbella, she also skilfully argued that her

---

85 Daybell, *Women Letter-Writers*, p. 256.

Composing and scripting letters 65

role constituted 'a great deale more' than any other maternal role because Arbella was a blood relative to the queen ('for the consanguynitye she ys of to her majesty'), for whom she (Bess) daily with 'zealous mynd' prayed to God. Her role as guardian and grandmother to Arbella, she emphasised, was one that she would fulfil not only as if she were a most devoted mother but also as her political and religious duty in direct service to the queen. That is, Bess took a stance that emphasised the alignment of her role as a mother to Arbella with her political role in service to the queen and the divine succession.

In order to interpret more precisely the nature of the power relations and emotions textualised in this letter of 6 May 1582, it is necessary to describe the broader context of the sequence within which it appeared. Immediately following the death of Elizabeth Lennox, it was the earl of Shrewsbury, Bess's husband, who, on 21 January 1582, wrote to Burghley and Leicester at Court with news of the bereavement and to ask for the child Arbella's financial entitlements. There was doubtless an awareness of epistolary decorum here and of the question of how soon after the death of a child it was appropriate for a mother to start petitioning for money. Shrewsbury's letter was signed only by himself and he explained that he had written himself because his wife Bess was too distressed to do so, having taken her daughter's death 'so grevouslie' that she 'neither dothe nor can thincke of any thinge but of Lamentinge and wepinge'.[86] Shrewsbury's report here of Bess's extremely debilitating state of grief helps us to corroborate Bess's own subsequent description of her emotional state in her letter of May. That is, while Bess's textualised emotion in her letter of May certainly had a rhetorical function, according to Shrewsbury's account it also reflected actual emotion that she had experienced. One week later, on 28 January 1582, Bess sent two letters to Queen Elizabeth's chief advisors, one to Lord Burghley and the other to Sir Francis Walsingham.[87] Both were penned by the same scribe, in a neat secretary hand, and were subscribed and signed by Bess herself. While the two letters made the same request, and were in the hand of the same scribe, they differed slightly in tone and pitch to reflect the unequal status of the two men and Bess's greater confidence in addressing Walsingham compared to Burghley.[88] To be specific, her letter to Burghley invoked negative politeness through the language of service and the linguistic scripts of 'humility and entreaty': he was repeatedly addressed as her 'honourable good Lordship', 'verry good Lordship' and as 'your Lordship' (sixteen times in a letter of only 315 words; 'you/your' were never used)

86 BL, Lansd. 34, fols 2–3.
87 BL, Lansd. 34, fols 4r-5v, ID 162, and TNA, SP 12/152, f 36r-36v (item 13), ID 144.
88 These differing modes of address are found more generally across letters to Burghley and to Walsingham; Daybell, *Women Letter-Writers*, pp. 241–47.

66 *Composing and scripting letters*

and she referred to her 'humble suitt' (twice) and used 'beseech' (twice).[89] By comparison, her letter to Walsingham sent the same day invoked positive politeness by being cast in the easier language of a more equal political friendship: she addressed Walsingham as her 'honorable good frende' and her 'approved good frende', she subscribed 'your assuryed louyng frend', referred to his 'frendelie care', and addressed him using 'you/your' seven times.[90] Her friendly but more equalising tone to Walsingham was continued through her use of linguistic scripts of 'supposal and assurance': she asserted confidently that it was her 'assured truste' the queen would grant her suit and would think the amount involved to be 'litle inoughe'. Neither letter made any mention of her emotional state of grief. Bess did mention to Burghley that she was sorry not to have written in her own hand and perhaps the implicit meaning here was that she remained so enervated by grief as to be unable physically to put pen to paper herself. However, as no explicit mention of her emotional state was made (she simply said, 'pardon me for that I am not able nowe to wryte to your Lordship with my owne hande'), the trope functioned primarily to signal her especial politeness and respect towards Burghley, which again was at a higher level than towards Walsingham, who received no such apology. In summary, Bess's letters of request sent in January carefully followed the conventional recommendations for a petition, fulfilling, as they did, the precepts of 'brevity and aptness' and tailored precisely to the relative status of the recipient. In neither letter did Bess textualise her emotion. In fact, the tone of these letters in no way recalled the image of the grief-stricken mother tearfully lamenting as described by Shrewsbury one week earlier, which in many ways sounded like a different woman.

Despite being, as it were, textbook productions, Bess's letters of petition sent in January did not achieve their desired response. Therefore, after a gap of three months, on 6 May 1582, Bess wrote another pair of letters to Burghley and Walsingham, which made the same request but this time recast in the persona of a grieving mother. As in January, Burghley was accorded a higher level of politeness and deference than Walsingham: so, repeatedly (seven times), he was addressed as 'your Lordship', 'your good Lordship' or 'my good Lordship', whereas Walsingham was never referred to with an honorific but as 'you' or 'your'. In other respects the two May letters were similar to one another. Whereas both of the previous (January) letters had been succinct, brief and to the point, both of the letters written

---

89 This letter is ID 162. Shrewsbury also addresses Burghley as 'Lordship' in ID 188 (Plate 14), and ID 189, which are both in his own hand. Bess's other letters to Burghley, whether in her own hand or Scribe A's, or by other scribes, all use this form of address and the language of service.

90 This letter is ID 144. Bess's other letters, whether in her own hand or Scribe A's, or other scribes, all use this kind of address to Walsingham.

Composing and scripting letters 67

in May were longer and each filled almost a full page.[91] The additions made to both functioned to insert her textualised grief and her account of stepping into the role of mother to Arbella in service to the queen, which have been described earlier. In both cases, the May letters were penned in Scribe A's italic hand and signed by Bess herself. It is possible that the choice of scribe was purely down to availability. However, we can observe that Scribe A was the scribe who most often penned Bess's letters to Burghley and Walsingham and that Scribe A's hand was not dissimilar to Bess's own.[92] In fact, that Bess included no apology to Burghley this time for using a scribe might suggest she anticipated he would not discern this letter to be by a scribe rather than penned herself, their hands being so alike. In her May letters, then, we see Bess trying a different tack in her petitioning strategy. Her revised approach was not to reduce her power by offering more submissive, humble or deferential letters. Rather, her tactic was, using Scribe A as copyist, to incorporate textualised emotion as a marker of sincerity and to mobilise the cultural model of 'natural' motherhood.

The revisions found between the January and May petitions remind us that the representations Bess sent out into the world in her letters were constructed and strategic. This is not to say that Bess did not experience emotion at the death of her daughter – according to her husband she experienced extreme emotion expressed as 'lamenting and weeping'. But we need to be aware that Bess was managing the image that was presented and fashioned in an attempt to elicit a particular response and achieve a particular goal. This management included: deciding how much time to leave before writing the first time and then before writing again; deciding when to, and when not to, mention emotion and how to textualise emotion so as to be persuasive; selecting from available linguistic scripts to inscribe perceived power relations according to the relationship with the recipient; taking into account that the letter was not only to Walsingham or Burghley but also for the queen; considering previous letters sent by herself or her husband and the current letter's relation to those in order to build a coherent case; and accounting for the scribe used and, where necessary, apologising for using a scribe. When we read these letters, then, we need to keep in mind the complex processes involved in their construction that underpin the decisions made about their language. Ultimately, none of these letters was successful and Bess never received any more money from the queen to support Arbella's upbringing and education.[93] But the letters reveal to us how Bess drew from a repertoire of existing scripts and forms available to her as a

---

91 Bess's January letter to Walsingham is 215 words long, whereas her May letter is 519 words; her January letter to Burghley is 315 words, whereas her May letter is 534 words.

92 Scribe A is discussed in section 2.3.

93 Durant, *Bess of Hardwick*, p. 23, records that Bess's first petitions on Arbella's behalf (i.e., after Arbella's father died) were successful, and he comments that this in itself was an achievement.

68 *Composing and scripting letters*

letter-writer and, in consort with her scribes, constructed a style, inscribed power relations and textualised emotion in the ways she perceived to be most appropriate to the intended purpose and function of each letter.

1.3 'I am the furst innosent wyffe, that euar was so very extremly vsed in thys realme, god make me the last': a letter to her estranged husband the earl of Shrewsbury written during their marital discord, 1585

Superscription, Scribe A:	To my Lord my husband the earle of Shrouesbury.//
Endorsement, *Shrewsbury:*	Answered & sente henry talbott therew^r
Letter, Scribe A:	My Lord, you know I neuar comytted any offence, wherby I should submyt my selfe, more then that I was bound in duty of a wyffe to doe to you; I beseache you charge me partecularly, that I may know my faults. I am assured, that non leueing, could be more dutyfull, trew, faythfull, and carefull to a husband, then I haue euar ben to you; I haue sought all means to haue pleased you yf yt would haue ben, and many years, you thought well of me; I well hoped of lat, when yt pleased you to saye to me, beare all thyngs that ys past, and let not appeare to the world the dyscontentment that ys betwext vs, and I wyll promys of my fayth to become anew man, in vowing most earnestly, you loued me so well that you also loued the stepes I trade one; thys was alettell before m^r myldmays coming and not past ij monthes before you sent me away; at wch tyme you pecked no quarryll to me, but alleged the lettelnes of your house, want of carryage for my stufe, and want of beds for my wemen and groumes./ my L. you cannot forget how much greued I was to part wth you (wch pronostycated that wch followed) and yet beleued your words, of my coming to you ageane wthin one monthe./ my L. you can not forget, how you set one your hole house to crye out of me, and to charge me wth that I was Innosent of, how I bare that and many other thyngs, I rather wyshe, that of your selfe you cauled them to remembarance, then I to wryte them./ you say I seme to excuse and iustyfye my selfe and chyldryn, yet you know the contrary, and charge me and them [*deletion*] wth wecked dealing, to the ovarthrow of you and your house; the almyghty knows my innocensye therin./ my Lord I pray you geue me leaue to say, that yf you thenke so, you doe me and them wronge, and I pray the lord so to prospar me as I haue ben carefull for you and your house, your extreme dealing, wch hath only ruinated me and myne, could not force me so much as in my harte to thenke, or onst to wyshe the ovarthrow of you or your house; and I beseache you not to condeme me for standing in my owne defence; your selfe forces me to yt, god put into your harte to weaye in equall balance

Composing and scripting letters 69

my desarts to you, and your dealing towards me yf I had
ben as you tearme me wecked, so I had not comytted
horedome, yt ys more then a suffeseyent reuenge, though
you contenew not styll in yt, to torne me away, to
w^{th}drawe the allowance from me you gaue me when I was
wth you, to enter into all the land was myne, and agreat
parte of others that was nether yours nor myne, and you
content styll to take a great parte of our leueings, and I
to leue in all want and meserye, my great debts not . . . to
you. thes extremetys wyll force my chyldryn to sell all they
haue for my meantynance, and to pay my debts; I haue not
left to leue vpon (rentes anuetys and many other charges
going out of the land being payd) cleare thre hondryth
pounds a yeare; for my chyldryns land I can not leue of
that wch most part ys owing for and they forced by thos
extremetys to sell that ys left, you may buy yt yf yt please
you, all thes thyngs and many other wrongs consedered
I trust non wyll condeme me in seking to helpe my selfe
by all good means./ but all thes and many more, greues
me not so much nor touche me so neare as that I se your
loue ys w^{th}drawne from me, but my constant duty and
affectyon contenews so to you, that yf my tyme weare
longe, as yt ys sure to be short, I shall nevar cease to seke
and sue by all good means, that I may lyue wth you as I
ought, and doubt not but in the end the almyghty wyll
torne your harte and make you thenke of me as I haue
dyssarued, and that we may leue together according to
hys lawes./ [*deletion*] my lord I may say wth grefe that I am
the furst Innosent wyffe, that euar was so very extremly
vsed in thys realme, god make me the last, for yt ys well
knowne to be adangarus example in aparson of your state,
but I beseache the almyghty god to torne your harte in
some tyme towards me, that we may leue together as we
ought, so wyll he be best pleased wth all your doings, you
better satysfyed in consyance and I obtayne that wch of all
worldly thyngs I most desyar, and non dyspleased but such
as are not good./ and so I cease beseaching you to except
of my good meaning./ at hygatt the xiiij^{th} of octobar.//

Superscription, Scribe A: your faythfull wyffe most sorrowfull
Signature, autograph: EShrouesbury
14 October [1585], Bess (countess of Shrewsbury)
writes from Highgate to her husband Shrewsbury, sent,
accordion folded, extra-large paper, Scribe A.[94]

In this letter Bess wrote to her estranged husband, the earl of Shrewsbury,
during their marital discord in an attempt to broach a reconciliation and
to offer her response to his accusations about her character and behaviour.
The letter was one of a sequence of seven existing letters exchanged between

94 Arundel Castle, Autograph Letters 1585–1617, No. 111, ID 229.

70   *Composing and scripting letters*

the feuding couple between 4 August 1584 and 5 August 1586.[95] While ostensibly between husband and wife, these letters were written with the advice of legal counsellors and in the knowledge that they may be circulated more widely and potentially used as evidence against the sender.[96] Such usage and wider circulation could be strategic, and we know that on at least one occasion during the marital dispute Shrewsbury had his secretary make a copy of one of his letters to forward to Lord Burghley.[97] From a rhetorical point of view, Shrewsbury's letters were extremely well crafted and measured: they were not letters wildly dashed off in the heat of the moment but carefully scripted character assassinations designed as much for the eyes of Burghley (and therefore the queen and Court) as for his wife. By this point the Shrewsburys' marital problems were the talk of the Court and these letters, while cast as 'private' missives between spouses, were everywhere infused with an acute awareness that the words on the page must be able to stand up to the possibility of 'public' scrutiny and judgement. This kind of fracturing between the 'private' form of the letter and its 'public' function is something we must be continually aware of when reading these letters, not least because the dispute started during the period when Shrewsbury and Bess were the custodians of the Scottish Queen, when any disruption or instability within their households constituted a state security risk. On more than one occasion Queen Elizabeth herself acted as mediator between the couple and Lord Burghley and other high-level figures were involved in drawing up agreements and settlements for them. That is to say, the earl and countess of Shrewsbury's marital problems were by no means just a personal matter confined to the domestic sphere, but were widely discussed at Court and had political implications.

95 Although not a complete sequence, we have examples of letters and direct replies. There are three letters from Shrewsbury: from 4 August 1584 (ID 119; unsent scribal copy), 23 October 1585 (Longleat House, Talbot Papers, MS 1, fols 194r-195v, ID 117; unsent scribal copy; a reply to Bess's letter of nine days earlier, ID 229) and 5 August 1586 (HMC Salisbury, III, p. 163, ID 251; scribal copy forwarded to Lord Burghley and now in the CP, endorsed by Shrewsbury's secretary in an italic script 'the copie of my lo: lre to the countesse his wyef'; a reply to Bess's letter of the previous day, ID 202). We have four letters from Bess: 26 August 1584 (Longleat House, Talbot Papers, MS 2, fols 267r-68v, ID 116; sent, Scribe A), 14 October 1585 (ID 229; sent, Scribe A; Shrewsbury's reply to this letter is ID 117), 9 June 1586 (ID 176; unsent draft by a scribe in a secretary script) and 4 August 1586 (Chatsworth House, Devonshire MSS, ID 202; sent, Scribe A; Shrewsbury's reply sent the next day is ID 251).

96 Apart from the tone of the letters implying the presence of legal advisers, in ID 119 Shrewsbury states that 'vppon deliberate advice of the Lerned I am now resolved to proceade by due order of Lawe with those my adversaries your sonnes'; and Bess writes ID 116 from Chancery Lane.

97 ID 251 scribal copy forwarded to Lord Burghley as it is now in the Cecil Papers, endorsed by Shrewsbury's secretary in an italic script 'the copie of my lo: lre to the countesse his wyef'; a reply to Bess's letter of the previous day, ID 202.

Composing and scripting letters 71

The stakes were extraordinarily high for Bess during the dispute with her husband: Shrewsbury had removed her allowance; evicted her from her beloved Chatsworth; denounced her character as wicked, malicious, greedy and duplicitous; refused to allow her to be in his presence; and he was taking legal actions against two of her sons, William and Charles Cavendish. Shrewsbury had also enlisted the support of Bess's other, eldest son, Henry Cavendish (who was Shrewsbury's stepson and son-in-law), and that Henry acted as bearer for Shrewsbury's reply to this letter of 14 October 1585 itself sent a message to Bess that husband and son were united against her.[98] Shrewsbury's letters sent to Bess and to his own network of powerful contacts and kin were bitterly vicious and full of malice.[99] They were also the letters used by Edmund Lodge as the basis for his biographical portrayal of Bess, which has been repeatedly cited ever since its publication in the eighteenth century. Bess's letters of response are nowhere near so well known, but they are compelling examples of attempts at defence and conciliation in the face of angry threats. They provide counter-narratives to her husband's accusations, and Bess's choice of language is revealing about her perception of her own position and of the options available to her. They show us her attitude with regard to the stances from which she could argue and positions she could occupy in order to forward her own cause most effectively. We find that Bess deployed a number of strategies across her four existing letters from this sequence, which are discussed next. These included the use of linguistic scripts and material forms to inscribe deference; the mobilisation of the cultural model of the 'good' wife; and the use of metaphoric language.

Linguistic scripts and material forms

Bess's letter to Shrewsbury of 14 October 1585 deployed several conventional forms associated with deference. The physical dimensions of the letter (the extra-large paper and accordion-folded letter packet) were means by which to inscribe politeness or humility.[100] Combined with these material features, the letter was structured around a series of linguistic scripts conventionally used to show deference and respect towards one's recipient. The opening address to 'my Lord' inscribed negative politeness, distance and formality. It contrasted with the address terms that characterised letters between the couple from the earlier, harmonious stage of their marriage,

---

98 ID 117.

99 For Durant they qualify as 'the most vituperative ever written by a husband to his wife'; *Bess of Hardwick*, p. 139.

100 A full discussion of these physical forms of letters having communicative functions is presented in section 3.4. We know that this letter had passed through Shrewsbury's own hands and under his own eyes (rather than being read aloud to him by a bearer or secretary before being filed away) because he endorses it himself in his own unmistakable handwriting.

72   Composing and scripting letters

which typically included terms of endearment, such as 'dear heart', to inscribe intimacy, relaxed familiarity, playfulness and trust.[101] In stark contrast here, Bess deployed 'my Lord' five times to structure the argument of her letter and to manage the opening of each of the letter's main clauses. A second category of linguistic form important to discourse cohesion within letters was speech-act verbs, and again we can observe a change in Bess's linguistic usage. Whereas earlier letters between the couple typically used 'I prey you' throughout, here we find requests from Bess made using 'beseech', which appeared four times in this one letter. Whereas 'I prey you' was a decorous choice of phrase for making a request to someone where there was minimal vertical and horizontal distance, forms such as 'crave', 'beg' and, most strongly of all, 'beseech' (all of which inscribed humility and deference) functioned to acknowledge much larger dimensions of vertical and horizontal distance. That is, they registered the perceived social superiority of one's correspondent, or the perceived emotional distance and lack of intimacy or familiarity, or the perceived large magnitude or urgency of a request, or, indeed, a combination of all of these.[102] That Bess's letters during the dispute all repeatedly deployed 'beseech', whereas none of her earlier letters had done so, again acknowledged the change in their relationship through the language of her letters.

The forms 'my lord' (used five times) and 'beseech' (used four times), then, provided a discourse-cohesive structure of polite and respectful linguistic scripts in the letter, necessary to acknowledge the actual change in the relationship between herself and her estranged husband. While this was so, elsewhere in the letter, Shrewsbury was addressed using 'you' (rather than the much more deferential 'my lord', 'your lordship's' or 'your lordship'): 'you' was used forty-six times compared to 'my lord' just five times.[103] Furthermore, the letter presented an argument that was forceful and sometimes confrontational in tone, as repeatedly Bess's argument in her own defence was structured around a claim or accusation against Shrewsbury beginning 'you', such as: 'you know I never', 'you cannot forget' (two times), 'you set on your whole house to charge me', 'you say', 'you know the contrary', 'if you think so, you do me and them wrong' and 'your self forces me to it'. The

---

101 The discussion in section 1.1 of the marital letters gives full references to and examples of these terms of endearment. We should note that Bess always used 'my lorde' as was conventional for the period, where letter-writers would use a more formal address on the outer letter packet (visible to the bearer) and more intimate terms would be used only inside the letter if a more private readership was anticipated.

102 To use the terminology from politeness theory, these scripts register larger dimensions of PDR, as discussed earlier in the introduction, p. 6.

103 The same pattern is found in ID 116 and ID 202, where Shrewsbury is addressed as <you> twenty-seven times and twenty-four times respectively, and as <my Lord> six times and six times respectively (82%:18% and 80%:2%), always with <my Lord> used in the superscription, opening and as the opening of the letter's main clauses.

Composing and scripting letters 73

switches between the deferential linguistic scripts used to cohere the main clauses of the letter ('my Lord' and 'beseech') and the argument characterised by confrontational you-centred assertions produced an unevenness of style. The apparent inconsistencies (between the deferential material forms and linguistic scripts on the one hand and the assertive argument on the other) resulted in an ambiguity of tone. The impression emerged, as a result, of Bess merely paying lip-service to the deferential conventions, which could seem like adornments included for the sake of correct decorum but incongruous with the substance of the letter.

The same ambiguity of tone was apparent in the conventional trope of wifely humility and submission deployed in the subscription: 'your faythfull wyffe most sorrowfull'.[104] Such formulae for subscriptions were well-worn by this point in the sixteenth century but they could nonetheless still be used sincerely. For example, in her letters to Shrewsbury sent during the harmonious stage of their marriage, Bess invariably and without irony or ambiguity subscribed as 'your faythfull wife'. Later, during the period of their brief reconciliation in 1587, after several years of estrangement and repeated petitioning to be allowed into her husband's presence, Bess wrote to Shrewsbury in her own hand a scrupulously affectionate and deferential letter, which used her most elaborate subscription of all, again without irony and doubtless here to express relief at their reconciliation: 'your louynge and most obedyante faythefull wyfe'.[105] While these formulaic subscriptions, then, could in some cases be sincere, where we find them following letters that were otherwise combative and argumentative their function changed and became ambiguous at least. Furthermore, as the subscription here in Bess's letter of 14 October 1585 could be seen to contribute to Bess's overall argument in the letter that she had been an unimpeachable wife, it could itself be seen as an implicit criticism of Shrewsbury. In the case of Bess's last letter to Shrewsbury during their marital discord, written on 4 August 1586, the choice of subscription must have seemed decidedly caustic: at the end of an especially combative letter she subscribed 'your obedynate faytheful wyffe'. That is, while it followed all the precepts for a wife addressing her husband, it concluded a letter so uncompromisingly critical in tone that it is difficult to read the subscription here as anything other than sarcastic and knowingly provocative.[106] These examples, then, remind us that we must be constantly vigilant of the pragmatic (interpersonal) context within which linguistic scripts and conventional formulae were deployed. While the form of these scripts was fixed and conventional, their communicative function could shift

---

104 The subscription in her previous letter was 'your humble wyffe most faythfull'; ID 116.
105 ID 186.
106 ID 202. Daybell, *Women Letter-Writers*, p. 214, makes the point that despite Bess's claims to dutifulness in her letters they were 'also almost certainly intentionally barbed'.

74   *Composing and scripting letters*

dramatically depending on context and use. So a set form of subscription could function at any number of points along a spectrum from sincere affection to acerbic gibe.

A 'good' wife

It was not only in the subscriptions but throughout these letters that Bess presented herself through the trope of the ideal Renaissance wife: patient, obedient, dutiful and unfailingly loyal to her husband.[107] In her letter of 14 October 1585 she opened with the assertion that she was 'bound in duty of a wyffe' to Shrewsbury, and a similar stance is found in her letter of the previous year where she beseeched Shrewsbury 'in all dutys of a wyffe'.[108] There is no doubt that Bess wanted to be seen to be in favour of reuniting with her husband, which she made known at Court. Her attempts at conjugal reconciliation may have reflected her own sadness about the estrangement, but there is no doubt they also represented a very shrewd legal move.[109] Indeed, Bess had taken legal advice by this point and her previous letter to her husband was written from Chancery Lane ('from my Loging in chanserye Lane'). That is to say, by taking the role of the 'good wife' seeking reconciliation with her husband, Bess activated a powerful and emotive cultural image, which also gave her the most advantageous position from a legal perspective.[110] To construct this image Bess emphasised her grief when she last parted from her husband, her sadness at seeing his love withdrawn from her and her sorrowful state. She depicted her unwavering and dutiful desire to be reunited with her husband: 'my constant duty and affectyon contenews so to you . . . I shall nevar cease to seke and sue by all good means, that I may lyue with you as I ought'. She closed her letter by reiterating her status as a wronged wife, patient in the face of her husband's

---

107   The classic accounts of construction of the ideal Renaissance wife and discourses of fictions of women include those by Hull, *Chaste, Silent, and Obedient*, Hutson, *The Usurer's Daughter*, and Jardine, *Still Harping on Daughters*.

108   ID 116.

109   It is a point also discussed by Lovell, *Bess of Hardwick*, p. 305.

110   Daybell, 'Scripting a Female Voice', discusses the 'emotive and powerful' image of the 'good wife' and summarises that it was 'culturally understood that women were able to manipulate male assumptions of women's social roles as "good" wives and "good" mothers, and of female incapacity', a situation which 'exposes the ways in which women could work within the limitations and constraints imposed by early modern society', p. 18. It is a strategy and stance used by other women of the period – for example, Dorothy Percy's letter to her estranged husband, which incorporates advice from her brother the earl of Essex on how to argue her point: 'On the one hand there was a need for the countess to be seen publicly to have been a dutiful wife; on the other hand, total submission and personal admission of sole responsibility for the separation were not compatible with the maintenance of the Devereux family honour. The letter, therefore, represents a carefully calculated response to these two considerations'; Daybell, *Women Letter-Writers*, pp. 77–78.

Composing and scripting letters 75

neglect, and she declared herself to be the 'furst Innosent wyffe, that euar was so very extremely vsed in thys realme, god make me the last'.

These performances of idealised wifehood evidently enraged Shrewsbury. In his letter of response sent on 23 October 1585, in tones clearly furious, he expressed scepticism about her epistolary performances and his contemptuous criticisms repeatedly referred to the words of Bess's letters: 'I mervell', said Shrewsbury, 'to see your earnestness, as you pretent by your letters to be with me' (pretent: *pretend*).[111] In particular, he challenged her deployment of the image of the 'good' wife and cited the many ways that, in his view, she had fallen far short of the cultural ideal prescribed for wives. He answered her particular claims for ideal wifehood point for point. So whereas Bess in her letter asserted that no wife had ever been so 'dutyfull, trew, faythfull, and carefull to a husband' as she had been, he, in response, called her a 'noe good wife' whose 'offences & faules' should be a warning to all men thinking of marriage. In another tit for tat, whereas Bess claimed she had 'sought all means to haue pleased you', he, in response, claimed that there could not be 'anie wife more forgetfull of her dutie & less carful to please her husbande than you haue bene'.

Shrewsbury's reception of Bess's letter of 14 October 1585 evidently did not deter Bess from appropriating the cultural model of the 'good' wife again, in her next letter, some eight months later, on 9 June 1586.[112] Again we must remember that this decision by Bess represented a shrewd legal stance. In addition she may also have recalled that, in their previous (brief) period of disagreement in 1577, her protestations of love had been effective in assuaging her husband's anger. According to Gilbert Talbot, who acted as their go-between, when he had told Shrewsbury of Bess's desire for reunion, her distressed 'perplexitie' of mind and her wish to relieve his griefs by taking them onto herself, Shrewsbury had 'melted' and had admitted his wrongs and their great love for one another.[113] It was both past experience and sound legal advice, then, that led Bess, on 9 June 1586, to frame her letter entirely using tropes of deference. Every time Shrewsbury was addressed in her June letter it was as 'your Lordship': sixteen times in total (i.e., there was no switching between 'your Lordship' and 'you/your' as in her October 1585 letter; 'your' is used only twice and never for an accusation). In her June letter she also overtly acknowledged that the ideal wife should according to contemporary doctrine patiently subjugate herself to her husband's authority: 'I owghte, bothe by the lawes of god nature & men, patiently to beare what correction by wordes or deedes, it shall please your Lordship to laye vppon me'. Yet (and while she acknowledged forbearance of punishment to be prescribed for wives), Bess explained that she was in 'great feare

111 ID 117.
112 ID 176.
113 ID 84, 1577.

76   *Composing and scripting letters*

of your Lordship's wrath' and 'the extreme rygoure of wordes' which had, in the past, caused her 'vexation of mynde' and the 'losse of my pore wytts & sences'. That is to say, Bess here invoked the cultural image of the patient and obedient wife as a means to explain and justify her own terrifying predicament and to remind Shrewsbury that the role of the loving and patient wife depended in turn upon a kind and patient husband. The implication was that Shrewsbury had not played his role or lived up to his responsibilities as a husband. To close the letter, Bess pictured herself in a posture of utter humility, as a supplicant, a religious worshipper down on her knees, who pleaded for her husband's blessing and sent prayers for him: 'Thus moste humblie on my knees becechinge your Lordship's blessing with my wonted bounden prayers for your Lordship's moste perfyte healthe, honour & longe lyffe, I humblie cease'. This letter, then, while underpinned by an implicit criticism of Shrewsbury, was cast in consistently deferential scripts, evoked the melancholic, sorrowful tone of the wronged wife and projected Bess's image of herself as the 'good', patient wife.[114]

It is worth recalling at this point that Bess had for many years associated herself, through visual art, with the classical figure of Penelope: the faithful wife, abandoned by her husband Odysseus, the epitome of patience and loyalty, waiting for her husband to return. Penelope was the period's most unambiguous example of feminine virtuosity and esteemed wifehood. While Bess evidently had a liking for a number of other mythic and iconic female figures, such as Lucrece, her strongest affinity was with Penelope and there were several visual depictions of Penelope at Chatsworth and, later, Hardwick.[115] The strength of Bess's affinity with Penelope was attested most clearly by the full-length embroidered figure she had had produced, commissioned within her own workshop at Chatsworth, which was both a depiction of Penelope and Bess's own self-portrait (Plate 8).[116] Bess's self-fashioning of her own identity through this mythic female figure was no coincidental or casual decision, but one she had developed over many years and would have been well known to anyone who had visited Chatsworth, where her embroidered self-portrait was prominently displayed. While in her letters Bess did not herself overtly or explicitly mention Penelope, her precise and sustained identification with the figure leaves us in no doubt that she was aware that identities could be fashioned and that cultural models and classical icons could offer roles to step into. In her letters, as in her textile art, we find that Bess took a rhetorical stance informed by contemporary discourses of ideal wives and virtuous women. Moreover, we do find a direct and explicit

---

114 Schneider, 'Affecting Correspondences', has shown that embodied images such as postures of supplication or kneeling were a conventional ways of textualising strong emotion and claiming sincerity of feeling at this period.

115 Kiefer, 'Architecture', p. 694, provides a description of the artwork, in various media, that featured Penelope at Chatsworth and Hardwick.

116 Frye, *Pens and Needles*, pp. 60–74.

Composing and scripting letters 77

reference to Bess's implied epistolary self-presentation as Penelope in one of her husband Shrewsbury's letters.

As we have seen, Bess presented herself to Shrewsbury via the cultural model of the 'good' wife, and given her well-established association with Penelope we might therefore detect an underlying reference to the Homeric narrative – that is, with Bess herself as a Penelope figure waiting for her husband, Shrewsbury, a wandering Odysseus figure, to come back to her. That Shrewsbury was very much alert to this underlying implied mythic narrative was apparent from one of his letters to Bess during this period where he recast the classical scene from his own perspective. His letter opened:

> Your letter . . . carrying so faire and vnaccustomed shewe of dutiful-ness & humilyte of spirite commeth now so late and so out of season that makes me suspect it to be a Sirens songe set for some other purpose then it pretendeth.[117]

Shrewsbury here presented himself as an Odysseus figure, but according to his version Bess was imagined not as the patient Penelope, his ever faithful wife at home, but one of the Sirens – female creatures whose beautiful-sounding but dangerous voices were used to lure sailors to shipwreck on the rocky coast of their island. That is to say, Bess's personal appropriation of the figure of Penelope, and her especial interest in classical and mythical women, should encourage us to be aware that Bess was self-consciously shaping the epistolary models available to her, and, in some cases, subverting these or using them for purposes of defence or to empower her arguments. Shrewsbury's counter-casting of the Odysseus myth provides evidence that these embedded references to mythical figures were very much alive in the reception of Bess's letters. While her letters may not be considered literary in the sense of including innovative conceits, intricate wordplay such as puns, or quotations in classical languages, they were literary through their reference to a broader context of personalised symbolic patterning and a readership who themselves fully identified with classical literary figures and iconographies.

Metaphoric language

Shrewsbury's letter of 4 August 1584, as well as its classical imagery, made reference to the everyday metaphors of 'marriage as war' and 'women's words as traps and weapons of war'.[118] Bess's words in her letter were 'a

---

117 ID 119, 4 August 1584, Shrewsbury wrote from Sheffield to his wife Bess (countess of Shrewsbury) at Hardwick, scribal copy, unsent.

118 The everyday metaphors MARRIAGE IS WAR and ILLNESS IS WAR can be tracked through the *HTOED* using the *MM* project's *Metaphor Map of English*.

78 Composing and scripting letters

Sirens song', which sound enticing but were 'set for some other purpose', as a dangerous trap for men. There were further examples of Shrewsbury's use of this metaphor in his letters: Bess was his 'bytter enemy', her ambitious aims in marriage were targets she shot at ('this was short of the mark you shott at & yet do') and her words in her letters 'appeare butifull' yet were 'mixed with a hidden poison' that he must avoid swallowing.[119] Shrewsbury, by this point in his life, was certainly an embattled man and a man suffering both psychological and physical pain. We also find him, during this period, describing his debilitating illness (the painful gout in his hands) using war imagery and in his letters he repeatedly conceptualised his illness as his enemy and adversary.[120] For Shrewsbury in the 1580s, life was a battleground and he felt himself to be attacked on many sides. These feelings of resentment, betrayal, mistrust and suspicion formed the background to the reception context for the letters Bess sent to him.[121]

To Shrewsbury casting himself as a war-weary Odysseus beset by enemies and traps, Bess responded with another strand of metaphoric language. Bess repeatedly drew on the metaphor (or metonym) of 'the heart as a container for the emotions'.[122] It is a metaphor that offered various advantages and around which Bess repeatedly structured her arguments in these letters during the marital discord.[123] As a well-worn, everyday metaphor, references to the heart had the advantage of sounding like plain, natural language (and therefore not artificial or contrived) and were therefore well suited to her claims of unadorned truthfulness and sincerity. The heart was also part of a wider pattern of embodied images deployed in contemporary letters, as well as other texts, to textualise emotion and claim sincerity of feeling.[124] Bess adapted the heart metaphor to support her case through the familiar

---

119 ID 119, ID 117 and ID 117.
120 Shrewsbury's painful illness and his metaphoric conceptualisations of it are discussed by Williams, '"My Evil Favoured Writing"'.
121 Durant, *Bess of Hardwick*, p. 123, surmises that by this point Shrewsbury was 'a very sick man'.
122 The everyday metaphor THE HEART IS A CONTAINER FOR THE EMOTIONS can be tracked through the *HTOED* using the *MM* project's *Metaphor Map of English*.
123 Images and metaphors of the heart appear in all three of Bess's letters to Shrewsbury: 'the innocency of my owne heart, 'my harte can not accuse yt', 'my harte . . . thyrstes after your prosperity', 'I trust you wyll quiet my harte' (ID 116); 'could not force me . . . in my harte to thence', 'god put into your harte', 'the almighty wyll torne your harte', 'I beseache the almighty god to torne your harte' (ID 229); 'the moste ioyed in harte' (ID 176).
124 The implications of using the heart metaphor and the ideology of sincerity in everyday early modern English are explored through early modern letters by Williams, '"That thought never ytt entered my harte"'. An exploration of the rhetoric of the heart across a range of early modern discourses, which includes literary considerations, is provided by Slights, *The Heart in the Age of Shakespeare*.

Composing and scripting letters 79

concept of the heart having its own autonomy: an organ separate from the mind and not subject to or capable of being controlled by the mind. By framing her words as coming from the heart, they were thus presented as sincere, genuine and beyond personal calculation. Moreover, the concept of the heart having autonomy became a way of asserting in her letters – and she said this very directly – that her heart was not only beyond the control of her own mind but also beyond her husband's power or control. In her letter of 26 August 1584 she repeatedly declared the 'innocency of my owne heart' and consistently emphasised that, despite the circumstances, her heart had an ardent and unwavering desire for Shrewsbury's love and favour. Then, in her letter of 14 October 1585, she more strongly emphasised the autonomy of her own heart and stated that no matter what Shrewsbury might do he could not force her, in her heart, to wish him ill:

> your extreme dealing, which hath only ruinated me and myne, could not force me somuch as in my hart to thence, or onst to wyshe the ovarthrow of you or your house.
> Gloss: hart: *heart*, thence: *think*, onst: *once*.

Shrewsbury could not, either through his actions or his legal cases against her, ultimately control her inner reality or turn her from being a loyal wife who hoped he would prosper. Bess then went further and called upon a higher authority than her husband. She asked God to put into her husband's heart a scale of justice so that he might judge her more fairly: 'god put into your harte to weaye in equall balance my desarts to you, and your dealing towards me'. Twice more before the end of her letter Bess referred to God as the supreme authority and to sanctified marriage as a higher law that must take precedence over Shrewsbury's legal cases against her, and which she was confident would ultimately win out:

> doubt not but in the end the almighty wyll torne your harte and make you thence of me as I haue dyssarued, and that we may leue together according to hys lawes . . . I beseache the almighty god to torne your harte in some tyme towards me, that we may leue together as we ought.
> Gloss: torne: *turn*, thence: *think*, leue: *live*.

In this way we see that Bess constructed a forceful argument and strongly defended her own position, and did so through the existing images and metaphors available to her and which were well known within her own culture. While the heart was a familiar, everyday metaphor, we see how it could be appropriated by Bess to serve her own purpose and defend her own credibility. In the end, despite Shrewsbury's incredulity and outrage, Queen Elizabeth found in Bess's favour. We might consider here that Bess's stance gained additional credibility because Shrewsbury's angry outbursts were

80   *Composing and scripting letters*

well known to be real, which lent integrity and validity to her claims.[125] Nevertheless, in the face of intimidating anger, Bess's letters tell us how early modern women could appropriate available cultural models and deploy everyday metaphorical language for powerful effect. In law and in the eyes of the queen, Burghley and the Court, Bess's behaviour and chosen stance were justifiable and ensured their support.

1.4 'My good sweete daughter . . . blesse you deare harte': a letter to her daughter Mary, countess of Shrewsbury, 1607

Superscription, Scribe A:	To the Right honorable my very good daughter the countys of Shrousbury / / /
Endorsement, secretary:	31. Nov: 1607. T[he countess] Dowag[r] of [Shrewsbury to my] lady
Letter, Scribe A:	my good sweete daughter; I am very desirous to heare how you doe./ I truste your Lord ys well or now ^of the goute^; and I desire to heare how all ours doe at London and the Lettell sweete Lorde mautrauars; I pray god euer to blesse you deare harte; and them all wth all [his] good blessinges; and soe in haste I cease at hardwecke this Laste of novembar
Subscription, Scribe A:	your Loueing mother
Signature, autograph:	EShrousbury
	30 November 1607, Bess (dowager countess of Shrewsbury) writes from Hardwick Hall to her daughter, Mary (Cavendish) Talbot, seventh countess of Shrewsbury, sent, Scribe A, Plate 22.[126] Gloss: or: *before.*

This brief note, signed in the very shaky hand of the octogenarian Bess, is her last letter to her youngest daughter Mary (Cavendish) Talbot, who had succeeded her mother as seventh countess of Shrewsbury some sixteen years earlier. Written during the final months of Bess's life, this note encapsulates something of the essence of their mother–daughter correspondence, which we can trace in over a dozen letters between the two women that extend across more than three decades, from 1575 to this final letter in

---

125 We know, from sources that include his own son Gilbert's letters to Bess, that Shrewsbury had a reputation for anger. For example, Gilbert had reported Shrewsbury's 'shewes' of 'angre' and 'evell will' towards Bess, his 'vehement coller & harde speches', his being 'exceedinge angrye' and uttering 'curell & bytter speches' against Bess. He also referred to his father's 'exceeding collor of sleyghte occasion' that was 'a great greife to them yat loves him to se him hurte him selfe so muche' and that make Gilbert wish himself anywhere but Sheffield, in his words rather 'a plowman then here to continew'; Gilbert Talbot to Bess (countess of Shrewsbury), October 1575?, Sheffield Archives, MD 6279, ID 218.

126 LPL, Talbot Papers, MS 3205, fols 59r-60v, ID 179 (Plate 22).

1607.[127] Their correspondence gives us an insight into how Bess styled her role as mother in correspondence with her daughter, which constitutes the only letters we have existing from Bess to any of her children.[128] We can be confident that their relationship included sustained and genuine emotional bonds, based on other sources that include the gifts carefully prepared by Mary for her mother to reflect their relationship; Bess's will, where Mary was remembered with the Cavendish heirloom of the Pearl Bed; Shrewsbury's refusal to see Mary during the marriage dispute because she would side with her mother, Bess, against him; the reports of Bess's extreme grief at the death of Mary's son George; and the reports that Mary suffered genuine distress when her mother died.[129] The argument made here is that while the letters have presented modern commentators with challenges of interpretation, when rigorously historicised they can be seen to yield information that bolsters our picture of a relationship that included affective bonds and warmth of feeling.[130]

We should first observe that certain elements of this letter were fixed conventions that never varied and therefore cannot be used to indicate the quality of the relationship. For example, the signature 'EShrousbury' is the one Bess invariably used once she became countess of Shrewsbury and that

---

127 The letter is penned by Bess's Scribe A, as are all six of Bess's letters to Mary; the remaining five are: LPL, Talbot Papers, MS 3205, fol. 72, fols 64r-65v, fols 75r-76v and fols 62r-63v, 1580 ID 185, 1580s ID 181 (also addressed to Gilbert), 28 February 1598 ID 187, and (also addressed to Gilbert) 15 January 1606 ID 180; Arundel Castle, Autograph Letters 1585–1617, No. 124, 18 February 1591? ID 233. There are five letters co-signed from Gilbert and Mary, Lord and Lady Talbot to Bess (countess of Shrewsbury): Folger CT, X.d.428 (112–115), 1 August 1577 ID 85, 19 September 1583? ID 86, February 1589 ID 87, and 1 July 1589 ID 88; LPL, Talbot Papers, MS 3197, fol. 287, 13 February 1579 ID 166. And there are two letters from Mary (countess of Shrewsbury) to her mother, Bess (dowager countess of Shrewsbury): Folger CT, X.d.428 (118 and 119), 8 July 1607 ID 89 and 30 December 1607? ID 90.

128 With the exception of a business-like letter that is co-addressed to her son William Cavendish jointly with Gilbert Talbot and one cousin Clarke. There are two letters from Bess's eldest daughter, Francis (Cavendish) Pierrepont, to her mother; one is discussed in section 3.3, and the other sends political news (April 1603, Folger CT, X.d.428 [68], ID 53). There are two letters from Bess's middle daughter, Elizabeth (Cavendish) Lennox; one is discussed in section 3.4, and the other (Folger CT, X.d.428 [51], ID 42) has been discussed by Magnusson, 'A Rhetoric of Requests', p. 53.

129 The gifts from Mary to Bess are discussed in section 3.3. Mary's genuine distress when her mother died is described by Durant, *Bess of Hardwick*, pp. 226–27. The bequest of the Pearl Bed to Mary was added by Bess in the nuncupative codicil to her will twenty days before she died. The information about Shrewsbury not wanting to see Mary appears in a letter from Gilbert to Bess where he said, 'the cause he wolde not have me carry my wife to London was for yat he thought your Ladyship wolde goe vpp to London & then wolde my wife ioyne with you in exclaiming agaynste him, & so make him to Iudge the worsste of me' (28 May 1576, ID 82).

130 For a discussion that surveys contemporary mother–daughter correspondence, see Daybell, 'Social Negotiations'.

82   Composing and scripting letters

never changed across any of her letters, as was the usual practice at the time. Other forms also fulfilled the required social etiquettes of address and included the precise use of her daughter's title the 'Right honorable' countess of Shrewsbury in the superscription. In letters in the other direction (from Mary to her mother) the forms selected emphasised daughterly humility and obedience, which were required by convention to register hierarchy within the early modern family. So, Mary framed her letter to her mother the same year with phrases that used scripts that invoke negative politeness to register their relative positions within the family: her letter opened 'My duty most humbly remembered', closed 'I humbly take my leue' and was subscribed 'your Ladyship's most humbell and obedient daughter'.[131] These terms of address were conventional for the period and, with slight variations in phrasing, regularly framed letters by daughters and sons (as well as by children-in-law, stepchildren and grandchildren, who typically refer to themselves simply as child, son or daughter). Mary's own daughter, Aletheia (Talbot) Howard, countess of Arundel, when writing to her grandmother Bess around the same time subscribed in a very similar way to her mother, Mary, as 'your Ladyships most obbedint daughter'.[132] These scripts can sound stiff and unnatural to modern ears and have led some historians to suggest (controversially) that relations between family members in the sixteenth and seventeenth centuries must have been cold and unfeeling. Yet, as they were forms required within letters for reasons of social decorum, they should not be read literally as markers of the quality of the relationship. We need to read beyond the conventional formulae if we are to assess more accurately the existence, or not, of affective and emotional bonds.

Problems of interpretation are posed not only by forms designed to inscribe distance through negative politeness but also by fixed phrases that use emotional language to inscribe intimacy through positive politeness. For example, Bess's subscription here as 'your loving mother' was a routine sign-off that was prescribed in epistolary manuals, which therefore may or may not relate to a relationship containing genuine warmth.[133] Nevertheless, and while certainly conventional, it is worth considering subscriptions and superscriptions and whether choice of wording could be indicative of

---

131   ID 185, ID 181.

132   The current location of the letter is unknown but there is an image available in Sotheby's sale catalogue, 26 June 1974, Lot 2840; 1606–8, sent, hand of Aletheia Howard, ID 237. Bess's granddaughter Arbella Stuart, aged twelve years old, subscribed: 'Your Ladyships humble, and obbediente childe', 8 February 1588, Huntington Library, MS HM 803, ID 106.

133   Daybell, *Women Letter-Writers*, p. 206, records the very widespread use of these forms: 'Most common were the phrases, "your wife" and "your loving wife" which were employed by some 67 per cent of letter-writers'; and emphasises that their customary employment 'possibly conceals warmer sentiments, in the same way that current usage of phrases such as "yours sincerely"', p. 207.

Composing and scripting letters 83

the quality of a relationship. So, we can observe that Bess consistently chose to include the descriptive additions 'very good' daughter, 'loving' daughter and 'loving' mother when writing to Mary. Not all mothers routinely added these touches of warmth when writing to their children: Lady Anne Bacon, for example, when writing to her sons, never subscribed with 'loving', always just as 'your mother'.[134] It is possible that Bess's choice of forms was conventional within her family as they mirror those used by her own mother.[135] To take another example, we can consider the case of letters from Bess's sons to their mother, where the subscriptions appear to be telling of their widely varying relationships. Whereas all her sons typically incorporated the expected and conventional phrase 'humble and obedient' son, we can observe that Bess's 'bad son' Henry's subscriptions were more deferential and were twice formulated as 'most bounden humble and obedyent' son.[136] By contrast, Charles Cavendish, Gilbert Talbot and Thomas Howard, with whom Bess had much more positive relationships, included 'loving', 'very loving' or 'affectionate'.[137] Similarly, when Gilbert Talbot co-signed with his wife, Bess's daughter Mary, they always subscribed as 'Your Ladyship's moste humble and obedient lovynge chyldren'.[138] While, then, to discern the quality of the relationships encoded by these conventionalised formulae is not straightforward, it seems we should not dismiss them out of hand and we should remain alert to variations in form.

Beyond the most formulaic opening and closing parts of the letter, we should consider the main body of the letter itself, which was typically the part that contained more relaxed and familiar language. In this letter from Bess we find terms of endearment and expressions of affection and we can observe, within the space of a short note, the density of such phrases. Bess addressed Mary as her 'good sweete daughter' and her 'deare harte', asked after her 'Letell sweete' great-grandson and sent blessings. All six of Bess's

---

134 Allen, *The Letters*. Bess's letters to Mary are superscripted to 'the Right honorable my very good daughter the countys of Shrousbury' and (earlier) to 'my Loueng daughter the Lady Talbott' and every letter is subscribed 'your Loveing mother'.

135 In the one existing letter we have from Elizabeth Leache to her daughter Bess (Lady St Loe) she superscribes 'To my right hertilie beloued doghttar ladie sayntlo' and subscribes 'be your louinge mother' – that is, she includes the personal touches 'right heartly beloved' and 'loving'; c. 1565, Folger CT, X.d.428 (48), ID 40.

136 Bess refers to 'my bad son Henry' and my 'vnnaturall sonne, Henry' on 10 March and 13 April 1603, CP 135/167 and 99/114, fols 218–9 and fols 1–2, IDs 135 and 140. Henry Cavendish used his more elaborately deferential subscription in his letters of c. 1570 and 6 November c. 1585, Folger CT, X.d.428 (9, 10 and 1), IDs 9, 10 and 1.

137 For example, Charles Cavendish has 'your Ladyship's most obedient and louine sonne', Gilbert Talbot has 'Your Ladyships moste obedient and very Lovinge sunne' and Thomas Howard, earl of Arundel, has 'Your Ladyship's dutifull and affectionate sonne to commande'; 18 June c. 1600, 28 May 1576 and 25 May 1607; Folger CT, X.d.428 (5, 109 and 1), IDs 6, 82 and 3.

138 IDs 88, 87, 166 and 85.

84 *Composing and scripting letters*

letters to Mary were generous in their deployment of such terms, and we find Mary addressed as 'Swete harte', 'my owne good daughter', 'good sweete harte' and 'deare sweete harte'; we find grandmotherly concern for 'all our Lettylons'; and we find Bess closing letters with blessings to her daughter, 'so praying god to blesse you', or to all the family, 'god blesse you both and our thre Iuyls with healthe honor and all happynes'.[139] Such expressions of endearment were reciprocal and we can observe that Mary and her husband Gilbert Talbot were aware of Bess's especial fondness for her young grandson George. They closed many of their letters with updates about the boy that indicated an ongoing affectionate relationship with his grandmother. To give one example: in a letter co-signed by Gilbert and Mary, a postscript described George in a way clearly designed to delight the young child's grandmother, his 'Lady Danmode':

> George is very well I thanke god, he drynkethe every day to Lady grandmother, rydethe to her often, but yet within the courte, and if he have any spyse, I tell him, Lady grandmother is comme and will see him, which he then will ether quyckly hyde or quyckly eate, and then askes where Lady Danmode is.[140]

This anecdote was part of an ongoing pattern whereby the couple were careful to include captivating stories to please Bess about 'Your Ladyship's pretty fellow' and 'your Ladyship's tale fellow George' (tale: *tall*).[141]

In Bess's letters to Mary we often find a more relaxed and familiar epistolary style than elsewhere. This epistolary style was characterised by its conversational tone, apparent in the tendency for these letters to be structured around reports of opinions, reactions, points of view and hearsay. So, Bess passed on nuggets of news or updates on opinions she had learned regarding friends or kin at Court, coming through from letters or spoken in person: 'I harde this day from my sonne parponnte', 'nan baynton tels me', 'I harde not from the court since monday', 'some make doubte', 'I never harde worde tyll master abrahale his now coming', 'I haue ben toulde by sondrye that come from London', 'my cosine choworthe toulde me that he harde', 'I haue sente into gloster shire, for some . . . who I am desirus to taulke with'.[142] This epistolary style was further characterised by its often personal subject matter focused around health issues. There was motherly advice with regard health, such as Bess's reminder to her daughter that 'this

---

139 IDs 185, 233 and 187. Dates from 1580 to 1607 and all Scribe A.

140 1 August 1577, Gilbert Talbot and Mary (Cavendish) Talbot write from Sheffield to Bess, hand of Gilbert, also signed by Mary, sent. Gloss: drynkethe: *drinks*, rydethe: *rides*, spyse: *spice (i.e., cheeky behaviour)*, ID 85.

141 ID 218 and ID 82; George is mentioned again in ID 84.

142 IDs 185, 233 and 187.

Composing and scripting letters 85

eayre is better for you both then London; and espetyally for you sweete harte after your ague' and request to her daughter that, following her son Charles Cavendish's illness, she 'write to him to kepe good dyate'.[143] There were updates from Bess about her own health, which included not only routine assurance of her general wellbeing, such as, 'I thanke god I am very well', but also more specific updates, such as, 'in cressonmas I was troubled with a coulde'.[144] The information at times ran to a level of detail that indicated intimacy and showed that Bess was confident of a kindly reception from her daughter:

> I haue ben contenewally greately paynd in my heade, necke, shouldars, and armes, and thenke yt much worse in the moyste wether./ this day I thanke god I am somewhat better and ventared to goe into the gardyn wher I was not this v. or vj weekes before.[145]

That Mary's letters to her mother were, indeed, attentive and sympathetic in this respect can be further confirmed by one of her existing replies: 'I am very glad to here that your la: helth is beter and that the payn in your hepe declineth'.[146] Another way in which Bess's emotional connection with Mary was textualised was through her expressions of longing to hear from her daughter regarding matters of health and wellbeing. So we find Bess saying, 'I desyre that I may some tymes heare from you, both how you doe haue your healthes'; 'I thanke you for your sendin[g] to me'; 'I shall be moste hartely glade to see you; you can not goe to any wher you shalbe more welcome'; 'I thanke god that your Lord you and all our Lettylons are well'; 'I shall thenke Longe tyll I see you both'; 'I pray you Let me heare this nighte how you and your good Lorde doth else shall I not slepe quiatly'.[147] These regular and strong expressions of desire to hear of their wellbeing, and expressions of longing to see and hear from her daughter, went well beyond the conventions required by protocol.

The desire for regular contact overlapped with one of the primary functions of early modern correspondence to parents: the supply of news. As one of the barometers of a parent–offspring relationship the quality and frequency of the news-letters exchanged are themselves indicative. Bess regarded the supply of news and updates as part of her children's filial

---

143 IDs 187 and 180.
144 IDs 180 and 187; cressonmas: *Christmas*.
145 1580, Bess (countess of Shrewsbury) writes from Chelsea to her daughter Mary (Cavendish), Lady Talbot, Scribe A, sent. Gloss: contenewally: *continually*, yt: *it*, gardyn: *garden*, v. or vj: *five or six*. ID 185.
146 ID 89 la:: *ladyship*; hepe: *hip*.
147 IDs 187, 180, 180, 185, 180 and 181.

86 *Composing and scripting letters*

duty, and throughout her life she laid emphasis on receipt of such news, which she evidently greatly looked forward to receiving. We must not underestimate the importance Bess placed upon her children (including her stepchildren and children-in-laws) sending news. As Mary's husband, Gilbert Talbot, made clear in the opening of one of his letters to Bess, to send news was her commandment and his required duty: 'To fulfyll your Ladyship's commandement, & in discharge of my duty by wryting rather then for any matter of importaunnce that I can learne, I herewith troble your Ladyship'.[148] Such were the expectations around sending news that Gilbert wrote even when he had very little to say because 'by salence I should neclect my duty', even though he had only written 'ij or iij dayes synce'.[149] While there was a social expectation that children send news to their parents, when we read the news-letters sent from Gilbert Talbot, often co-signed with his wife Mary, we can observe the high quality of these exchanges. The importance of tailored news-letters from a trusted source is evident from these letters, which were written in Gilbert's own hand and often ran to several pages. Much time and effort clearly went into writing lengthy and detailed reports about current national and international events that included political, military and Court news. Extra attention was given to matters of particular interest to Bess or anticipated to please her, such as the progress of particular bills going through parliament; the praise given by the archbishop of Canterbury for her husband Shrewsbury's entertainment of him; the false rumour that Shrewsbury had been taken ill; and the 'hartie commendacions' sent from Frances, Lady Cobham at Court, who 'asketh daly how your Ladyship dothe' and who has been 'saynge openly' that she 'remayneth vnto your Ladyship as she was wonte, as vnto her deereste frend'.[150] Likewise, when Bess's sons William and Charles Cavendish wrote to their mother, their duty was fulfilled in the form of regular news and well wishes. Charles's news-letter of 1587 in particular must have been a great pleasure for Bess to receive: at four pages long it gave detailed accounts of some of her favourite topics that included her granddaughter Arbella's generous reception at Court and current building designs, a topic in which they had a shared interest. Charles included details of Lord Burghley's building works at Theobalds House, which included a roof 'lyke the low gallery at

---

148 28 July 1574, Gilbert Talbot wrote from the Court at Greenwich to his stepmother and mother-in-law Bess (countess of Shrewsbury) in his own hand, sent. ID 80. Gilbert opened another letter to Bess saying, 'I hope your Ladyship will houlde me excused rather in wrytinge altho I know nothynge worthy advertising, then is by salence I should neclect my duty', ID 82.

149 ID 82.

150 20 February 1576, LPL Talbot Papers, MS 3197, pp. 133–36, ID 165; ID 165; 28 June 1574, Folger CT, X.d.428 (107), ID 80; and ID 80.

Composing and scripting letters   87

Chattesworth', a fashionable decorative bird-and-rocked-themed hidden cupboard, lights set into the ceiling like stars, and the exact footage of the gallery (which, incidentally, Bess outdid when she built her own gallery a few years later at Hardwick New Hall).[151] It again reminds us again that, while sending news was a social convention that demonstrated duty, and that it had a political function (e.g., providing updates on Bess's legal cases and suits), it also fulfilled an emotional need and gives us insights into Bess's relationships and the areas of common ground she shared with her children.

The six letters from Bess to Mary are of further especial interest because they tell us something about what was distinctive within letters written between women. While most of Bess's existing letters are between herself and male correspondents, about 20 per cent (46 of her 242 existing letters) are to or from other women. We have letters between Bess and twenty-one different female correspondents, who included her daughters, stepdaughters and daughters-in-law as well as her mother, half-sister, kin, contacts at Court, Queen Elizabeth and the Scottish Queen. Some of these letters were written in the hands of hired secretaries, in the language of curial prose or political friendship, and on issues of estate business, legal matters or politics, and in these respects resembled closely letters to and between men. For example, a letter from Mary Percy, countess of Northumberland, concerned a dispute over cattle; Bess's letter to Elizabeth, Lady Kitson, asked for legal documents; and a letter from Bess's daughter Frances Pierrepont (in her own hand) sent political news.[152] But we also find letters written to Bess by other women that offered a female perspective, which included letters that concerned health around pregnancy and childbirth.[153] We also gain glimpses of her network of female friends at Court, who were vital barometers of Court politics, factions, fashion and favour.[154] When Bess was in

---

151 1587, Chatsworth House, Devonshire MSS, H/143/16 (HL/2), ID 209. Burghley was building Theobalds House 1564–85, and Charles here reports in 1587 that the gallery was 'very fayre . . . I take it to be a hundred and xxvj foot longe, xxj foot brood; a xvj foot hy' (38.4 × 6.4 × 4.8 meters), which can be compared to the larger size of the Long Gallery at Hardwick New Hall, recorded by Mark Girouard, *Hardwick Hall*, p. 16, to be 51 × 6.7–12 × 8 meters.

152 Folger CT, X.d.428 (62), 27 May 1555? ID 51; 8 April 1594, ID 236; and ID 53.

153 8 and 29 May 1575, Folger CT, X.d.428 (121 and 122), ID 92 and ID 93. Bess's stepdaughter-in-law Anne Talbot (née Herbert) wrote on 8 May 1575 to apologise for not writing by the last messenger with news of the health of her pregnant sister-in-law, Bess's stepdaughter, Katherine Herbert (née Talbot), countess of Pembroke. In her next letter, three weeks later, on 29 May, she explained that she 'would haue wrytene oftener, yf I could haue learned, any newes worthy the wryrtynge' and to assure Bess that she would have sent word immediately if she had news of her sister Pembroke's 'good delyuery'.

154 These women included Elizabeth Wingfield (née Leche), Lady Dorothy Stafford (1526–1604) and Frances Brooke (née Newton), Lady Cobham (b. after 1530, d. 1592). For

88   *Composing and scripting letters*

her darkest days during her marital dispute, through letters she activated this network of female friends at Court, and we gain occasional glimpses of how they played a role in ensuring that Bess's predicament was favourably presented to the queen. So, Elizabeth Wingfield wrote to Bess to inform her that 'Lady cheke had Longe talke with her magisty latly of my Lord's harde dealing and the quene gaue many good words what she woulde do for yow honor'.[155] While these letters between Bess and her female friends tend to exist in isolation, from their style, as well as contextual information, it is apparent that they are snapshots of what were much larger, ongoing correspondence sequences and portray relationships based on loyal friendship and established ties of affection. We have seen, throughout this chapter, that Bess's letters textualised anger, humour, playfulness, deference, grandeur, grief and fear, but in these letters we also see the more familiar styles that textualised everyday companionship and affection. As such, they are a part of the complex and varied landscape of relationships revealed to us by Bess's letters.

---

example, Elizabeth Wingfield described how she 'longe confarde' with Bess's old friend Frances, Lady Cobham, over the most appropriate gift for Bess to give to the queen and their efforts to find some 'fine reare thinge' to present; 8 December [c. 1585], Folger CT, X.d.428 (131), ID 98.

155 ID 98.

2 Reading and writing letters

2.1 'A little deske to write on guilded': situating epistolary production within textual cultures at Hardwick Hall, c. 1601

> In my Ladies Bed Chamber . . . my Ladies bookes viz: Calvin uppon Jobe, covered with russet velvet, the resolution, Salomans proverbes, a booke of meditations, too other bookes covered with black velvet, a looking glass, an hower glass, too brushes, a payre of pullies lyned with black taffetie, a great iron chest paynted, three great trunckes, too little trunces, three deskes covered with lether whereof one a great one, a lyttle deske to write on guilded, a little cofer guilt, a little cofer covered with lether, a little cofer covered with black velvet, three flatt cofers covered with lether, a boxe paynted and guilded with my Lordes and my Ladies armes on it, a yellowe cotton to cover it, an other boxe covered with grene velvet, too trussing cofers bounde with iron, fyve wood boxes.[1]

The 1601 inventory of Hardwick New Hall here vividly depicts Bess's bed-chamber as a locus for reading and writing activities during the final years of her life. The presence of the books and desks confirms that the bedchamber was a space where reading and writing took place, which is further indicated by the various gilded, painted, leather- and velvet-covered coffers and boxes, listed next to the desks, suitable for storage of documents.[2] In terms of the mode and nature of these literate activities, the furniture and architecture here in January 1601 give a mixed picture. On the one hand, their location in her bedchamber itself implies a desire to create opportunities for greater privacy, away from the more overtly public apartments on the ground and second floors. The sense of the bedchamber as a personal space is suggested by her six books, customised possessions with their russet and black velvet bindings, which include those on meditative themes. That these books appear next to her mirror, brushes and 'payre of pullies' (knee armour) lined

---

1 1601 inventory for 'the newe building at Hardwick'; Levey and Thornton, *Of Houshold Stuff*, pp. 53–55 (the document is the copy held in the archives at Chatsworth House).
2 Levey and Thornton, *Of Houshold Stuff*, p. 13.

90 Reading and writing letters

with black taffeta further suggests an aspect of Bess's literate practice which was contemplative, perhaps with the 'pullies' designed to support time in prayer that was hard on the knees.[3] That is, it suggests that aspects of Bess's literate practice included the kind of silently conducted inward activities and mental processes associated with the books of meditation.

On the other hand, it is impossible to conceive of Bess's bedchamber as in any sense primarily a space for inward contemplation or where, if ever, time was spent alone without company. Her bedchamber was far from a modern bedroom and the furniture and furnishings indicate it functioned much more in the way of an office-cum-sitting-room, which must have had the ambience of a plush, upscale corridor or dormitory. Parallels with a royal bedchamber do not seem out of place and would align it with Bess's pretentions. Its numerous pieces of portable furniture and moveable and stackable storage receptacles mean the bedchamber was undistinguished from the multiple adjoining and surrounding chambers, outer chambers, passageways, half-landings, doorways and closets inhabited by Arbella, Bess and their gentlewomen. Together this group of connecting rooms formed a fluid, adaptable space with folding tables, moveable stools, trunks and boxes, portable wicker screens, beds on landings that could be converted into chests, and pallets in doorways that could be used as beds. To give a sense of the flexibility and the communality of the atmosphere of this section of Hardwick New Hall: the full inventory entry records that this part of the building housed at least eleven beds, fifty-seven trunks, boxes, coffers, chests or standards, six chairs, nineteen stools, five screens and six tables.[4]

Bess's bedchamber itself was replete with furniture that included not one but four desks, as well as two more 'wood deskes' stored in the adjoining 'Maydes Chamber': a total of six desks in or connected to Bess's bedchamber. The only other desk listed at Hardwick New Hall was a rather decorative-sounding object in the best bedchamber, above on the second floor, described as 'a little deske of mother of pearle'. By contrast were the more functional desks in Bess's bedchamber, three leather-covered, one of which was large, and a fourth which was small and gilded being 'to write on' and no doubt would have been portable, like the two stored in the Mayde's Chamber.[5] The assemblage of these desks together suggests

---

3 We know that Bess had problems with her knees and hip in later life; for example, Sir John Harpur to Gilbert, seventh earl of Shrewsbury, 31 July 1606, where he reports that Bess (dowager countess of Shrewsbury) walks with a stick but is well for her age and impatient regarding the earl's suit against her; LPL, Talbot Papers, Vol. M, fol. 349.

4 Levey and Thornton, *Of Houshold Stuff*, pp. 53–55 and pp. 66–67. For broad-ranging accounts of the history of notions of privacy see Chartier, *A History or Private Life*, and Braudel, *Civilization and Capitalism*, especially the discussion (from p. 308) which considers the layout of houses.

5 The contents of the Maydes Chamber and the best bedchamber and the location of these are from Levey and Thornton, *Of Houshold Stuff*, p. 54, p. 46 and pp. 66–67. The conclusion that the desks must have been portable desks is proposed by Thornton, p. 13.

this space to have been the hub for her writing activities in 1601, which included her correspondence. Most importantly, it is a reminder that when Bess produced or received a letter, it was often not a solitary process but an activity that involved others.

There would certainly have been advantages for Bess of using the bedchamber as the focal point for her literate activities. She may have used the adjoining closet or withdrawing chamber in combination with the bedchamber by moving the portable desks, stools and screens, although the use of the closet as storage space and the more formal set-up of the withdrawing chamber suggested she chose not to and that her bedchamber was her command centre. Propriety around male secretaries has been suggested as one of the reasons women did not withdraw into closets with the regularity of their male peers.[6] However, for the seventy-nine-year-old countess, living out the Derbyshire winter, it was more likely that comfort and practicality were reasons to prefer the bedchamber to the closet as a locus for letter-writing. Bess's need for warmth and physical support is indicated by not only the knee armour but also the heavy precautions against drafts and cold. The full inventory for the bedchamber lists instruments for attending to the fire along with numerous quilts, fustian blankets, Spanish blankets, fledges, coverlets, curtains, rugs and hangings with which she cocooned herself against the cold. Her comfort was further ensured by her fine russet satin chair, with silver stripes and fringes, complete with a matching scarlet woollen footstool and an embroidered cover. Surrounded by these luxury items, her bedchamber was organised so as to facilitate the reception and accommodation of scribes, servants, bearers and family members (they could come to her). Arranged around her russet satin chair were four stools – listed in the inventory as 'a highe Joyned stoole, too other Joyned stooles, an inlayde stoole' – for her grandchildren. The payments for these, and for the 'too Chares for Children' in the withdrawing chamber off Bess's bedchamber, appear in the accounts for a year or so earlier:

	[s]	[d]
payde to bramley for tow lettell cheares for James	ij	
payde to bramley for a hye joyned stoulle		xij
. . .		
To the Joyner for a little cheare for James		
xijd & a little stole for him xijd	ij	
To the Joyner for a hye stole for my La. chamber		xij.[7]

---

6 Daybell, *Women Letter-Writers*, p. 59. The closet as a site for closer relationships between masters and secretaries is discussed by Stewart, *Close Readers*.

7 Account Book, 1599/1600, Hardwick MS 8, fol. 81v; transcribed from Durant Papers MS 663/2/1/16/2.

92   *Reading and writing letters*

The chairs were for her second son William Cavendish's younger children, 'little' James, daughter Frances and eleven-year-old William (his oldest son, Gilbert, was a teenager by this point). It was perhaps while sitting on these chairs and stools and resting on the portable desks that in early November 1600, little James, Frances and William were supervised by their grandmother Bess as they added subscriptions to one of her letters to their father. In his letter of reply, on 12 November 1600, he acknowledged and thanked her for her careful tutoring: 'I humbly thank your Ladyship for the handes of the three litle honest folkes subscribed in your Ladyships letter, I know by Iames writing; where he lerned his skill'.[8]

The necessity for six desks can be further explained by the presence of another of Bess's grandchildren: Arbella Stuart, who, aged twenty-six in 1601, inhabited this section of Hardwick New Hall with her grandmother. Both women were frequent letter-writers – Arbella, says Bess, 'never restes wryting and sending' letters[9] – and both used scribes and bearers in various capacities. While Arbella had her own chamber nearby, her bedstead, where she slept, with its canopy of 'blewe and white with guilt knobs', was next to that of her grandmother. Such close proximity was an arrangement that, at least for Bess, had certain advantages, given that she was under direct orders from the queen to monitor Arbella's whereabouts and contact with other people.[10] In addition to Arbella and visits from younger grandchildren, such as little James, we know that Bess was accompanied in her bedchamber by her women, who included her long-standing attendants Mistresses Elizabeth Digby and Mary Cartwright. Their almost ubiquitous presence at the end of Bess's life can be glimpsed in a document regarding amendments to her will made on 1 February 1608, which recorded their joint 'remembraunce of sondry speeches used and spoken' by Bess over the previous ten days.[11] Their recollections depicted Bess's favoured son William regularly attending on his mother in her bedchamber during this period and included moments when she was well enough to rise from her bed and speak to him from her russet and silver chair. They recall conversations overheard between Bess and William at various moments, such as the words spoken to him 'in the hearing of mistress Digby whoe was holding my La: stomack' and the series of additions to her will spoken with 'mistress Digby being present'. Their remembrances give us a sense of the relative concept of privacy at this period and it is clear that Bess was rarely entirely alone. Only the most

---

8 12 November 1600, Folger CT, X.d.428 (22), ID 20.

9 10 March 1603, Bess (dowager countess of Shrewsbury) writes from Hardwick to Sir Henry Broncker, CP 135/167, fols 218–9, ID 135.

10 For Bess's struggles over the security of Arbella see ID 130, and for Bess's report that Arbella tells 'any bad bodie' she can find 'that she is kept as a prisoner' and the rumour that one of Arbella's supporters 'had a pillion to carry a woman behind him & covered it with a cloke' see ID 135.

11 Chatsworth House, Hardwick MS Drawer 143.

Reading and writing letters **93**

intimate conversations were one-on-one and these were remarked upon as being exceptional, such as the moment Bess sent her women away for half an hour while she warned William to 'look about him' and briefed him of her fears for him in the future:

> At an other tyme, my Lord Cavendishe attending on her in her weaknes in this moneth of January lat; she tolde him that she laye waking much of the night thinking of matters that might concern him much and which perhaps he never thought of, and that it stode him vppon to looke about him, and withall willed vs all to depart, and then had now half an howers talk with him, whereby wee sawe her contynuall care and love towardes him.[12]

William's future kept Bess lying awake at night during her final days, and these exchanges offer us a detailed depiction of her circles of intimates. At the centre was William, her closest confidant, but Digby and Cartwright were privy to all but their most highly confidential exchanges. On a par with them was one other person: Timothy Pusey, Bess's secretary, who copied the remembrances in this document. It may have been that Timothy Pusey was away during this period in early February, which resulted in the need for him to make these notes from the women's memories and spoken testimonials after the event. He certainly had access to all the details of Bess's business dealings and many of her most high-security and sensitive letters from this period. Unlike Bess's receiver, William Reason (who was paid the same), he had no room of his own at Hardwick. Durant suggests he most likely slept within calling distance, uncomfortably lodged on a pallet out on a nearby landing.[13]

Bess's bedchamber at Hardwick New Hall, then, was not private in the modern sense, but it did involve certain levels of privileged access. It was a flexible, adaptable space that Bess could manage in her final years for her own comfort and convenience and for different activities and levels of intimacy. Furthermore, it was a space which was often communal, but where Bess had control over levels of individual access to herself and to Arbella.[14] We will return again to Bess's bedchamber later in this chapter and the next, in order to consider in further detail the roles of William Cavendish, Arbella

---

12 'A remembraunce of sondry speeches vsed and spoken by the Right honorable the Countess of Shrouesbury dowager in the hearing of Mistress Elizabeth Digby and Mistress Mary Cartwright, subscribed by them the first daye of february 1607[/8]', hand of Timothy Pusey, Hardwick MS Drawer 143 (17).

13 Durant, *Bess of Hardwick*, p. 200. Timothy did have a room at Chatsworth, described ahead, p. 133.

14 The spaces for writing and control over space are discussed further by Roberts, 'Shakespeare "Creeps into the Womans Closets about Bedtime"', and Stanbury, 'Women's Letters and Private Space in Chaucer'.

94 *Reading and writing letters*

Stuart, Timothy Pusey, Bess's ladies-in-waiting and children like little James when it came to Bess's letter-writing and reading. Most important, here, are the impressions gained from the architecture and furniture – the sense of mixed circumstances, and of different people entering and exiting the spaces within which reading and writing took place – which are compatible with the broader picture that emerges from the letters Bess sent from different locations and at different stages across her life. It is a picture of letter-writing that involved a spectrum of different modes of composition and levels of privacy or security; and it included a range of collaborative and semi-collaborative scenarios involving scribes and secretaries. We need to imagine, in 1601, Hardwick New Hall to have been the locus where Bess's secretariat, or favoured son William, or her grandchildren or attendants, could collaborate with her on the twin activities of reading and writing documents and letters in a combination of different collaborative scenarios; and we need to imagine this situation as contiguous with practices throughout her life and with the broader culture of early modern letter-writing.

The existence of detailed inventories for Chatsworth and Hardwick Old and New Halls in 1601, combined with contemporary letters, accounts and other documents, offers us an extraordinary opportunity for historical reconstruction. As has been shown, this combination allows us to imagine, in some detail, individuals, at a specific historical moment, inhabiting a building that we can still walk around today in something close to its original state. We have seen that letter-writing was communal, rarely if ever an activity that took place entirely alone. The inventory allows us further insights into aspects of literate culture within the household and the nature of Bess's own literacy. It is important to emphasise that Bess's literacy extended well beyond sending and receiving letters. Her letter-writing was just one part of an interrelated set of literate skills that were contiguous with one another. It is worth outlining these skills and activities in order to show both the extent and the limits of Bess's own literacy, and the interconnectedness between her letter-writing and other literate activities. To this end the 1601 inventory provides further information and a stimulus for reconstructing the range of Bess's literate activities and her bedchamber and its associated rooms as a locus for activities.

Numeracy, inventories and accounts

The 1601 inventory lists 57 boxes, trunks and coffers in and around Bess's bedchamber. While their contents were not recorded by the inventory clerks, we can cross-refer to information from Bess's Account Books, letters and other documents, including other of Bess's inventories, in order to offer some informed speculation, and in some cases hard evidence, as to what they contained. Many of the receptacles were iron-bound vaults of various sizes, such as the 'great painted iron chest' and the 'too trussing cofers bounde with iron' mentioned in the inventory and designed with security in

Reading and writing letters 95

mind. Further references from the Account Books to iron-clad chests and to locks and keys for boxes can be added here; for example, there were earlier payments for 'an Iron bounde chest ix^{li}', an 'Iron cheste' and 'a Locke and key for a box for my La twelve pence – xij^d'.[15] The final two of these entries follow a list of 'plate bought of Sr Wm Hatton' and 'of Wm hunt the gould smith', which were among Bess's most valuable possessions stored in the boxes. Linen and textile furnishings have been suggested as items likely to be among the contents of the trunks and boxes as a form of stored wealth.[16] Lockable iron-clad trunks would have been safe enough for Bess's most costly fabrics and texts, which we know included velvet decorated with precious metal threads or studded with pearls.[17] Other valuables we know that Bess owned, and that would have posed a security risk, included jewellery and, of course, money. In fact, the Account Books specifically mention that Bess accessed money from trunks at Hardwick New Hall in 1599:

	[l]	[s]	[d]
This was taken out of a trunk at the newe building of this	xxi	iijj	iij
xx layed out	xvij	xii	iij.[18]

To this payment can be added an earlier reference from 1583, which mentions that money was stored along with jewellery by Bess in her coffer at Chatsworth: 'delyvered to my sone wyllame of ^out^ of my juwell coffer at chattysworthe the ~~xxx~~ xxjth of september thre – honderyth ~~threscore~~ forescore ponde'.[19] There would have been no need for the clerks of the household inventory to list the contents of Bess's jewellery coffers: it had already been recorded in a series of other, shorter, inventories, some of which still survive from among the remnants of Bess's Papers. The extant bundled assortment of differently sized pieces of paper, dating from various periods, includes several short inventories of jewels and plate, in places written or annotated in Bess's own hand or the hands of her personal assistants.[20] These point to various boxes containing treasures, such as the 'fane with a handyll of gould in a woode

---

15 Purchased during Bess's trip to London; Chatsworth House, Hardwick MS 7, 27 November 1591, 21 December 1591 and 20 January 1592, fols 7, 11v and 15v. There is also a reference to a gilt cup taken out of 'the plate trunke', Hardwick MS 8, fol. 145r.

16 Levey and Thornton, *Of Houshold Stuff*, p. 13, citing Hall, p. 65.

17 It is worth recalling the very expensive cost of such fabrics, as seen in the records for Bess's shopping trip to London in 1591. Payments for velvet, satin and taffeta rival those for plate and jewels, such as the £33 'Payd the xxijth of the same for xxx^{tie} yards of velvet at xxijs the yard Thirtie three pounds – xxxiijl'; Chatsworth House, Hardwick MS 7, 21 December 1591, fol. 11v.

18 Hardwick MS 8, 1599, fol. 52.

19 Hardwick MS 5, 1583, fol. 32.

20 'List of Jewells Plate &c belonging [to] Elizabeth Countess of Shrewsbury 1567 to 1599', Sheffield Archives MS MD 6311, previously owned by Thomas Phillipps; and in the Devonshire MSS at Chatsworth. The hands of both Timothy Pusey and Scribe A appear, whose roles as scribes are discussed in section 2.3.

96 *Reading and writing letters*

boxe wherin is many other tryffels'.[21] Included is Bess's main jewellery coffer ('my Juyll coffar'), the contents of which was listed on 27 July 1593 in the hand of Scribe A and signed off by Bess. The coffer stored her iconic 'fore ropes of greate perle', as well as various gold chains, a ruby ring, black-and-white enamelled gold buttons to be given to Grace Manners and 'a bone lace with thurtye perles for a cornyte geuen to my juyll arbella'.[22] Bess's specific references to 'my juwell coffer', then, in the Account Books and here in the inventory, suggest an organised system and one to which only Bess and her closest assistants had access. Furthermore, the reference to Bess herself taking money from her coffers adds to the impression of her control over cash flow and her hands-on approach to the day-to-day finances. The storage of money and jewels in the boxes and coffers, along with the presence of the brass and lead weights and balance in the bedchamber, reminds us that Bess's letter-writing activities overlapped with her other activities involved in running her businesses. That is, it reminds us that Bess's literacy extended to include skills with numbers and account keeping. The Account Books dating from the 1550s to the 1590s with entries in Bess's own hand show both her training and her role in the daily financial transactions of household and estate, which were contiguous with letters that contained her instructions for payments and purchases. As such, we can see the direct links between letters and documents such as Account Books.

The complexity of Bess's accounting activities in later life is presented to us in all its spectacular detail in the Account Books for the 1590s, which extend well beyond household items, impressive as these are in Bess's case. To use the words of Durant: Bess was running a business empire; her receivers and solicitors, men such as William Reason and Edward Whalley, were key figures 'on what can be called her board of management'. Her son and heir William Cavendish undertook a great deal of work under his mother's direction, and one man with enormous responsibility was her chief secretary, Timothy Pusey, a man with legal training who 'might be termed a managing director under the chairmanship of Bess'.[23] The layers of transactions that appear in these records illustrate the skills in literacy involved, as well as the scale of the finances.[24] By 1600 Bess's gross annual receipts were estimated to be around £10,000 (or double this if income from lands made over

---

21 Sheffield Archives, MS MD 6311/5, hand of Scribe A; fane: *fan*.

22 bone lace: *bone-lace*; cornyte: *cornet*, i.e., the veil that covered a woman's hair. The four-strand rope of pearls was worn by Bess for her portrait (Plate 2), and these may also be the same pearls worn for their portraits by her daughter Mary (Cavendish) Talbot and granddaughter Arbella Stuart; images of all three portraits are in Steen, 'The Cavendish-Talbot Women', pp. 150–52.

23 Durant, *Bess of Hardwick*, pp. 166–69 and p. 181.

24 Here summarising the figures calculated by Durant, *Bess of Hardwick*, pp. 181–84.

Reading and writing letters 97

to William, Charles and Arbella is included), a staggering sum that made her the richest non-royal woman in the country. Income came from payments relating to the management of the estate, which included the sales of wool and livestock as well as payments for wages and fines, and money loaned and repaid. There were the rents received from various properties, estates and lands. In 1596 there were fourteen rent collectors or bailiffs working for Bess who brought in a total of £7,685, and seventeen bailiffs in total were operating for her in the 1590s. As well as these were receipts for rents on coal pits and for the sale of coal, charcoal, glass and iron: Bess received revenue from coal mines at Bolsover and Hansworth, both Talbot lands where she paid colliers wages, and at Bolsover she had another shaft sunk in 1595. Her own coal mines and lead mines were farmed out and exploited by others, who included her son William, but she had ironworks and glass works, smelting industries which involved blast furnaces and hammers at Wingfield, run by her iron master Sylvester Smyth, and she prospected for alum in 1593. All of these payments (for rents, iron, coal, charcoal and glass) were gathered by Bess's receiver William Reason, who kept detailed records in his own hand; these totals were checked and authorised by Bess herself and the money taken in and the amounts summarised by Timothy Pusey. In addition to these there are accounts for the ongoing extensive building work at Hardwick, mainly kept and recorded in the hand of Sir Henry Jenkinson. There were payments for legal experts, in part channelled through Bess's London solicitor Edward Whalley, who was key to seeing through to successful conclusion various court cases. We also find larger one-off payments, such as, in the late 1590s, the record made by Bess in her own hand of £640 given to Arbella to buy Skegby, and payments for luxury goods, such as jewellery and clothing during her trip to London in 1591. Bess's hand appears on almost every one of the many hundreds of pages of these financial records. We can track her presence through her entries, annotations and signatures, which attest to her impressive mastery of this aspect of documentary culture.

Tools and materials for writing, sealing, storage and filing

Hardwick New Hall had a muniments room purpose-built to house the majority of the paperwork: cool and dry, with a vaulted ceiling, this was the place Bess had built to store legal documents, receipts, deeds of ownership for her lands, mines, quarries and properties. However, for items in current use, a system of inboxes was perhaps among the functions for which the many coffers listed next to the desks in the 1601 inventory were employed. Three of these were described as being flat and leather-covered, so certainly sounded suitable for holding papers. The other five were all covered in different ways: there was a box covered in green velvet; three little coffers variously gilded, covered in black velvet and covered in leather; and a box painted and gilded with heraldic arms which had a yellow cotton cloth cover.

98   *Reading and writing letters*

The descriptions suggest these were luxury objects in themselves, and their distinctive coverings would have made them suitable as sorting containers where objects, valuables or paperwork would be readily accessible and locatable (and, again, comparison with royalty does not seem out of place here). Bess's letters from this period do not contain any endorsements, though it is not clear why not (it certainly was not due to any lack of the funds needed to employ a secretary for this task). Perhaps the use of the boxes, combined with the muniments room, provided an information storage system that meant further annotations on the letters themselves were not necessary.[25]

No standish, which would have contained an ink pot and other writing materials, was mentioned in the 1601 inventory, although we know that Bess was regularly signing letters, adding subscriptions and postscripts and signing and annotating documents right up until her death. The accoutrements of writing are likely to have been contained inside one of the desks and we know she purchased these throughout her life.[26] Almost exactly fifty years earlier, in December 1551, the Account Book of Bess and Sir William Cavendish recorded purchase of 'a penknyve . . . balance & weaghts . . . paper . . . waxe . . . & an ynkhorne', all of which 'was to furnish my ladys wryting deske' and which were followed by subsequent references to purchases of 'ij penhornes & ij ynkhornes for my master & my lady', 'reddewaxe', quires of 'whyt paper' and 'browne paper' and 'ij dossen swanne qwells'.[27] By 1591 we know that Bess was distinguishing between paper quality in her purchases, which included buying high-quality imported paper. So, as the newly financially independent dowager countess of Shrewsbury, when she embarked on a major shopping trip to London for several months (in 1591–92), she took the opportunity to stock up on letter-writing supplies that included red wax and fine, expensive imported paper from Frankfurt and Venice:

> Paid more the same for two Reame of pott pap ~~six~~ xij[s] shillinges –   vj[s] xij[s]
> for six quire of franckfordd pap[er] at ten pence the quire –   v[s]
> for six quire of Venice paper Three shillings Eyght pence –   iij[s] viij[d]
> for ij [Pound] of hard waxe Twelve pence –   xij[d]
> for one Pound of Soft waxe xijd⁻   xij[d].[28]

25 For other examples of women using caskets and trunks for the storage of their letters see Daybell, *Women Letter-Writers*, p. 56.

26 Also suggested by Thornton, *Of Houshold Stuff*, p. 14. An illustrated guide to early modern tools for writing is Stewart and Wolfe, *Letterwriting*, pp. 13–20.

27 Hardwick MS 1, 1552–53, fol. 8 (December 1551). The Account Book evidence indicates the validity of the suggestion by Thornton, *Of Houshold Stuff*, p. 13, that a standish and similar items must have been contained in one of the desks. The other references are from: Chatsworth House, Hardwick MS 1, 1552–53; the inkhorns are on fol. 39r, the red wax is on fol. 40r, the swan quills are on fol. 48r and payments for quires of paper appear throughout.

28 Hardwick MS 7, 29 July 1592, fol. 31, and fol. 30, 24 July 1592.

Reading and writing letters   99

That the trip was also an opportunity for letter-writing is suggested by the regular purchases of paper made: 'Paid for ij quire of pap[er] ^for my Ladie^ Eyght pence – xvj', 'paid for a quire of paper – iiij^d' and 'paid for a quire of paper foure pence – iiij^d'.[29]

We also know that during her stay in London, in addition to these various kinds of paper and wax, Bess invested in two new seal rings: 'for ij Seale Rings for my Ladiee foure pounds Ten shillings iiij^l x^s'.[30] A seal could authenticate and authorise a letter, it could identify the sender and, potentially, it could encode symbolic meanings through the use of coloured wax or by a personalised image embossed into its surface. It was the seal ring, or seal matrix, that was used to emboss the wax. The many forms seals could take and the functions they performed were both practical and iconographic. Across Bess's correspondence we find many letters where traces of wax and a seal tear indicate that a seal was once present but has been lost. The seals that are intact all appear on letters from Bess dating from between 1583 and 1603 and all feature Bess's own Hardwick shield.[31] For example, when Bess (dowager countess of Shrewsbury) wrote to Elizabeth I on 9 January 1603 and then to Lord Burghley one month later, on 6 February, she locked these letters with wax seals stamped with her own Hardwick Cross, a heraldic symbol that also appeared throughout the visual schemes in place at Hardwick and Chatsworth at this time and featured a saltire engrailed, in chief three eglantines, surmounted by a countess's coronet (Plate 7).[32] While we have no letters with intact seals from earlier stages of Bess's life, a couple of copies exist, made by Canon Jackson when he examined Bess's original letters some time in the nineteenth century at Longleat House. Jackson's copy of Bess's letter to Sir John Thynne, sent to Longleat on 25 February 1558, features his drawing that shows Bess's original seal was stamped with the Hardwick Cross, which he labelled 'Seal of Hardwick'.[33] It did not, at this stage, feature the countess's coronet, which was added later, some time after she rose to the status of countess in in 1567. Bess's use of the Hardwick Cross to seal her letters, then, spanned at least half a century: from the time she was married to her second husband, Sir William Cavendish, right up until the final years of her life as dowager countess of Shrewsbury.

But we know that in the 1550s the Hardwick Cross was not the only symbol she used to stamp her letters. Jackson's drawing of the seal on another of Bess's letters to Sir John Thynne, this one from 15 March [c. 1550s],

29 Hardwick MS 7, fol. 18v, 13 March 1592; fol. 26, 5 June 1592; fol. 27, 28 June 1592.
30 Hardwick MS 7, 29 July 1592, fol. 31.
31 These letters Bess sent that have existing seals intact are: from 1583?, ID 116; from 11 April 1591, TNA SP 12/238, ff 173r-174v (item 116), ID 159; from 2 April 1597, ID 239; from 9 January 1603, DP 135/112, fols 146r-v, ID 128; from 29 January 1603, ID 129; from 6 February 1603, CP 91/105, fols 190–1, ID 131; and from 10 March 1603, ID 135.
32 IDs 128 and 131.
33 ID 112.

100   *Reading and writing letters*

includes a drawing of Bess's original seal stamped with the arms of her husband Sir William Cavendish, which features three bucks heads. It is an insignia that later came to be regularly used by her sons and that appeared throughout the heraldic schemes at Chatsworth and Hardwick Hall. Bess's three sons used various different insignia associated with the Cavendish family when sealing their letters: the Cavendish arms featuring three bucks heads, the Cavendish serpent knotted on a cushion and the Cavendish stag, all of which Bess used elsewhere in the visual schemes she developed at her properties (Plate 6).[34] We do not have any other existing examples of other symbols she used on her seals; for example, we have no evidence that she ever used her fourth husband Shrewsbury's motto, the Talbot dog. We know that the iconographic schemes within her interiors of her households incorporated all of these symbols – that is, her own Hardwick cross, combined in various ways with the shields and crests of her last three husbands, Sir William Cavendish, Sir William St Loe and George Talbot, earl of Shrewsbury.[35] It is possible that these were each also used when she sealed letters; however, without any other existing evidence of actual seals we cannot be sure. What we do have are the examples of the Hardwick Cross and Cavendish arms being used when she was Lady Cavendish, and then the Hardwick Cross incorporating a countess's coronet after she became countess of Shrewsbury. Furthermore, we should be aware of Santina M. Levey's observation that, as dowager countess, Bess chose to revert to the Hardwick arms displayed alone (rather than impaled with the arms of her last husband) but surmounted by her countesses coronet, and with the Cavendish supporters of two stags (rather than the Talbot supporters that she would have been entitled to as the widow of a peer). This chosen heraldic insignia was one that was distinctively her own. Its visual references to her previous marriages are self-referential as they concern her own status and dynasty: her status as countess (represented by the coronet) and her dynastic line (represented by the Cavendish stags as supporters).

The ability to compare the use of seals across families, or across different stages of an individual's life, can potentially reveal information about how individuals, couples or groups forged and consolidated their identities. As more examples become available in the future, it may well be instructive to

---

34 The Cavendish arms featuring three bucks heads (6 November c. 1585?, ID 5), the Cavendish serpent knotted on a cushion (18 June c. 1600?, ID 6) and the Cavendish stag (4 July 1604, Folger CT, X.d.428 (23), ID 21). Bess's servant James Crompe gives us an example of a non-heraldic embossed image: his seal is stamped with a heart and cross ID 17 and ID 18.

35 The heraldry of each is described and illustrated by Levey, *The Embroideries*, pp. 32–35, followed by a catalogue that gives numerous examples of the incorporation of these heraldic insignia, as well as those of her children, into the textiles from Bess's households. The households, as Levey describes, were 'liberally decorated' with these motifs, often impaled with each other or in different combinations, across a variety of materials, such as was typical of wealthy Tudor households, p. 32.

compare Bess's deployment of her seal insignia with other contemporary women. We can observe that Bess retained, throughout her life, in the form of the Hardwick Cross, an insignia that was her own and was independent of any of her husbands. Whether this was conventional and predictable in the era, or whether Bess was innovative in this respect, is a question which will be answered only by further examination of seals used by other early modern women. The information about wax, paper, sealing, seal matrixes, the tools for writing and the storing documents all reminds us of the various material aspects to epistolary literacy. The preparations involved in writing and producing documents could be laborious and, in themselves, an investment in equipment. The evidence from Bess's Account Books reminds us that she had the required resources but also that her use of seals was carefully managed and was continuous with the elaborate iconography she had developed around herself over many years.

Books

We must, then, envisage valuables (that included linen, clothing, money, plate and jewellery) as well as documents and writing materials to have been stored in the various desks, chests, trunks, boxes and coffers in and around Bess's bedchamber. But there is another category of item we should also consider: Levey has suggested the many boxes in and around Bess's bedchamber were packed with her books.[36] In fact, the only books mentioned in the entire 1601 inventory, apart from 'a great olde bible' in the Low Wardrobe at Chatsworth, are the six found here in Bess's bedchamber on her dressing table listed as 'my Ladies bookes'.[37] All six are notable for their religious content, gravity and sobriety, as well as for their russet velvet and black velvet covers. The inclusion of these books seems likely to have been due to their cost, evident from their covers, and we must remember that the inventory was not intended as a complete record of the contents of the house but was made for the purpose of preparing bequests for Bess's will. We may also detect an element of late-life self-fashioning in the books arranged on the dressing table the day the inventory was taken, which set out a weighty programme of Protestant spiritual reading. There was, bound in russet velvet, Calvin's 752-page *Sermon Upon the Book of Job* (translated by Arthur Golding in 1574, reprinted in 1580 and 1584); and bound in black velvet: 'the Resolution', probably *A Brief Resolution of a Right Religion*, by C.S. (1590); a commentary on Solomon's proverbs, of

36 Levey, *The Embroideries*, p. 14.
37 Levey and Thornton, *Of Houshold Stuff*, p. 28. There is also an account book reference in December 1601 for purchase of 'Master Smithes sermons for my La: vjs'; Hardwick MS 10a, *The Sermons of Master Henry Smith* (1591; reprt. 1601), discussed by White, '"That whyche ys nedefoulle"', p. 275.

102   *Reading and writing letters*

which there were several versions in existence; a book of meditations and the two unnamed books. Bess's mind was at this point in her life turned towards spiritual concerns, although these six books should not be taken, literally, to be the sum total of Bess's books, nor should they be taken to represent the scope of her literary and cultural interests. Whereas biographical accounts have tended to cite these books as evidence she was 'not much of a reader', there is a need for caution here and this is certainly to underestimate her reading interests.[38] We know that, at least from the seventeenth century, there was a library at Hardwick Old Hall, although no book-list now exists.[39] We know from Bess's letters that she avidly read news, both news-letters sent to herself and news-letters sent to her husband and other family members who would share their letters. She was disappointed if she did not receive regular lengthy missives that kept her up to date with a range of national and international events and included topics that her correspondents knew she was interested in.[40] But there are also a number of specific reasons why we should further extend our view of Bess's reading to include other kinds of books and textual materials.

First, as has been mentioned, Bess's textile creations referenced numerous contemporary and classical printed sources. Some of these have been tracked down, such as Bess's Diana and Actaeon cushion, based on an engraving by Virgil Solis from Ovid's *Metamorphoses* printed in 1563.[41] However, the printed sources for many more of Bess's remarkable needlework creations have remained elusive, despite the efforts of art historians to infer these from the existing textiles. While Levey has acknowledged that Bess's workmen (men such as John Balechouse, known as John Painter) may well have accrued collections of prints and patterns, she concludes that, out of all the forty-three (by her count) trunks, chests and coffers in Bess's bedchamber, 'some surely contained her books and also woodcuts and engravings in

---

38 For example, Durant has commented that Bess 'never showed a taste for reading'; *Bess of Hardwick*, p. 64; Hubbard, *A Material Girl*, p. 15, has commented that Bess had 'little or no intellectual interests'; Williams, *Bess of Hardwick*, p. 4, concluded that Bess 'was never a great reader and, like many of her contemporaries, seems to have confined her reading to books of a religious character'. The limitations of the 1601 inventory have been assessed, through comparison with Bess's will, by White, '"That whyche ys nedefoulle"', pp. 267–68, who concludes that while the inventory is no doubt of great value as historical evidence, it was created for the specific intention of making bequests 'not for listing the entire contents of Hardwick' and therefore 'some of the house's actual contents may have been excluded from it'.

39 Worsley, *Hardwick Old Hall*, pp. 33–34.

40 Daybell, '"Suche newes"', and discussed in section 1.4.

41 Frye, *Pens and Needles*, pp. 63–67. Other print sources have been suggested by Wells-Cole, *Art and Decoration*, p. 256, mostly from Antwerp but also from France, such as Claude Paradin, *Devises heroïques* (Lyons: I. de Tournes and G. Gazeau, 1557), and Pierre Belon, *La nature et diversité des poissons* (Paris: Ch. Estienne, 1555) and *L'histoiure de la nature des oyseaux* (Paris: G. Cavellat, 1555).

Reading and writing letters   103

books, or as sets and separate sheets'.[42] When we add to Bess's textile art her interests in garden design, architecture, heraldry and interior decor, and her achievements in these fields, it is hard to believe she did not have a stock of reference materials at the very least. To these speculations we can add, given Bess's activities as a letter-writer, that she may have owned copies of epistolary guides, such as those published by Angel Day or William Fulwood. It is evident that Bess was well aware of contemporary recommended epistolary norms and structures, such as those suggested by Day, although, as Peter Mack's study of early modern correspondence has shown, women's knowledge of epistolary conventions was often likely to have derived from contact with the form, through receiving letters, rather than manuals.[43]

Second, we know of other books Bess owned, which were not mentioned in the 1601 inventory. The 1550 Northaw inventory lists a book containing commissioned portraits of herself and her husband Sir William Cavendish bound with gold and precious stones: 'my greate booke of gould sett with stones, with her fathers Picture and my pictures drawne in yt'.[44] In its deluxe form and commemorative function, this gold and jewelled book must have been on a par with the finest items from royal libraries and was consistent with Bess's preference for self-fashioning and expression through visual and material means. We know that this bejewelled book was still in Bess's ownership at the end of her life as it was given in her will to her eldest daughter, Frances. The c. 1550 Northaw inventory also lists a copy of Chaucer, and we know that other contemporary households owned copies of printed *Works* of Chaucer, which attracted female readers. It was perhaps from Chaucer's lively and entertaining stories that Bess read versions, in English, of the classical lives of virtuous women that came so to define her textile art for the next decades and which also, as has been seen, influenced her letter-writing.[45] The copy of Chaucer certainly

42 Levey, *The Embroideries*, p. 26.
43 Discussed by Daybell, *Women's Letter-Writers*, pp. 22–23, and in section 1.1, pp. 1–2, p. 49.
44 The 1550 Northaw inventory is now held within the Devonshire Collection at Chatsworth House. For the same year Bess and Cavendish's Account Book (Folger CT, X.d.486, fol. 37) records the commission of the book that included gold, rubies and a diamond, the cost of which is listed in the accounts for 1550 at £13 6s. The book is mentioned in Bess's will in 1601 (cited).
45 The Northaw inventory lists 'iij englysche boks Chawcer ffroyssarte cronicles & a boke of ffrenche & Englysche', pp. 5–7. That the book is listed as a 'Chawcer' suggests it was a *Works* of Chaucer, that at this date would have been one of William Thynne's *Works of Chaucer* (London: T. Godfray, 1532; W. Bonham, 1542; R. Grafton, 1542; N. Hill, c. 1550). The place of women within Chaucer's early modern readership is discussed by Wiggins, 'Frances Wolfreston's Chaucer'. The embedded reference to Penelope in Bess's letter writing is discussed in section 1.3. We can observe that the five 'Noble Women of the Ancient World' selected for the full-length wall hangings at Hardwick New Hall all appear in Chaucer: Lucrecia (which is also the name given to Bess's daughter who died in infancy) and Cleopatra have their own stories in the *Legend of Good Women*, Artemisia is mentioned in the *Franklin's Tale*, Zenobia in the *Monk's Tale* and Penelope (Plate 8) is regularly cited as an example of virtuosity.

104   *Reading and writing letters*

indicated literary interests. If books reflect something about a person's biography, then these two volumes seem a very appropriate reflection of Bess's life as a whole, although they were not the ones she chose to present on her dressing table, to be recorded in the 1601 inventory, which certainly had a partly representative role.

Third, that Bess engaged with other cultural activities is indicated by the performances she enjoyed, attested by numerous references to payments to musicians and troops of players for dramas and theatricals staged at Hardwick New Hall. For example, in September 1599 Bess was entertained at Hardwick by the Nottingham waits, the Earl of Rutland's musicians and those of the Earl of Essex; and in 1600 by the queen's players who perhaps played Shakespeare in the hall while Bess watched from the gallery. While Bess's piety was Protestant she was certainly was far less strict in her practices than, say, her acquaintance and contemporary Lady Anne Cooke Bacon, something which is reflected in her enjoyment of the arts. Hardwick New Hall must have been a lively place to be around 1600: there are also references to payments to clowns and jesters and Hardwick even had its own bowling alley.[46] The image of the sober black-clad dowager countess that comes down to us in her later portrait (Plate 2) and in the six books on her dressing table is certainly one which was cultivated as appropriate to later life, but one which we should be careful not to take too literally nor generalise to her whole life.

Whatever conclusions we might draw about Bess's own reading habits or book ownership there is no doubt that she set great store by education for the next generation.[47] The presence of Arbella Stuart within the household, one of the most well-read women of her day, itself tells us this was a place of many books, even if they were not recorded anywhere in the 1601 inventory.[48] Sir John Harrington memorably recorded how he was eyewitness to Arbella's impressive displays of learning 'severall tymes at Hardwicke' as well as at Chelsea and Wingfield, where she had him read to her from Ariosto's *Orlando Furioso*, and aged twelve she 'read French out of Italian, and English out of both, much better then I could'.[49] The accounts kept by

---

46 Durant, *Bess of Hardwick*, p. 185. Durant also gives an account of Bess's attendance at Court for the Christmas period 1591 where 'the Court jester, was given 20s (£1) for amusing her at New Year, and there would have been music, dances, banquets and masques; possibly a play by William Shakespeare', which he contrasts with her old acquaintance Lady Anne Bacon, a firm Protestant with a 'Horror of Plays and Masques', p. 168.

47 The financial investments Bess made in the education of her own children and grandchildren, as well as those of members of her household, including her workmen in some cases, are recorded by Levey, *The Embroideries*, p. 14. The discussion in section 1.2 shows Bess petitioning for funds to support her young daughter Arbella Stuart's education.

48 There is a subsequent reference, in a letter of March 1603, to Arbella sending her page for 'somm books into my quondam study chamber'; Steen, *The Letters*, p. 156.

49 Harrington, *A Tract*, p. 45.

Plate 1 Bess of Hardwick (Lady Cavendish), by an unknown artist, c. 1555–57, oil on panel, at Hardwick Hall, Derbyshire. The painting was later incorrectly inscribed 'Mary Tudor'. © National Trust Images/Angelo Hornak.

Plate 2 Bess of Hardwick (dowager countess of Shrewsbury), c. 1590, oil on canvas, unknown artist. © National Portrait Gallery, London.

Plate 3 Hardwick New Hall, Derbyshire, seen from the East Court part of the garden. © National Trust Images/Andrew Butler.

Plate 4 Hardwick New Hall, rooftop pavilions, 1590–97, which feature the 'ES' initials of Elizabeth, countess of Shrewsbury, surmounted by a countess's coronet. Author's own image.

Plate 5 Embroidered red velvet panel bearing the 'ES' monogram of Elizabeth, countess of Shrewsbury. © National Trust Images/John Hammond.

Plate 6 Velvet panel with padded applique of cloth of gold and silver showing the Hardwick crest, which features the Cavendish stag and 'ES' monogram. © National Trust Images/John Hammond.

Plate 7 Detail from Bess of Hardwick's tomb designed by Robert Smythson in 1603, All Saints Parish church, Derby, now Derby Cathedral, featuring the Hardwick Cross: an heraldic symbol with a saltire engrailed, in chief three eglantines, surmounted by a countess's coronet. Author's own image.

Plate 8 Detail of Penelope in the wall hanging of Penelope flanked by Perseverance and Paciens in the Museum Rooms at Hardwick Hall, Derbyshire. © National Trust Images/Andreas von Einsiedel.

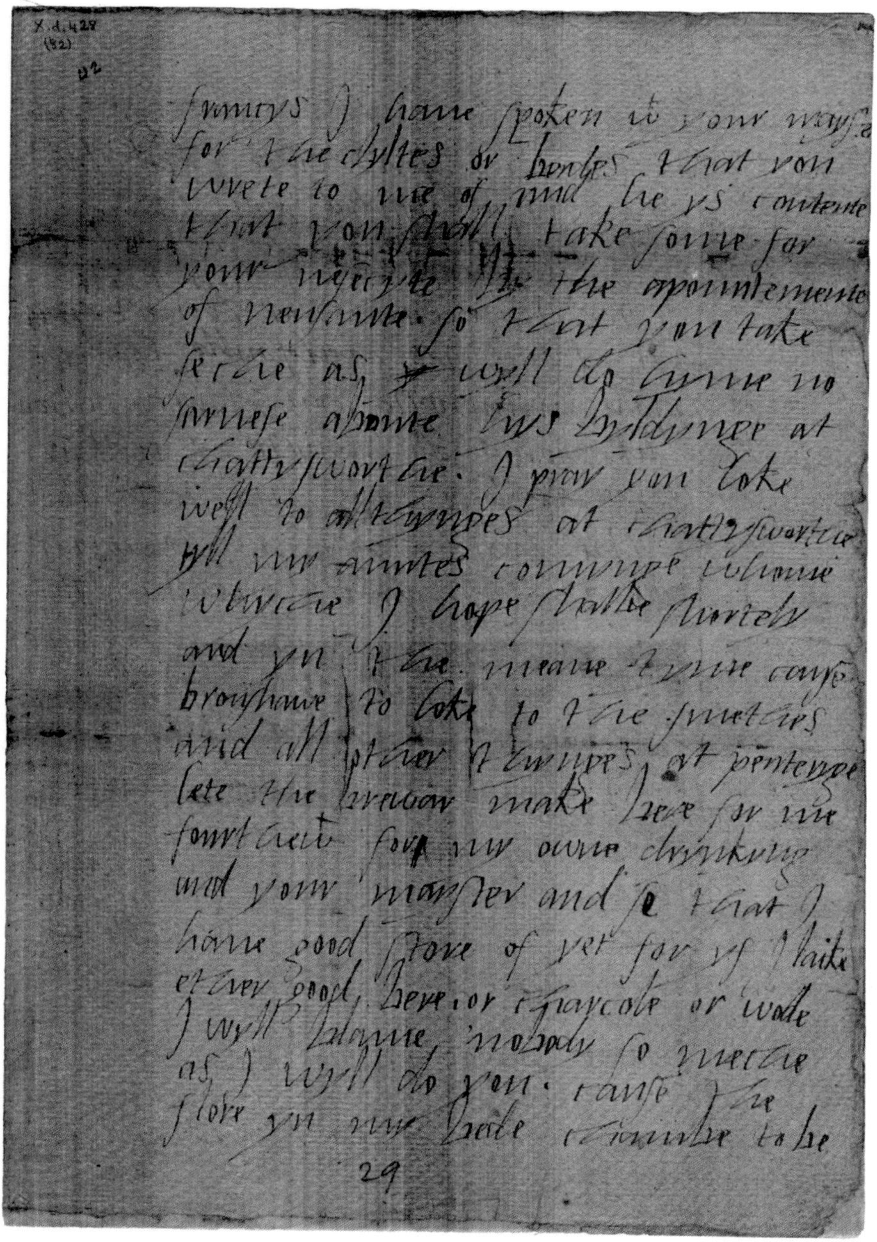

frances I haue spoken to your mays[ter]
for the dytes or bontes that you
wrete to me of and he ys contente
that you shall take some for
your nycyte yn the apoyntemente
of newaute so that you take
sertie as I well do came no
harmese aboute hys byldynge at
chattysworthe I pray you take
well to all tymber at chattysworthe
yll my aunte commyge tolumme
wherine I hope shalbe shortely
and yn the meane tyme cause
browghtone to loke to the pantres
and all other tymber at pentere
lete the brewar make here for me
fourtene foys my owne drynkyng
and your mayster and se that I
haue good store of yet for yf I laike
eyther good bere or charcole or wode
I well blame nobody so meche
as I well do you. cause the
store yn my bele chambre to be

29

Plate 9 Letter from Bess (Lady Cavendish) to her servant Francis Whitfield, 14 November [1552], sent, in her own hand, slit-and-band letter packet. Folger CT, X.d.428 (82), ID 99. By permission of the Folger Shakespeare Library.

yowr lordshypp letters dyrected vnto my lord my
husband and to me yn hys absence bearyng
dayte the xviij of thys instant monthe of
Januarye wos not delyuered vnto me before
the xx daye of the same at vj of the clocke
yn the evenynge / surelye my L. J wos muche
greued becawse ther wos nomore haste yn
delyuerye of the sayd letters consyderyng the
weyghtye and great cawses dependyng therypon
and my humble dewtye and servyse to be
shewed yn the dyspache of suche thynges
as the quenes mayestye requyreth to haue
yn redynes wythyn tutbury castell the
house beyng vnredye yn manye respectes for
the receavyng of the scottyshe quene comynge
at sodayne. J haue cawsed workmen to make
furthwyth yn redynes all suche thynges as ys
moust needfull to be downe before her
comynge and god wyllynge J shall
cawse furthwythe thre or fowre lodgyngs
to be furnysshed wyth hangyngs and other
necessaryes and rather then J shuld not be
trewe and ffaythfull hart answere the trust
reposed by the quenes mayestye J wyll lacke
furnyture of lodgyng for my selfe. thus yt
my contynuall prayer to god for the
preseruacyon of the quenes most excellent
mayestye and my hartye comendacyons
unto your good lordshyppe J cease to truble
you any further at thys present ffrom tutbery
the xxj of Januarye

yowr L. assuryd frend
E Shrouesbury

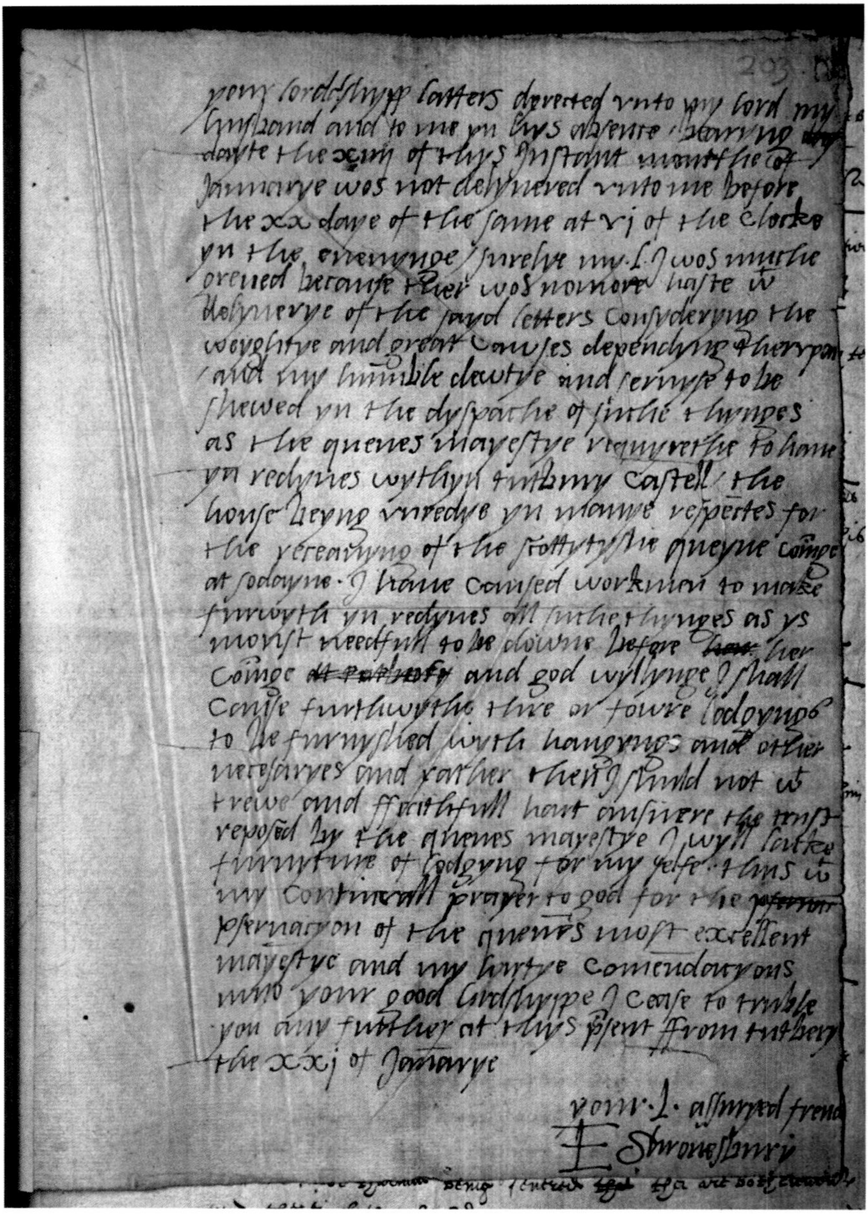

Plate 10 Letter from Bess (countess of Shrewsbury) to Robert Dudley, earl of Leicester, 21 January 1569, sent, in her own hand, slit-and band letter packet. Magdalene College Library, Pepys, MS 2503, pp. 203–6 (image of p. 203), ID 107. By permission of the Pepys Library, Magdalene College Cambridge.

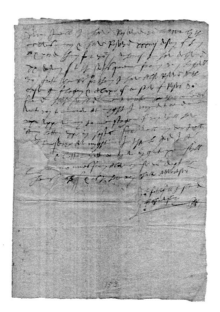

Plate 11 Letter from George Talbot, sixth earl of Shrewsbury, to his wife Bess (countess of Shrewsbury) [c. 1571], sent, in his own hand, tuck-and-fold letter packet. Folger CT, X.d.428 (92), ID 70. By permission of the Folger Shakespeare Library.

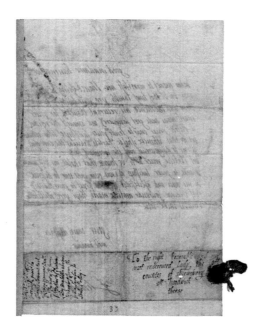

Plate 12 Letter from Elizabeth (Cavendish) Stuart, countess of Lennox, to her mother, Bess (countess of Shrewsbury) [1574?], sent, in her own hand. The letter packet (shown) was accordion folded and locked with a red wax seal embossed with the Lennox Stuart arms over goldish-ochre coloured silk floss. Folger CT, X.d.428 (50), ID 41. By permission of the Folger Shakespeare Library.

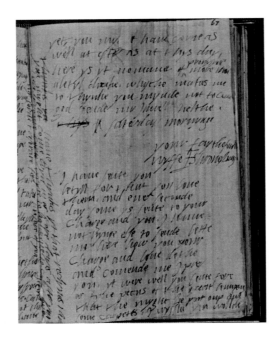

Plate 13 Letter from Bess (countess of Shrewsbury) to her husband George Talbot, sixth earl of Shrewsbury [1577], sent, in her own hand, tuck-and-fold letter packet. The letter covers three sides of paper and the image shows the final page with the postscript. LPL, Talbot Papers, MS 3205, fols 66r–67v (image of fol. 67r), ID 182. By permission of Lambeth Palace Library.

Plate 14 Letter from George Talbot, sixth earl of Shrewsbury, with a postscript by his wife Bess (countess of Shrewsbury), to William Cecil, Lord Burghley, 14 May 1578, sent, in their own hands, slit-and-band letter packet. LPL, Talbot Papers, MS 3206, fol. 885, ID 188. By permission of Lambeth Palace Library.

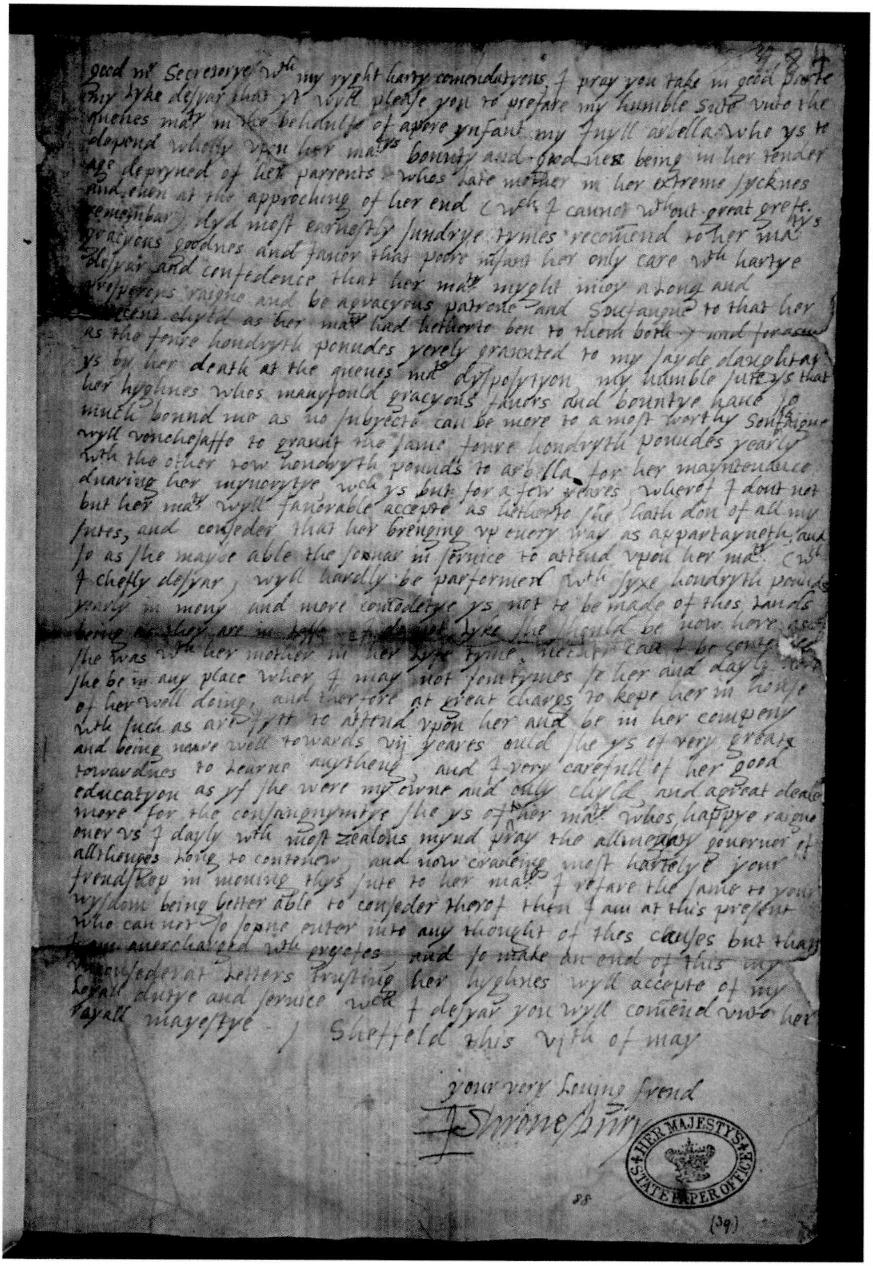

Plate 15 Letter from Bess (countess of Shrewsbury) to Sir Francis Walsingham, 6 May 1582, sent, letter in the hand of Scribe A, signed in her own hand. TNA, SP 12/153, fol. 84r-84v (item 39) (image of fol. 84vr), ID 145. By permission of The National Archives.

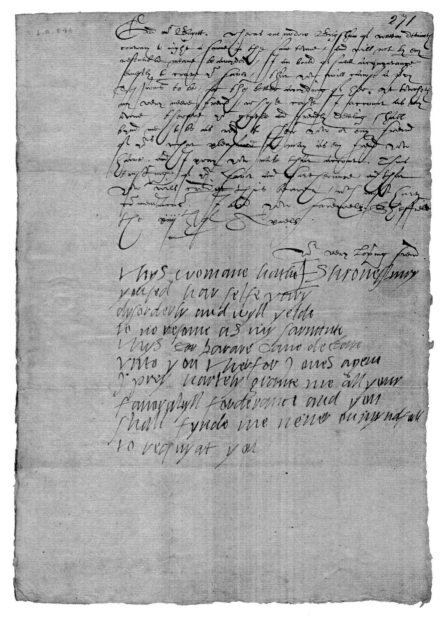

Plate 16 Letter from Bess (dowager countess of Shrewsbury) to Walter Bagot, 14 April [1600?], sent, letter and subscription in the hand of a secretary, signature and postscript in her own hand, tuck-and-fold letter packet. Folger Bagot, L.a.844, ID 2. By permission of the Folger Shakespeare Library.

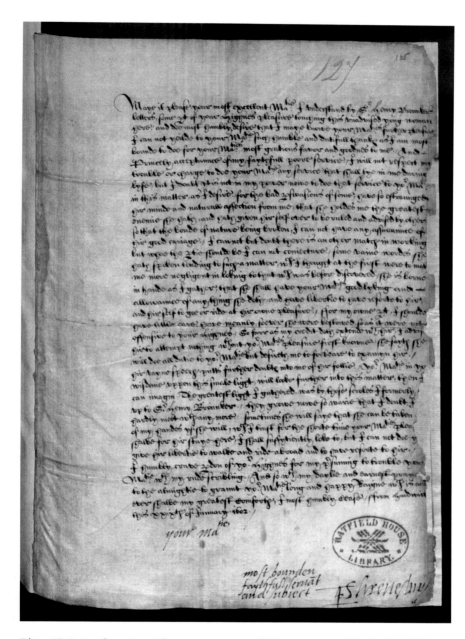

Plate 17 Letter from Bess (dowager countess of Shrewsbury) to Elizabeth I, 29 January 1603, sent, letter in the hand of Timothy Pusey, split subscription in the hand of Scribe B, signed in her own hand. The tuck-and-fold letter packet was locked with a red wax seal embossed with Bess's arms that feature the Hardwick cross (Plate 7). CP 135/127, fols 165–6 (image of fol. 165r), ID 129. By permission of the Marquess of Salisbury.

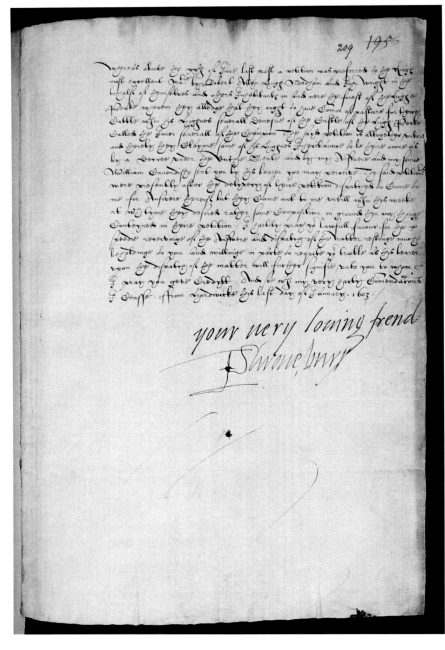

Plate 18 Letter from Bess (dowager countess of Shrewsbury) to Sir Julius Caesar, 31 January 1604, sent, letter in the hand of Scribe D, subscription in the hand of Scribe B, signed in her own hand, tuck-and-fold letter packet. Cover image. BL, Add. 12506, fols 209r-10v (image of fol. 209r), ID 161. © The British Library Board Add. 12506, f209.

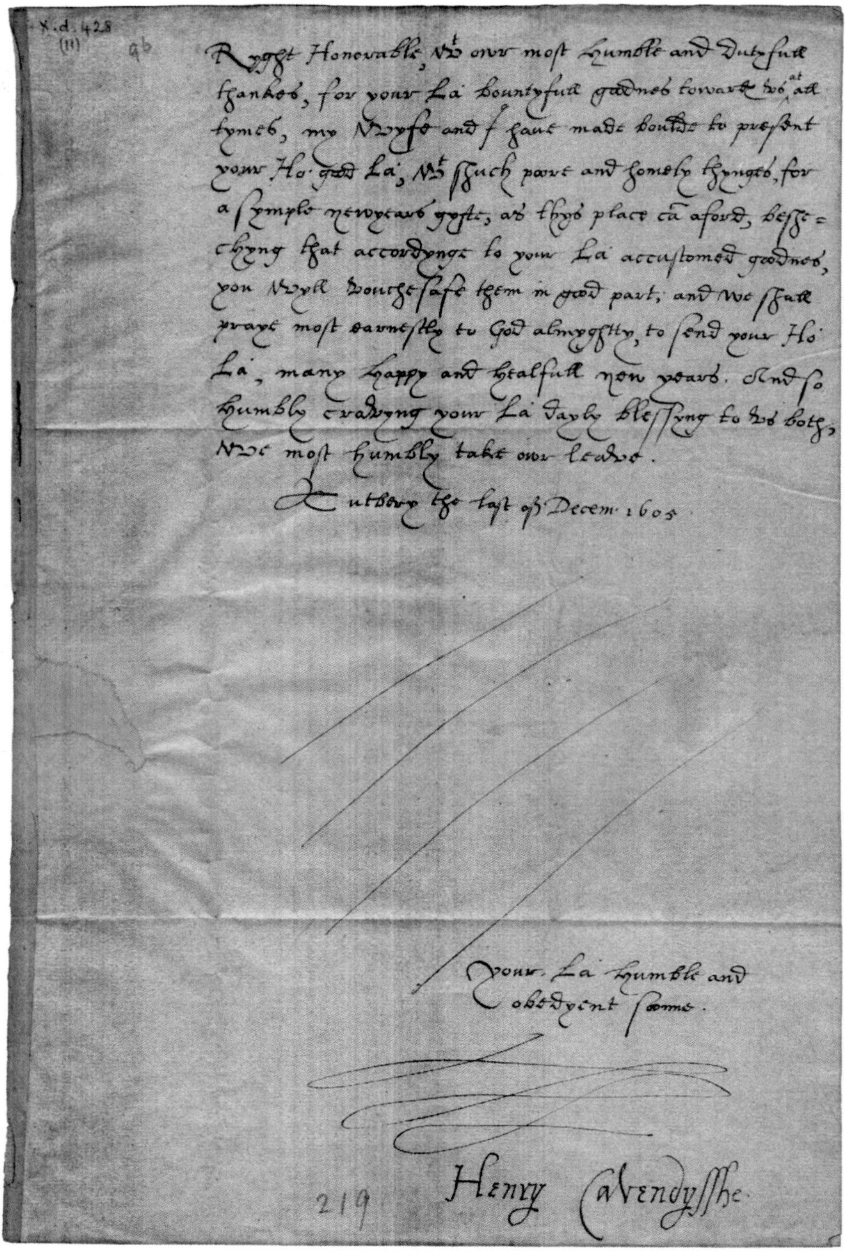
X.d.428 (11) 96

Ryght Honorable, wt our most humble and dutyfull thankes, for your La: bountyfull goodnes towardes us, at all tymes, my wyfe and I have made bould to present your Ho: good La: wt such poore and homely thynges, for a symple newyeares gyfte, as thys place can afford, besse=chyng that accordynge to your La: accustomed goodnes, you wyll vouchesafe them in good part, and we shall praye most earnestly to God almyghty, to send your Ho: La: many happy and healthfull new yeares. And so humbly cravyng your La: dayly blessyng to us both, we most humbly take our leave.

Tutbery the last of Decem. 1605

Your. La: humble and obedyent sonne.

Henry Cavendysshe

219

Plate 19 Letter from Henry Cavendish to his mother, Bess (dowager countess of Shrewsbury), 31 December 1605, sent, in his own hand. The tuck-and-fold letter packet was locked with a red wax seal embossed with the Cavendish arms that feature three bucks heads cabossed. Folger CT, X.d.428 (11), ID 11. By permission of the Folger Shakespeare Library.

Plate 20 Letter from Thomas Howard, earl of Arundel, to his grandmother-in-law Bess (dowager countess of Shrewsbury), 25 May [1607], sent, in his own hand. The letter packet (shown) was accordion folded, locked with two red wax seals, with arms embossed over pinkish-plum coloured ribbon. Folger CT, X.d.428 (1), ID 3. By permission of the Folger Shakespeare Library.

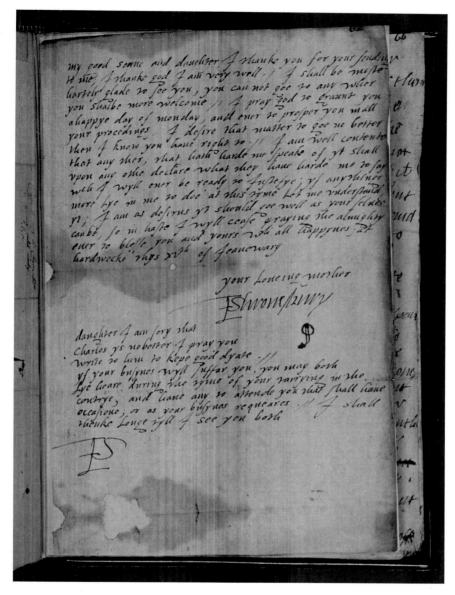

Plate 21 Letter from Bess (dowager countess of Shrewsbury) to her son-in-law and stepson Gilbert Talbot and her daughter Mary (Cavendish) Talbot, seventh earl and countess of Shrewsbury, 15 January [1606], sent, the letter and postscript are in the hand of Scribe A, the signature and initials after the postscript in her own hand, tuck-and-fold letter packet. LPL, Talbot Papers, MS 3205, fols 62r–63v (image of fol. 62r), ID 180. By permission of Lambeth Palace Library.

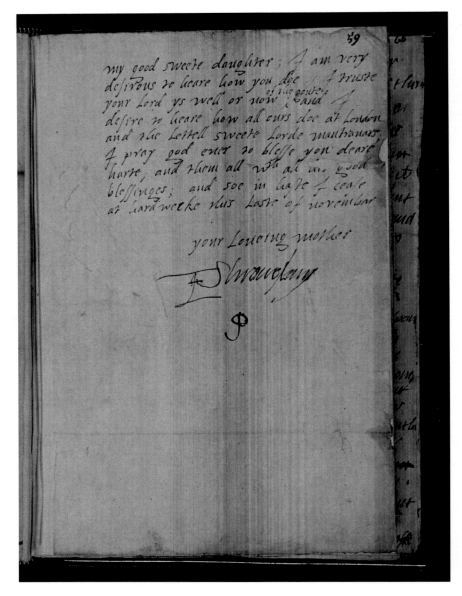

Plate 22 Letter from Bess (dowager countess of Shrewsbury) to her daughter Mary (Cavendish) Talbot, seventh countess of Shrewsbury, 30 November 1607, sent, hand of Scribe A, signed in her own hand, tuck-and-fold letter packet. LPL, Talbot Papers, MS 3205, fols 59r-60v (image of fol. 59r), ID 179. By permission of Lambeth Palace Library.

Reading and writing letters   105

William Cavendish from 1599–1607 include regular payments for books, such as those for September 1600:

To the booke binder for bookes v^s vj^d –	000 05 06
ffor two Italian bookes xx^s –	001 00 00
Singing bookes xj^s –	000 11 00
ffor a pamphlett iij^d –	000 00 04.[50]

We have already seen little James reading and writing with his grandmother. We might be tempted to speculate that he perhaps was responsible for hiding the French ABC printed for children in the 1570s, which was pushed down the back of the dining room panelling only to be discovered in 2003 and now on display at Hardwick New Hall.[51] While we cannot be sure this was his book, we know that when it came to the education of Bess's own children, some forty years earlier, they were well provided with reading materials: 'bokes for ye children / ffor iij grammers in frenche for the Children the same day ij^s / Cosmografie de levant – iij^s / psalmes in frenche with notes – iij^s'.[52] Hardwick New Hall was a hub for the arts and learning and rang with music, drama and humanist languages, as is glimpsed by a surviving note, jotted by a scribe on a scrap of paper on 16 November 1602 and signed by young William Cavendish and his father. The note set out an agreement that young William would be rewarded with a dagger and other items if he spoke only Latin to the men and Arbella for a week:

> The xvith of November in the foure & fortyth yeare of her Majesty raigne 1602. That my Master and Master William have Covenanted & agreed that if Master William Doe speake lattin till lent assizes next to my Lady Arbella . . . Master Oath Master Chaworth Master Parker Master Brodebent Master Heywood Master Owyn Roger ffrotwell Robert Parker & Hall . / Then my Master will geue Master William a rapyer and dagger, an imbrodered girdle & hanger and a payre of spurres.
>
> W Cauendysshe [*autograph, William Cavendish*]
> William Cauendysshe [*autograph, young William Cavendish*][53]

It reminds us that while Bess was not proficient in Latin herself, and is not listed here, we should not think of her as hermetically sealed off from humanistic learning. These languages were alive within her immediate environment, spoken within the household and displayed in graphic form

---

50 Hardwick MS 23, September 1600.
51 Girouard, *Hardwick Hall*, appendix. I am grateful to Nigel Wright for the reference.
52 Chatsworth House, St Loe Accounts August 1560 – December 1560, fol. 21.
53 Hardwick MS H/143/12 (HL/2), followed by notes about the delivery of linen.

106   *Reading and writing letters*

scattered throughout her embroideries at Hardwick Hall. In Bess's needle-work and textiles, Latin tags, title and quotations appear frequently. Without having training in the language herself, she was nonetheless clearly alert to its emblematic function and symbolic capital.[54]

This discussion has shown that while Bess did not start out in life with the benefits of a humanist education or legal training, she nevertheless developed levels of proficiency in several areas of literacy during her life. As a young woman she had received basic training in account keeping, as appropriate to a gentlewoman and necessary for running a household; by the end of her life she had developed a formidable level of knowledge and expertise in accounts, legal and business matters. As a young woman she had been taught needlework; by the end of her life she had created among the most extraordinary examples of architecture and textile art from the period, and become adept at fashioning her own iconography. As a young woman she had been taught the skills of reading, writing and composition, as appropriate to her social status; by the end of her life she had developed a level of epistolary literacy that allowed her to navigate the webs of Elizabethan power though dexterous deployment of epistolary forms. She participated in higher-level literary activities, which included daily devotional reading, cultural interests in the arts and an avid consumption of news. Altogether, these provide us with a broad picture of Bess's literacy. There remains the more precise question of Bess's technical abilities when it came to the linked but separate skills of writing and reading – of manually putting pen to paper herself or casting her own eyes over a text. The following section considers her literacy in this respect: her handwriting, idiolect and reading competency. There has been no previous attempt to historicise Bess's language, so the account begins by considering the context of early modern English.

2.2   'Your honour's hand': autograph writing and Bess of Hardwick's idiolect

Victorian editors of Renaissance women's texts attempted to resurrect their author's reputations by 'improving' their writing. Typically this meant regularising the language in order to bring it in line with standard modern English, as well as tempering its tone in various ways. Sara Jayne Steen makes the case for retention of original punctuation and spelling in editions of

---

54   For example, Latin inscriptions appear in the borders of the thirty-three octagonal embroideries featuring plants; these are based on the adages of Erasmus, of which many compilations were published in the sixteenth century, while the source for the plants was the herbal produced by Italian Pietro Andrea Mattioli. Another example would be the Latin titles that appear in the numerous panels depicting figures representing the Liberal Arts (Astrologie, Perspective, Logiqve, Mvsiqve, Architectvra, Arithmetiqve, Grammatica and Rhetorica) as well as the Vitures, Pastoral Nymphs and Goddesses, the Elements, the Senses and Personifications. Levey, *The Embroideries*, pp. 111–78 and pp. 344–45.

Reading and writing letters 107

Renaissance women's writings on the basis of feminist principles. Original spelling and punctuation were, says Steen, 'wrenched from Renaissance women by nineteenth-century editors who desired to make them conform to a later code of literacy so as not to seem embarrassingly uneducated to a general audience'.[55] These well-intentioned Victorian editors, such as E.T. Bradley, whose regularised edition of Arbella's letters *The Life of the Lady Arabella* appeared in 1889, enacted, in Steen's view, a new kind of oppression on their subjects. As Steen puts it, Bradley denies Arbella her anger and emotion and suppresses her self-expression by normalising her language. We have already seen examples of how Bess's early biographers made substantive changes to her letters – either to expurgate perceived indelicate emotions, or to superimpose an angry-sounding tone of voice, according to their own biographical agendas.[56] Bess's early editors and biographers also replaced forms characteristic of Bess's personal spelling system with modern standard English equivalents. For example, Bess's <nedefoulle, hare, yet, yousede, whome> become Williams's and Lovell's <needful, her, it, used, home>.[57] It reflects an attitude to Bess's written language as if it were a difficult problem to overcome, something that gets in the way of reading and that constitutes a barrier to extracting nuggets of information.[58] By contrast, the argument here is that Bess's written language is itself a topic for scrutiny and a source of information.

Fictionalised depictions and dramatisations of Bess have repeatedly attempted to mark her as a social climber through her language. Typically these elide regional dialect with a style of speaking that amalgamates straight-talking and earthy colloquialism with 'the tongue of an adder'.[59] Such depictions cast Bess into the limited role of an Eliza Doolittle–type figure – Rawson sees in the young Bess 'a touch of Becky Sharp' – a girl thrown into high society who needs to learn to 'talk proper'.[60] It is an anachronistic stereotype, one that reflects the linguistic situation in modern Britain, where regional accents have become stigmatised and prejudicially

---

55 Steen, 'Behind the Arras', p. 232.
56 Discussed in section 1.1, pp. 35–36, 44–46.
57 Williams, *Bess of Hardwick*, p. 24; Lovell, *Bess of Hardwick*, p. 80.
58 Lovell, *Bess of Hardwick*, mentions the problems she experienced reading the documents, including difficulties posed by 'handwriting, styles, inconsistent and archaic spelling, incomprehensible words', which rendered some 'impossible fully to decipher', pp. xvii–xviii.
59 Williams, *Bess of Hardwick*, p. v, citing John Neale; other similar portrayals are discussed by Williams and earlier in the introduction, pp. 11–12.
60 Rawson, *Bess of Hardwick*, p. 3. The rise of accent as social symbol has been charted by Lynda Mugglestone, *Talking Proper*. Hubbard, *Bess of Hardwick*, p. 20, likewise inappropriately and incorrectly links Bess's social position to having a regional accent: in her comments on Bess's gentry status and her gentry traits of 'prudence, pragmatism and . . . rigour . . . applied to household accounts' saying that 'she retained those traits (just as she retained her flat Derbyshire vowels) . . .' Bess was born in Derbyshire, but we do not have evidence of her spoken language, and little can be reconstructed from her written language.

108   *Reading and writing letters*

associated with a lack of education. Bess lived at a time when there was no accepted standard form of spoken English and only an emerging ideology of standardisation. While there were debates over correctness in language, the decisions had not yet been made over which forms, geographical or social, were 'better', more prestigious or more valuable than others. And while, as we have seen, Bess was not trained in Latin or other learned languages, it in no way automatically followed that the variety of English she used must therefore have been stigmatised. We need to describe Bess's language on the terms of her own culture, not according to our own cultural assumptions, and not through the ideology of standardisation, which was not defined until later in the seventeenth century. There has been no previous attempt to historicise Bess's language, but before we can interpret her letters it is important to do so, just as much as it is important to historicise any other of the other materials relating to her life. The aim of this section, then, is to provide an accurate and systematic historicisation of aspects of her idiolect – handwriting, spelling and punctuation – as found in her autograph writing.[61]

Bess's handwriting shows she had learned to write as part of the usual training for a gentlewoman and that she knew the italic script.[62] She wrote in a large, rather angular hand, fluent and clear to read (Plates 9, 10, 13, 14 and 16 give examples of her handwriting from 1552, 1569, 1577, 1578 and c. 1600). Her handwriting was congruent with her social status, education and gender, by comparison with, say, the more up-to-date and Italianate styles of handwriting we see used by some of her younger and better-educated correspondents (Plates 19 and 20), or the neat secretary scripts of her hired scribes (Plates 17 and 18).[63] Her handwriting remained consistent throughout her life and, apart from a slight tremor that appears in some of her later signatures (Plate 22), can be described as very fluent and steady. Her writing demonstrates that she was efficient, adept and competent with the pen. There is no evidence in Bess's handwriting of advanced training in calligraphy (e.g., loops and hooks, or clubbed ascenders and descenders, or

---

61 For a recent introduction to these issues see Hope, *Shakespeare and Language*, Chapter 4, 'Fritters of English: Variation and Linguistic Judgement', pp. 98–137 (especially pp. 126–33). Hope's critique of the models and conceptualisations of early modern English proposed by Adam Fox and Paula Blank (pp. 123–24), which are underpinned by modern cultural assumptions, is in contrast to his own more direct and uncompromising stance on tolerance of variation in early modern English. While Hope refers to material that is printed and literary, his position coincides with, and can be extended by, the findings of the analyses presented here based on manuscript letters.

62 An account of how Renaissance women learned to write is provided by Wolfe, 'Women's Handwriting'.

63 Comparisons can be found in Wolfe, 'Women's Handwriting', and Daybell, *Women Letter-Writers*, pp. 64–66, where he discusses women's training in handwriting and compares Francis Willoughby's 'clearer and more modern Italianate hand' that is distinguishable from that of his sister and those of lower social status.

elegant fluctuations in the line thickness created by adjustments in pressure and turning the nib of the pen).[64] In a few of her earlier letters, from the 1550s, it is possible to discern some attempts towards flourishes or extensions on certain letter forms (Plate 10), although these were not consistently applied or particularly well executed. We have several examples of her handwriting from after 1568, when she became countess of Shrewsbury (Plates 13 and 16), and there were generally no such efforts towards neatness or calligraphy.[65] It is not surprising nor is it necessarily a disadvantage, given that such visual niceties and precision may have been associated more with schoolgirls and hired scribes than with grand countesses. As Mel Evans, Graham Williams, H. R. Woudhuysen and others have shown, when it came to the most powerful individuals in the land, such as Burghley, Shrewsbury and Elizabeth I, bad handwriting was both a burden and a badge of grandeur.[66] While Bess's writing was easy reading by comparison with theirs, she had nothing to gain, by way of authority or respect, through neatness.

Like her penmanship, Bess's spelling and punctuation provide information about her control and mastery of writing. Again, we find competency without evidence of very much formal training. For example, capitalisation was rarely used by Bess and, where it was, the decision to use a majuscule form was determined as much by spatial as grammatical function. So, majuscules were not always used by Bess for proper nouns, but they were found in use for the first word of a letter (ID 123) and, often, for <C> or <L> in the word-initial position. Another example of competency without formal training was Bess's use of allographs: while <u> and <v> were usually in complementary distribution, with <u> being in the word-medial position and <v> word-initial, this practice was not consistently executed, so we find both <uenysone> and <venyson>.[67] Another example relates to abbreviations: the only abbreviation used regularly by Bess was <wᵗ> WITH, which was used either as a stand-alone word or in compounds in the initial, medial or terminal position. Occasionally a macron was used to abbreviate a nasal,

---

64 Nor is special training visible in the handwriting of Bess's daughters, a point observed by Wolfe, 'Women's Handwriting', p. 32. However, as Wolfe notes, Bess's granddaughters seem to have be renowned for their skills with the pen, not only Arbella but also Mary, Elizabeth and Alethea, to whom a copybook was dedicated in 1593, p. 24.

65 It is interesting to see the one example we do have of Bess attempting to include some neat decorative features in her letter written in her own hand to her husband Shrewsbury in 1587 during the brief period of their reconciliation. It was a visual feature to communicate, at this moment, particular respect towards her husband, with whom she had been asking to reconcile for several years. It seems to be the exception that proves the rule – that is, that Bess did not elsewhere deploy such features indicates that they inscribed particular respect and deference.

66 Evans, *The Language*; Williams, '"My Evil Favoured Writing"'; Woudhuysen, 'The Queen's Own Hand'. The 'scrawling almost illegible hands' that mark 'aristocratic reserve' are discussed by Daybell, 'Material Meanings', p. 653.

67 <uenysone> ID 184 l. 42 and <venyson> ID 183 l. 26. See also <uary> and <very>.

110   *Reading and writing letters*

though usually this practice was adopted at the edge of the page where space was running short. This usage, combined with the occasional use of a macron to abbreviate a vowel, suggests some hesitancy over how to use these forms and Bess's limited formal training. Her punctuation was very light and generally included only two marks: a full stop and a mark that is something between a comma and a short virgule. These marks did not serve to point out grammatical structures in the manner of present-day English writing but, rather, functioned rhetorically or for emphasis, such as 'to youse my tanantes. as I trouste. they. shall' ('use my tenants as I trust they shall') and 'I wolde I coulde parswade you that your neryste waye to London. were to come by Chattysworth or ells. that you wolde chouse thys tyme to go see your lande yn yourke shyre'.[68] The option to punctuate rhetorically rather than grammatically was one that was legitimately available to writers at this time, though one that Bess's academically trained scribes and correspondents tended not to prefer and which was therefore a marker of her level of training.

It should be emphasised with regard to Bess's handwriting, spelling and punctuation, while these do not display high levels of formal training, they do remain remarkably consistent throughout her life and are in line with what would be expected of the level of training for a gentlewoman. So, with regard to her personal spelling system: Bess repeatedly selected the same spelling forms over several decades, even though a range of different forms were available in early modern English writing. It is necessary to emphasise this stability because Bess's spelling tends to give the *appearance* of being unstable or erratic. There are specific reasons why her spelling system would seem to give this impression, at least to modern readers on first glance or after only a cursory or superficial analysis.[69] The first reason is that, by comparison with her academically trained scribes, Bess's writing in her own hand displayed a higher degree of tolerance for minor variations. One example here will stand for many. To take a high-frequency word: Bess's typical spelling of FAITHFULL was <faythefoull>, which appears eight times. However, on another six occasions she tolerated minor variations, such as use or not of final <-e>, use of single or double <-ll> and variation in the choice of vowel (typically between <o> and <ou>). The result of these was five different spelling forms for this word: <faythefull, faythfoull, faythefoull, faythefoul, faythefall>. The same is true for the suffix – FULL: Bess's typical spelling of this suffix, as seen in the case of FAITHFULL, was <-foull>, which was used another four times, but as well as this form she

---

68 ID 198, l. 8 and ll. 9–14.

69 Further discussion of this issue, and of the methodologies involved in analysis of Renaissance women's writings, is presented by Sönmez, 'Perceived and Real Differences', and Nevalainen, 'Women's Writings'. The following analysis here is based on Bess's existing autograph writing from her letters, a total of around 5,200 words.

Reading and writing letters **111**

also used the forms <-full,-fulle,-foulle>.[70] In these cases, as elsewhere, Bess's spelling can be described as focused around a predictable set of forms; the level of 'noise' created by tolerance for minor features, such as non-grammatical final <-e>, doubled final consonants and variation between certain vowels, especially <o> and <ou>, should not distract us too much from its core stability and predictability.

It is worth adding here that tolerance of spelling variations of this kind was not unusual in early modern English manuscripts. Early modern women's writing has developed something of a reputation for 'bad spelling', by which, it seems, is generally meant that it gives the impression to modern readers of being less stable or 'more phonetic' than the spelling of their male contemporaries.[71] However, as Margaret Sönmez has shown, this reputation that has been acquired somewhat unfairly, largely as a result of the tendency to compare women's manuscript letters with printed literary texts. If we compare Bess's autograph writings with that of her fourth husband, the earl of Shrewsbury, we find his spelling was, if anything, less stable than hers. For example, Bess has been shown to have had a repertoire of five spelling forms for FAITHFULL, but her husband Shrewsbury had seven: his typical forms were <fathefull> (7x) and <fethefull> (5x) but he also used <fathfull, fathef[u]ll, faythefull, fethfull, fethef[u]ll>.[72] There were many other aspects of Shrewsbury's spelling and orthographic profile that likewise displayed his high tolerance for variation and which showed greater instability than Bess. For example, Shrewsbury's usual forms for the present participle suffix – ING were <-ynge> and <-enge> (18x and 15x), but he also used <-yng,-eng,-inge,-ing>, whereas Bess generally used only <-ynge> and <-yng>, occasionally <-enge> and <-inge>.[73] Likewise, for SH- Bess

---

70 ID 107 (Plate 10) has been excluded here as it is an exception, discussed ahead. Methods of scribal profiling, spelling questionnaires and the need for systematic methodological approaches to late medieval and early modern spelling are discussed by Evans, *The Language*, pp. 209–10; Horobin, 'The Criteria for Scribal Attribution'; McIntosh, Samuels and Benskin, 'General Introduction' to *A Linguistic Atlas of Late Medieval English*, pp. 1–28; Benskin and Laing, 'Translations and *Mischsprachen*'; Doty, 'Telling Tales'.

71 Sönmez, 'Perceived and Real Differences'.

72 fathfull (ID 68); fathefull (IDs 72, 71 x2, 70, 69, 68, 64); fathef[u]ll (ID 66); faythefull (ID 66); fethfull (ID 154); fethefull (IDs 78, 77, 76, 75, 74); fethef[u]ll (ID 67). This survey is based on seventeen of Shrewsbury's autograph letters, all of which are written to Bess and are held by the Folger Shakespeare Library (ID 64–79 and 154, excluding one scribal letter). Shrewsbury's extensive correspondence would no doubt reward further investigation; however, this study has been limited to seventeen of his autograph in order to provide an approximately equal word count to Bess's eighteen autograph letters. On the methodological issues involved in such a comparison see Sönmez.

73 -yng (Remainyng ID 65; comyng 64); -ynge (swetynge, Redynge, delynge, delynge ID 154; cummynge ID 78; nothynge ID 77; etynge ID 76; commynge ID 71; commynge ID 68; cummynge x2 ID 66; kepynge ID 66); -enge (causenge, wyschenge x2 ID 154; brekenge, askenge ID 78; consyderenge x2, waverenges, byldenge ID 77; consyderenge ID 74; st[r] yfenge ID 66; havenge ID 66; havenge, wrytenge, metenge ID 65); -eng (brengeng ID 78;

112　*Reading and writing letters*

generally used <sh-> but Shrewsbury alternated between <ch> and <sh> in the initial position (so, <che> SHE alongside <shall> SHALL and <shuld> SHOULD) and between <sch> and <sh> in the medial or terminal position (so, <folysch> FOOLISH, <furnysche> FURNISH and <wysche> WISH, alongside <fenyshed> FINISHED and <wyshe> WISH).[74] Shrewsbury did not show any commitment to the niceties of precise punctuation: his letters were punctuated, capitalised and abbreviated just as sparingly as those of his wife, and he was even less predictable when it came to the distribution of <u>/<v> allographs.[75] In fact, the only place we find stability and predictability in spelling and punctuation in the letters from Bess and Shrewsbury is in those penned by their hired scribes. For example, Bess's secretary Timothy Pusey always used <sh->, such as <she> throughout; he always used <-ing> forms, such as <praying>, <importuning> (ID 132), <reading>, <wryting>, <comming>, <spending> (ID 134); and the two times he wrote FAITHFULL they were the same spelling, differentiated only by the use of capital <ff>, itself a trained feature: <faythfull> (ID 129, Plate 17) and <ffaythfull> (ID 140). As these observations indicate, spelling instability and the use of rhetorical rather than grammatical punctuation were not gender-based, nor did they depend entirely on educational training; rather they were dependent upon a combination of training, status and social role.

The second reason, and as can be seen from these examples, for the initial *appearance* or *impression* of instability in Bess's personal spelling system relates to the perceptions of modern readers. A high proportion of Bess's linguistic choices were forms that did not, subsequently, become part of modern standard English. For one thing, Bess did not use Latinate spellings, many of which subsequently became standardised into modern English. In Bess's day no fixed decision had yet been made and there was no single correct form; therefore, Bess's non-Latinate forms represented an entirely acceptable alternative to their Latinate competitors. For example, for the word DOUBT Bess's spelling was <dowte> (3x) – that is, she did not insert the <b> to reflect the Latin cognate. For MAJESTY and SUBJECT Bess's spellings were <magystye(s)> (15x) and <subgett> (2x). And Bess again used the non-Latinate form for words which tended to include a <t> when written by trained scribes; so, Bess's forms for ADDITION, AFFECTION, DISCRETION and INFECTION are <adecyone>, <affeccyone>, <dyscrescyon> and

---

wryteng ID 74; acordeng); -inge (doinge ID 74, goinge ID 71, myndinge ID 67, proubinge ID 66; fyndinge ID 65; thyngking, wyllinge ID 64); -ing (sending ID 71).

74　<folysch> ID 154; <furnysche> ID 77; <wysche> 74; <fenyshed> ID 77; <wyshe> ID 65. See also the variation between <sen(d/t)> and <cen(d/t)> that occurs throughout his letters.

75　For an example of his unstable use of <u>/<v> see ID 68, which features <v> in the initial position whether voiced <vyle, very> or unvoiced <vnto, vndar, vpp>; <v> in the medial and terminal positions whether voiced <evare, loves, hav, gyve, have> or unvoiced <cvm> and used interchangeably with <u>, so <hur, you, burne, tuesday>.

<ynfeccyone>.[76] These forms might seem marked to modern readers, but there is no reason to think they would have been so to Bess's readers. These were available variants at that point in time, when the question over which forms were preferable had not yet been decided. In each of these cases we see that Bess's personal spelling system did not reflect the (Latin) etymology. It may have been that certain aspects of her personal spelling system reflected dialect or pronunciation, such as HER <har>, PUT UP <pott oup>, THOUGH <thought>, HOME <whome>, OWES <woyes>, I UNDERSTAND <yonderstand> and EARLY <yerly>.[77] However, without sound recordings, it is difficult to be certain about the precise relationship between Bess's spoken and written language. In early modern English, just as today, spellings did not necessarily or exactly reflect pronunciation.[78] There is no doubt that Bess was aware of a range of other spelling choices available to her: she was exposed to many different personal spelling systems through her extensive reading of a wide range of letters from correspondents across the social and educational scale. Given all of this exposure to different spellings, we must conclude that Bess found no good reason to go to the trouble of adapting her own spelling system, which she perceived to be acceptable, or even advantageous or prestigious, as it was.[79]

Again, it is important to point out that her spelling profile resembled that of her husband Shrewsbury in this respect. Like Bess, Shrewsbury did not typically use etymologically reconstructed Latinate spellings, such as the <b>-form of DOUBT; his primary forms were without the <b>: <dout>, <doute> and <douted>. It was not that he was unaware of the existence of the <b>-form; indeed, that fact that he used it on one occasion, <dobted>, indicates that the form without <b> was not the limit of his repertoire but was his preference.[80] Likewise, we find Shrewsbury using non-Latinate

---

76 <dowte> ID 200 l. 10, ID 123 ll. 5, 16. <magystye(s)> ID 110 l. 22; ID 122 ll. 16, 19, 29; ID 120 superscription and ll. 1, 3, 6. 14, 18, 23, 26; ID 123 ll. 4, 8 and superscription. <subgett> ID 123 l. 8, and ID 120 l. 27. <adecyone> ID 123 l. 17. <affeccyone> ID 123, l. 4. <dyscrescyon> ID 99 l. 33 (Plate 9). <ynfeccyone> ID 183 l. 9. <esspecyall> ID 109 l. 20. <gracyous> ID 120 ll. 7, 15, ID 110.

77 <har> is used throughout Bess's writing; <pott oup> ID 182 (Plate 13); <thought> ID 111; <whome> ID 200; <woyes> ID 184; <yonderstand> ID 120; <yerly> ID 186>.

78 For example, Bess's spelling DAUGHTER <dowter> may have indicated pronunciation without the velar fricative (which was sometimes, in the spellings systems of other early modern English writers, indicated by medial <gh>). However, it is difficult to be absolutely certain and, of course, we must remember that our present day English form <daughter>, although written with medial <gh>, is widely pronounced without the velar fricative. On the relationship between pronunciation and spelling, and methodological issues involved in the use of historical sources here, see Meurman-Solin, 'Letters as a Source'.

79 It is interesting to recall the findings of Evans's study of Elizabeth I's language, *The Language*, pp. 191–98, which considers that the clutch of distinctive spelling forms Elizabeth I retained when she became queen may have functioned as a prestige marker associated with writing in her own hand.

80 IDs 65, 72, 74, 76, 77, 78. The case of <dobted> is in ID 65.

114   *Reading and writing letters*

spellings for <deskresyon> DISCRETION and <affecsyon> AFFECTION, as well as various forms that may or may not be phonologically explicable, such as rhoticism, perhaps suggested by <grettarr>, <harvm> and <warom> (GREATER, HARM, WARM), and long- and short-<a>, perhaps suggested by <smawle> and <laghe> (SMALL, LAUGH).[81] Bess and Shrewsbury shared these features which, again, contrasted with their academically trained secretaries and hired scribes. For example, Bess's secretary Timothy Pusey used the <b>-form of DOUBT <doubt> on all six occurrences of the word in his writing; he also used Latinate <i> or <j> spellings, such as <coniecture> (3x) CONJECTURE, and <t> spellings, such as <affectionate> (1x) AFFECTIONATE, as well as <spetially> (1x) SPECIALLY and <gratious> GRACIOUS (5x) (which can be compared to Bess's <esspecyall> 1x and <gracyous> 3x). Again, then, the decision as to whether to use etymological spellings and dialectally colourless forms was not one determined by gender or by education alone, but by a combination of training, status and social role.

It can be difficult for modern readers fully to grasp and accept that Latinate spellings like <doubt> in early modern English (especially where these subsequently happened to have been incorporated into the standard modern language) were not somehow 'better' than their non-Latinate counterparts like <dout>. For the sake of perspective, then, it is worth recalling Shakespeare's views of such forms, that he expected his audiences to recognise, which are cast as academic pretentions. Concern over the use of these forms is presented as the viewpoint of the character Holofernus, known throughout *Love's Labour's Lost* as 'Pedant' and satirised for his pettyminded obsessions and overly fastidious opinions about surface matters over content. Holofernus may well have sneered at Bess's spellings <dowte> DOUBT and <dowter> DAUGHTER. His preference would have been for the etymologically restored form <doubt> and the older form <doughter>, both of which he proposed, additionally, should be followed in speech, with the <b> and velar fricative pronounced to follow the spellings. In the Pedant Holofernus's words, his rival Armado should be condemned along with all others who

> speake dout *sine* b, when he should say doubt: det, when he shold pronounce debt; d e b t, not d e t . . . neighbour *vocatur* nebour; neigh abreuiated ne: this is abhominable, which he would call abbominable.[82]

These forms (dout, det, nebour) were not dialect forms: the <b> was artificially restored to <doubt> on academic grounds, and the loss of the velar

---

81 <deskresyon>, <smawle>, <laghe> ID 154; <affecsyon> ID 66; <grettarr> ID 75; <harvm> ID 74; <warom> ID 72.

82 *Love's Labour's Lost*, V.I; probably written in 1594–95, the first surviving quarto is from 1598; the quotation is from the First Folio of 1623.

fricative in words like DOUGHTER and NEIGHBOUR was part of the ongoing widespread disappearance of the sound from southern English.[83] Holofernus's objection to them was on the basis of his peculiarly prescriptive ideas about English and his views on which rules should be applied for its improvement. Shakespeare, on the other hand, made clear though his satirisation that his position was on the other side of this debate. For Shakespeare, who was not a university man himself, Holofernus's prescriptivist attitude to language represented the tedious preserve of pedants and schoolteachers; rigid and rather ridiculous, it was certainly not the concern of great poets or grand countesses.

The discussion so far has emphasised the tolerance of variation in English during Bess's era, and has stressed that we cannot think in dichotomous terms ('correct and incorrect' or 'better and worse') when it comes to sixteenth-century spelling. Instead, we must assess linguistic forms in terms of their place on a spectrum where education and gender were not the only factors determining choice, but must be combined with factors such as status, social role, genre and pragmatic (interpersonal) context. However, if we are to be wary of anachronistic prescriptive views or hierarchical models of language, a key question arises for editors: what counts as an error and which forms could be described as legitimately requiring editorial emendation? It is a question that is of importance to editors as well as to all readers of Renaissance writing, and it is one that takes us close to more fundamental questions about perceptions and attitudes towards language. It is worth looking at some examples here of cases from Bess's autograph letters which all, from an editorial point of view, would require a decision over whether the form should be classified as an error in need of correction, or represents a legitimate spelling variant, regardless of whether reflecting pronunciation:

Item	Forms
PERFECT	<perfytt> (ID 120 l. 23; missing <c>?)
FRIENDSHIP	<frenshep>, <frenchepe> (ID 123 l. 7, ID 200 l. 26; missing <d>?)
BALDWIN	<balwene> (ID 182 l. 74; missing <d>?, Plate 13)
ENGLAND	<enlonde> (ID 122 superscription; missing <g>?)
LENGTH	<lenth> (ID 109 l. 1; missing <g>?)
THANKFULL	<thanfoull> (ID 120 l. 12; missing <k>?)
WORKSOP	<worsope> (ID 184 l. 16; missing <k>?)
TROUBLE	<trbyll> (ID 200 l. 2; missing <o>?)
CHAMBER	<chambe> (ID 99 l. 23; missing <r>?)
FRANCIS	<francy> (ID 101 l. 1; missing <s>?)

83 A discussion of this passage is in Burnley, *The History*, pp. 237–43.

116   *Reading and writing letters*

One editorial approach would be to classify all of these as errors – that is, as slips involving accidentally missed letters. Support to indicate that this was so (that these were errors) could be garnered from other cases where Bess corrected the same error – for example, where she changed <frene> to <fren^d^e>, which shows that, at least some of the time, she perceived this to be a form in need of correction.[84] Further support might be gathered from other examples of the same word in Bess's own hand where the suspected missing letter is in place, such as <lenghte>, <trobyll>, <trobeled>, <chambers> and <francys>.[85] However, given that forms such as <chambe> and <trbyll> may nevertheless reflect aspects of pronunciation (e.g., rhoticism), and given that Bess has not corrected them in all instances, there is still a case to be made for retaining them as they are.

On this point about the perception of spelling forms, it is worth remembering that, from a linguistic perspective, loss or addition of a single letter had the potential to differentiate between a socially marked or an unmarked form. For example, in Bess's language we find various categories of /h/-dropping and /h/-insertion; so, she sometimes left off initial <h> in a native word, as in <oubende> HUSBAND and <beouldynge> BEHOLDING, or inserted an unetymological /h/ as in <hotheres> OTHERS.[86] Nevalainen has shown that there was no general stigma attached to /h/-dropping or insertion in early modern English, which were features that became stigmatised only towards the end of the eighteenth century.[87] In further support of this view, it is worth observing that Bess dropped <h> in letters to her husband the earl of Shrewsbury and Sir Francis Walsingham, and that Shrewsbury also used these forms, such as /h/-deletion in the native suffix <lyklyoddes> LIKLI-HOODS.[88] That is to say, these examples offer further evidence that in early modern English /h/-dropping was not stigmatised and was admissible among the higher gentry and nobility. While these spellings may have been frowned on by Holofernus (who preferred etymologically reconstructed forms) and

---

84 ID 123, l. 26. A detailed study of the potential value of corrections and revisions in handwritten texts, although for the earlier period, is Wakelin, *Scribal Correction*; Steen has shown the value of corrections and revisions in relation to the interpretation of early modern letters; 'Behind the Arras'.

85 ID 198, l. 2; ID 200, l. 17; ID 109, l. 36; ID 99, l. 27 and l. 1 (Plate 9).

86 <oubende> ID 184, l. 42; <beouldynge> ID 123, l. 2; <hotheres> ID 111, l. 12 and l. 39.

87 Nevalainen, *An Introduction*, pp. 127–28, emphasises that the situation involved a range of usages in early modern English. Görlach, *Introduction*, p. 75, by contrast, classifies these as stigmatised forms in early modern English: while he acknowledges they were not stigmatised as strongly as they were from the nineteenth century, all the same, he says, 'loss of initial [h] was typical of dialect and "vulgar" speech'. Görlach does not cite the historical sources and he is simply, it seems, reluctant to free himself from the nineteenth-century prescriptive tradition, where /h/-dropping had a prominent role. Further discussions of /h/-dropping are in Wyld, *A History of Modern Colloquial English*, pp. 295–96, and Mugglestone has a chapter on the topic in *Talking Proper*, pp. 95–134.

88 ID 66.

Reading and writing letters **117**

avoided use by university-educated scribes, outside of such academic pedantries, for the earl and countess of Shrewsbury, no such concerns prevailed.

All of these examples indicate the value of original-spelling editions. It is worth reviewing and reiterating these, given the ongoing debate over original spelling and modernisation in editions of early modern texts.[89] First, and as Steen as argued, original spelling is justifiable from a feminist perspective: it allows the woman writer full agency in terms of her self-expression, without constricting her language based on later cultural assumptions (a justification that could also be applied to other non-elite social groups). Second, original spelling has value from a linguistic point of view as it provides a bank of data for historical linguistic analysis, of the kind that can provide insights into textual production and consumption, literacy and social trends in language use. Third, original spelling delineates between scribal and autograph writing and tracks the shifts between these. These shifts are, in reality, less clear-cut than the terms 'scribal writing' and 'autograph writing' might imply and here, in tracking the boundaries between them, is another function for original spelling. That is to say, at times the relationship between scribal and autograph language is blurred and indistinct, and the modulation between the two, where it is discernible at all, can be detected only in minute shifts of spelling and orthography.

As the boundary between autograph and scribal writing is an issue that has further implications that are fundamental when it comes to defining what we mean by Bess's language or letters, it is worth giving an example. Of particular relevance is the letter from Bess to the earl of Leicester of 21 January 1569 concerning the imminent arrival of the Scottish Queen at Tutbury Castle, in which we find Bess adapting her personal spelling system.[90] We know that this was Bess's own hand based on the characteristic visual features (i.e., allographs, duct, aspect and orthography) as well as certain typical spellings (e.g., <wos> WAS and <moust> MOST). What is remarkable are the departures from these usual features. It is possible that, in this letter, the anomalous forms that appear were selected spontaneously from Bess's own memory (from her 'active repertoire'). However, more likely is that it indicates she copied this letter from a scribal draft, carrying over the spellings in the process (from her 'passive repertoire').[91] That the latter was

---

89 The recent issue of a second volume of Elizabeth I's letters, this second volume being in original spelling, was in response to a perceived need to supplement the first volume, which was a modernised edition; Marcus, Mueller and Rose, *Elizabeth I: Autograph Compositions*. A range of detailed discussion of modernisation and its various advantages and limitations, taking in different perspectives, appear in Phillips and Williams, *Editing Early Modern Texts*, by Gavin Alexander, Joseph L. Black, Joad Raymond, Neil Rhodes, Roger Kuin, Henry Woudhuysen and Alison Wiggins.

90 ID 107, Plate 10.

91 The definitions of active and passive scribal repertoires are given in Benskin and Laing, 'Translations and Mischsprachen'.

118   *Reading and writing letters*

indeed the case is further, and compellingly, confirmed by two visual features of palaeography and orthography that are also unique within Bess's spelling profile. The first is the one (and only) example of a secretary script allograph in Bess's writing: a terminal sigma-shaped <s> in <lodgyngs> (the final word of line 20, Plate 10). The second is the use of the abbreviation <p*er*> in 'p*reser*uacyon' and 'p*res*ent' (lines 27 and 30); this abbreviation, developed for Latin, normally took the form of a hook through the descender of <p>, although here Bess used a line below <pseruacyon> and a macron above <psent>, which suggest her uncertainties about the exact use of this form. Her spelling anomalies in this letter are as follows (Plate 10):

Item	Bess's usual spelling	Bess's spelling in this letter
ANSWER	<ansore>	<answere>
FAITHFULL	<fay-> types	<ffaithfull> (also <ffrom> in this letter)
HER	<har>, <hare>	<~~herr~~ her>
HUSBAND	<hosbande>	<husband>
-ING	<-yng(e)>	<-inge> (2x)
MAGESTY	<magystye(s)>	<mayestye> (3x)
MUCH	<meche>	<muche>
SERVICE	<sarues>	<seruyse>

Each of the forms listed here, used in this letter to Leicester, was either anomalous or very unusual in Bess's autograph writing, although, in each case, the forms used here tended to be those more common among formally trained writers. For example, <her> and <hir> forms of HER were far more common among professional scribes and academically educated correspondents in Bess's network than her own usual form <har>.[92] We can add to these the use of grammatical (rather than her usual rhetorical) punctuation in this letter, and features of the style of curial prose, which have been discussed in section 1.1 and which were also associated with the language of academically trained scribes. In addition, the single use of the Latinate form of MAJESTY <mayestye> here in this letter and the palaeographic features typical of secretary script, <p*er*> and sigma <s>, suggest that Bess had copied this letter from a scribe's draft written in a secretary script, carrying over some of the features as she did so.

This letter therefore allows us to gather more information about Bess's reading abilities and, specifically, confirms she could decipher secretary script. That Bess went to the trouble of copying out a scribal draft tells

---

92 None of her later spelling suggests that she was interested in switching to the forms used by scribes, such as <her>, <-ing> and <much>. For example, Bess used her usual <har> in her final three autograph letters dealing with the important issue of Arbella's portion and written to the queen, Burghley and Walsingham in 1578.

us she perceived it to be crucial that this letter to Leicester was written in her own hand. The reason may have been its content, which, concerning the arrival of the Scottish Queen, had security implications, and use of her own hand would confirm her presence and ensure maximum control over the content. Alternatively, it may have been thought barbarous, from an interpersonal point of view, to write to the earl of Leicester in anything other than her own hand, as was also her husband's preference.[93] Finally, this letter tells us about possible methods of composition available to Bess. The syntax, phrasing and punctuation indicate the text was drafted through collaboration with the scribe, as the scribe's influence on the structure of the language is evident.[94] There must have been advantages to this chosen method of composition, the most obvious of which seem to have been the efficiency of having a scribe undertake the laborious task or writing a draft (rather than Bess having manually to produce both a draft and a final copy herself). That is, the letter suggests Bess's preference here, in this case, for composition through oral modes (we might envisage a situation involving a mixture of discussion with a scribe, dictation and spoken instructions) rather than through the process of physically putting pen to paper herself. It is not surprising that Bess used this mode of composition and it is one that we know other letter-writers deployed, such as Queen Elizabeth.

It is necessary to distinguish, then, between writing that is 'in an individual's own hand' and writing that is 'single-authored'. For one thing, this notion is misconceived from a technical point of view. Autograph writing, at this period, did not guarantee authorial or single-authored writing: a letter could be collaboratively composed, or scribally composed, but then copied out in the hand of the sender. Features of palaeography, spelling and punctuation can help to delineate and diagnose more precisely the shifts between scribal and autograph writing. It is not just an issue for editing women's letters, but for men's correspondence too, and in any cases where concepts of authorship are to be interrogated.[95] Here we are again reminded of the collaborative nature of letter-writing, where it is possible to distinguish between not only scribal and autograph but also moments where the two can be seen to blur and become a hybrid voice. The shifting lines of autograph and scribal writing are never stable and sometimes not at all distinct. Original spelling helps us to track these boundaries and we find a range of collaborative scenarios at different periods that show the flexibility

---

93 Daybell, *Women Letter-Writers*, p. 108: 'Although it was customary to employ amanuenses for formal correspondence, many female letter-writers judged it important to correspond personally with officials where there existed bonds of political friendship'.

94 Discussed in section 1.1.

95 For example, Burlinson and Zurcher, '"Secretary to the Lord Grey Lord Deputie here"', observe the blending of Lord Grey's idiosyncratic personal spelling system with those of his scribes in cases where a scribal letter has been copied from an autograph draft. Such examples remind us of one of the values of original-spelling editions.

120 *Reading and writing letters*

of the letter form. The next section will examine further this shifting and flexible relationship between scribal and autograph epistolary writing. It begins with a consideration of cases where Bess wrote letters in her own hand, and then moves on to consider her use of various types of scribes during her lifetime.

2.3 'I am not able nowe to write . . . with my owne hande': scribal writing and idiolects

As is apparent from the existing letters that Bess sent, when she had the opportunity to use a scribe, she would do so. Her surviving early letters were all written in her own hand (all five of those we have from the 1550s) but after 1560 we see Bess using scribes. Once she became countess of Shrewsbury in 1568, Bess evidently had ready access to scribes and letters sent from her appeared in a range of scribal hands. Her own hand, by contrast, was reserved for particular kinds of communications. We have seen in the discussion so far examples of Bess using scribes or using her own hand for different occasions, but it is worth reviewing these here before introducing the scribes themselves.

Bess used her own hand for all four of her five of letters to her husband Shrewsbury written during harmonious periods of her marriage and, on the other side of their marital correspondence, his letters to her were also in his own hand except where prevented by illness.[96] It was customary for Tudor husbands and wives to write to each other in their own hands; they did not always do so, but there was an expectation that they would. There were obvious advantages to writing in one's own hand to a spouse and the opportunities for confidentiality – either for business or political purposes, or for reasons of intimacy – were valued by Shrewsbury in his correspondence. Awareness of these expectations was certainly indicated in Bess's final letter in her own hand, of 1587, during her reconciliation with Shrewsbury, where she added a postscript: 'sure swete harte with my bletynge, of late I haue yoused to wryte letyll. with my owne hande but coulde nott now for bayre'.[97] That Bess used a scribe for her letters to Shrewsbury written during their marital discord is itself a marker of the increased distance and the loss of intimacy between the couple. To use one's own hand was a marker of a close relationship and allowed for freer communication between couples.[98] So we see Shrewsbury self-censured and adjusted his usual terms and modes of address to Bess when a third party was involved: rather than his usual

---

96 She subsequently switches to using Scribe A during their acrimonious separation around 1582, but returns to her own hand for one more letter written during their brief enforced reconciliation in April 1587, ID 186.

97 ID 186.

98 Daybell, *Women Letter-Writers*, p. 104.

terms of endearment, such as 'my dear none', 'my jewel' and 'my sweet heart', with which he almost exclusively opened his letters to Bess during the first decade of their marriage, when he used a scribe or asked Gilbert to read his letter, he addressed her as 'Wife'.[99] More generally, letters between family members were more likely to be in a writer's own hand, which marked the closeness of the relationship and allowed for inclusion of content of an intimate or personal nature.[100]

By contrast, for routine business letters, or for more formal letters where there was not a personal relationship between sender and recipient, it was appropriate to use a scribe. In these cases, the presence of an amanuensis functioned to inscribe distance and as a marker of status: to use a scribe was to possess the means to avoid the arduous task of writing routine letters oneself. While Bess used scribes for such routine business letters, she would sometimes add a postscript in her own hand, which functioned to add a personal inflection, to emphasise a particular point made in the letter or to add more intimate information. The situation was rather different when writing on business or political matter to officials, where there was a desire to inscribe bonds of political friendship. Therefore, Bess used her own hand when writing to high-status individuals, especially those who intersected or overlapped with her husband's political networks. These included letters sent to the earl of Leicester, Elizabeth I, Lord Burghley and Sir Francis Walsingham, which often concerned the Scottish Queen or Arbella's entitlements. We also see that Bess used her own hand to add postscripts to her husband's letters to these individuals, which functioned to cultivate her own networks as well as to enhance the personal nature and bonds of friendship in her husband's letter – another example of the way in which their dual epistolary activities were mutually advantageous. That it was usual or expected that she would use her own hand in these cases was indicated by her comment in the scribal letter of 1582 to Burghley which beseeched him to 'pardon me for that I am not able nowe to wryte to your Lordship with my owne hande'.[101] Evidently, Bess judged it important to write in her own hand in these letters to officials, partly for security purposes and partly for interpersonal reasons. That is, choice of handwriting constituted another layer of the language of political friendship and social courtesy, and was one of the

99 11 September and 10 October 1580, IDs 154 and 79.
100 Daybell, *Women Letter-Writers*, pp. 102–4, observes that family letters are more likely to be holograph and gives a range of examples from the period to show that 'the more personal and intimate the relationship between sender and recipient, the more likely it was for a letter to be personally written'.
101 Examples of business letters in the hands of scribes, letters of political friendship to Court contacts, Bess and Shrewsbury adding postscripts to each other's letters, and Bess's apology to Burghley for not writing in her own hand are all discussed in section 1.1, and examples are given as Plates 10, 14, 16 and 18. Daybell, *Women Letter-Writers*, p. 108, discusses autograph writing and the 'bonds of political friendship'.

122 Reading and writing letters

ways in which we find that the boundary is blurred between visual/material and linguistic in early modern letters.

As countess of Shrewsbury, then, Bess used her holograph hand when writing to her husband the earl, or to his powerful Court circle of political contacts when there was a need for security reasons or to show a particular level of respect. This practice contrasted with her remaining letters written from the period of her separation from Shrewsbury around 1582 through to her death in 1608. Apart from the one letter (already mentioned, written during her temporary reconciliation with Shrewsbury in 1587), none of these letters was in her own hand. It is a pattern that may be a result of archival survival; however, given that there are over sixty scribal letters extant after 1582, it seems reasonable to suggest that there may well have been a shift towards scribes around about this time. It is possible that by this stage in her life, when she aged from her sixties to her eighties, Bess was having eyesight problems and that it was this factor, more than anything else, that motivated her decision to use scribes. However, we know that she could write competently until her death and that she was authorising her Account Books and letters with her signature, annotations and postscripts well into the 1600s. This is to say, it seems that her ability to write herself was always there, but was something to be kept in reserve and called on only if absolutely required. To put it another way: when married to Shrewsbury, and during the keeping of Mary, Queen of Scots, there were repeated occasions when only her holograph hand would do, both for her husband and for herself. But once separated from Shrewsbury, and as dowager countess, most of her correspondence could be sent with only her signature as authorisation.

As dowager countess, one of the advantages of using scribes would have been time and efficiency if we bear in mind she was running the equivalent of a large business empire. As we have seen, Bess's personal spelling system was less regularised than those of most of her scribes, which, in itself, would make writing more laborious. Evans has made this point in relation to Elizabeth I: when Elizabeth came to the throne she switched from a varied to a more regularised personal spelling system, probably because it was much more efficient given the volume of her correspondence.[102] Bess's use of scribes may have been for similar reasons of efficiency. While this was so, we also need to consider local factors at particular moments, which related not only to the use of a scribe but also to the choice of scribe. In some cases, the choice of scribe could be determined by the need for particular rhetorical,

---

102 *The Language*, pp. 191–98. It is worth emphasising Evans's observation that, while Elizabeth I's spelling became more consistent, a number of the fixed forms were quite distinct from those of her administrators and courtiers, a demarcation that was perhaps consciously retained as a kind of prestige marker. Daybell, *Women Letter-Writers*, p. 102, surveys the letters of petition women sent to Julius Caesar 1582–1603, two thirds of which were in the hands of secretaries, by contrast with family letters, which were far more likely to be in a woman's own hand.

legal or technical skills. In others, the choice of scribe could be determined by style of handwriting, and the need to create distance or formality rather than the intimacy of her autograph hand. In other cases again, the choice of scribe might be determined by issues of security, privacy or trust according to the content of a letter. While it is not possible here to propose any sort of rigid typology, it is appropriate to provide some illustrative examples and these point to certain trends in Bess's use of scribes during the years from the 1550s to 1608. These trends correlate with and are determined by the various stages in her life and her relationships with her husbands and, in many ways, define these different eras.

Bess's use of two scribes who wrote in italic scripts (1560 and 1570s)

As the discussion so far has indicated, Bess made use of scribes whose writing was distinguishable from her own in its palaeographic forms and spelling features. But it is important to emphasise that Bess used a range of scribes during her life, themselves of varying levels of proficiency and competency. That is, not all her scribes were equal in their level of literate proficiency and it is worth comparing two of her italic-hand scribes as an illustration. From around 1560, when Bess was Lady St Loe, exists an entirely scribal letter sent from Court to her servant James Crompe at Chatsworth. The letter, as has been discussed in section 1.1, was evidently dictated verbatim to the scribe. The handwriting, while similar in some respects to Bess's own, such as duct, can be distinguished by visual features (that include allographs and punctuation) as well as by a comparison of spelling forms:

Item	Bess's usual spelling	Spelling of the letter to Crompe
CHATSWORTH	\<Chattysworth(e)>	\<chattesworth>
LITTLE	\<letyll>	\<letell>
MUCH	\<meche>	\<muche> (2x)
THINK	\<thynke>	\<thenke>
VERY	\<uary, vary>	\<very>
WHICH	\<whyche>	\<weche>
WILL	\<wyll>	\<well, wyll> (3x each) \<wyl> (1x)
WOULD	\<wolde>	\<would(e)>

This scribe's writing is also distinguishable from Bess's own by the rudimentary quality of penmanship – that is, from the unevenness of line spacing, letter sizes and pen pressure, as well as the overall stilted appearance of the hand. It is possible that the scribe was an attendant, perhaps a young one, based on the penmanship, or perhaps one of Bess's children: in 1560 she had a daughter and three sons aged between seven and twelve years

124 Reading and writing letters

old. It is also possible that the use of this scribe was exceptional for some reason, although the use of an italic-hand scribe was not, in itself, unusual. There are other italic hands, such as the only other entirely scribal letter, this time from the period of Bess's marriage to Shrewsbury and written from Chatsworth. The letter reprimanded Lord Thomas Paget for persuading her son Henry to negotiate an agreement with 'the boses' and asked him to take Henry's side.[103] The entire letter was written in a scribe's hand, including the signature, which differed from Bess's own both in both palaeography and spelling: <E Shrowesburye> compared to Bess's own <EShrouesbury>. The letter was carefully written by a proficient hand and has neat clubbed ascenders and flourished calligraphic features.

These two letters in italic hands are unique among all of the letters Bess sent for being entirely scribal sent letters (i.e., including the subscriptions and signatures), but they are otherwise rather different from one another: one gives instructions to a servant, whereas the other deals with business matters, and one is penned by a novice-looking scribe to whom Bess dictates, whereas the other is attractively written and well executed. We do not know the identity of either scribe. However, these two letters serve as a reminder that we should not rule out women and girls as being used by Bess as scribes. These two were not necessarily penned by female scribes; it is just that men and women, or boys and girls, are equally likely candidates here. There is no doubt that Bess certainly did use female scribes for some letters as her husband Shrewsbury referred to having received 'your lettar of your gyrrelles hande' (8 August 1574).[104] That is, he specified a letter in 'your girl's hand', which was certainly a reference to handwriting rather than delivery.[105] Furthermore, we can observe that at Chatsworth by 1601 the 'Closet to the maydes Chamber' (i.e., the maid's chamber off Bess's own bedchamber at Chatsworth) was a site for writing as it contained 'a Desk with tills' (tills being boxes or caskets for secure keeping of valuables or documents).[106] That Bess used female scribes should not seem especially surprising. There are other examples of contemporary women using female relatives and companions as amanuenses; among others, lady-in-waiting Mistress Blanche Parry, for example, was known to have drawn

---

103 1570s, Keele UL, Paget Papers, MS 10, fols 43–44, ID 210.

104 ID 73.

105 That is, based on the phraseology. For example, among the letters already discussed is that in which Bess referred to Arbella's Declaration as being 'sett down with hir owne hand' (ID 130) and another in which Bess asked her 'jewel' (the term Bess commonly used for Arbella and other children and grandchildren) to write out two letters 'with your owne hand' (ID 175).

106 *OED* till, *n.1*, 1 'A small box, casket, or closed compartment, contained within or forming part of a larger box, chest, or cabinet; sometimes one that could be lifted out, sometimes a drawer in a cabinet or chest of drawers; used for keeping valuables, documents, etc., more safely.'

Reading and writing letters 125

up inventories of Elizabeth I's jewels.[107] It is an example that suggests we should extend the possibility that Bess used female amanuenses to include the various scribes who, in italic hands of differing qualities, added entries to Bess's numerous Account Books and inventories. To build on the picture in a meaningful way would require more details about the identity and biography of these individuals. But the impression gained from the letters and accounts allows us to speculate that Bess had no qualms about using available members of her inner circle of attendants for scribal tasks, men and women, *ad hoc* and as required.

Bess's use of the Sheffield secretariat before 1583

Bess's marriage to the earl of Shrewsbury in 1567 brought not only wealth and powerful networks but also a greater abundance of resources, not least among which were professional scribes. It is illustrative, for example, to review Bess's letters to Sir John Thynne, which spanned the period of three of her marriages and therefore allow us to track her social progress during the decade up to 1567. Her first four letters were all written in the 1550s, when she was Lady and then widow Cavendish, and were in her own hand. In them we find Bess offering thanks or appealing to Thynne to ask for his support in a case in parliament. However, by the time of her next letter, of 25 April 1560, she had become Lady St Loe and the letter was in the secretary hand of a professional scribe. Here again we find Bess asking for Thynne's help: this time, requesting the loan of his plasterer for her building works. Her final letter to Thynne is the earliest dated letter we have from Bess after she became countess of Shrewsbury: written from Sheffield on 27 August 1567, in the secretary hand of another professional scribe, it informed Thynne that she had been unsuccessful in interceding with her husband Shrewsbury to grant Thynne's suit. By 1567, then, it was Thynne who was approaching Bess to call in favours. That we find Bess writing from her powerful husband's seat at Sheffield, using one of his hired scribes there and presenting Thynne's suits to the earl, shows Bess benefiting from her husband's epistolary networks at a number of levels.

From her marriage to Shrewsbury in 1567 up until their acrimonious separation in 1582 we regularly find Bess using secretary-hand scribes from Shrewsbury's castle and manor at Sheffield.[108] Over these fifteen years we can identify seven more existing letters written from Sheffield in various

---

107 Doran, *Elizabeth*, p. 107. Daybell gives various examples of women acting as secretaries, who included Kat Ashley; *Women Letter-Writers*, pp. 73–74. North, 'Household Scribes', tracks the roles of literate servants in copying literary manuscripts.

108 There were other professional secretary-hand scribes used by Bess to write letters from different locations too, such as the one written to Sir Francis Walsingham on 8 June 1576 from Leicester House (ID 234). See also ID 157 and 175 from Chatsworth in 1568? and 1582; and ID 102 from Chatsworth in 1594.

126 *Reading and writing letters*

secretary hands that all dealt with routine business matters. Bess wrote to Thomas Paget regarding accusations against her servants; to Thomas Paget and Gilbert Talbot about a proposed marriage between her son Charles and Margaret Kitson; and to Burghley and Walsingham regarding Arbella's portion.[109] There is no doubt that Bess's marriage to Shrewsbury opened up epistolary networks and resources and one further letter from Bess illustrates the point. Again written from Sheffield in a secretary script by a hired scribe, this letter was to Shrewsbury's London agent Thomas Baldwin to ask him to conduct business on her behalf. At the end of the letter were written three autograph postscripts, two by Shrewsbury and one by Bess, adding further authority to the content of the letter, as well as a further request from Shrewsbury (to 'send a pott of grene iengar in siroppe that is very good for my self').[110] It reminds us that Bess's use of servants, networks and scribes overlapped with those of her husband Shrewsbury, and that she benefitted from regular access to the earl's secretariat.[111]

Bess's use of 'Scribe A' after 1583

Dramatic changes occurred in Bess's life after her separation from Shrewsbury sometime in the spring of 1583. During the seven-and-a-half-year period that followed, up to Shrewsbury's death in November 1590, he refused to admit Bess into his presence for extended stretches of time. Unsurprisingly, there are no letters from the Sheffield secretariat from this period, and in fact there is no evidence that Bess was ever permitted to return to Sheffield Castle or Sheffield Manor again during Shrewsbury's lifetime. From this era of estrangement we have one autograph letter from Bess and one unsent scribal draft, but the remaining total of eleven letters Bess sent were all written in the italic hand of one scribe, designated here as 'Scribe A' (Plates 15, 21 and 22).[112] On a superficial glance there are similarities in duct and aspect between Bess's autograph hand and that of Scribe A, such as might easily lead to confusion between them. However, examination reveals consistent and distinctive allographs (e.g., Scribe A's dotted <h>), punctuation (e.g., Scribe A's <wth> compared to Bess's <w^r>, and Scribe A's wider repertoire of punctuation marks) and spelling systems that allow the two hands to be

---

109 IDs 103, 227, 228, 104, 144, 162 and 105.

110 This letter can be compared to two from Shrewsbury to Baldwin to which Bess added autograph postscripts: ID 193, 28 December 1578, Shrewsbury to Baldwin regarding Bess's business matters, scribal; ID 195, 8 February 1582, from Sheffield, Shrewsbury sends instructions to Baldwin.

111 It seems, from preliminary examination of the Shrewsbury and Talbot Papers at Lambeth Palace Library, that these scribes formed an efficient secretariat at Sheffield Castle and Sheffield Manor and it is a topic that would reward further investigation.

112 The autograph letter is ID 186 and the scribal draft is ID 176.

readily distinguished from one another. Some examples of their spelling differences include the following:[113]

Item	Bess's usual spelling	Scribe A
ANSWER	<ansore->types 4x	<answe(a)re> 2x
CHATSWORTH	<Chattysworth(e)> 9x	<Chatsworth> 1x
DAUGHTER	<dowter>-types 7x	<daught(a/e)r> 13x
DOUBT	<dowte> 3x	<doubte>-types 3x
		<dout> 1x
FROM	<frome> 16x	<from> 19x
	<frome> 2x	<from> 2x
-FULL(Y)	<-foull(e)> 7x	<-full>-types 12x
		<-full(e)> 5x
LETTER	<lat(t)er(s)> 11x	<letter(s)> 8x <leter(s)> 2x <lettar> 3x
LITTLE	<letyll> 13x	<lettell> 4x
MUCH	<meche> 13x	<much> 5x
SUBJECT	<subgett> 2x	<sub(i/y)ect(es)> 3x
WOULD	<wol(l)d(e)> 19x	<would(e)> 8x

There were eleven letters penned by Scribe A during the three-and-a-half-year period from 6 April 1584 to 6 October 1587: three were to Shrewsbury to protest her innocence and defend herself against his accusations; six were to Burghley and Walsingham to ask for their support with regard to her dispute with her husband and his refusal to reconcile or provide her with provisions or shelter; and the remaining two were short notes to her daughter Mary (Cavendish) Talbot. As a group they are remarkable among Bess's letters because they were written during a period when she was under intense pressure as a writer: she was required to compose counter-narratives to those of her husband, which were under public scrutiny as their marriage breakdown became a political issue. Written during the heat of their marriage collapse, her three letters to Shrewsbury were very well articulated and in them she attempted to portray herself as the ideal Renaissance wife, patient, obedient and dutiful: a Penelope figure, waiting and wanting to be reconciled with her husband. In her letters to Burghley and Walsingham she drew on petitionary strategies to make her case for support. The rhetorical features of these letters, as well as the public nature of ostensibly private letters, have been discussed in section 1.3, but of interest here is her choice of a scribe. We do not know for sure whether the use of Scribe A represented Bess's preferred choice, or Scribe A just happened to be conveniently at

---

113 ID 107 (Plate 10) has been excluded here, for the reasons discussed earlier; it includes the anomalous forms <answere> 2x, <ffrom> 1x and <muche> 1x.

128 *Reading and writing letters*

hand, or, indeed, was the only person available. But there are a number of reasons why Scribe A might have been Bess's scribe of preference. The similarity between Bess's own hand and Scribe A's hand could have had obvious potential advantages from Bess's point of view, if recipients of her letters were not able to distinguish between them.[114] That is, if her correspondents routinely took Scribe A's hand to be Bess's own, that would allow her the opportunity of using a scribe while appearing to be writing herself (thus gaining the interpersonal benefits of manually penning one's own letters while avoiding the arduous task of actually doing so).[115]

Another reason for preferring Scribe A may have been trust and confidentiality. We know of the examples of secretaries to the countess of Lennox and the Scottish Queen, who had roles as political confidants.[116] Given that Scribe A pens letters for Bess when so much is at stake, we may reasonably expect there to have been a close and confidential relationship between mistress and scribe. Another question is whether Scribe A was involved in shaping the form, content and language of these letters or, alternatively, Scribe A's role was that of a silent amanuensis. We might think of the example of Hannah Wolly acting as a scribe for her mistress, who went to 'great pains' in order to represent her mistress well and used her skills carefully to shape her letters.[117] There is no doubt that Bess's letters written during this period were carefully crafted and that the exact wording was thoughtfully and scrupulously managed.[118] However, there are reasons why we cannot automatically assume Scribe A's role in the compositional process. In particular, we must acknowledge the existence of two unsent scribal drafts of letters

114 That this was the case – that Bess's recipients would find her hand indistinguishable from that of Scribe A – may be suggested by her two letters to Lord Burghley in 1582, one in the hand of a secretary-script scribe and the other in the hand of Scribe A. Out of politeness Bess apologises to Burghley for using a scribe in the secretary-script letter, but she does not do so in the letter penned by Scribe A. Discussed earlier in section 1.2. On the other hand, it seems that Shrewsbury was able to distinguish between Scribe A and Bess's own hand, given Bess's comment in ID 186 that she is writing in her own hand now but is sorry not to have done so recently – apparently referring to Scribe A's letters to Shrewsbury penned during their marital dispute.

115 The tricks played in *As You Like It* and *Twelfth Night* rely upon characters not being able to distinguish between women's hands: Rosalind recognises Phoebe's hand herself but seeks to convince Silvius otherwise, and Maria impersonates her mistress's handwriting in order to dupe Malvolio. Daybell discusses these fictional examples alongside the case of Anne, countess of Warwick, who was able to differentiate between letters from Robert Cecil in his own hand and that of a secretary; *Women Letter-Writers*, pp. 70–71.

116 The countess of Lennox's secretary, Thomas Fowler, was interrogated after the clandestine marriage of Elizabeth Cavendish and the countess's son Charles Stuart, earl of Lennox; Mary Queen of Scots's secretaries Gilbert Curle and Claud Nau were examined because of their roles as political confidants; Daybell, *Women Letter-Writers*, pp. 72–75.

117 Daybell, *Women Letter-Writers*, pp. 72–75.

118 Discussed in section 1.3.

Reading and writing letters 129

from the 1580s, both in secretary-script hands: one to Thomas Cornwallis in July 1582, the other to Bess's estranged husband Shrewsbury in June 1586.[119] The letter to Cornwallis includes a note from Bess in the hand of Scribe A saying 'good jewel take pains to write out these in your own hand'; that is, the note suggests that the sent version of this letter (which no longer exists) was copied out from the draft by a second scribe. As the note refers to the second scribe as her 'jewel' (an affectionate term Bess reserved for close family members and used elsewhere for individuals who included her husband, children and grandchildren), this suggests this second scribe was one of her intimate circle. The other letters we have from Bess to Cornwallis and to her husband during this period are sent letters that are in the hand of Scribe A. We can therefore conceive of a production economy whereby a draft letter was crafted by Bess with a male collaborator (in a secretary script) and then copied out by one of her inner circle, such as Scribe A (in an italic script). We can rule out the possibility that the copies we have in secretary scripts were made later by secretaries for record-keeping purposes, given that these letters contain the kinds of reworkings and revisions to wording that we would expect of a draft rather than an administrative copy. These revisions include: 'vexation of ~~spiritt~~ ^mynde^ thorrow conceyte of a dutyfull [*deletion*] ^unkyndnes^', 'yor ~~greate~~ grief', '~~vse hym~~ dele wth hym' and '~~any~~ ^one^ of my owne'. While the precise contribution of Scribe A, then, cannot be determined, we are reminded of the layered nature of the process of epistolary composition and production.

One thing is for sure: Bess had an uncertain and somewhat peripatetic existence during part of the period when Scribe A was penning her letters. Shrewsbury not only denied her access to his own houses but also drove her from her beloved Chatsworth, which he claimed as his own, and had her son William imprisoned in the Fleet. Bess was forced from her home, required to garner support for herself and her children from her connections in London and then, subsequently, ordered by the queen to live at Wingfield in Derbyshire. As a result, the eight letters from Bess where the location is specified were written from seven different locations in just over three years. That is, from 2 August 1584 to 6 October 1587 Bess wrote from: Hardwick in Derbyshire, then her lodgings at Chancery Lane in London, then Wingfield in Derbyshire, then Highgate near London, then from the Court at Richmond Palace, then Chelsea near London and then Wingfield again. Scribe A, who penned all of these letters for Bess, from all of these locations, was, is seems, constantly at Bess's side during these years, despite the numerous moves and the uncertain and fragmented state of Bess's household. While we cannot be sure as to the identity of Scribe A, the travelling involved during this period and Bess's reduced circumstances indicate we must look for this

119 These letters are: 15 July 1582, LPL, Talbot Papers, MS 3198, fol. 172, ID 175; and 9 June 1586, LPL, Talbot Papers, MS 3198, fol. 331r-v, ID 176.

130   *Reading and writing letters*

individual among Bess's inner circle of attendants who were constantly with her. We know that, after the death of Shrewsbury in November 1590, Bess continued to use Scribe A for many years at Hardwick Hall. Immediately following Shrewsbury's death in November 1590, Scribe A was on the scene and penned three letters between December 1590 and April 1591.[120] When Bess's life regained stability and she rebuilt her household and recruited new servants, Scribe A's letters are fewer and farther between, though there are three more from many years later (from 1598, 1601 and 1607), as well as regular entries into the household Account Books for this period.[121] We would therefore certainly expect this individual, Scribe A, to be listed in the wage books and New Year's gift lists for the 1590s.[122] Candidates might include Bess's gentleman attendant George Knyveton, or her gentleman servant John Digby (the husband of Bess's most important female attendant, Elizabeth), who had his own room at Hardwick Old Hall.[123] Alternatively, Scribe A may have been one of Bess's women of the bedchamber, such as Mistresses Cooper, Skypwyth or Lyslye or, as we have seen earlier, Mistresses Digby or Cartwright, who were the highest paid of Bess's servants and rarely far from their mistress's side.

One further candidate should be mentioned here, although she is a more elusive figure in the historical record: Bess's half-sister and lifelong companion Jane (Leach) Kniveton, who we know would act at Bess's representative when Bess was away from the household herself.[124] We know from a passing comment from Gilbert Talbot in 1575 that Jane would sometimes write for Bess: Gilbert told Bess that if 'my cosen Iane will wryte what your Ladyship sent for, we shall sende them'.[125] We do not have this letter that

---

120   IDs 231, 233 and 159. The earliest letters we have in Scribe A's hand are from a couple of years before the split with Shrewsbury: 24 November 1582?, Chatsworth House, Devonshire MSS, ID 204; 6 May 1582, 145; and 7 February 1583, TNA SP 12, ff 160r-160v (item 58), ID 148. The intended recipient of ID 143 is unknown and the letter is discussed in section 1.1.

121   IDs 187, 180 and 179.

122   Chatsworth House, Hardwick MSS 7 and 8.

123   'Mr. Digby's Chamber' contained only a bedstead, trestle board and andiron. The lack of a desk in his chamber does not exclude the possibility he could have been involved in preparing documents: Master Reason had the chamber next to him, which also contained no desk, but we know Reason prepared Bess's rent books. Levey and Thornton, *Of Houshold Stuff*, p. 37 and p. 41.

124   Jane was the daughter of Ralph Leche and Elizabeth, widow of John Hardwick. She was married to, and outlived, Thomas Kniveton of Mercaston and they had one son, Sir William Kniveton. I can identify one letter to Jane at Hardwick sending news from her son William Knyveton, 27 May 1604; Folger Shakespeare Library, Cavendish-Talbot Papers X.d.428 (40).

125   ID 217. We also see Jane receiving letters on Bess's behalf. So, Gilbert noted, 'I wrot[e] . . . passyng ij or iij dayes synce to your Ladyship and was then dryven [to] sende my letter to my Aunte knyveton for yat my selfe . . . not of any messenger to carry hit, so yat vnle[ss] . . . happ she knew how to convey the same' (ID 82). Another example is discussed in section 3.2.

Gilbert mentioned, although we can observe, incidentally, that all the existing letters we have from Bess to Gilbert and Mary were written in the hand of Scribe A. If Jane did pen this letter then it is no longer extant, although we know that she was on the scene well into the seventeenth century as she was consistently mentioned in Bess's Account Books as a recipient of New Year's gifts. Further evidence of her high status within the household can be inferred from her own well-appointed bedchamber at Hardwick New Hall; next to the nursery and below Bess's own bedchamber, it was impressively furnished with darnix hangings and with a bedstead canopy of cloth of gold and mulberry-coloured velvet.[126] Without samples of handwriting from these individuals, in particular from Jane Kniveton, it is difficult to build on these deductions or to pinpoint the identity of Scribe A. Nevertheless, Scribe A remains a figure of compelling interest, although he or she has never once been mentioned by any of Bess's biographers, who may have mistaken the hand as Bess's own. Nevertheless, this individual had a key role as one of Bess's intimates and was a stable presence through her life during periods of both good and bad fortune.

The Hardwick Hall secretariat, 1590–1608

When Shrewsbury died in November 1590 Bess was at liberty to rebuild her household. As the power structures shifted so too did the roles and responsibilities of those in Bess's circle. We know that Scribe A was still available. We also know that Bess was seeking to recruit new secretarial staff as part of the rebuilding of her household, as by 1593 Bess had written to Susan Grey asking her to recommend a clerk to enter her service.[127] However, most important were the two figures who became vital to Bess's epistolary activities after 1590. The first was Bess's favoured second son, William Cavendish, who we know acted as scribe and bearer to his mother, as seen in the letter he penned for her in September 1592:

I am inforced to vse the hand of my sonn William Cavendysshe, not beinge able to wryte so much my self for feare of bringing great payne

---

126 Levey and Thornton, *Of Houshold Stuff*, p. 39 and p. 56, 'Mrs Knyvetons Chamber'. Jane also had her own chambers at Hardwick Old Hall ('Mrs Knyveton's Chamber', close to Bess's bedchamber, William Cavendish's chamber and the nursery) and at Chatsworth House ('Mrs Knyvetons Chamber', again close to Bess's bedchamber); Levey and Thornton, *Of Houshold Stuff*, p. 39 and p. 27. It may be that we should think of Jane Knyveton directing the writing of letters, rather than, or as well as, penning them herself.

127 26 January 1593, Susan Wingfield (née Bertie, dowager countess of Kent, b. c. 1552, d. after 1611) wrote to Bess to say she has not yet heard of 'ani one that is ffite ffor the office of a Clarke'; Folger CT, X.d.428 (38), ID 32.

132   *Reading and writing letters*

to my hed, he only is pryuy to your Lordships letter, & neyther Arbell nor any other lyuinge, nor shalbe.[128]

The letter referred to concerns about plots to trick Bess and kidnap Arbella, or as Bess put it, 'wicked and mischeuous practises . . . deuysed to intrap my pore Arbell & me'. Bess's reassurances to Burghley that only William 'is pryuy to your Lordships letter' indicated shared concerns over security, as well as Bess's absolute trust in William. There were seven letters from 1581 to 1602 in which Bess directly mentioned her use of her son William as bearer and typically these dealt with sensitive negotiations or high-security issues. In each case, the letter functioned to introduce and authorise William's role. To take one example, Bess's letter to Robert Cecil of 18 January 1602 served to introduce 'my sonne this bearer' who had 'come vp to attend your pleasure in some matters touching Master Thomas Gerrard who hath exhibited a complaint to her Maiestie'.[129] As is apparent from this and other letters, while Bess was reliant upon William, he was acting on his mother's behalf and for her benefit (rather than under his own initiative).[130] Bess's faith in William allowed her to utilise him in the role of negotiator at Court, for which he possessed the required combination of legal and diplomatic skills. It was a mother–son alliance that defined many of Bess's high-level epistolary transactions, especially during this later period of her life.

The other important figure, who had appeared on the scene by 1591 and who was to become Bess's main source of secretarial support, was Timothy Pusey, almost always referred to in the records simply as 'Timothy'.[131] He was perhaps in his early or mid-twenties in 1591 when he joined Bess's service, given that by this point he already had high-level legal training but did not die until the time of the Civil War.[132] He was ambitious and by the end of his life had become a very successful man. Paul Hammer has shown the opportunities that the appointment as secretary could offer a man and the

---

128 Bess (dowager countess of Shrewsbury) writes to Lord Burghley, 21 September 1592, ID 163. Other examples of sons penning letters for their mothers, or other family members for each other, are given by Daybell, *Women Letter-Writers*, p. 75.

129 ID 139.

130 William is mentioned acting as bearer or delegate for his mother Bess (countess and then dowager countess of Shrewsbury) in the following letters: 28 January 1582, ID 144; 6 October 1587, TNA SP 12/207, f 44 (item 31), ID 156; 6 October 1600, CP 250/16, ID 126; 2 June 1600, CP 80/9, ID 125; 18 June c. 1600?, ID 6; and 18 January 1603, ID 139.

131 There is no mention of Timothy Pusey in the 1584 notebook of accounts kept in Bess's own hand (Chatsworth House, Hardwick MS 5). On the wages paid to Pusey see Durant, *Bess of Hardwick*, p. 183.

132 Durant tracks the progress of Pusey's successful career: after Bess died Pusey stayed on and, when he left William Cavendish's service, 'married a daughter of John Clay of Crich, another of Bess's occasional servants . . . bought Selston Manor, was a justice for Nottinghamshire for over twenty years, and Sheriff of the County in 1625'; *Bess of Hardwick*, p. 184.

Reading and writing letters 133

social horizons it opened up: this certainly seems to have been the case for Timothy, whose life after his time with Bess saw him as a landowner and a stalwart of midlands communities.[133] Once he started working for Bess he quickly proved himself to be indispensable, to the extent that he became her right-hand man in business matters for more than fifteen years, up to her death in 1608. By 1601 he had his own very comfortable-sounding room at Chatsworth, itself an indication of his status within the household.[134] By tracking Timothy's distinctive and scrupulously neat secretary hand through the letters (Plate 17), Account Books and other documents, a striking impression emerges of his intimate knowledge of all aspects of the businesses.[135] It is worth profiling his various roles here, in order to make clear his areas of skill as well as the level of trust Bess had invested in him.

On the one hand, Timothy was involved day-to-day in running the businesses, which included keeping accounts, such as checking and totalling the household expenses recorded by Roland Harrison, as well as receipt of large sums of money and calculation of expenditure and receipts. Timothy would take in money for rents and industrial works from individuals such as William Reason; he would then pass this to Bess, who would check and authorise the accounts and secrete the money in one of her locked security chests in her bedchamber. In addition to these tasks, Timothy had a key role in legal matters that included the drafting of indentures and complaints, as well as seeing though cases and taking every possible measure to ensure success. To give one example: during Bess's trip to London in 1591, Timothy collaborated extensively with Bess's London solicitor Edward Whalley in order to prevent Gilbert Talbot, the newly installed seventh earl of Shrewsbury, from bringing the case over the will of his father (Bess's deceased husband, Shrewsbury) to London. They employed the tactics that Shrewsbury had previously used against Bess: effectively, and at large expense (£430), they paid off every single attorney and sergeant in London, so as to make it

133 Hammer, 'The Earl of Essex, Fulke Greville and the Employment of Scholars'. PROB 11/202, fols 340r-v, will of Timothy Pusey.

134 In 'tymes Chamber' (*Tim's Chamber*) were five tapestry wall-hangings depicting the Old Testament story of Solomon – an archetype for wise justice and therefore a seemingly appropriate choice of subject for Bess's legal advisor – a cupboard, an inlaid table, six carpets, a long board with a green cloth carpet, two stools, a 'forme' (bench) covered with purple cloth 'garded' (trimmed) with velvet, and a velvet cushion embroidered with gold; Levey and Thornton, *Of Houshold Stuff*, p. 25 and p. 32. As there was no bedstead, it seems this was a room for working (for receiving visitors and preparing documents) and that Timothy slept elsewhere when he was at Chatsworth, presumably in one of the various rooms called 'the Servantes chamber' or one of the 'other' chambers that contained bedsteads, chamber pots and pallets, and could have accommodated one or more servants, pp. 24–27 and p. 31.

135 We have examples of Pusey's signature, such as in Bess's will and in the letter he verifies as a witness 'vera copia ex *per* Tymothie Pusey / Ro: Parker'; Gilbert Talbot to Thomas Smethwicke, 27 July 1604, Folger CT, X.d.428 (117).

134 *Reading and writing letters*

impossible for Gilbert to find anyone to present his case. Surely and systematically, they closed every loophole to Gilbert. Bess had learned from past experience, and through Timothy and Whalley ensured her own and her children's entitlement to her many properties was secure.[136] In subsequent years, it was Bess's astute practical understanding of the law that allowed her to consolidate her wealth and secure the inheritance of her children. She had legal advisors and strategists placed in different regions, such as John Hacker of East Bridgford and George Chaworth of Annesley in Nottinghamshire, but at the centre of all these dealings was Timothy.[137]

In addition to these accounting and legal roles, Timothy acted as scribe for letters from Bess. He was not the only scribe employed in this capacity and, typically, when he penned a letter he was not the only scribe involved. The working patterns suggest the sort of collaboration that would be expected of a secretariat with allocated roles. To be specific: we have fifteen letters that together infer, at least by the early 1600s when Bess was installed at Hardwick New Hall, the existence of something resembling a formal professionalised secretariat under Bess's command. All fifteen of these letters were copied at Hardwick Hall by three scribes: Timothy and two others, here designated as 'Scribe B' and 'Scribe D'. We do not know their identities. Scribe D wrote in an extremely neat, professional-looking secretary hand that indicates a trained clerk, perhaps one of the men recorded in the wage lists. Scribe B wrote in an elegant and assured italic hand that could have been produced by the pen of any one of Bess's higher gentleman or gentlewoman servants. Possible candidates include individuals from among Bess's inner circle recorded in the wage lists and New Year's gift lists at Hardwick after 1590 (i.e., those already discussed earlier in relation to Scribe A). For now their identities and biographies remain unknown. Nonetheless, it is rewarding to outline the roles of these scribes in more detail here, as they provide insights into the processes of epistolary production at Hardwick Hall.

In 1603 Timothy copied a total of seven letters from Bess to Queen Elizabeth, Robert Cecil and Sir John Stanhope. Scribe B added the subscriptions to six of these (only one being subscribed by Timothy himself), although Timothy added the superscriptions and, in one case, a postscript.[138] That is

---

136 The full account of these legal dealings, paraphrased and summarised here, is in Durant, *Bess of Hardwick*, pp. 168–74.

137 Durant, *Bess of Hardwick*, p. 184, describes in full the 'mysterious comings and goings' of John Hacker and the advisory role of Bess's kinsman George Chaworth; see p. 189 for Pusey's involvement in a rigged Derbyshire jury.

138 That is, for IDs 129, 131, 134 and 135 Timothy copied the letter and superscription and Scribe B copied the subscription; for CP 135/150, fols 195–6, ID 132, Timothy copied the letter, postscript and superscription and Scribe B copied the subscription; for ID 130 (which was sent and endorsed but has no superscription on the address leaf) Timothy copied the letter and Scribe B the subscription; and for ID 140 Timothy copied the letter,

Reading and writing letters   135

to say, once a fair copy of a letter had been penned by Timothy, it was then either subscribed by himself or, more usually, passed to Scribe B to be subscribed, before being handed to Bess to add her own autograph signature, and then returned again to Timothy for postscription and/or superscribing (Plate 17). The distinct changes in ink colour and thickness of stroke between the different parts of these letters attest to changes of pen between these stages – that is, of the kind that may imply gaps of time and location and that suggest we should not envisage Bess, Timothy and Scribe B sitting down together in one room. Rather, the system involved a workflow comprising a series of distinct stages. Bess first formulated a draft with a scribe, presumably Timothy here, either by dictation or by giving more general directions (perhaps orally) as to the type and theme of letter required. Timothy would then produce the fair copy. This fair copy was subsequently passed to Scribe B to be checked and subscribed, before being passed to Bess for final authorisation and her autograph signature. The final version was then returned to Timothy for superscription and dispatch, and postscription if necessary. It is a model familiar from elsewhere among Bess's contemporaries and outlined in detail by Christopher Burlinson and Andrew Zurcher in their analysis of Edmund Spenser's role in Lord Grey's secretariat. As Burlinson and Zurcher observe, for Grey's letter-writing there could be up to six stages with various hand-to-hand exchanges in between: draft, fair copy, subscription, signature, superscription, dispatch. Bess, it seems, was very much applying, within her household, a tried and tested model that was also deployed by her male contemporaries, such as Lord Grey.

There are three more letters from the same period where we find this model applied but where Scribe D, rather than Timothy, was the main scribe who also added the superscription (Plate 18 and cover image).[139] In each case the subscription, as before, was added in the assured italic hand of Scribe B. In addition, and as well as subscribing this total of nine letters by Timothy and Scribe D, there were at least three occasions where Scribe B copied the main part of the letter and, in some cases, also the subscription and/or superscription.[140] That is to say, the extant letters suggest a leading role for Scribe B as he or she was the only scribe who subscribed both his or

---

subscription and superscription. He had also subscribed for himself the one earlier letter we have penned by him, from 1594, ID 1.

139 These are IDs 127, 139 and 161 (Plate 18 and cover image), written in 1601, 1603 and 1604.

140 That is, for ID 126 Scribe B copied the main letter and subscription and another, unknown secretary hand, copied the superscription; for ID 121 Scribe B copied the main letter and superscription and Bess subscribed; for IDs 124 and 125 Scribe B copied the main letter, subscription and superscription. It also seems to be Scribe B who added the subscription to ID 128. Incidentally, it seems that the scribe who wrote the subscription may also have folded and sealed the letter, based on the differences in folding patters between letters superscribed by Timothy, Scribe B and Scribe D.

136   *Reading and writing letters*

her own letters and those of other scribes. Therefore, while we have only a relatively modest total portion of writing for Scribe B (four letters and nine subscriptions), we should be careful not to dismiss the potential importance of the role of this individual for Bess's later letter-writing. Burlinson and Zurcher's conclusion that Spenser was 'chief secretary' within Grey's secretariat was drawn largely from the fact that Spenser was often responsible for subscribing the letters of other scribes. It is a task that implies a responsible or managerial role, which included liaison with the sender, by comparison with the drudge-work of copying the main letter.

In order to reflect further on the roles of these scribes, it is worth making a comparison with other contemporary documents within the household. Across the Account Books, as we have seen, Timothy's role was to manage and co-ordinate the various accounts. Men such as William Reason and Roland Harrison did have responsible roles, but these were lower down the pyramid and involved routine collecting and compiling, whereas Timothy would bring in the calculations of men like Reason and Harrison, check and re-total their amounts, and then take these to Bess for final authorisation and signature. That is to say, when it came to the Account Books, Timothy was the man immediately below Bess and her 'chief secretary' in this department. However, based on the extant letters, epistolary transactions seem to have involved a slightly different personnel structure. Timothy still often had a key role as he wrote the main body of letters dealing with high-security or sensitive issues, and was trusted to check and subscribe his own letters. Scribe D was sometimes employed to write Bess's letters, though is not found to subscribe the two letters we have. By contrast, Scribe B seems to have had a role equal or above both of these: one that included copying and subscribing his or her own letters, but also subscribing the letters of Timothy and Scribe D. Given what we know of Timothy's role it would be difficult to argue that he was subordinate to Scribe B in some way. It seems more likely that both scribes ranked at the top of Bess's hierarchy of trust, but that Scribe B took the lead when it came to Bess's letter-writing. Perhaps this division of responsibility is understandable, given how busy Timothy must have been and his frequent excursions on legal, business and purchasing matters.

In summary, the letters from Bess were written in a range of scribal hands and tracking these reminds us of, and provides us with evidence for, letter-writing as a collaborative processes. It reminds us that letters were multilayered sources and that, certainly in the case of Bess's letters, it is not enough simply to distinguish between 'scribal' and 'autograph' writing. Wherever possible, we must consider the identity of the scribe, his or her relationship with Bess and his or her own language and palaeography. The linguistic form and structure of Bess's letters were determined by the scribe: their language was mediated in different ways depending on the particular scribe and the nature of his or her own language. The contents of the letter were also determined by the scribe: only the most trusted scribes would be permitted access to the

Reading and writing letters   137

most sensitive or secure information, whether political, intimate or legal. In a number of cases, Bess used scribes who were part of her inner circle, or close family members. The level of trust and intimacy and the personalised nature of the role of scribe related to what could or could not be said in a letter. Fuller acknowledgement and understanding of the roles of scribes bring us much closer to the conditions and circumstances within which early modern letters were produced and received.

2.4   Letters from 'the palace of the sky': Bess of Hardwick's signature

Hic locus est quem si verbis audatia detur haud timeam magni dixisse Palatia caeli.
This is the place which, if boldness were given to my utterance, I should not hesitate to call the palace of the sky.

Ovid, *Metamorphoses*, Book 1, lines 175–76

This piece of Latin graffiti was carved onto one of the columns near the front entrance of Hardwick New Hall around 1600. As Durant observes, the content and style of elongated italic writing indicate that it was 'obviously put there by an educated hand'.[141] It was a quotation that greeted callers arriving at Hardwick New Hall around 1600 in an entirely appropriate way. As a literary, humanistic reference it heralded the entrance to Hardwick New Hall as a cultural centre, a palace of the finest learning, art, architecture, drama and music. At the same time it directed the eyes of the visitor upwards, skyward. There the visitor would see the building's striking silhouette, the most distinctive feature of which were the 'ES' ciphers emblazoned against the sky, flagging the top of the building and multiplied around the turrets (Plates 3 and 4). These letters, carved against the sky, make it absolutely clear that by the time Bess built Hardwick New Hall she was in full control of the iconographic schemes through which she chose to represent herself to the world. It was the apotheosis of an iconography Bess had been developing ever since her marriage to Shrewsbury in 1567. It reminds us that we should think again about Bess's very distinctive signature and what it meant to receive a letter signed by her hand. By 1600, as we have seen, the main function for writing in Bess's autograph hand was signing. Scribes of various kinds were employed for more onerous writing tasks, but when it came to signing, Bess's autograph hand was essential and she reproduced her signature on many types of documents, literally hundreds of times, between 1590 and 1608. This concluding section reviews the form and function of Bess's signature as an aspect of her letter-writing that deserves particular attention.

141 Durant, *The Smythson Circle*, pp. 144–45.

138   *Reading and writing letters*

Bess's signature changed its form throughout her life. These changes were as a result of her various marriages (something that makes archival research more challenging), but we also find changes in her attitude towards her signature over time. We do not have any letters or examples of Bess's signature from the period before she was married or during her first marriage, to Robert Barlow. However, there are several examples of Bess signing her name in her own hand in letters written during her second and third marriages, to Sir William Cavendish and Sir William St Loe. These examples show different forms of her name each time and therefore display Bess's impartiality and indifference as to which combination of spelling and execution was preferable:

Elyzabethe Cauendyssh
Elyzabeth Cauendyssh
E Cauendyssh
Elyzabeth ~~Cauendyssh~~ ^Seyntlo^
E Seyntlo
Elezabeth Seyntloo

At this stage, as we can see from these signatures, Bess had made no decision over whether she preferred the full form of her first name or the initial 'E'. In addition, while the spelling of 'Cauendyssh' is stable in these instances, there is variation between 'Seyntlo' and 'Seyntloo' and in one case the two names are confused. While it might appear to us to be an embarrassing error, it seems not to have been sufficiently embarrassing to go to the trouble of starting the letter again: the letter was sent to Thynne as it was and is still there at Longleat House today. These variations and instabilities in Bess's signature during the first half of her life are not especially surprising; rather they are very much of their time.[142] Far more remarkable is the change that occurred when she married her fourth husband.

All such instability and indifference ceased in 1567 when Bess married George Talbot, sixth earl of Shrewsbury, and became countess of Shrewsbury and then in 1590 dowager countess. Throughout this period she was highly consistent in how she signed her name, which appeared more than sixty times in the letters, always as (Plates 10, 13, 15, 16, 17, 18, 21 and 22):

EShrouesbury

There is one exception but it is an unequivocal error, whereby <ou> had been accidentally written twice: <EShrououesbury>.[143] The conclusion is

---

142 A well-known example is Shakespeare's name, for which more than fifty spellings are known from the early modern period.

143 ID 190.

that as countess Bess's signature was extremely stable and it was also how she signed off other documents, of which there are numerous examples in the hundreds of pages of books of accounts, inventories, wages and rents received. Her signature did not vary between these different types of documents. Nor did it vary in the letters when writing to different correspondents: the form was <EShrouesbury> whether she was writing to her husband, Lord Burghley, a servant, one of her daughters or anyone else. It was the address terms and subscriptions that were modulated in relation to the correspondent, not the signature. The reputation of early modern women for 'bad' spelling, discussed earlier, is, as Sönmez observes, 'hardly surprising' when examples of personal types of female writing in manuscript are set alongside more public-facing published writings by men in print.[144] Bess's signature provides us with a rare but welcome example of public-facing writing by a Tudor woman, and it is one that is defined by its stability. Her husband the sixth earl showed no such consistency in his spelling of <Shrewsbury>, which appears in his letters to Bess most commonly as <Shrewsbury> twenty-one times, but also, one or two times each, as <Shrewesbury, shrewsbury, Shrevesbury, shrowsbury>. There can be no doubt that the very stable form of Bess's signature after 1567 was a conscious decision on Bess's behalf and its fixity was precisely well suited to its twin functions.

On the one hand, the form of Bess's distinctive, reliable and recognisable signature was ideally suited to its function for practical security purposes as a mark of authorisation. That security could be a real issue for Bess and those in her circle is described in a letter from her servant Nicholas Kynnersley on 22 April 1589. In a postscript he reassured Bess, telling her to 'take no thowght botte be merye', as special security measures had been put in place at Wingfield:

> your honour shall nede to take no thowght botte be merye for you shall fynd all thynges here I truste in as good order as you leafte them for we nether wyll yeld to commandment nor forsse except your honour's hand & yett we wyll lett your honour vnderstand & haue a second comandment by on off your owen men vnder your hand leaste ye fruste be counterfett.[145]

The Wingfield household, Kynnersley explained, would follow no orders unless these were authorised by 'your honour's hand' (i.e., Bess's own signature). Even then, were such orders to come, the procedure would be to

---

144 Such as when, in the case of handbooks, a woman's manuscript letter is sandwiched between selections from Evelyn and Milton; Sönmez, 'Perceived and Real Differences', pp. 407–8.

145 Nicholas Kynnersley wrote from Wingfield to Bess (countess of Shrewsbury), 22 April 1589, Folger CT, X.d.428 (45), ID 38.

140 Reading and writing letters

contact Bess and to wait for a reiteration of the same orders from one of her own men, which would also need to be authorised a second time 'vnder your hand leaste ye furste be counterfett'. Cases of counterfeit signatures are well known from the period: in 1579 Gilbert Talbot wrote to Bess to tell her of the trial of four Court messengers found to have used fake signatures to swindle the queen out of more than £3,000 and punished by public humiliation and having 'theyr eares cutte of'.[146] Counterfeiting, then, was a serious matter. Perceived threats to the running of the Wingfield household were a constant issue during the late 1580s, when the relationship between Bess and Shrewsbury remained fraught.

On the other hand, the predictable visual form of Bess's signature was likewise well suited to its second function, which was iconic and symbolic. The signature 'EShrouesbury' had a fixed graphical form where the first two letters (the initials of Elizabeth and Shrewsbury) were linked together to form a distinctive 'ES' ligature. Bess incorporated this 'ES' ligature into her signature or used it on its own as a monogram to authorise written documents, such as the postscript to her letter to Gilbert Talbot and Mary (Cavendish) Talbot on 15 January 1606 (Plate 21). Today Bess's 'ES' monogram is perhaps best known in the context of the visual schemes she developed at her properties. From masonry to textiles to plasterwork, the 'ES' monogram is still rarely out of sight at Hardwick New Hall, where it is the leitmotif of Bess's self-aggrandising personal iconography incorporated across metalwork, stonework, needlework and plasterwork (Plates 5 and 6). Whether we approach Hardwick New Hall by car or on foot, along the drive that cuts through the surrounding fields, our eyes are drawn upwards to the striking silhouetted stone 'ES' monograms multiplied around the buildings' turrets (Plates 3 and 4). Emblazoned against the sky, Bess's initials continue to express her authority and presence, almost as if she had intended the house to be a letter sent to the future.

The appropriation of her own signature was a self-conscious decision on Bess's part and an idea which seems to have grown in her mind over time, finding its ultimate expression at Hardwick New Hall.[147] This use of her signature can be compared to the authorising function of signatures of other contemporary women letter-writers concerned with both security and self-fashioning, most famously Elizabeth I. Just as we have seen Bess collaborate with highly trained and trusted scribes to fashion her public persona through letters, so too did she harness the skills of builders, plasterers, architects, professional embroiderer and textile artists to realise her self-aggrandising visions for Hardwick New Hall. Her success in operating

---

146 Gilbert and Mary Talbot to Bess (countess of Shrewsbury), 13 February 1579, ID 166.
147 The deliberateness and consciousness behind Bess's development of a range of interlocking visual schemes have repeatedly been commented on – for example, White, '"That whyche ys nedefoulle"', p. 269.

within early modern culture and society came from her ability to orchestrate such projects, and to create and control her own iconography. Her 'ES' monogram became a form of visual branding that followed her, as countess and dowager countess, for over forty years, from her marriage to Shrewsbury in 1567 to her death in 1608, and beyond. It reminds us that writing had both visual and linguistic roles to play in the construction of agency and authority. Moreover, it reminds us that if we are more fully to appreciate how Bess communicated and operated within contemporary epistolary culture, we must attend to the visual features of her handwritten letters and to the material contexts within which they were written and received.

3 Sending and receiving letters

3.1 'Geven to one that brought a letter': situating epistolary reception within early modern postal and delivery networks

Item geuen to my norcys hosbande when he broughte lateres frome my myd wyffe –	ij^s [June 1549]
Item paid to hew Awsoppe for brenginge iiij capons & caring ij lettrs to derby –	vj^d [January 1553]
unto Simson the footeman at his goinge to Bittsbie with a letter Three shillings foure p –	iij^s iiij^d [November 1592]
geven to one that brought ^a^ letter from Weadson that tends the grounds at uden xij^d –	xij^d [May 1593]
geven to one that brought a letter from Master Topclyffe –	xij^d [May 1594]
geven to a boy that brought a lettre from agars the mason twelve pence –	xij^d [August 1594]
geven to Laurence at his going ^at sondry tyms^ to sheifield wth ^a^ letter three shillings foure pence – iij^s iiij^d and to houlmes the labourer for goinge ^thither likwise^ an other tyme –	xij^d [Septemper 1594]
Geven the Last of June unto Standishe at his goinge to London wth letters ten shill –	x^s [June 1595]
To one that brought a lettre from my Lady of Cumbrland three shillings fore pence –	iij^s iiij^d [November 1595]
to one of my Lo: of shrewesburies men that brought a lettre to your Lapp/ –	v^s [October 1597]
geuen to a pursevante that broughte letters for my subsetye –	v^s [December 1598]
To the carrier that brought letters from harthill –	xij^d [February 1600]
geuen to a collyar of ballebrough that brought a letter from harry leake fyfe shellings –	v^s [December 1600]
to the post his fees –	iij^s [1600/1]
Henry Smythes charges for watching the cattle sending letters and keeping the cattle and for coppies of the replevies –	vij^s iiij^d [April 1601]
Master Manners footboye brought letters –	xij^d [June 1601]

Sending and receiving letters 143

These Account Book references record payments made for the delivery of letters into and out of Northaw, Chatsworth and Hardwick.[1] They offer a series of snapshots, across particular dates and locations, of the wide range of means and methods by which Bess could send or receive a letter. That not a single one of the letters mentioned in the Account Books can be matched to an extant letter is indicative of the number of letters that must have been lost, as well as of the slippage that occurs between historical sources. Nevertheless, combining Bess's letters with her Account Books opens up a wealth of information about distances, delivery, payments and personnel. It is information that reveals the layered and multifaceted nature of early modern postal networks, of which it is worth providing an overview here, before moving on to consider particular aspects that inflected the delivery and reception process. The postal network, including its development and logistical mechanics, has been documented by Philip Beal and Mark Brayshay.[2] However, by focusing on the letters of one individual in this chapter it is possible to gain a vantage point from which to survey its complexities from, as it were, the inside out, and from the user's point of view. The advantage here is in the opportunity to reconstruct how one individual could utilise so many different facets of the postal network, as well as the motivations and circumstances for doing so. There is also the opportunity to add further evidence for letter-writing as a process, one which involved multiple stages and was implicated within various social connections and relationships. At the same time, by considering how Bess utilised the transport and delivery options available to her, we gain further insight into how she so successfully operated within and negotiated her way through the structures and hierarchies of early modern culture and society.

First are informal and *ad hoc* deliveries, such as Bess's nurse's husband ('norcys hosbande'), who brought letters from her midwife to Northaw after the birth of her second daughter Temperance in 1549; or, some fifty years later, in 1598, the miner who came down with a letter from Bilbrough

---

1   The Account Books are: Folger CT, X.d.486, 1548–50; Chatsworth, Devonshire Collection: Bess and Earls Misc. II, An inventory of the contents of Northaw, c. 1540–52; Hardwick MS 1, 1551–53; St Loe Accounts August 1560 – December 1560; Hardwick MS 5, 1579–84; Hardwick MS 7, 1591–97; and Hardwick MS 8, 1596–1601. The quotations cited here are taken from the transcriptions in Nottingham MS 663 David N. Durant Papers and White, '"That whyche ys nedefoulle"', vol. 2, Appendices. A full survey of all references to payments of letters in Bess's Account Books has been undertaken and an article on this topic is in preparation.

2   The standard work is Brayshay, *Land Travel and Communications*, and Chapter 6, 'Communication by Messenger and Post before 1635', provides an overview of available modes and methods of letter delivery. Scholarship that tracks the development of the official postal network and the growth of transport routes includes: Beale, *England's Mail*; Brayshay, 'Royal Post-Horse Routes in England and Wales'; Brayshay, Harrison and Chalkley, 'Knowledge, Nationhood and Governance'; Brayshay and Harrison, 'Post Horse Routes'. For an overview of the delivery, reception and reading of Tudor women's letters see Daybell, *Women Letter-Writers*, Chapter 5, from p. 127.

144 *Sending and receiving letters*

in North Yorkshire ('a collyar of ballebrough'). Had these letters survived, perhaps they would have been among the most appealing to modern readers, given our interest today in the histories of ordinary people and everyday life. As they are, these references remind us, as Alan Stewart has demonstrated in his seminal study, that early modern letters were not sent through a regularised and anonymised mail service.[3] Moreover, the social or occupational category of 'bearer' or 'messenger' was relative and had the potential to be occupied by a wide range of individuals. Persons from across the social spectrum could temporarily or sporadically enter the role and become involved in the delivery process, as and if occasion required. The fluidity and flexibility of the category of bearer, bringer or messenger mean it had a wide potential for use and customisation in the delivery process in early modern culture and anyone could, potentially, step into the role of bearer. This was a culture within which messages were carried by those who ranged from poor boys to Court favourites, serving maids to educated diplomats, anonymous strangers to trusted intimates. None were excluded – there was even the case of the message taken to the king tied to the neck of a hunting hound.[4] This enormous degree of flexibility and fluidity was intrinsic to the personalised and customised culture of handwritten letters. As we shall see, it was a situation revealed in Bess's letters and Account Books, in the various references to people who temporarily took on the role of bearer as an extension of their other roles and responsibilities, from colliers, labourers and maids to solicitors, secretaries, husbands and kin.

These kinds of *ad hoc* and informal uses of messengers existed at the same time, and in parallel with, more routine bringers of goods. An important layer of the official network was the Carriers, who transported goods and people along set routes with stops at inns according to regular timetables.[5] Travelling with their team of carts and packhorses, Carriers were typically mentioned bringing larger items; so in Bess's Account Books we find payments to the Chesterfield Carrier for 'bringing ffruit trees from London' (40s 2d), for 'carring one runlyte of muskyedyne and one runlyte of sacke weaying ij hondrethe and ij^{li} at a pennye the pounde' (18s 10d) and 'for the carriage of fyftene yardes of grene penystone at a penyye the pounde'

---

3 Stewart, *Shakespeare's Letters*, pp. 11–12 and throughout.

4 LPL, Talbot Papers, Vol. K, fol. 231: Edmund Lascells to Gilbert 4 Dec 1604, the note asked the king to leave the area where he had been hunting at Royston as the locality was no longer able to support the demands of the Court.

5 For analyses which consider a variety of methods of communication and transportation, including the Carrier system and the case of early modern Derbyshire, see: Stewart, *Shakespeare's Letters*, Chapter 3, 'Shakespeare and the Carriers'; Brayshay, *Land Travel and Communications*, pp. 244–47, and 'Waits, Musicians, Bearwards and Players'; Crofts, *Packhorse, Waggon and Post*; and Hey, *Packmen, Carriers and Packhorse Roads*.

Sending and receiving letters 145

(3s 4d).[6] Or letters were sometimes among the items sent, and we find payments from Bess for sending and receiving letters by the Carrier at various stages in her life, such as 12d to 'borage the caryar that broughte lateres' to Chatsworth in October 1548, 6d to 'a cariar that brought letters from London' to Hardwick in March 1592 and 12d to 'the carrier that brought letters from harthill' in February 1600.[7] While this was an official service (in the sense of being open to all who could afford it) we should not think of it as anonymous nor disconnected from the community. On the contrary, the men who were Carriers were, typically, well-known individuals within their locales. During Bess's marriage to Sir William Cavendish in the 1550s the couple regularly used 'Young Alsope' for deliveries; this was young Thomas Alsope, the Carrier of Derby, who was simultaneously kept in the employ of Sir William Cavendish and Bess (Lady Cavendish) – they had a coat made for him and rewarded him for prioritising their deliveries. Among the advantages of this arrangement were that Young Alsope would bring bulk deliveries from London directly to Chatsworth House itself, such as the thirty dozen candles in four baskets and 'rundlett of ranyshe wyne'. Or, if required, he would delay his departure time to accommodate their deliveries, such as the 'horse lod of stuf from london' for Cavendish that he 'taryed one day longer for' in December 1551 and for which his expenses were covered.[8] When Bess married Cavendish, then, she gained not only a husband but also priority access to the delivery network.

During her next marriage, to Sir William St Loe, Bess's utilisation of the Carriers continued. The most regular and sustained record of use is for the period 8 August to 31 December 1560, when St Loe left Chatsworth to attend the queen at Court. His Account Book for this five-month trip contains eleven records for the delivery of letters. These show St Loe regularly sending his servants, Greves, Cottesmore and Griffen, to and from the Carriers with letters, as well as one reference to hire of 'an olde man' to take letters from Somerset House to Bosoms Inn, the depot for the Derby Carrier

---

6 Chatsworth, Hardwick MS 8 and Hardwick Drawer 143 43–46. For a description of the teams of packhorses, wagons and carts that Carriers travelled with, see Hey, *Packmen, Carriers and Packhorse Roads*, pp. 88–91.

7 Folger CT, X.d.486, fol. 11r; Chatsworth, Hardwick MS 7, fol. 53v and Hardwick MS 8, fol. 82v. Harthill was a village six miles west of Worksop; see Hey, *Packmen, Carriers and Packhorse Roads*, p. 211, who gives the example of the flitch of bacon sent from Worksop to London in 1604 by the Carrier of Harthill.

8 Chatsworth, Hardwick MS 1, fol. 6r: he is paid 14s 4d for the delivery and another 15s 4d for his 'chargs'. The reference to the coat is in November 1551, fol. 4v: 'paid for iij yards di of [i.e. 3 and a half yards of frieze, a type of cloth] to make Thomas Alsope the caryer a cote at xxd the yard'. The reference to the delivery of candles and wine is on fol. 6r. 'Young' Alsope was distinguished from 'Old' Alsope, who also brought deliveries that included 'yron worke that pertyneth to ij portalls' and 'an ounce of fyne gold and an ounce of fyne silver' (fol. 5v) and who may or may not have been the same person as 'Hugh Alsope', who brought capons and hens (fol. 44r) as well as for 'caring ij letters to derby – vjd' (fol. 43r).

146 *Sending and receiving letters*

where St Loe also stored his baggage. Twice during this period St Loe wrote to Bess at Chatsworth from his lodgings at Master Mann's House (in one case we have his record for purchase of the actual paper he wrote to Bess on: 'for paper the same night to wryte home – iij^d').[9] Alongside his letters, St Loe used the Carriers to send Bess thoughtful gifts that included specialty items, such as frankincense, virginal wire, canvas and a fashionable bongrace.[10] We know their exchanges were two-way, as in a third letter St Loe asked Bess to send 'by the nextt caryar . . . soche stvff' that his servant Mowsall had 'left packt in a schete' (stvff: *stuff*, schete: *sheet*) that included 'hand towels and other thyngs'.[11] When in London herself a few years later Bess likewise routinely communicated with those back at Chatsworth via letters sent with the Carrier. In fact, her letters and packages sent by the Carrier seem to have become part of the weekly rhythm and routine of the Chatsworth household and her reliable servant James Crompe came to expect a regular delivery: 'I thought I shulde a receuyd no lettur ffrom yowr ladyshippe this wyck it was xj of the clocke of weseday or the caryer cam with it to chatteseworth' (a: *have*, or: *before*).[12] Here Crompe mentioned the clock tower at Chatsworth and we know that Bess also had a watch at this period.[13] Crompe's surprise at the Carrier's lateness suggests they were generally reliable for time. That the Carriers may have been less dependable when it came to money (and this was one of the risks acknowledged in contemporary criticisms of Carriers) is shown when Crompe sent cash to Bess in London in the charge of her trusted man Dyckyns, who would travel with the Derby or Tutbury Carrier: 'dyckyns shalbe with your Ladyship at london god wylling on Sondaye the xth daye of marche next with as moche moneye as I can get ethur he shall com with the caryer of derbye or with the caryer of tutburye'.[14] The case of Dyckyns reminds us that different networks of carriage could overlap: here

---

9 Chatsworth, St Loe Accounts, p. 48. The two letters he wrote home to Bess during this period are 4 September 1560 (ID 59) and 12 October 1560 (ID 60).

10 *OED*, 'bongrace', n. 1. 'A shade or curtain formerly worn on the front of women's bonnets or caps to protect the complexion from the sun; a sunshade'. The earliest citation was from 1530 and by 1617 they were referred to as worn by 'Gentle-women of old' and 'now altogether out of vse with us'.

11 ID 61.

12 'I thought I should have received no letter from your ladyship this week it was 11 o'clock on Wednesday before the carrier came with it to Chatsworth', ID 17.

13 The reference to Bess's watch is found in her and Sir William Cavendish's account books for the period: 'Item payed for mendyng my wache – vs'; Folger CT, X.d.426, fol. 19r. Her letters from Chatsworth show more a precise concern over time than those written in her later years at Hardwick, where there was no clock tower, which show a vagueness of time: 'about two of the clock', 'at dinner time' or 'written late at night'.

14 James Crompe wrote from Chatsworth to Bess (Lady St Loe), 26 February 1566?, Folger CT, X.d.428 (19), ID 18. On the liability of Carriers see Stewart, *Shakespeare's Letters*, pp. 146–48.

Sending and receiving letters 147

both a personal servant and a Carrier are utilised, a combination that would ensure both security and reliability.

This brings us to a third method of delivery: as appropriate to her station, Bess regularly used personal servants to send letters. For example, from the period when she was dowager countess of Shrewsbury, there are records for payments to 'Simson the footeman' for taking one of Bess's letters to Bittsbie, to Laurence at various times for taking letters to Sheffield and for Standishe for taking letters to London. Likewise, Bess's correspondents frequently sent letters to her by the hand of a member of their own personal retinue, so we find letters received by Bess from, for example, 'one of the earl of shrosburys men', 'one of my La: of Shrewsburies men', 'one of the Earle of Sallops men', 'my Sonne williams ffooteboye', 'charles hys man', 'master Chaworths man' and 'Master Manners footboye'. Similar references recurred within the letters themselves, which sometimes included other people's servants being used, so Bess noted in a letter to Burghley in 1592 that: 'I reseuyd your Lordships letter on wedensday towards night being the xxth of this September, by a seruant of Master Iohn Talbotts of Ireland'.[15] In these ways, trusted retinue members populated early modern epistolary culture and inflected the discourse of letter-writing. Katy Mair has demonstrated in compelling detail the problems with bearers experienced in the 1590s by Bess's close contemporary Lady Anne Cooke Bacon when writing to her son Anthony, a situation which impacted upon the content of her letters and which caused her continual anxiety over their reception. By contrast, the evidence suggests Bess occasioned trustworthiness and loyalty in her bearers at various points in her life. There were advantages to using personal servants who could be relied upon for responsible roles, and that Bess was able to trust servants such as James Crompe, Francis Whitfield and Dyckyns, and then, later, Timothy Pusey, Robert Harrison and Edward Whalley, was important to the success of her business dealings.

It is worth emphasising that the issue of trust not only concerned handling cash. Rather it was that the role of bearer or messenger overlapped with other service roles – that is, as an extension of an individual's capacity as, say, project manager, solicitor or accountant. For example, during the period of early building work at Chatsworth Bess's servant Master Hyde switched between the role of bearer and that of project or estate manager. In one letter Bess sent Hyde to Sir John Thynne at Longleat to give an update on his handling of estate matters at Chatsworth: 'for that I haue no tyme to wryte a length mayster hyde cane declare unto you of all oure prosedynges here I thanke hym he hathe taken meche ^payne^ to brynge my dysordered thynges yn to some good order'. Subsequently we see Hyde's involvement in the building of Chatsworth: when seeking to establish the trustworthiness of Thynne's plasterer, Bess requested the information be transmitted

---

15 ID 163.

148   *Sending and receiving letters*

via the person of the bearer, Hyde, as a word-of-mouth recommendation: 'spare me your ~~mason~~ ^plaisterer^ that flowred your halle . . . Praing you to aduertise me by this bearer whether I may truste to hym or not'. Hyde was then further charged with passing on Bess's directions to the plasterer: 'I wolde gladly have [the plasterer] furthwith to be sent either to my howse at Chattesworthe whiche way Master Hyde can instructe hym'.[16]

This method of having a trusted bearer speak for her continued throughout Bess's life and she was entirely typical of her time in this respect. As James Daybell's authoritative account has demonstrated, bearers were widely used by both men and women who had the available resources: they were an integral part of early modern epistolary communication and their verbal contributions were often the most effective method of personal representation.[17] We must envisage Bess receiving bearers as well as sending them and, certainly in important matters, messengers would have spoken with Bess face to face. George Clifford, earl of Cumberland, made clear his faith in his bearer when he ended his letter with a direct appeal to Bess (dowager countess of Shrewsbury) that she too should trust him:

> I will not nou troble your Ladyship with wrytyng answere to the speech that passed betwyxt hus concernyng my doughter, nor with a further sute that I am forced to macke to you, but refer all to this berer, whom I pray your Ladyship trust, he is the man that I most dooe [nou: *now*, hus: *us*].[18]

A bearer could bring particular skills and knowledge to the communicative encounter. Especially important to Bess were those who could elucidate the detail of a business transaction, such as would be excessively tedious in a letter, as well as open to ambiguity and interpretation. In these cases, a live discussion of the legal intricacies involved in a particular marriage settlement or land transaction could ensure accuracy and that the written words were not misappropriated – a feature that can be regarded as typical of a manuscript-based culture where trust in orality was strong compared to writing.[19] So, in a letter where Bess gave her support in the form of £3,000,

---

16 Bess (Lady Cavendish and then Lady St Loe) to Sir John Thynne, 31 March 1550s, ID 198, and 25 April 1560, ID 113. On 15 March 1550s, Hyde was bearer and we find him bringing news in the reverse direction, to Bess at Chatsworth from Thynne at Longleat: 'I trousse mayster hyde wyll kepe hys aponntode day with me. And by hym I trouste to here frome you', ID 200.

17 Daybell, *Women Letter-Writers*, p. 148, and throughout this chapter, which includes assessments of intimacy, trust and agency. As Daybell observes, 'bearers acted as personal representatives entrusted with women's intimate business interests and empowered to operate on their behalves in their absence', p. 132.

18 June 1603?, Folger CT, X.d.428 (20), ID 19.

19 The key study is Clanchy, *From Memory to Written Record*.

the bearer Henry Willoughby had responsibility for concluding the fine details according to her agenda: 'My cosin Henry Willoughby will shoe you my mynd at more length.'[20] In another example, Bess's letter to Sir Julius Caesar functioned as an authorising note for two more letters, enclosed, one from Bess herself and one from her son William, both of which refuted a petitionary claim for rights to common land made by men of the High Peak. Her instructions to Caesar were to recognise her authority in both the written letters and in the spoken words of the bearer, who 'vpon the dispatch of the matter will further signifie vnto you to whom I pray you geve credytt'.[21]

In other transactions, while still dealing with business matters, the role of the bearer was signalled by the letter to convey something of Bess's strength of feeling, or to inject urgency or a heightened sense of importance into the encounter. Perhaps the most dramatic example is Bess's letter to Burghley of 2 August 1584, during the height of her marital quarrels, where she subscribed herself as your 'dystresed sorrowfull frend' and stated in her letter that 'I was neuer more dystresed then now' due to Shrewsbury's intent, within the next few days, 'to take away chatsworth' along with her goods and allowances. In her plea to Burghley for intervention, Bess specifically asked him to hear the bearer's account of her personal distress in the matter: 'I beseche your Lordship lycence thys bearar to declare more parteculary vnto your Lordship my most lamentable state.'[22] That is, the bearer's role was to reinforce the words of the letter by ensuring they were charged with a particular set of moods and emotions, to convey something of Bess's distressed and pitiable condition, or to use her own phrase, her 'lamentable state'. To take one more example: a scribal letter dealing with one Widow Bagshaw's unlawful claim to a farm ended with a request that the recipient 'creditt this bearer'. This was followed by a postscript in Bess's own distinctive handwriting that reiterated the main points of the letter: 'thys womane hathe yoused har selfe vary dysorderly and wyll yelde to no resovne as my saruante thys barare cane declare vnto you'.[23] Bess's resounding autograph postscript indicated her position in no uncertain terms and thereby ensured the bearer's words were heard loudly and clearly as an authoritative echo of her own. In these ways, it was through bearers in which she had confidence that she managed negotiations. As we shall see in the next section, the bearer's role as negotiator was especially vital in the context of high-stakes requests presented at Court and fraught family encounters.

In some cases, then, the person introduced the letter, but in other cases the letter introduced the person in the sense that it served to authorise his or

---

20 Bess (dowager countess of Shrewsbury) wrote from Chatsworth to Sir Francis Willoughby at Wollaton Hall, 8 May 1594, sent, unknown scribe, Nottingham UL, Middleton MSS, Mi C23, ID 102.

21 ID 161 (Plate 18).

22 TNA SP 12/172, ff 64r-65v (item 50), sent, Scribe A, ID 150.

23 14 April 1600?, ID 2 (Plate 16).

150 *Sending and receiving letters*

her presence and words. These included cases whereby a letter functioned as a recommendation for permanent residence within the household: the combination of bearer and letter was the method by which individuals were brought into service. The beginning and end of Bess's marriage to Shrewsbury featured by such letters, as the household was reconfigured at the start of a new reign. There was the case of the letter of introduction from Edward Manners, carried by the bearer 'Mistres Higgens', an 'ould servant' to Shrewsbury's first wife, Gertrude, who presented herself to Shrewsbury's new wife, Bess, with her claim to 'aparaunt' – that is, her right to remain employed in the family's service.[24] Then, following the death of Shrewsbury in November 1590, Bess set about establishing her own household and received recommendations from a number of her contacts and connections. On 23 March 1591, Robert Devereux, second earl of Essex, wrote to Bess from Court a letter of recommendation to be presented by the bearer, one Christopher Hannam, who hoped 'to be entertayned in service by yow' as a 'gentleman vsher'. Essex added that Hannam had been particularly recommended by his, Essex's, own 'good frend Sir Ihon Wingfield' (Sir John Wingfield), as well as by the 'iudgment of my Lady of Kent' (Susan Grey, dowager de jure countess of Kent), both of whom 'thowght him meete for your service', to which he added his own consent and preferment, as well as (this being 'not enoughe') 'these lettres in his commendacion'.[25] Likewise, on 26 January 1593, Susan Grey, dowager de jure countess of Kent, responded to Bess's request 'to desire me to help yow to a clarke and a porter' with the report that 'as yet, I can not hear of ani one that is ffite ffor the office of a clarke' but 'for yowr porter, the bearer hearof I take to be a very fitt man, & for whose truethe I dair answeare/ otherwise I would haue been loothe to write or speake in his behalfe, and I hoope yowr Ladiship shall find him willinge dilligent and redy to please'. Her choice of words here in her recommendation, which endorsed the bearer as 'willinge dilligent and redy to please', coincided precisely with contemporary views as to what made a good messenger, with 'diligent' having the specific meaning of speedy and swift.[26] As the new dowager countess of Shrewsbury, Bess

---

24 18 April c. 1570, Folger CT, X.d.428 (71), ID 56. The full reference is: 'I: am bould to recommend to your Lady shippes good furtherances this berer Mistres Higgens an ould servant of my late awntes your predecessor who claymeth a paret from my Lord your husband as by his deed it semeth that he hath granted'. Shrewsbury and Bess married in or by 1567 and the catalogue dates the letter to 18 April [ca. 1570]. I am grateful to Graham Williams for advice on this letter.

25 23 March 1591, Folger CT, X.d.428 (26), ID 24.

26 A discussion of the term 'diligent' meaning 'speedy' in relation to messengers is provided by Stewart, *Shakespeare's Letters*, p. 205. The letter cited is ID 32 and there is also a reference to Bess acquiring a new porter when she was at Chelsea in 1591, Hardwick MS 7, fol. 28v: 'unto a new porter vjs viijd'. Further examples can be found among Gilbert Talbot's letters, as incoming earl after the death of his father: Lambeth Palace Library, London, Talbot Papers, Vol. H, fol. 181, 27 November 1590, John Savage sent a suitor for the earl's

Sending and receiving letters 151

surrounded herself with the best team of representatives she could find. References in 1591 to the purchase of new coats for her wagon men remind us that Bess's employees must have been a familiar and distinctive sight as they travelled around the country dressed in their blue livery.[27]

To summarise, so far we have seen the roles of friends, relatives and kin ('my norcys hosbande', 'My cosin Henry Willoughby'), redeployed employees ('a collyar of ballebrough', 'houlmes the labourer'), the regular Carrier service ('the carrier from harthill', 'the carrier of Chesterfeeld', the caryer of derbye', 'the caryer of tutburye') and personal servants whether named ('old Awesope', 'Laurence', 'Simson the footeman', 'Standishe', 'Otwell Greves', 'Dyckyns', 'Mistres Higgens') or attributed (a person's man, page, footboy or footman) and travelling either locally or to and from London. To these should be added the various wagon men, coachmen and porters employed on the estate, such as the one recommended by Susan Grey; their main role was in transporting large items, heavy goods and livestock, but we cannot entirely rule out the possibility that they may also sometimes have carried accompanying notes or letters.[28] To these should further be added references that mentioned pursievants and the official post bringing letters.[29] All together these references depict an overlapping and multilayered reticulated network of transport and transit options available to Bess. In order to add to our sense of the intricacy of the picture, we must think beyond Bess's own letters and take into account the networks that intersected with her own. To be specific, in order to provide a fully textured map of the delivery traffic in and out of Bess's social sphere, we must mention three further factors: (1) the custodianship of Mary, Queen of Scots, (2) the place of informal workers, including the poor and women, in Bess's households and (3) international trade and import-export activities. Each of these adds to our sense of the landscape of Bess's everyday life at particular periods, as well as to our conception of

---

solicitorship or secretaryship, and fol. 187, 29 November 1590, Thomas Leigh sent his son to offer his services to the earl, who had studied law at Oxford and Lincoln's Inn for seven years.

27 See the reference, whilst on the trip to London, to money 'Paid for iiij yards and an halfe of blewe cloth for iij liveries ten shill the yd. – xlvs' (Chatsworth, Hardwick MS 7, 29 July 1592, fol. 31, Nottingham University Library, Special Collections, Durant Papers MS 663/2/1/13–1–8). For a reference to livery coats for wagon men see Chatsworth, Hardwick MS 7, 1591, fol. 44v.

28 On the role of porters see LPL, London, Shrewsbury Papers, MS 701, fol. 189 'Memorandum of the Duties of the Office of Porter of Tutbury'.

29 As wife to the custodian of the Scottish Queen, Bess (countess of Shrewsbury) may also have had privileged access to the royal post. Discussion of some of the challenges around travel and transportation associated with the Scottish Queen during her time in the custodianship of the Shrewsburys is offered by Brayshay, *Land Travel and Communications*, pp. 158, 282 and 235, and includes the provision of extraordinary posts during times of emergency, p. 302.

152 Sending and receiving letters

the social range and geographical reach of her communication and delivery networks.

First of all, then, we must remember that for sixteen years, from late 1568 until November 1584, Bess and Shrewsbury were the keepers of Mary, Queen of Scots, which dramatically transformed the nature of epistolary transactions into and out of their various households. Although in fact their prisoner, the Scottish Queen, as befitted her royal status, was accompanied by a substantial court-in-exile and her servants included individuals she used as bearers, such as Monsieur Doln, her treasurer. It was an ambiguous arrangement whereby some access to channels of communication was allowed, but at the same time there was vigilant monitoring of both oral and written interactions. For example, in a letter to Burghley of 2 August 1572 Shrewsbury made report of a visit from a secretary to the French ambassador to the Scottish Queen permitted by Queen Elizabeth: he reassured Burghley that the meeting was short, of little consequence and all within his own hearing, and went on to mention that the Scottish Queen had sent letters to Queen Elizabeth and the ambassador, which Shrewsbury had himself opened and read before sending.[30] As this example illustrates, there was to be an appearance of allowances being made, that included gestures towards epistolary privileges, but at the same time all of the Scottish Queen's communications were to be rigorously scrutinised and checked. Likewise, while certain deliveries were permitted, they were nevertheless to be treated as thoroughly suspicious: such as the book and box left by Curcelles, servant to the French ambassador, apparently received from Mistress Seeton, which was carefully searched just as the Scottish Queen's letters were scrupulously read and their content reported back to Queen Elizabeth.[31]

In this way, Shrewsbury and Bess were forever searching crevices and corners. In this climate of relentless surveillance everyone, including themselves and members of their own household, was potentially the bearer of a

---

30 LPL, Shrewsbury Papers, MS 697, fol. 90.

31 For an example of Monsieur Doln as letter-bearer see LPL, Shrewsbury Papers, MS 701, fol. 153, 11 May 157[6], Sir Edmund Brudenell to Shrewsbury. The book and box sent to the Scottish Queen, along with other items, accompany a letter from Thomas Baldwin to Shrewsbury in 1583, Shrewsbury Papers, MS 705, fol. 33. The Talbot Papers at LPL contain numerous letters regarding Shrewsbury and Bess's monitoring of the Scottish Queen's movements and transactions, especially her letters. For example: Vol. E, fol. 229, Queen Elizabeth to Henry Hastings, 22 September 1569, he is to guard the Scottish Queen while Shrewsbury is ill and she is not to have any visitors or send any letters without Queen Elizabeth's knowledge; Vol. P, fol. 579, Shrewsbury to Lord Burghley, 19 November 1571, he has intercepted a messenger, Bastien, with unauthorised letters from the Scottish Queen to the French ambassador; Vol. P, fol. 633, Sir Thomas Smith to Shrewsbury, 31 March 1574, asks him to broach the subject of the enclosed letter with the Scottish Queen; Shrewsbury's note indicates he has secured a letter from the Scottish Queen to James Boyd, Bishop of Glasgow.

Sending and receiving letters   153

secret letter, and every letter was potentially suspicious.[32] There were continual stories of secret letters having been smuggled in by ingenious methods, and the household was forced repeatedly to ramp up security measures and endlessly reassure Queen Elizabeth of their loyalty and vigilance. In one memorable effort to soothe the fears of the Court, Shrewsbury's son Gilbert Talbot declared that unless the Scottish Queen 'could transform herself to a flea or a mouse, it was impossible that she should escape'.[33] Gilbert's barely concealed tone of exasperation acknowledged that the responsibility for monitoring the Scottish Queen's letters was a frustrating, anxiety-inducing and at times impossible task. Part of the difficulty was that while Queen Elizabeth expected Shrewsbury to be ever watchful over his charge, at the same time she expected him to track down suspicious letters coming in from all directions. On one occasion Shrewsbury was informed of a suspected letter for the Scottish Queen carried by a French woman who had just left London, whom he must ensure was apprehended. Another report informed him of a rumour about secret messengers who had left Scotland with letters for the Scottish Queen, whom Shrewsbury should ensure were captured.[34] These letters were needles in haystacks and the incessant stalking and shadowing took its toll on Shrewsbury's physical and mental health. We can glimpse Bess's direct involvement in identifying rogue messengers in a letter to her from Gilbert Talbot, in which he passed on information provided in 'the hastie lettres from Sir Iohn cunstable' which 'advertise yat there are ij Scotts yat travell with ~~lyne~~ lynen clothe to sell yat have lettres of importance to this Quenes thone of them is brother to curle'.[35] When Bess was assigned

32 For an example of Shrewsbury intercepting suspicious letters and then forwarding these to Bess for her perusal, see ID 154: 'last nyght I intarcepted bagshaw found folysch lettar where in you may see his delynge . . . it were good you loked to sutton ho is made a spye to gyve bagshaw intellygens / & for bentles lettar cend for him to you & delyvar him his lettar your celfe openyd & intarcepted by me & show him that he may perseve you vndarstand bagshaw his inderecte delynge I have no more to say butt that I made my selfe sport at his lettares'.

33 LPL, Talbot Papers, Vol. F, fol. 79, Gilbert Talbot to Shrewsbury, 11 May 1573; his comment was in response to Dr Wilson's question about provision for guarding the Scottish Queen during her removal to Sheffield Lodge while the castle was cleaned.

34 LPL, Shrewsbury Papers, MS 709, fol. 89, n.d., unknown correspondent to Shrewsbury; Talbot Papers, Vol. F, fol. 145, 29 March 1576, Sir Francis Walsingham to Shrewsbury.

35 The linen sellers appear in ID 84; 'Sir Iohn cunstable' is Sir John Constable (1526–79) of Burton Constable and Halsham, Yorkshire; 'curle' is Gilbert Curle, one of the Scottish Queen's attendants. For further discussion of these and related issues see Durant, *Bess of Hardwick*, pp. 74–76, and Daybell, 'Secret Letters'. The Talbot Papers at Lambeth Palace Library contain numerous letters relating to the security of the household of the Scottish Queen. Repeatedly, letters concern suspicions over particular members of the household – for example, those who came under suspicion included Bess (Vol. G, fol. 286, earl of Leicester to Shrewsbury, 14 December n.a., the queen had been suspicious of the countess, but is now well satisfied), Gilbert Talbot (Vol. P, fol. 701, Shrewsbury to the earl of Leicester, 14 May 1574, he keeps Gilbert with him as some at Court hold him to be a spy),

154 *Sending and receiving letters*

the role of co-keeper of the Scottish Queen, then, her household became a living panopticon: every person monitored and monitoring others, every epistolary exchange surreptitiously scrutinised for signs of espionage and every situation a potential security risk, from conversations with her husband to the purchase of linen from travelling salesmen.

The rumoured plot to use disguised linen sellers brings us to the second factor under consideration here: the plot relied upon the fact that humble and poor people plying their trades were part of the regular unofficial traffic into, out of and around Bess's households. Although there are few extant Account Book records for the period of the Scottish Queen's custodianship, those for the 1590s reveal in spectacular detail that these individuals were part of the fabric of daily life in and around Bess's estates. We can observe the enormous social range of visitors to her houses who brought a variety of goods, services and messages and included hawkers and pedlars bringing items for sale, figures elsewhere elusive in the historical record.[36] Among these individuals, coming into and out of Chatsworth and Hardwick, were women of ordinary and poor means, not necessarily or usually bringers of letters, but who came with other items and requests, some of which, we can reasonably speculate, may well have involved now lost notes, bills and verbal messages. There are numerous payments to women for running errands, which range from the 40s to Mistress Bainton's daughter when she took a gilt cup to her mother from Bess, to far more modest payments to wives, daughters, maids and girls, often walking or riding miles across the tracks and fields to Chatsworth or Hardwick – for example, 10s to Dr Jones's daughter when she collected payment, 10s to 'Tefealles daughtr that came from shefield', 6s 8d to Mistress Chapman for bringing plums, 5s to 'Isbell hardye of sheffield that brought chekins', 2s 4d to a poor women for bringing cakes, 2s to the gardener's wife who brought a present, 12d to 'my cosyn choworths mayde for

---

Shrewsbury (Vol. P, fol. 691, Shrewsbury to Lord Burghley, 16 April 1574, defending his loyalty to Queen Elizabeth and referring to the Scottish Queen as 'a stranger, a Papist, and my enemy') and servants of the household (Vol. P, fol. 1023, Shrewsbury to Lord Burghley, 3 March 1574/5, thanks the queen for telling him that she has been told some of his servants convey letters and messages for the Scottish Queen, he says that if so they are very secret about it; Vol. G, fol. 120, Shrewsbury to Thomas Baldwin 10 February 1581/2, comments that 'I have too many spies in my house already'; Vol. G, fol. 170, Shrewsbury to Thomas Baldwin, 15 July 1582, complains of spies around him; Vol. G, fol. 274, Sir John Somers to Thomas Stringer, 16 February 1584/5, concerning one of Shrewsbury's servants of twenty-eight years, a coachman called Sharpe, who has been attending the Scottish Queen and is under suspicion).

36 For example, see Folger CT, X.d.426 fol. 20r: 'Item geuen to a prentes that broughte sylkes – iiijd'; fol. 20v: Item payed for fyne threde that I bought of a pedeler – ijs ijd'. For mention of a poor man travelling between Derbyshire and York selling caps and other goods see LPL, Shrewsbury Papers, MS 696, fol. 23, George Talbot (later earl of Shrewsbury) to his father, 22 February 1557. For further examples and discussion see Hey, *Packmen, Carriers and Packhorse Roads*, p. 195; Fumerton, *Unsettled*.

Sending and receiving letters 155

brenging fore grene gesse', 6d to 'widowe Plates mayde yat brought goose & apples', 4d 'in reward to fynshe [French?] maid for brenging a kydde' and 2d to 'a gyrll thatt brought a newers gyfte to my lady'. Further payments go to poor women who came to the house without anything to deliver, such as 12d to the 'poore woman yat came out of Lancashire' and 2s 'To a poore woman of dronfeild'. These should be considered alongside the many entries for small payments to women engaged in menial tasks around the estate, such as the payment of 2s 4d 'To xiiij poore women that did weed in the garden ij^d a peece'.[37] There are many of these kinds of examples of women bringing small consumable items, or simply bringing themselves, in hope of payment.[38] As will be seen in the discussion of enclosures ahead, they speak of a context and a culture within which letters were only one means through which communication occurred within a locality.

These references to payments – which range from royalty to pedlars and poor women – map out the wide social terrain of Bess's transactions and deliveries. But in order to gain a sense of the geography involved we must consider the larger communicative networks that Bess was able to activate. We must remember that while Bess was based in Derbyshire for extended periods, she was simultaneously managing business remotely in London. A key figure in this respect was Bess's solicitor Edward Whalley, whose 1589–92 Account Book outlined the communicative activities he undertook on her behalf in the capital; a typical example recorded Whalley's payments

> for goinge & cominge by water to Chelsey & to other places aboute your honors busines & to porters for caridge of venison & the caryers for caridge of sundreye lettres from your honer & for paper & harde waxe wherewith I made & sealed your honors lettres the some of ~ Three poundes sixe pence.[39]

At the same time, and beyond London, Bess's husband Shrewsbury and his son Gilbert Talbot were engaged in international trade and communications

---

37 Chatsworth, Hardwick MSS 7 and 8.
38 Bess was following practices typical of her time in this respect. For comparative examples see Hey, *Packmen, Carriers and Packhorse Roads*, pp. 187–90, on the steward's accounts of Sir George Vernon of Haddon Hall, also in Derbyshire, for 1549–51 and 1564–65, which include supply trips to Chesterfield, payments to the 'egg woman' and local people bringing items. See also William's comments on the Howards of Naworth Castle in the early seventeenth century and their practice of regularly rewarding 'bringers of presents with sums that were two to four times as large as the daily wages they were paying to their labourers. It was a curious practice, deeply embedded in a paternalistic view of social and economic relationships'. See also Durant, who comments that despite famine and disease 'stalking the country' in 1594–97, due to heavy rains, 'life at Hardwick went on as if there was no distress outside'; *Bess of Hardwick*, p. 185.
39 'Edward Whalley's Accompts Steward to Elizabeth Countess of Shrewsbury. 1589–1592', Folger, MS V.b.308, p. 19.

156 Sending and receiving letters

through their extremely successful import-export businesses: they had beaten off the competition to become the primary exporters of lead, which was shipped by water out of the manor of Bawtry in Derbyshire to London and Hamberg.[40] Shrewsbury's ship, *The Talbotte*, was used for this purpose and would return with bulk items, such as wine, leather and barley, as well as luxury goods, such as velvet and rarities from Paris as New Year's gifts, and which included items bought on behalf of his wife and for which she paid.[41] For any items he could not import himself, Shrewsbury was in direct and close contact with leading London merchants. For example, trader and venturer Sir Edward Osborne (c. 1530–92) on 20 September 1585 sent Shrewsbury two samples of ten pounds of nutmeg, along with news that a ship had arrived from Turkey laden with carpets he might be interested to buy.[42] There were other examples of international travel and trade that involved family members: Gilbert Talbot and Henry Cavendish wrote to Bess and Shrewsbury from Padua in Italy in 1570 and mentioned their stops in Venice (then the centre of the Levant trade), Paris and Hamburg; in 1582 Shrewsbury's agent Thomas Baldwin travelled to France with Edward Talbot and Henry Cavendish; in 1589 Henry Cavendish wrote from Constantinople; and from its founding in 1600, Bess's son William Cavendish was directly involved in the East India Company.[43] That Bess benefitted materially from

40 For an account of Shrewsbury's lead exporting activities see Hey, *Packmen, Carriers and Packhorse Roads*, pp. 109–14. Bess's later direct involvement can be tracked in her Account Books – for example, Chatsworth, Hardwick MS 8, 1600–01 contains her iron and glass-works accounts and records for haulage costs to and from Hull and Bawtry.

41 On Shrewsbury purchasing goods for Bess see Levey, *An Elizabethan Inheritance*, p. 106, note 33. There are numerous examples of Shrewsbury's import-export activities in the Talbot and Shrewsbury Papers at Lambeth Palace Library – for example, Talbot Papers, Vol. G, fol. 185, Shrewsbury to Thomas Baldwin, 19 November 1582, *The Talbott* has had an unsuccessful voyage, but he will have rarities sent from Paris as New Year's gifts; Shrewsbury Papers, MS 697, fol. 83, Anthony Barly to Shrewsbury, 23 June 1570, regarding the importing of handguns and helmets (calivers and burgonets) from Hamburg, a shipment of wine and the difficulty of getting velvet and of selling lead; MS 697, fol. 135, Richard Torre to Shrewsbury, 24 July 1579, regarding a shipment of fourteen little barrels of red lead and leather; MS 698, fol. 77, Richard Torre to Shrewsbury, 15 May 1586, regarding a cargo of lead and orders to buy barley and wine.

42 LPL, Shrewsbury Papers, MS 695, fol. 27.

43 Henry and Gilbert's letters from Padua are IDs 171 and 226. That this trip was at least in part a trade venture is suggested by its mention in other letters from merchants and traders: Lambeth Palace Library, Shrewsbury Papers, MS 697, fol. 71, Edward Osborn to Shrewsbury 1 November 1571; and MS 697, fol. 83, Anthony Barley to Shrewsbury, 23 June 1570. On Thomas Baldwin's journey to France with the earl's sons Edward and Henry see Shrewsbury Papers, MS 704, fol. 151, Shrewsbury and Bess to Baldwin, 8 February 1581/2. Henry's remarkable journey to Constantinople is mentioned in his wife Grace's letter to Bess ID 80, 27 June c. 1589. Further information about his journey can be found in his manuscript journal, now at Chatsworth House, and available in the edition by A.C. Wood, 'Mr Harrie Cavendish His Journey to and from Constantinople 1589, by Fox, His Servant', Camden Third Series, 64 (London: Royal Historical Society, 1940), pp. 1–29.

Sending and receiving letters 157

such international trading connections is evident from the spectacular domestic interiors she created, as recorded in the 1601 inventory and, in some cases, still there at Hardwick New Hall today. From these we know that she imported European silks and fabrics to custom-make furnishings for her houses, and that she imported ready-made items from further afield that included her Persian and Anatolian carpets, Gujarati embroidered bedcover, Bengal quilt and Chinese woven silk damask cushion backs.[44]

We must be careful, then, when we read accounts of early modern Derbyshire that describe the county as wild and remote, or that depict Chatsworth and Hardwick as desolate islands surrounded by howling and treacherous terrain. Travel could certainly be challenging, especially in bad weather and on open moorland. Daniel Defoe's famous observation on visiting the Peak, that it was perhaps 'the most desolate, wild, and abandoned county in all England', was anticipated a century earlier in a letter from Viscount Lisle, who hoped Gilbert Talbot had returned safely to Sheffield, which, from his perspective at Court, was 'half way to the North Pole'. Other encumbrances that slowed the progress of communications included an inevitable range of human factors, such as the delay for several days of Gilbert Talbot's servant in London by a widow who claimed he had contracted marriage with her. But while we should not disregard the challenges communication could present, nor downplay the bleakness of a Derbyshire winter, nor should we overstate or romanticise an image of Bess cut off in a remote outpost. Her position was at, or close to, the hub and helm of myriad means, methods and networks of communication, local, national and international. While she spent extended periods at in Derbyshire, in many senses, the world came to her in an array of forms.[45]

This sense of multiple layers of communication, and of Bess regularly switching between different methods of delivery and tapping into interrelated

---

Durant suspects Henry may have 'gone on this difficult trip at Bess's bidding' to ship pepper and explore options for trading spices and other eastern exports; *Bess of Hardwick*, p. 153.

44 Levey, *An Elizabethan Inheritance*, pp. 26–29; and *The Embroideries at Hardwick Hall*, pp. 29–30, and in that volume, Rosemary Crill, 'Appendix One: The Hardwick Hall Bengali Quilt', pp. 389–90. As Levey observes, there is a distinction to be made between 'real Turkish carpets' – that is, those imported from Anatolia (modern Turkey) – and 'carpets of English turkey-work'; the furnishings of Chatsworth and Hardwick included both.

45 The letter from Viscount Lisle is LPL, Talbot Papers, Vol. L, fol. 63, 11 September 1606. The letter to Gilbert Talbot regarding the delay of his servant is Talbot Papers, Vol. K, fol. 62, from Richard Bancroft, Bishop of London, 27 September 1602. See also Talbot Papers, Vol. M, fol. 353, Sir William Bowes to Gilbert Talbot, 29 October 1606, saying that severe weather and bad roads have prevented him from visiting Sheffield. There is also the letter from Burghley to Bess that pictures her amid the 'rocks and stones', discussed earlier in the introduction, p. 20. On the remoteness of Derbyshire see Durant, *Bess of Hardwick*, p. 3, and Hey, *Packmen*, p. 12 and Chapter 10, where he discusses the Defoe comment. On Bess's position at the centre of news networks see Daybell, '"Suche newes"'.

158 Sending and receiving letters

networks, is repeatedly found in the letters. Regularly, we find Bess interacted with several bearers, servants and Carriers simultaneously or in rapid succession. To give an example, it is worth considering the opening lines of her letter to Burghley in 1591, regarding her ongoing dispute with Gilbert Talbot, at this point seventh earl of Shrewsbury, over her right to claim her widow's third on the death of her husband:

Letter, Scribe A:	My moste honorable good Lord; your Lo:ᵖˢ ould saruante my good frend m.ʳ Bradshaw coming by me in his retorne toward the cowrte, I mighte not suffare him to pas wᵗʰout my Letters of moste hartye thankes to your Lo:ᵖ for all your honorable fauors towards me, and wᵗʰall to segnefye partly to your Lo:ᵖ how matters now reste betwene the earle of shrousbury and me, wᶜʰ I should haue thoughte fully concluded yf be fore I had not had tryall of his strange and vnkynde dealing; the xjᵗʰ of marche Laste mʳ markham being sente hether to me from the earle of shrousbury and my daughter for to make offars in respecte of my wedows parte, I tould him yt was in veane for me to enter into taulke wᵗʰ him for that the earle hertofore had refused such articles as he had set downe; whervnto mʳ markham replyed that he had full commetione from the earle to conclude all matters and whatsoeuer he should now set downe he would be bounde the earle should parforme them, so that the xijᵗʰ of marche Laste ther weare artocles set downe by mʳ markham betwen the earle of shrousbury and me and m.ʳ markham bounde in syxe thousad pounde that the earle should parform them, before the Laste of marche; the effecte wherof I segnefyed to my solesytor whaley emediatly vpon the conclusyone, and commandid him forthewyth to wayte of your Lo:ᵖ at your Leasure and to declare the wholl vnto your Lo.ᵖ wᶜʰ was Longe for slowed by the neclegence of the carryar that stayed my Letters as Whaley hath wrete to me;
	Extract from a letter from Bess (dowager countess of Shrewsbury) written from Wingfield to Lord Burghley, 11 April 1591, sent, hand of Scribe A.⁴⁶

Bess opened with a conventional-style reference to the bearer passing as a motivation for writing, but she customised this convention by referring to the bearer as 'your Lordships ould saruante my good frend Master Bradshaw'. It was a personal addition to the language of political friendship and social courtesy. It is not clear whether Bradshaw had in fact been sent up to Derbyshire by Burghley to investigate the goings-on between Bess and the new earl and countess, Gilbert Talbot and Mary (Cavendish) Talbot, or whether the letter was genuinely a spontaneous response to a bearer who happened to be passing. Either way, Bess certainly took the opportunity to

46 ID 159.

Sending and receiving letters 159

frame the letter as one written on her own initiative and a reflection of her confidence in her excellent relationships with Burghley and Bradshaw. Bess then went on to recount how, on the 11 March, the earl and countess had sent Master Markham to negotiate with her over her claim. Here we see the way in which a highly trained personal servant was authorised ('had full commetione from the earle') to undertake legal negotiations by proxy on behalf of his master and mistress; we also gain a glimpse of Bess's formidable competency when it came to her own participation in such matters of legal negotiation. The matter concluded, Bess then told how she wrote immediately to her solicitor Whalley in London and instructed him to speak with Burghley in detail about the issue. Unfortunately, she added, her letters to him were delayed by the slowness of the Carrier, but certainly Whalley would speak to Burghley in due course. Here, then, we find, in a short space, Bess interacting with one of Burghley's trusted and named personal servants (Bradshaw), legal advisors and solicitors who executed the technicalities of the negotiations and paperwork (Markham, Whalley), as well as the routine Carrier service. The delays, protractions, chance meetings and overlaps in time involved depict a dynamic system, one which was uneven and unregulated, which relied upon personal contacts and in which letters were only one part and were contiguous with other verbal and written discourses.

Epistolary circulation and delivery dynamics

The modes and methods of early modern epistolary delivery that have been described so far are, in many respects, familiar from recent scholarship and the models and examples presented here confirm and consolidate the findings of a number of studies. Most importantly, the examples from Bess's letters add further welcome detail to Mark Brayshay's account of the early modern travel and postal network routes; Alan Stewart's seminal account of the highly personalised nature of letter bearing; James Daybell's theorisation of bearers as 'corporeal extensions' of the letters they carry; and Katy Mair's demonstration of the way trust or distrust of the bearer impacted upon the content of letters. The remainder of this discussion considers a series of case studies, focused on individual letters to or from Bess, in order to further test and develop these models. The intention here is not to recast the theories of letter bearing presented by Brayshay, Daybell, Mair and Stewart, nor to dispute their narratives of the delivery process and accounts of letter reception and exchange. Rather, the aim is to augment and reflect upon their findings with reference to the particularly rich set of materials offered by Bess's letters. The model of delivery that emerges from this examination is characterised by two particular facets, and it is worth summarising these here.

First, it is a model that emphasises the flexible and unstable nature of the relationship between letter and bearer; that is, it acknowledges that the relation of the written words of the letter and the oral message supplied by the bearer was not fixed or predictable. On the one hand, the main locus

160 *Sending and receiving letters*

of agency and authority could reside within the letter; in these cases the role of the bearer was restricted to bringing the letter and, sometimes, bringing back a letter of reply. On the other hand, the primary locus for meaning could be with the spoken words of the bearer; in these cases the letter functioned to introduce and authorise his or her oral message, a warm-up act for the main performance. In between these two points was a spectrum of scenarios in which the locus of meaning could shift and slide between texts and persons and between written and oral. For example, the locus of meaning could switch from letter to bearer during the course of an epistolary transaction; in these cases the initial role of the bearer may have been to bring a letter, but then the moment of reception could give rise to a second message, typically his or her own report on the letter's reading. At this point the bearer became the receptacle for a memorised oral message back to the sender, or wrote a letter him- or herself. In other examples we see the letter designed as a prop that could be produced, as and if the occasions demanded, to aid the bearer's improvised negotiations. The next section examines, through a series of illustrative case studies, these possible scenarios and encounters between sender, bearer, recipient and letter.

Second, it is a model which emphasises not only the role of the bearer in the process of delivery but also the role of enclosures and the physical features of the letter packet itself. All three of these material and corporeal components – bearer, enclosure and letter packet – were found in a variety of combinations and remind us that the moment of reception was experienced through the senses. Alongside the sound of the bearer's voice, Bess's letters provided commentaries and covering notes for a range of material objects, from rose-petal conserve and red deer pies to books, garden seeds and ermine. When the letter packet was handed over, the recipient may have found him- or herself holding a stained, scruffily assembled postcard-sized rectangle of paper, or may have looked down at a neat white oblong tied with gold silk and folded as small as a packet of chewing gum. These physical objects and material features were extensions of both the written words on the page and the spoken words of the bearer, and, again, we find that the location of meaning and agency was not fixed or stable: a letter's material accompaniments might have functioned as mood music to cajole the recipient into a suitable frame of mind, but in other cases they functioned as the main locus for meaning, or existed coevally or in synergy with the words. These are features of Bess's letters that draw deeply on the interwoven conventions of epistolary practice, oral custom and gift-giving culture. The third and fourth sections of this chapter consider these material dimensions – enclosures and then letter packets – and the ways in which they had the potential to carry and generate meaning through their relation with the sender, bearer, recipient and letter. Ultimately, these provide a basis of empirical examples which make it possible to begin to outline the limits and boundaries of the proposed mobile and dynamic model of delivery.

3.2 'Delyver therwith vnto him, so great thankes & good wordes as yow can devyse': letters with bearers

> Sonne Gilbert this other lette^r wch I have writt to yo^{r}self yow may shew it to Sr Thom*as* Cornewallys wth all and I pray yow delyver therwth vnto him, so ^great thankes &^ good word*es* as yow can devyse.
>
> 31 January 1581, Bess (countess of Shrewsbury)
> writes from Sheffield to Gilbert Talbot, William Cavendish
> and Master Clarke, sent, scribal with autograph
> subscription and signature[47]

On 31 January 1581 Bess (countess of Shrewsbury) wrote to her stepson and son-in-law Gilbert Talbot, her second son, William Cavendish, and Master Clark a long letter concerning the arrangements for a proposed marriage agreement between her third son Charles Cavendish and Margaret Kitson (ID 227). The instructions from Bess, quoted earlier, appeared at the end of this letter and told Gilbert Talbot what to do with a second enclosed letter (ID 228), which she referred to as 'this other letter'.[48] The enclosed 'other letter' concerned Gilbert's upcoming visit to Sir Thomas Cornwallis to negotiate the details of the marriage agreement.[49] The 'great thanks & good wordes' she told Gilbert to improvise were intended to smooth the path of these negotiations and win over Cornwallis. More subtle was Bess's suggestion that Gilbert actually show Cornwallis her enclosed 'other letter'; she said 'you may shew it to Sir Thomas Cornewallys'. Her enclosed 'other letter' was not a simple authorising note to introduce the bearer, as seen elsewhere and described earlier. Rather, it was, to all appearances, a letter from Bess to Gilbert that was never intended for Cornwallis's eyes. By giving Gilbert such a letter, which could be revealed during his negotiations, Bess created an opportunity for Gilbert to display evidence of transparency and to establish proof of plain dealing. That is to say, the enclosed 'other letter' had a double function: first, it was a set of instructions to Gilbert in which Bess set out how she would like him to conduct the negotiations; second, it was a prop for Gilbert to show to Cornwallis if the moment demanded, as proof of her intentions. After Gilbert became seventh earl of Shrewsbury in 1590 he developed something of a reputation for violent quarrelsomeness, yet here in his earlier life he seemed to have possessed the skill of diplomacy, a quality Bess appreciated in him. That he was a close lifelong friend of Charles Cavendish may explain Gilbert's willingness to act as negotiator in this case, which concerned Charles's marriage, but it was also a role he

---

47 Arundel Castle, Autograph Letters 1585–1617, No. 89, ID 227.
48 Arundel Castle, Autograph Letters 1585–1617, No. 90, ID 228.
49 For more on Cornwallis's letter writing see Scott-Warren, 'News, Sociability, and Bookbuying'.

162 *Sending and receiving letters*

adopted elsewhere for Bess while she was countess of Shrewsbury and for his father, the earl.

Here we have, then, one of Bess's close family members being deployed as letter-bearer. Daybell's observation that bearers were often 'shadowy and historically invisible' figures is partially true in relation to Bess's letters.[50] As we have seen, Bess's Account Books record payments to many faceless individuals, now only partly traceable in the historical record and therefore largely unknown to us. But Bess also regularly employed bearers, such as Gilbert Talbot, from among those in her inner circle, individuals for whom we have substantial biographical information and who were employed for high-level personalised communication. These are letters that reveal to us the overlapping dynamics of family, household and political allegiances and allow us to consider at close quarters how Bess negotiated and navigated her way through the structures of power. They contribute to our understanding of the notions and workings of the interrelated concepts of secrecy, privacy, intimacy, diplomacy and trust at this period. Furthermore, they illustrate Bess's astute awareness of the importance of the timing of delivery and the person of the bearer when it came to winning over a correspondent.

As this 'other letter' from Bess provides an insight into how she could delegate to a bearer, as well as into how she wanted to be seen (by Cornwallis) to have delegated to a bearer, it is worth quoting in full here:

Superscription, unknown scribe:	To my loving sonnes Gilbert Talbott William Cavendyshe and my cosyn Clark
Endorsements, unknown scribe:	Charles v.^{Cli} presently. v.^{Cli} terio Trimtertes. 1581 v.^{C} in ffesto tour pro x. 1581 vltimo dec. 1582. ^{vCl}
Endorsements, Gilbert Talbot:	*lettres* from my L. ^& Lady^ at my beynge at London in february & marche. 1582 My La. *lettre* to my brother ~~Charles~~ ^William^ Cavendyshe m^r Clarke & my selfe concernynge my brother Charles Caven*dish's* marryage vltimo *January* 1590
Letter, unknown scribe:	Sonne Gilbert: I have receaved the artycles sett downe in behalf of a maryage betwixt Charles my sonne and Sr Thom*as* kidstons dought^r, wch truly in dyvers pointes are too obstricte, and the same I have noated in the margent of the booke wth my answer and mynde to every suche partycule whervnto I refer yow/ I pray yow delyv^r to ^good^ Sr Thom*as* Cornewallys most harty salutacions from me: wth thank*es* for his

---

50 Daybell, *Women Letter-Writers*, p. 127.

Sending and receiving letters 163

paynes taken in the matt[r] and willingnes to have it a
matche/ w[ch] wth all my hart I wishe and will strayne
myself to the vttermost, and farr more than shall
stand wth my ease, bothe for the vertuous demeanure
of the younge gentlewoman herself/ and that my
sonne is to ioyne wth so good frendes/ Yet my hope is
that S[r] Thom*a*s Cornewallys/ will thinke my offer to
the artycles very large and sufficyent/ and be a meane
that no further bonde be required, than conveniently
I may in reason graunt vnto/ Looke what I have sett
downe that shalbe assured in what stet they hold
best/ and yf further increase for Charles livinge be
stood vpon/ as also eny great Som*m*e to be bestowed
of land and assured to Charles/ that my worde
may take place, w[ch] I will not faile to *p*erforme.
And furth[r] declare, that as he hathe wysely done in
forbearing to wryte vnto me for the respecte alledged/
so do I now forbeare in lyke mann[r] to troble him
w[th] eny letter from me/ onely making ernest request
for his favorable contynuance in concluding the
maryage that yt may be dyspatchte before Lent/ and
so the enemie wilbe p[r]vented from wurking damage/
My hope is, it will not be taken in so ill degree as is
expected/ What soever chaunce lett him rest assured,
that I and all the frend*e*s I am able to make shalbe
imployde to labor the cause. and thus having referred
my mynd vnto yow/ I beseche god to blesse yow.
Sheffield the last of January 1580

Suscription, autograph: your louynge mother

Signature, autograph: EShrouesbury

31 January 1580/1, Bess (countess of Shrewsbury)
wrote from Sheffield to Gilbert Talbot, William
Cavendish and cousin Clarke, scribal with autograph
subscription and signature.[51]

Here Bess described her own letter as one which 'refers her mynd' to Gilbert, a conventional term that means she had described her views in detail to Gilbert so he could represent them accurately and in full to Cornwallis. She did so through her annotations on the paperwork related to the marriage negotiations: Bess told Gilbert that she had set out her 'answer and mynde to every suche partycule'; that is, she had indicated her responses and opinions in the form of marginal notations against each and every relevant point in the written agreement, so that Gilbert could be in no doubt as to her particular views in every respect. Having set out the technical specifications of her position, Bess went on to give directions as to how she would like Gilbert to approach Cornwallis. She made a show of emphasising that Gilbert should convey her warm greetings and appreciative thanks and reassure

51 ID 228.

164   *Sending and receiving letters*

Cornwallis of her sincere and genuine efforts to go above and beyond what was required to make the match happen. She then slipped in, in the form of a reminder to Gilbert, her good opinion of the 'vertuous demeanure' of Margaret Kitson, and the fact that the Kitsons were such 'good frendes' as of especial importance and reflected in her generous offer. Bess then skimmed over the nitty-gritty of the business, which was reduced to a clear-cut reminder of the single most important issue for her: that the marriage go ahead but that 'no further bond be required'.

Next, she deftly circumvented the lack of a reply from Cornwallis to her previous letter of two months earlier (24 November 1580, ID 204), which she managed under cover of a point of clarification and reassurance to Gilbert. In a move which re-appropriated Cornwallis's lack of response to her letter, she mentioned that she found Cornwallis's decision not to reply to her to be a wise one ('wysely done') and a good sign, a signal that they must be in complete agreement. She inverted the 'trouble taking' linguistic script so that it functioned to assert her own confidence and assurance of Cornwallis's positive reception of her last letter. So, rather than (as would be conventional in expressions of 'humility and entreaty') apologising for troubling him, she instead stated that she had decided to emulate his lack of response in 'forbearing to wryt vnto me' by herself forbearing 'in lyke manner to troble him with eny letter from me'.[52] There was, she said, no need for more letters, given that they were so clearly in agreement and all that was needed now was to conclude the marriage as soon as possible. Ultimately, her method was to embed her own message to Cornwallis within a letter ostensibly to Gilbert the bearer; it allowed Bess to communicate covertly. The finely balanced etiquette of when to write and when not to write, how much to say and how to select and utilise the bearer for maximum impact was a factor in the success of the communicative process.

As is clear from the Kitson negotiations, by 1580, when Bess was in her fifties, she was aware of these factors and adept when it came to their application: Charles Cavendish and Margaret Kitson were married in 1581.[53] Bess had had the opportunity to hone her skills in such matters during the earlier years of her life, an insight into which comes from a letter of a few years earlier, this time written from Gilbert Talbot himself, in which he relayed advice from the earl of Leicester regarding the strategies Bess must employ when writing to Queen Elizabeth. Again, great emphasis was placed upon the utmost importance of the personalised role of the bearer and upon the careful construction of sincerity and transparency in order to establish trust. Leicester was visiting the baths at Buxton for a swelling in his leg, an event Gilbert had dreaded ever since Leicester had 'threateneth' to come the

52 The linguistic scripts associated with 'humility and entreaty' are discussed in section 1.1, p. 49.
53 Margaret Kitson died soon after the birth of their first child in 1582; see ID 175.

Sending and receiving letters 165

previous spring.[54] In the first part of the letter we find Gilbert in attendance, shuttling between the demands of his father, the earl of Shrewsbury, the earl of Leicester, Bess (countess of Shrewsbury) and various other powerful individuals, appeasing and placating the one and then the other. The letter as a whole was addressed to both Shrewsbury and Bess, but the following segment was the part intended for Bess:

> I shewed y^t *lett*re of my La. Len*n*oxe yor daughter to my L. of Lec. who sayde, that he thoughte it were farre better for him to deferr her sutes to her ma.^{tie} till his owne com*m*inge to the courte then otherwyse to wryte to her before, for y^t he thynkethe her ma.^{tie} will suppose his *lett*re ~~were~~ if he sholde wryte were but at yor La. requeste & so by an other *lett*re wolde streyghte answere it agayne & so it doe no great good but at ^his^ metynge yor La. he will (he saythe) advyse in what sorte yor La. shall wryte to the Q. ma.^{tie} wch he will carry vnto her, and then be as earneste a solisitor ^therin^ as ever he was for any thing in his lyefe, & he doubtethe not to prvayle to yor La. contentac*i*on.
>
> 30 June 1578?, Gilbert Talbot from Buxton to Bess (countess of Shrewsbury) and Shrewsbury, holograph[55]

Here we learn that Bess had given Gilbert Talbot a letter ('y^t lettre') from her recently widowed daughter, Elizabeth (Cavendish) Lennox. The letter contained suits to the queen concerning her three-year-old daughter, Bess's granddaughter, Arbella Stuart's claim to the Lennox earldom.[56] Gilbert was to give the letter to the earl of Leicester so that he (Leicester) may write to the queen to press the suit. Here, in his letter of 30 June 1578, Gilbert reported back to Bess with Leicester's advice, which was: to wait until he (Leicester) could act as bearer himself and then for her (Bess) to write a letter directly to the queen, which Leicester would present himself in person. Leicester's reasoning was that, were he to write now, from Buxton, the queen would immediately suspect Bess to be behind the letter (which, of course, she was). The queen would then therefore write straight back with a negative response: 'stryghte answere it agayne & so is doe no great good'. Instead, Leicester proposed that when he next meet with Bess in person he would advise her on precisely how to phrase her own letter to the queen ('advyse in what sorte yor La. shall wryte to the Q. ma.^{tie}'), which he would then carry to the queen himself and guarantee to present her daughter Lennox's case as persuasively as possible and with every confidence of

---

54 LPL, Talbot Papers, Vol. F, fol. 237, Gilbert Talbot to Shrewsbury, 3 May 1578.
55 ID 83.
56 The issue of Arbella's claim appears in several letters between March 1578 and October 1578; see IDs 120, 188, 197, 121 and 122; for a full account see Durant, *Bess of Hardwick*, pp. 101–3.

166 *Sending and receiving letters*

success. In this way, Leicester explained the benefits of a more direct letter from Bess, one which would not arouse the queen's suspicions or cause her to raise her defences, presented personally and therefore creating the opportunity for the bearer (Leicester) to use his judgement as to the most persuasive line of approach. Here, then, we see Bess appealing to Leicester for help with the drafting and delivery of a letter. Within weeks she had also enlisted the direct support of her husband Shrewsbury, who wrote himself to the queen to press the suit.[57] Ultimately, Bess decided her own presence was required, and in October 1578 Leicester arranged for accommodation at Court for Bess so that she could present her suit to the queen herself in person.[58] Durant concludes that Bess's efforts, which resulted in annual pensions for Elizabeth Lennox and Arbella of £400 and £200 each, were something of a triumph given the circumstances; he comments that it 'says something for Bess's determination that she was able to get anything at all'.[59] Again, we see Bess's success as a letter-writer, which involved the use of letters within the context of the wider management of her social relations and interactions.

Shifts in power relations and personal status meant that the most appropriate person to act as bearer was constantly fluctuating and could change in an instant. Leicester's marriage in September 1578 resulted in his demotion in the queen's favour, which meant he became a less valuable channel to the queen after that point and after this date a range of other courtiers were preferred as bearers and intermediaries. Similarly, Gilbert's elevation to the position of earl of Shrewsbury in November 1591 raised him out of Bess's orbit, added to which were Gilbert's disputes with Bess. From the 1590s Bess came to rely increasingly upon her own favoured son, William, and her dependable legal advisors Timothy Pusey and Edward Whalley as conduits for communication. Yet, just when all seemed settled later in life, perhaps when Bess was least expecting it, she entered into what were to be among her most fraught communicative dealings in relation to the extraordinary drama surrounding her granddaughter Arbella Stuart in 1603. The events

57 He wrote two letters (co-signed with Bess): to Burghley, 14 May 1578 (Plate 14, ID 188), and to Leicester, 2 August 1578 (BL, Cotton, MS Caligula C. iii, fols 561r-62v, ID 197).

58 On 23 September 1578 Bess wrote to Lord Burghley from Chatsworth about her forthcoming visit to Court, to thank him for his friendship towards her daughter Elizabeth Lennox and granddaughter Arbella Stuart, and in anticipation of the 'comforte' she shortly hoped to receive 'by being in hir majesties presence' when she came to Court. On 24 October 1578 Bess wrote to Lord Burghley from Richmond Palace to describe her accommodation at Court and to note that she had not yet moved any suit to the queen (ID 122).

59 Durant, *Bess of Hardwick*, p. 102. Another example that provides us with 'a first-hand glimpse into the mechanics of personal letter-carrying and message delivery in elite circles' is given by Stewart, *Shakespeare's Letters*, p. 198.

that unravelled took place when Arbella – twenty-eight years old but still unmarried and deeply frustrated by her restrictive life at Hardwick Hall with her elderly grandmother – took matters into her own hands. She somehow persuaded one of Bess's trusted old servants, John Dodderidge, to take a memorised message in secret to Edward Seymour, first earl of Hertford, to propose marriage between herself and his sixteen-year-old grandson, Edward Seymour. Arbella's rather fanciful plot proposed that the boy Seymour should ride to Hardwick, trick his way in and identify himself to his betrothed via a token, such as a letter from Jane Grey. Hertford, sensibly suspicious, was having none of it, and took the matter straight to Sir Robert Cecil. So on 2 January 1603 it was not the boy Seymour who rode up to the gates of Hardwick Hall to seek Arbella, but courtier Sir Henry Bronker, sent by Cecil and Queen Elizabeth as bearer-ambassador to manage the situation. The extant sequence of letters is very well known and unfolds the events in detail.[60] Most relevant here (for our consideration of letter bearers), the sequence convinces us that Henry Bronker must have been a most eloquent and skilled diplomat; in Bess's words, citing Arbella's description of him, 'a verie discreete gentleman'.[61] That he successfully befriended both Bess and Arbella while relaying information between them, all the while reporting back to the queen, suggests a man of considerable personal charm and integrity.

In addition to the sketch of Henry Bronker the bearer that this sequence of letters gives to us, it reminds us how the precise micro-dynamics of Bess's family and households had wider political implications: how domestic tensions became enmeshed with intricate negotiations that implicated statesmen and courtiers. Moreover, Bess and Arbella's fractious relationship superbly illustrates that the reason for sending a letter was not always due to geographical distance, but that letters and bearers could be called into service in attempts to bridge emotional separation between correspondents in close physical proximity. The chasm of bad feeling between the two women meant that, at one point, they could bring themselves to communicate only by letter, even though they were living under the same roof and sharing the same bedchamber. Having been placed in the most difficult of circumstances, the situation must have been excruciating for them both, although, eventually, a reconciliation did occur.

While it might seem difficult to surpass Bess and her granddaughter's relationship for dysfunctionality, it was certainly rivalled by that with her eldest son, Henry Cavendish. A consistent disappointment to his mother, Henry's debts deepened and his problems spiralled during the course of his life. In

60 Steen, *The Letters*.
61 ID 131.

168   *Sending and receiving letters*

the 1580s Bess sent another of her sons, William Cavendish, as bearer to upbraid his brother for his incessant gambling. In Henry's defensive letter of response he protested his innocence and blamed rumour and hearsay:

> I receyved a lettar from your Ladyship by my brother Wyliam: and whear as your Ladyship wrytes yt ys sayed with you that, I am gonne onely vp to London to playe at dyse, and [the] sayer, or speaker of yt in tyme, wyll be asshamed of hys occupacyon.[62]

Communications failed to improve between mother and eldest son after this point. In 1603, when he sided with Arbella against her, Bess referred to him as 'my bad sonne Henry' and 'my vnnaturall sonne, Henry Cavendishe'.[63] Eventually Henry was cut from Bess's will, never to be restored.

Something of the desperation of Henry's financial situation can be seen in the following letter from Edward Talbot (Henry's brother-in-law) to Bess in 1604. With Henry having pawned the family silver and with debtors literally lining up at his door, it was no surprise that communications between family members were fraught and limited to tense exchanges involving intermediaries:

Superscription, unknown scribe:	To the right ho:[ble] and my very good Lady and mother in Lawe the Lady Elizabeth Countesse of Shrewsbury dowager: at Hadwicke *delivered* §
Letter, unknown scribe:	My duty most humbly remembred to yo[r] ho:[r] may please you be aduertised that yesterday beinge ffryday, I receyued a *lettre* from my Servant Townro[w] from London, wherin he writeth that he hath not as yet got any answere from my sister Grace; of the *lettre* w[ch] I writt vnto hir, w[ch] your ho:[r] knoweth of; but said y[t] she would writ vnto me an answere, but as yet hath not: and he writeth further that she deliu[r]d the *lettre* to my brother hir husband, who he him self did see read it, and he saith that it semeth by his speaches that he did well accept therof, and thanked me for my remembrance, and wished he had bene ther before my Comm*i*nge downe: and intreated my man in his next *lettre* to commeand him kindly vnto me, after which his speaches my sister spake privately vnto him, and as he writeth (said these wordes) w[ch] he thought should not haue proceded from hir, w[ch] were these: Assure my brother I am and euer wilbe, as sorry to doe any thing that may be eyther

---

62 ID 10, 6 November c. 1585.
63 ID 135 and ID 140.

Sending and receiving letters **169**

hurtfull to him, or the house wherof I came;
as any sister or woman in the world, except
great and extreame necessity doth inforce me
thervnto, wch nowe god knowes is much, and we
are hardly delt with, both by my ould Lady and
my Lord: Addinge furth^r y^t I should assure my
self that assoone as my Lord, did move any such
matter vnto hir, as she protested as yet he hath
not done; I should knowe of it: which answere
accordinge to my *Lett*re dated from Newarke he
made acquainted to m^r Will*i*um Cavendishe who
returned him this speech: Assure your self, she
will not doe it, without a great some of money,
which my Lord can not giue; without they will
take ther payment in wordes, and that will pay
no debtes; nor releiue ther present want, but they
are wise enough for that, and if my sister should,
yet the Recou^ry will not be good vnlesse your
ho:^r consent thervnto, wch I hoope you never will:
and this is all he adu^rtiseth in those matters But
he writeth that the Earles Iewells and platt are
laid to pawne, and that ther is as many suters
euery day at his chamber, as at the most noble
men in the Court; but they come onlye to Crave
ther debtes: Alsoe ther is not any thinge done by
the Earle in Parliament, nor like to be that he can
learne Thus with my wifes most bounden duty and
my owne vnto ~~hir~~your ho: most humbly cravinge
your blessinge to vs both, doe most humbly and
hartely beseech the contenuance of your honorable
fauour, with the like humble thankes for your
most hon:^ble bounty towardes vs: Soe wishinge you
most long and happy yeares: doe humbly take my
Leave: Bothell the xij^th of Maye: 1604:

Subscription:

Yo^r hon:^rs most humble and faithfully affected
Sonne to be commaunded//
§

Signature:

Edw Talbott

12 May 1604, Edward Talbott wrote from Bothell
to Bess (dowager countess of Shrewsbury) at
Hardwick, sent.[64]

Here Edward Talbot wrote to Bess to tell her he had received a letter sent
from London from his servant Townrow. In the said letter, Townrow told
Edward that he (Townrow) had not yet had a reply from Grace (Talbot)
Cavendish (Henry's wife and Edward's sister) to Edward's earlier letter,
this letter being the one 'which your honor knoweth of' (indicating it was
written at least with Bess's approval, if not at her instigation). The line of

64 Folger CT, X.d.428 (81), ID 63.

170 *Sending and receiving letters*

communication ran from Bess to Edward to Townrow the bearer to Grace, who passed the letter to her husband Henry; then back again from Henry and Grace to Townrow (the bearer) to Edward to Bess. The multiple stages of transmission are indicative of the deadlocked state of Bess and Henry's relationship, where communication could be broached only through concentric circles of intimates. Bess's second son, William Cavendish, was also involved, and Edward closed his letter by reporting his younger brother-in-law's views as to the couple's irretrievably debt-ridden state.

At the centre of this letter is the bearer Townrow's detailed report on Henry's reception of Edward's letter. As Stewart has shown, to observe a letter being read, and then provide the sender with an account of its reception, was an expected element of letter bearing.[65] The scene depicted by Townrow gives us an insight into his entry in the circus of this family's domestic disputes. He described, as it were, a miniature five-part drama involving three people, shifting interpersonal dynamics and ending in a betrayal:

1 Townrow brought Edward's letter to his (Edward's) sister Grace and stood witness as she showed it to her husband Henry.
2 Henry was observed by Townrow and Grace as he read the letter.
3 Henry reacted to the letter and by his 'speaches' Townrow concluded he has accepted its contents.
4 Henry thanked Townrow and asked that he commended him to Edward in his next letter.
5 Grace, apparently present throughout, 'spake privately' to Townrow, uttering words he 'thought should not haue procedd from her'.

It is not clear exactly what was meant by 'spake privately' here, whether it meant private in the modern sense of Grace and Townrow being entirely alone, or, more likely, whether it was closer to the modern sense of 'individually' and meant they spoke one-to-one but with others still present. As a result, it is not possible to tell whether Grace took Townrow into another room where they talked alone; or, alternatively, whether they were in the same space with Henry, and perhaps others, present, where she drew Townrow to one side; or, alternatively again, whether she managed to whisper in his ear at some opportune moment. Certainly, Grace's words, quoted in direct speech and intended for her brother Edward, were sufficiently inappropriate in implicating her husband to suggest he was out of earshot: she apologised to Edward for her involvement in any behaviour that would be damaging to him or to the Talbot name; assured him she would do such a thing only if forced 'out of great and extreame necessity'; and she complained of being dealt with severely by 'my ould Lady and my Lord' (her mother-in-law Bess and her husband Henry). Grace was hard-pressed and

---

65 See the discussion in Stewart, *Shakespeare's Letters*, p. 199.

Sending and receiving letters 171

her whispering to Townrow the bearer was a desperate measure, a distress flare or a message in a bottle to her brother Edward. It reminds us that, as conduits for communication, a bearer could become party to the most intimate secrets, disloyalties and indiscretions.

These events and indiscretions may have been the final straw for Grace and Henry. The following year, on 22 April 1605, Bess's right-hand man Timothy Pusey wrote to William Cavendish to inform him that his mistress Bess

> this night is informed by a gentlewoman here, that a gentleman of good credit now here sayeth there is no good agreement between Master H Cavendish and ye Lady Grace and that he hath lately charged her to be a harlot to some of his men and names men to her.[66]

These were serious accusations from a husband to his wife and, as Durant comments, Bess may have reflected that it was all 'too much coming from Henry who had scattered his own bastards throughout Staffordshire and Derbyshire'.[67] Now cut off from his inheritance, Bess had washed her hands of Henry and their communications shrank to only the most strained of formal gestures. Henry's Christmas and New Year letters to his mother in December 1605 were all surface: restricted to the stiffest of rhetorical and palaeographical conventions, they rehearsed the brief formalities of exemplary politeness. While in another context, and from another person, such formalities might be read as straightforward expressions of polite and deferential respect, here they reflected a sub-zero emotional climate. That he wrote at all may suggest he was hopeful his mother may have a change of heart and revert him to her will, as rumours had been circulating of Bess's declining health.[68]

We know that Henry's wife, Grace (Talbot) Cavendish, in previous years, had made her own approaches to Bess on her husband's behalf. The following letter shows how Grace attempted to present a suit from her husband Henry to his mother, Bess, through lines of female contact. As Daybell has observed, 'the circles of women surrounding leading courtiers, government officials and regional magnates were targeted by female petitioners seeking to circumvent official channels of power'.[69] Grace tried just this tactic by appealing to Jane (Leach) Kniveton, Bess's half-sister and lifelong companion and one of the most intimate of the inner circle of women with which

---

66 The letter from Timothy Pusey is Chatsworth House, Hardwick Drawer 143 (14).
67 Durant, *Bess of Hardwick*, pp. 217–18.
68 Henry's Christmas letter is from 6 December 1605, and his New Year letter from 31 December 1605 (ID 207; and ID 11, Plate 19). As Durant states, Henry Cavendish and Gilbert Talbot were left nothing at all in Bess's will, 'not even a small sum to buy mourning-rings', and they do not seem to have attended her funeral; *Bess of Hardwick*, pp. 224–25.
69 Daybell, *Women Letter-Writers*, p. 147.

172   *Sending and receiving letters*

she constantly surrounded herself. It is clear from Grace's letter that the women closest to Bess could be key players when it came to the delivery and reception process:

> Good aunt mr Cavendysshe hath sent hear inclosed a letter to my honorable good la. whych he desireth you to delyuer. it is a sutt he hath to her honor whych I trust she wyll not be offended wyth hym for I haue presumed to send her honor ij fatt capons , whych ar not so good as I desier the wer but I hope to haue better shortly now wee haue corn in the barner and a hundred of wardins , the best frute our cuntrey wyll afford thys year whych good aunt delyuer to her honor , wyth my most humble duty and lyke desier of her honors dayly blessinge : thynkeinge my selfe most bound for her honors bounty euer to me : whych I can no ways deserue . but wyth my prayers for her ho: helth and happynes in all thyngs : good aunt comend ^v^vs ~~me~~ most louyngly to my swet nephew and nece . to whom I haue sent adosin wardins and thus wyth my harty , comendatyons to yourselfe I take my leue tutbury thys x of october
>
>   your assurede louinge nece
>   Grace Cavendysshe
>
> 10 October c. 1585?, Grace (Cavendish) Talbot
from Tutbury to Jane Kniveton[70]

The chain of contact ran from Henry to Grace to Grace's bearer (unmentioned) to Jane to Bess, and Grace included with her letter two fat capons and a hundred wardins – birds and fruit intended, as it were, to leaven and sweeten the communications. Writing in the context of a high-level of horizontal distance, the attempt was made to reach Bess through her inner circle of women and through reconciliatory gestures of food. Women such as Grace and Jane, wives and companions, could lubricate social relations and potentially transmit communications in diplomatically tricky situations. The skill was to know which family member to interact with at a particular moment in order to get your message through. Delivery dynamics map onto household, family and political dynamics. Henry's message to his mother was embedded in concentric circles of relationships and couched in the customs of obligation and gift-giving. That is to say, Henry's message involved not just the rhetorical and practical tasks of composing and then sending a letter, but also negotiation through the layers of customs and etiquettes through which epistolary culture operated. We do not know for sure whether Grace's letter enclosing Henry's suit met with success, although there are various references in Bess's Account Books to donations made to Henry, collected by his bearer named 'Swift', which may well have been

---

70 Folger CT, X.d.428 (7), sent, in her own hand.

Sending and receiving letters   173

responses to letters such as this one.[71] The usefulness of consumable and material accompaniments to a letter should not be underestimated: it was a feature that recurred repeatedly throughout Bess's letters, sometimes to powerful effect, and is the focus of the next section.

3.3   'A note that came with the stuff': letters with enclosures

> Tymperley came yesternyght, it apereth by a note y^t came wth the stuffe y^t there is such thinges comme as nicholas steward wrytt for, as thredd & silke or suche like, but it is lapped amonge so many other roulles of the lyke, and nothing wrytten on the backsyde, y^t we can not tell wch is for y^r La. from other folkes.
>
> 13 October 1575, Gilbert Talbot from
> Sheffield to Bess (countess of Shrewsbury)[72]

This reference to 'a note y^t came with the stuffe', now lost, reminds us that many items delivered were accompanied by a bill, a note, a letter, notes written on the thing itself or other sorts of verbal messages. We can speculate that many more of these, unmentioned in the Account Books, and by their nature highly ephemeral items, are now lost or invisible in the historical record. Sometimes a letter may have been entirely unrelated to the object it accompanied, carried only out of convenience, such as those that, as far as we can tell, just happened to arrive with butter and cheese when Old Alsop came to Chatsworth in December 1552: 'paid unto ^old^ Awesope by my ladis commandyment for brenging serten leters & other stuff buter & ches – ijs'. In other cases there was a close relationship between the letter and the enclosure or accompanying item, between the words and the things; in fact, the nature of the enclosure regularly determined the form and function of the letter. To comment on an enclosure in some way could be the whole function of a letter, or occupy just a small part of a letter's purpose. Most

---

71 Other food gifts from Grace are recorded in Bess's Account Books for the 1590s – for example, 'geven to one that brought ij Capons from my Ladie grace – xijd' (Chatsworth House, Hardwick MS 7) and 'To one that brought Rosemarie from my La: grace – xxd' (Hardwick MS 8, 1596). Henry Cavendish's messenger Swift is mentioned by Gilbert Talbot in ID 217 as well as in payments recorded in Bess's Account Books – for example, 'to swefte henry Cavendish hys man tow shellings – ijs' and 'To swyft ijs vjd' (fol. 120v) and 'To Swyft Master Henry Cavendishes man ijs vjd' (Hardwick MS 8). There are also references to passing money to Henry via Grace in May 1583: 'Item to my dowter cavendyssh to sende to har hosbande threscore ponde' and 'Item to my dowter cavendysshe the xiiij of maye to sende to har hosbande one honderyth ponde' (Hardwick MS 5, fol. 34).

72 Sheffield archives, MD 6278, ID 217, sent, in his own hand.

174 *Sending and receiving letters*

usual in this respect were those cases where a letter functioned as a commentary on a second, enclosed, letter. We might term these 'bye-letters' as they are additions to the main package being delivered.[73] We have already seen examples of these: they included news-letters circulated among kin, accompanied by a bye-letter in the form of a shorter covering note or marginal annotation; and letters sent to bearers, typically accompanied by a bye-letter in the form of specific instructions for delivery. There were three other commonly found ways, in the letters to and from Bess, that a letter could function in relation to an enclosure: (1) as a set of practical instruction, often associated with supplies or enclosed household items, (2) as part of a regular discourse of relationship maintenance, usually to accompany food and consumables, or (3) as a commentary on a costly luxury item, sometimes a unique symbolic gift. Examples of each of these allow us to examine how commentaries provided by letters and bearers related to the enclosures they accompanied. These examples remind us that Bess's letters were part of an ongoing process of material exchange in which enclosures were material extensions of letters and that they could determine the words on the page and carry just as much meaning.

The first category involved bye-letters that gave practical instructions related to items and objects used within the household or garden. For example, on 8 March c. 1560 Bess wrote from Court home to Chatsworth describing her wish that her aunt Marcella Linacre create a new herb and flower garden which was to be sown with 'al kynde of earbes and flowres and some pece of yt with malos'. She concluded her letter with words that functioned as a covering note to several enclosed bundles of garden seeds, themselves annotated by her gardener William Marchington, and she promised to write again with further instructions for their particular use: 'I haue sende you by this carerer iij bundeles of garden sedes all wreten with wellem marchyngtons hande and by the next you shall know how to youse them yn euery pynte'.[74] When Marchington himself wrote to Bess on 13 January c. 1560 from his letter we see that the transaction of items between Bess at Court and her servants at Chatsworth was two-way; he sent 'by this carryer iiij pottes ij of them tonnes/ & ij with covers'.[75] Such practical exchanges were part of the wider discourse of routine request and receipt that permeated many of the letters. Especially notable here were those from the early years of Bess's marriage to Shrewsbury, when he regularly supplied her with provisions and their letters track the transit of sack, beer, ale, rye, malt, hops, barley, venison, salt venison, offal, plate and iron as they left one household, were expected at another, then arrived and were received,

---

73 There is a discussion and definition of 'bye letters' in Daybell, *The Material Letter*, p. 127.
74 ID 100.
75 ID 47.

Sending and receiving letters 175

in relation to the frequent movement of the Scottish Queen between their various households in the 1570s.[76]

There is a distinction to be made between, on the one hand, exchanges of household or estate supplies that included the weekly allowance of barley, rye and offal sent from Shrewsbury to Bess and, on the other, items which fell more closely into the category of gifts. Often the line between the two was rather thin. In some cases, the content of a covering letter, or bye-letter, can help to elucidate the origins and intended use of an item, and therefore aid in establishing its point on the fuzzy continuum between purchase, exchange, supply, donation, reward, token, bribe and gift.[77] However, in other cases, and more often, the relationship between note and stuff is oblique and fractured and therefore does not necessarily offer clarification. So, in the following letter we find Shrewsbury in the midst of multiple deliveries and where letters were utilised to order items or confirm receipt:

> My iuelle I have resevyd your lettar by the erles man & have resevyd xxxiiij dosen of him & payd him for youres/ whereof I have delyvered xx dosen to the scotes quene from you ho gyves you gret thankes for them I have also resevyd the casteng flagon & a boxe of consarv of roses.[78]

The dosens (woollen cloths or blankets) could be classified as essential supplies, although they had nevertheless been procured with effort and were received with gratitude by the Scottish Queen ('ho [who] gyves you gret thankes for them'). The box of rose-petal conserve or jam ('boxe of consarv of roses'), on the other hand, might more appropriately be classed as a small token or food gift. Together these items show Bess in her role as co-keeper of the Scottish Queen, delivering choice items of luxury foodstuffs to generate good will and improve her custodian's comfort.

The rose-petal conserve brings us to the second category of letters with enclosures: letters concerned with relationship maintenance sent with food or consumables. Not all foods were equal and some could be prized luxuries if they were difficult to find or grow, or were seasonal delicacies or imports from warmer climates.[79] If food was the currency of relationship maintenance, then a jam or jelly that involved bales of rose petals as an ingredient certainly ranked as fit for an earl or a queen. Other desirable items included citrus fruits, which were regularly imported, as mentioned in Shrewsbury's letter to Bess of 8 August 1574: 'I sent you this day iiij^{xx} [i.e. fourscore, 80] and xx

---

76 The letters tracking supplies and provisions are IDs 73, 178, 182, 183 and 184.
77 These distinctions are made by Zemon Davis, *The Gift*, pp. 22–35, and throughout.
78 c. 1571, George, sixth earl of Shrewsbury to his wife Bess (countess of Shrewsbury), sent, ID 70, Plate 11.
79 Heal, 'Food Gifts'.

176 *Sending and receiving letters*

orenges by your caryar'.[80] We know that Bess and Shrewsbury regularly exchanged delicacies that included lettuce and butter, and also mentioned were salt venison and two 'boxses of comfettes'. This was the stuff of harmonious marital discourse and we likewise find her previous husband, Sir William St Loe, sending Bess lemons, olives, cucumbers and other food items to signify his affection. It was not a practice restricted only to husbands and wives and similar tangible expressions of friendship, affection or respect came from other family members. So on 8 February 1588 the twelve-year-old Arbella Stuart wrote to her grandmother Bess to thank her for 'the token' she had sent and to send in return 'a pott of gelly, which my seruante made', along with her own hair trimmings, which were customary to send to a loved one. With these items came a letter written in Arbella's exemplary calligraphic hand, with its curled flourishes and clubbed ascenders, and her good wishes couched in her self-consciously precise Latinate prose (seen in, for example, her choice of the words 'certified' and 'disposition'): 'My Aunte Cauendishe was heere on Monday laste, she certified me, of your Ladyships good health, & dispositione'. It was a package of three items concocted by the young Arbella to acknowledge her relationship with her grandmother in linguistic, corporeal and culinary form. That the young Arbella managed to express appropriate thanks and respectful affection, while displaying her own accomplishments, gives us an early insight into her epistolary competency.[81]

Early modern epistolary rhetoric, then, was paralleled by an ongoing patterned rhetoric of gifted food, which articulated aspects of shared identity, mutual friendship, respect and deference. Many food items were sent without letters and remind us that Bess's letters existed within a wider cultural milieu of material transactions. There was not only domestic harmony but also pride and prestige to be gained from giving fine and exotic consumables. Shrewsbury's ship *The Talbott* was used to import a quantity of wine from Bordeaux in May 1573, from which portions were distributed as gifts to the Lord Keeper, Lord Treasurer and earl of Leicester. While Shrewsbury's gifts were of magnificent proportions, it was a practice repeated across the social scale and items received by Bess correlated against the spectrum of those in her social network. Numerous items defined and articulated social hierarchy and status within an acknowledged structure of exchange – a customary means of establishing social bonds and competing for favour. There is a strong impression of a continual flow of items being sent and received, some over long distances but many more exchanged among family and kin between the houses of Chatsworth, Hardwick, Wingfield and

---

80 ID 73.
81 ID 106. For comparison see Jonathan Gibson's discussion of Elizabeth I's accomplished and painstaking italic handwriting that appears in texts she wrote before she came to the throne, 'The Queen's Two Hands'.

Sending and receiving letters 177

Oldcotes, which were all within a few miles of each other. The poor brought apples and spiced cake and neighbours and kin sent seasonal delicacies of fruit, such as strawberries, apricots and peaches, or luxury vegetables, like 'hartyechokes' and fresh young peascods.[82]

The most marked or 'gift-determined' of high-status foods was venison. Deer parks defined the nobility and higher gentry, and elite control over game kept it separate from the market and therefore the ultimate in luxury foods.[83] Venison was the lifeblood of Bess's elite network and she regularly involved herself in its circulation among her exalted contacts and connections. The earliest records are from the 1550s Account Books, which mention deliveries of red deer pies and venison pasties from among the great and the good given to Bess (Lady Cavendish) and her second husband Sir William Cavendish:

> Item geven to Master mylner man for brenginge a pye off Redde derre – vjd
>
> Item geven to Master berand mane for brenginge pastes off venysone – xijd
>
> Item ~~paid for~~ geven in reward to a mane off my lorde off huntingtons for breng a pastye off venysonne by my lady command – xijd
>
> Item geven to one off my lorde off suffolke mane for brenginge one sydde off venysone – vjd.[84]

A few years later, Bess married a man well able to supply her with any imaginable quantity venison. There are numerous references to Shrewsbury's largess when it came to the distribution of venison-based gifts. Typically, Shrewsbury dispatched batches of pies and pasties from Sheffield to his agent Thomas Baldwin in London, accompanied by covering letters giving directions as to their distribution. One such letter of 14 October 1580 refers to seventy red deer pasties to be distributed to the earl of Leicester, Roger Manners, Sir Henry Tirrell, Sir Walter Mildmay, Sir Ralph Sadler, Sir Christopher Hatton, the Comptroller of the Royal Household and others; similar letters written on 14 November 1579 and 16 October 1583 indicate that this was an annual event.[85] Other letters referred to Shrewsbury's gifts of venison to, among others, the archbishop of York, Sir Richard

---

82 For discussions of comparable gift patterns and gift networks see Zemon Davis, *The Gift*, pp. 66–68, and Heal, 'Food Gifts', pp. 55–56. On other forms of symbolic capital in letter writing see Magnusson, 'A Rhetoric of Requests', pp. 51–66.

83 Here paraphrasing Heal, 'Food Gifts', pp. 57–58, who shows how venison was 'marked out from the rest by cultural consent' as a 'status food', the most 'determined' and 'gift-ascribed' item, separated from the market and commerce.

84 Chatsworth House, Hardwick MS 1, fols 44, 46, 47, 48.

85 LPL, Shrewsbury Papers, MS 699, fol. 31, and Talbot Papers Vol. P, fol. 981 and Vol. G, fol. 218.

178 *Sending and receiving letters*

Knightly and Robert Radcliffe, Viscount Fitzwalter; these are sometimes on request but always with the implication that the compliment would be returned.[86] Particular pride was attached to the presentation of venison captured by a female huntress, such as the fat stag killed by a lady and presented by Sir Henry Lee to Shrewsbury in May 1588, or the one killed by Bess's daughter Mary (Cavendish) Talbot, countess of Shrewsbury, and presented by her husband Gilbert Talbot to Thomas Cecil, second Baron Burghley, in September 1602.[87] As talking points for high-table entertainment, their hints towards the huntress goddess Diana would have appealed to elite pretentions and self-fashioning.

We can observe Bess's involvement in the distribution of venison in one of her first letters following her marriage to Shrewsbury. A delivery from the newly married earl and countess was presented at Court on the couple's behalf, along with their good wishes, by Anthony Wingfield. His wife, Elizabeth (Leach) Wingfield, who was head of the maids of honour of the royal household, immediately wrote to her half-sister Bess to report on the gift's reception.[88] On the reverse of this letter Bess jotted down a list of her and her new husband's connections at Court, all of whom were very likely recipients in what must have been a venison extravaganza:

> the quene
> the lady cobham
> the lady clenton
> the lady howarde
> the lady knolles
> the lady strange
> the lady cescell
> the lady k̶ baken
> the lady myldmaye
> the lady cattelyne
> my cossen garate
> my syster wynfelde
> blanche
> marberey
> the lorde great sealle
> the lorde tresorare
> mayster atorney
> mayster solysyter

---

86 LPL, Talbot Papers, Vol. G, fol. 138, Robert Loughter to Shrewsbury, 3 May 1582; Vol. I, fol. 21, Sir Christopher Hatton to Shrewsbury, 30 July 1589; Vol. H, fol. 119, Edward Russell, third earl of Bedford, to Shrewsbury, 29 October 1590.

87 LPL, Shrewsbury Papers, MS 698, fol. 73 and Talbot Papers, Vol. K, fol. 52.

88 On Elizabeth (Leach) Wingfield's position within the royal household, see Daybell, *Women Letter-Writers*, p. 156.

mayster ~~ob~~ osborne
the lorde cheffe joustys
mayster creswell
my l
my lady h
my lady r
my lady ny
my lady g

Item of countery wemen[89]

Elizabeth Wingfield went on to describe to Bess how the queen, having received the venison, talked for 'one longe owre with Master wyngfeld', during which time she expressed her great love and affection for the earl and his new countess. The queen, reported Elizabeth Wingfield, had emphasised her particular desire to see Bess at Court, quipping, 'I haue bene glade to se my lady sayntloa but now more dyssirous to se my lady shrewsbury'. Furthermore, she added, the queen had loaded particular praise on Bess, saying, again quoting her majesty's words, that she hoped 'my lady hath knowne my good opennon of her and thus muche I assure you there ys no lady y[n] thys land that I beter loue and lyke'. This striking praise from the queen has become a favourite quotation among Bess's biographers and has understandably been taken as evidence of a special bond between the two women, monarch and subject.[90] That the queen favoured Bess is in no doubt, but the wider context of the letter reminds us that the queen's words here were prompted by what must have been a bumper donation of venison given to the Court and to an array of courtiers. Bess had expert knowledge of Court circles, having only recently left the privileged and intimate position as one (of only five) of the queen's Ladies of the Privy Chamber.[91] In this intensely competitive environment, where gifts were the currency through which favour was generated, we know from the consistent success of Bess's New Year's presents to the queen that she had a talent for judging gifts. Here, in the very early days of her marriage to Shrewsbury, we should be in

89 Frances Brooke, Lady Cobham (b. after 1530, d. 1592); Elizabeth Fiennes de Clinton, Lady Clinton (1528?–1589); Lady Katherine Howard (1545 × 50–1603); Dame Katherine Knollys (d. 1569); Margaret, Lady Strange (1540–96); Dame Mildred Cecil (1526–89); Dame Anne Bacon (d. 1610); Dame Mary Mildmay (1527/8–77); Anne, wife of Gilbert Gerard (d. 1593), attorney general; Elizabeth Wingfield, half-sister to Elizabeth, countess of Shrewsbury; Blanche Parry (d. 1590); Sir Nicholas Bacon (1510–79), lord keeper of the great seal; William Paulet, first marquis of Winchester (1474–72), lord treasurer; Gilbert Gerard (d. 1593), attorney general; Richard Onslow (1527/8–1571), solicitor general; Sir Robert Catlin (d. 1574), lord chief justice.
90 21 October 1567, sent, Folger CT, X.d.428 (129), ID 96.
91 By 1567 Bess had remarried and left the Privy Chamber, by which point Elizabeth had only four women of the Privy Chamber, Blanche Parry, Lady Stafford, Elizabeth Knollys and Dorothy Bradbelt; Durant, *Bess of Hardwick*, p. 50.

180   *Sending and receiving letters*

no doubt as to Bess's ability to make the ultimate high-status food gift work in her own and her husband's favour.

Bess's role in the deployment of venison to maintain her and her husband's networks continued during their marriage, and she sent venison and puddings to London in November or early December 1568, which were to be sent on to Shrewsbury at Court. In an affectionate letter back to Bess, Shrewsbury was keen to assure her that, while he was enjoying some of the puddings himself in the privacy of his own chamber, three dozen of them had been appropriately and publically distributed at Court, given specifically to Bess's friend Frances Brooke, Lady Cobham (b. after 1530, d. 1592), to William Herbert, first earl of Pembroke (1507–70, lord steward from 1567–70) and to the earl of Leicester. He offered her further reassurance that the venison had been sent for:

> I thank you swete none for your podenges & venyson/ the podenges have I bestoud in this wyes dosen to my lade cobbam & as many to my Lord steuard & to my Lord of Leystere & the reste I have resarved to my celfe to ete in my chaumbar the venyson is yett at london but I have cente for it heddar.[92]

But just as the harmonious early days of Bess's marriage to Shrewsbury were marked, in the letters, by gifts of venison, so too was its acrimonious end. On 29 September 1586 bailiff William Deckenson wrote to Shrewsbury that Mistress Elinor Brytten had put so much wine and spirits into the venison pasties that they had broken in transit. Elinor Brytten was the woman from whom Shrewsbury sought comfort and consolation during the final years of his marriage to Bess, following their widely known and notoriously bitter separation. Little is known of her, other than she was a woman of his household and that she engaged in prolonged litigation with Gilbert Talbot when he became seventh earl after his father's death over her entitlement to gold and jewels she claimed Shrewsbury had given her. That she had taken over management of the pasties by autumn 1586 is another marker in the decline of the Shrewsburys' marriage.

Most of the enclosures that have been mentioned so far no longer survive because they were perishable or consumable. More durable items were sent but we have few of these either, presumably lost, decayed or discarded, although a few are extant. Those most likely to be mentioned constitute the third category of letters with enclosures under consideration here: letters with costly, luxury items. For example, we have a record of 20s payment for delivery in 1599 made to 'a carrier that brought the Quenes picture from

---

92 December 1568, Shrewsbury from Hampton Court to Bess (countess of Shrewsbury) at Tutbury, sent, in his own hand, Folger CT, X.d.428 (86), ID 65.

Sending and receiving letters   181

London'.[93] This picture, painted by the workshop of Nicholas Hilliard, can still be seen at Hardwick New Hall today and shows the queen modelling an extraordinary dress embroidered with images of sea monsters.[94] As Roy Strong has shown, by 1599 the ageing queen no longer sat for portraits, but the Hilliard workshop was given access to her jewellery and dresses, into arrangements of which they would inset an officially sanctioned formalised mask of the sovereign. The Hardwick portrait is typical of one of these productions: while the queen appears rather frozen-faced, her dress is vividly drawn from life and rendered in detail. It seems, in fact, to have been the dress that Bess was particularly interested in when she commissioned this full-length portrait. The dress may even have been a New Year's gift from Bess, such as the one mentioned by Elizabeth (Leach) Wingfield in her letter sent from Court some twenty-three years earlier, on 2 January, probably 1576. Her account of the success of the gift would have been welcome news to Bess and Shrewsbury, who were confined to their Derbyshire households, dutifully guarding their charge Mary, Queen of Scots, unable to attend at Court to represent themselves in person:

> her majesty neuer liked any thinge you gaue her so well the color and strange triminge of the garments with the reche and grat cost bestowed vpon yat hath caused her to geue out such good speches of my lord and yovr ladyship as I neuer hard of better she toulde my lord of S Lester and my lord chamberlen that you had geuen her such garments thys yere as she neuer had any so well lyked her/ and sayd that good nobell copell the show in al things what loue the bere me.[95]

The dress was a sensation. Given the queen's reaction and her public lauding through 'good speches' of 'that good nobell coupell' (the Shrewsburys), we can only imagine the kind of spectacular garment Bess had masterminded into existence. It would be tempting to suggest that this was the same sea-monster's dress that came to feature in the painting some twenty-three years later, in which case the 'strange triminge' would refer to the dress's distinctive embroidered front panel. If so, then the 1599 picture, painted when both women were well into their senior years, memorialised the long-standing bond between queen and loyal subject through reference to a gift that recalled their heyday. It would certainly have accorded with Bess's wider project to tell the story of her remarkable life through the carefully managed visual schemes at Hardwick New Hall.

93 Chatsworth, Hardwick MS 8, fol. 56v, 1598–99.
94 Known as the 'Hardwick' portrait; there is a discussion of this portrait by Strong, *Gloriana: The Portraits of Queen Elizabeth I*, pp. 147–51; and by Ashelford, *The Art of Dress*.
95 2 January 1577, Elizabeth (Leach) Wingfield to Bess (countess of Shrewsbury), sent, in her own hand, Folger CT, X.d.428 (130), ID 97.

182 *Sending and receiving letters*

Regardless of whether it refers to the sea-monster's dress itself, Elizabeth Wingfield's report illustrates how letters could function in the construction of meaning between gift, giver and recipient. It is no surprise, in this culture of consumption, that unique and imaginative gifts were important to Bess's ability to manage her relationships at Court, especially with her female contacts and from the distance of Derbyshire, and there are other examples. There are the exchanges between Bess and her long-standing friend Lady Frances Cobham: in a letter to Bess (Lady St Loe) of 21 October c. 1564 a heavily pregnant Frances Cobham wrote to her friend that 'i loue dearely and most desyr to see' wishing that Bess should 'be as grete a strangvr in in darbi shere as now yow ar in london'. She enclosed 'the brede and lenthe of a caylle' (a kind of netted cap or headdress worn by women) for Queen Elizabeth, with advice to Bess that 'the faysshyne ys much altered sense yow were heyr' at Court and that 'x yarde ys innoufe for the rounks of the sneke and handes'.[96] This kind of information was a means for Bess to keep her finger on the pulse of life at Court, and during her marriage breakdown it was her female contacts at Court who put Bess's case to the queen.[97] While in later life Bess's interests in competing at Court declined, her network of women remained active and their letters were useful in decoding and making judgements around gift-giving. For example, a letter from Lady Dorothy Stafford written 13 January 1601 referred to a disappointing New Year's gift from the queen to Arbella Stuart; it is, Dorothy regretted, 'not so good as I could wish it nor so good as her Ladyship deserveth in respect of the rarenes of that whiche she sente vnto her Maiestie'. She asked Bess to 'keepe it to your selfe not making anie other acquainted with it' because the implications of such a gift could be potentially damaging to the young Arbella.[98]

The objects described so far have been seen to stand for social bonds, to define hierarchies of relationships or to serve to maintain and nurture contacts and connections. These functions were vital to the management of Bess's networks and relationships at every level. But, with the notable exception of elaborate New Year's gifts to the queen, the symbolic value of the items sent could not be described as intricately constructed. Nor could any of the objects discussed so far themselves be said to enshrine or symbolise uniquely personal or emotional connections. However, there were certain objects sent to or from Bess where there is evidence of emotional engagement with the object itself, as delineated by the accompanying letters. These were the gifts exchanged between Bess and her daughters, which, among Bess's enclosures, were the most carefully constructed. We must be wary of Victorian sentimentality when considering emotion in relation to attitudes to objects, but what distinguishes these items are the precise commentaries

96 Gloss: x yarde: *ten yards*, innoufe: *enough*, rounks: *runkles, i.e., pleats*, sneke: *neck*. Folger CT, X.d.428 (16), ID 15.
97 Discussed in section 1.4, pp. 87–88.
98 Folger CT, X.d.428 (120), ID 91.

found in the letters, the wording of which, and its exact vocabulary, helps us to define the relation between feeling, object and person. Lena Cowen Orlin has shown that there were only two representational strategies deployed for bequeathed objects in wills that we can use as indications they stood as carriers of relationships. Both engaged 'the potentially affective faculty of memory': in the first the objects were referred to as 'remembrances' or 'tokens', often given with 'good will'; in the second objects were 'identified by means of their own remembered histories of ownership'.[99] These criteria are pertinent to the letters and, as is the case with wills, these are prominent phrases that stand out amid the sea of other material objects mentioned. To take one example, for the New Year, probably in 1575, Bess's eldest daughter Lady Frances (Cavendish) Pierrepont sent her mother Bess (countess of Shrewsbury) a piece of lawn (a kind of fine linen resembling cambric) and a drinking glass: 'I haue sent vnto your honoure a peece of lawne and a drinckinge glasse'. The letter that accompanied these enclosed New Year's gifts specified that these items were to stand 'as a remembrance of my intyre louynge dutie'.[100] The particular specification here, that these two objects were to be taken 'as a remembrance of' Frances's unconditional and affectionate loyalty towards her mother, shows how the letter functioned to define in very particular terms the emotional intentionality of the object given as a gift.

More elaborate are the gifts exchanged between Bess and her youngest daughter Mary (Cavendish) Talbot, seventh countess of Shrewsbury, during the final year of Bess's life. As has been shown in section 1.4, Mary and Bess had a relationship that included genuine emotional bonds: Mary wrote regularly with news or to ask after her mother's health, and her grief at her mother's death in 1608 was a cause for comment.[101] But their close relationship achieved clearest articulation through the exchange of carefully prepared gifts, which were commented upon in their letters. On 18 July c. 1607 Mary thanked her mother for the gift of an object 'wrought in metall' that had been passed to Bess from another, unidentified, woman:

> My duty most humbly remembered with like humbel thankes for your ladyship's fayre and well wrought Armen ~~which god willing~~ which god willing I will kepe as a gret iuel both in respect of your ladyship and of her from hom your ladyship had it ther can nothing be wrought in metell with mor life.[102]

---

99 Lena Cowen Orlin, 'Empty Vessels', in Hamling and Richardson (eds.), *Everyday Objects*, pp. 299–308.
100 Folger CT, X.d.428 (67), ID 52.
101 LPL, Talbot Papers, Vol. O, fol. 139, Anne, countess of Arundel, to Gilbert, seventh earl of Shrewsbury, n.d. [March 1608], she was sorry to hear of the grief of Mary, countess of Shrewsbury, over the death of her mother Bess (dowager countess of Shrewsbury).
102 ID 89. I have been unable to discover what kind of metal object an 'Armen' is, though perhaps a kind of jewellery, after *OED* 'armil, *n.* 1. A bracelet'.

184   *Sending and receiving letters*

Mary explained that she would revere the object as a 'gret iuel [jewel]' and would do so 'in respect of' her mother and her mother's predecessor, as an object passed from woman to woman down the female line. That is to say, she acknowledged that the object's worth went beyond the economic and aesthetic value and, through memory and lineage, had accrued affective meaning and symbolic capital. In a postscript to the same letter, Mary referred to a second gift, a christening gift of ermine: 'the ermen was as well brought vp: as was posibell it shall li by my daughter of arandall the day of the cresning'. In declining health, and well into her eighties, it seems understandable that Bess was unable to travel from Hardwick to attend the christening of her great-grandson, James Howard, Lord Maltravers (1607–24) at Whitehall Palace, Westminster. However, Mary gave her mother's christening gift pride of place during the ceremony, next to the infant James's mother, her daughter and Bess's granddaughter Aletheia Howard, countess of Arundel (d. 1654). As such, Mary's thoughtful public display took the opportunity to use the gift to make the absent person present.

At the end of the same year, Mary sent a New Year's gift to her mother Bess of a 'quission which is mad iust by the pateron of my daughter of arandals bed: and sparuer and do besech your Ladyship to yous it euery day at your prayer to learne of it which I pray god you may doe with all comfort'.[103] Here the letter functioned to elucidate how the cushion would serve Bess as a daily reminder of the loving bond between three generations of women. Made in the same pattern as Mary's daughter Aletheia's bed and canopy, the cushion provided a visual link between mother (Bess), daughter (Mary) and granddaughter (Aletheia). The letter functioned as a covering note for the cushion, which must have been a most appropriate gift for Bess in these final few weeks of her life, for a number of reasons. For one thing, we know that Bess had trouble with her knees, so her daughter's concern she have something 'to leane of' is partly a practical one: we know that, by the time Mary sent her letter, the octogenarian Bess was walking with a stick, and the plush furnishings of her bedchamber were specifically designed with warmth and comfort in mind against the cold of the Derbyshire winter.[104] Second, we know that Bess appreciated commissioned textiles, especially those that told the story of her life in visual and heraldic form that filled Hardwick New Hall, so the cushion's decorative link to her granddaughter was a fitting one. Third, and perhaps most importantly given this was a prayer cushion, in her final years we know that Bess's mind was focused on

103 A 'cusion which is made exactly in the pattern of my daughter of Arundel's bed and a sparver, and [I] do beseech your Ladyship to use it every day at your prayer to learn on it which I pray god you may do with all comfort', ID 90, 30 December c. 1607. Middle English Dictionary: 'sperver (n.(2)) A canopy for a bed; ~ wise, with a canopy'.

104 The reference to Bess walking with a stick but being well for her years appears in a letter from John Harper to Gilbert Talbot, 31 July 1606 (LPL, Talbot Papers, Vol. M, fol. 349). The reference to Bess's knee armour is given in section 2.1.

Sending and receiving letters 185

spiritual matters. As it was to be used by Bess during her daily prayer, the cushion simultaneously attended to care of the body (it protected her knees) and the soul (it supported her during prayer).

When Mary told Bess 'to learne of it . . . with all comfort' she was asking her mother to draw from the object comfort which was physical, spiritual and familial. This symbolic commentary, and that the cushion was a feminised textile object, must have made an ideal gift for Bess.[105] Certainly, we know, by Bess's final gift to her daughter, that Mary was in favour that January. Within a few weeks, in January 1608, believing herself on her deathbed, Bess made a last amendment to her will witnessed by her chief woman of the bedchamber Mistress Digby and subsequently added as a codicil to her will by her secretary Timothy:

> Yesternight being the last of January, she sent for the Lord Cavendishe to come to her, and tolde him (Mistress Digby being present) that she had no hope of lyfe, she fownde her self extream sick at her hart, That she would have him to give to her daughter Shrouesbury from her, her Pearle Bed, with that belonged to the bed, but she would give no hanginges.[106]

Even without the hangings, the Pearl Bed and its accoutrements constituted a substantial bequest and were rivalled only by the one in the 'Best' bedchamber as the most magnificent bed at Hardwick New Hall. The Pearl Bed had a carved gilt bedstead, a tester bed's head and double valances of black velvet that were studded with pearls, embroidered in silver and gold thread with 'sivines and woodbines' (raspberries and climbing vines) and trimmed with gold, silver and black silk fringes. Its many coverings included a rich counterpane of black velvet striped with silver and worked with pearls and 'purl' (coiled silvered wire).[107] The bed's monetary and aesthetic values are in no doubt, but it also had a place in the armorial and iconographic schemes through which Bess told her dynastic story at Hardwick New Hall. Dating from the time of Bess's marriage to Sir William Cavendish, the Pearl Bed commemorated their union in heraldic form and featured 'my Ladies and Sir William Cavendishes Armes in the bedeshead'. By the time of the bequest, the bed, which she had shared with Mary's father Sir William Cavendish, had been with Bess for almost sixty years. The

---

105 On sewn gifts and how they construct relationships between women see: Calabresi, '"You sow, Ile read"'. See in particular the emphasis on the inclusion of sewn pieces in accounts of women's literacy as it 'usefully complicates what has at times become a constricting dualism of reading and/or writing in discussions of early modern literacy', p. 100.

106 January 1608, Chatsworth House, Hardwick Drawer 143 17, notes in the hand of Timothy Pusey.

107 See the commentaries by Levey and Thornton in *Of Houshold Stuff*, p. 43, and p. 10, pp. 15–16 and p. 69.

186 Sending and receiving letters

nature of the bequest, combined with the context of the other recent gifts between mother and daughter mentioned in the letters, gives extra credence to Durant's postulation that the 'pearl bed had ties of sentiment' for Bess and Mary.[108] As much as any woman of her time, Bess was in control of her own personal iconography and attuned to the value of visual and material display for self-fashioning. There may have been other narratives and commentaries, now lost to us, that drew on memory, lineage or shared identity in order to personalise objects that perhaps still furnish Hardwick New Hall today. These examples remind us of another way, to add to those discussed in sections 2.2 and 2.4, in which Bess's interior design projects involved the interweaving of texts and textiles.

3.4 'Hauinge no betar menes to manifast mi thanckefolnes': letters with floss and accordion folds

Superscription, Elizabeth Lennox?:	To the right honorable and my most reuerenced Lady the countes of shrewsbery att hardwick thease
Letter, Elizabeth Lennox:	good madame hauinge no betar menes to manifast mi thanckefolnes to youer onar bot bi thes lines i umbli pra your ladiship to axsept them and ine theme mi reuerant thanckes for youer onares mani ande gret fauoueres and amonest the rest that it plesed youer onar to lende ^me^ youer ladishipes litar whiche bot for that i thincke i sholde hardeli ^haue^ ataned the ende ofmi gurni so dangouroues was the weonhores backe ——————— bot i beseche youer [*deletion*] ^onar^ to be leueme that i holde mi selfe somoche bouende to youer ladiship as i wil euar inde uar to deserue bi mi duti and afeckesinat [*deletion*] serues to youer ladiship thos prainge youronar maliue mani hapi yeres withehelthe i umbli tacke leue – [*significant space*]
Subscription, Elizabeth Lennox:	your onares daftar most bondane [*significant space*]
Signature, Elizabeth Lennox:	Elizabeth cauendishe
	Elizabeth (Cavendish) Stuart, countess of Lennox, writes to her mother Bess (countess of Shrewsbury), holograph, before October 1574, sent, red wax seal embossed with the Lennox Stuart arms over goldish-ochre floss, letter packet accordion folded.[109]

Before Bess (countess of Shrewsbury) had opened this letter she would have known immediately, from glancing at the outside of the letter packet,

108 Durant, *Bess of Hardwick*, p. 222.
109 Folger CT, X.d.428 (50), ID 41, Plate 12.

Sending and receiving letters   187

that it was a note of deferential gratitude from her daughter.[110] The packet was sealed with the Lennox Stuart arms, which would have indicated to Bess the identity of the sender. The purport of the letter was anticipated by the carefully written calligraphic script on the outer packet, which featured clubbed looped descenders, as well as by the overtly deferential and scrupulously respectful wording of the superscription: 'To the right honorable and my most reuerenced Lady the countes of shrewsbery att hardwick thense'.[111] But the content of the unopened letter was most clearly signalled by the outer packet's most eye-catching feature of all: the gold-coloured silk floss beneath the wax seal.[112] This combination of features on the outer packet set the tone for the letter itself, and it was the earliest of five existing letters with brightly coloured silk or ribbon that were sent to Bess. All five were short notes confected from a mass of politeness formulae, all non-committal offerings that expressed gratitude, thanks or apology. The deployment of elaborate linguistic scripts continued inside in these letters, to register family hierarchy and to fulfil the rhetorical requirements of social courtesy. These letters were among the most content-light of all those received by Bess: brief insubstantial puffs of politeness. It would be tempting, as a modern reader, to suggest that the shiny floss on the outside is a suitable forewarning of the fluff on the inside. More helpfully, we might describe these letters as the products of a culture of epistolary politeness, and as gifts in themselves.[113]

110 Magnusson, 'A Rhetoric of Requests', discusses the elaborate linguistic scripts deployed in another letter from Elizabeth Lennox to her mother, Bess.

111 This one can be compared to the more straightforward superscriptions from Bess's other daughters – for example, IDs 52 and 53 from Frances (Cavendish) Pierrepont, c. 1575 and April 1603, 'to my Lady'; and IDs 89 and 90 from Mary (Cavendish) Talbot, countess of Shrewsbury, 8 July and 30 December c. 1607, 'To my Lady'.

112 It is not possible to be exact when describing the colour of aged silk ribbon, due to the wide spectrum of shades of variation which result from uneven wear and fading on the different parts of the tie. However, in order to aid the process and as a method of providing a more realistic approximation, the Michel-Farbenführer Colour Guide has here been used for recording purposes. The ribbon on this letter falls between 9–5–7 (dunkelgelbocker, dark yellow ochre) and 9–0–8 (schwärzlichocker, blackish ochre) but with similarities to 9–0–5 (lebhaftocker, vivid ochre) and 5–16–8 (schwärzlichrötlichgelb, blackish ginger); Michel-Farbenführer, p. 11 and p. 15. I am grateful to Heather Wolfe and Erin Blake for pointing out this colour guide to me and for discussion of these matters.

113 The other extant letters to Bess with ribbon are as follows (for the colour referencing system used here, see earlier). Elizabeth Smyth to her daughter's godmother Bess (countess of Shrewsbury), 10 December 1578, with yellowish-green ribbon close to 5–2–8 (schwärzlichgraugelb, blackish grey-yellow) but with similarities to 5–7–6 (olivgelb, olive yellow) and 5–7–5 (lebhaftolivgelb, lively olive yellow); LPL, Talbot Papers, MS 3205, fols 34r-35v, ID 168. Alethea Howard, countess of Arundel, to her grandmother Bess (dowager countess of Shrewsbury), written between 1606 and 1608, the current location of this letter is unknown but the Sotheby's sale catalogue mentions its 'white silk' ties; ID 237. Thomas Howard, earl of Arundel to his grandmother-in-law Bess (dowager countess of Shrewsbury), 25 May and 27 June c. 1607 with, respectively: pinkish-plum ribbon

188   *Sending and receiving letters*

Whereas letters with enclosures make us think about the relationship between words and things, letters with ribbon and floss remind us that letters are things themselves. Historians of the book and of reading have shown us how the physical form of the codex can impact upon literary interpretation. In a comparable way, the physical form of a letter could extend or inflect its meaning just as much as the spoken words of an accompanying bearer or the presence of an enclosure. There were various visual and material aspects of early modern letters that were designed to communicate meaning or encourage a certain kind of reader-response. These have been documented by Stewart in his scholarly 'grammar of early modern letter-writing', which elucidates the 'complex letter-writing etiquette' firmly in place by this time and the interplay of spatial, material and visual forms.[114] A range of such features can be found in the letters to Bess and, in many cases, were the means by which different writers found ways to register their subordinate relationship to her. Thus, in order to express humility, deference or politeness, we see a number of Bess's correspondents used, variously, not only ribbon but also space on the page, calligraphic penmanship and decorated paper.[115] For example, when Bess's eldest son, Henry Cavendish, wrote to his mother at New Year 1605, he used a widely spaced split subscription, calligraphic flourishes, neat handwriting and placement of his signature low on the page, all to register deferential respect and politeness (Plate 19). Henry's efforts to express humility and respect graphically on the page perhaps reflected his hopes of being reinstated in his ageing mother's will (which did not happen). But while his efforts here were polished and carefully executed, there was nothing exceptional about registering respect to a parent through use of space above the signature: it was a feature we find across letters from Bess's (adult) children when writing to their mother.[116] The other correspondents who registered respect or deference to Bess using

---

somewhere between 25–11–7 (dunkelbraunpurpur, dark purple-brown) and 11–19–3 (hellkarminbraun, light carmine-brown) but with similarities to 25–11–3 (hellbraunpurpur, light brown-purple) and 11–17–3 (hellrotbraun, light red-brown); and pale pinkish-lilac ribbon close to 2–19–3 (hellkarmingrau, light carmine-grey) but with similarities to 1–21–6 (rosaweiß, pink and white) and 2–19–6 (karmingrau, carmine-grey); ID 3 (Plate 20) and ID 4 (Folger CT, X.d.428 (2)). On autograph letters as personal tokens see Steen, 'Reading beyond the Words', pp. 57–58.

114   *Shakespeare's Letters*, Chapter 1, 'The Materiality of Shakespeare's Letters', pp. 39–74 (quotations at pp. 40–41 and p. 50, and on the concept of a 'grammar of letters', as a set of historically specific material practices, see p. 5). See also Daybell, *Women Letter-Writers*, Chapter 2, from p. 47.

115   On the registering of deference, humility and hierarchy through the use of space see: Braumuller, 'Accounting for Absence: The Transcription of Space', and Gibson, 'Significant Space in Manuscript Letters'.

116   Where space was available it was included above the signature, often with a split subscription, in the letters from all of Bess's sons and daughters (IDs 5, 7, 10, 20, 23, 41, 52, 53, 88, 90) as well as in letters from her stepchildren or (grand)children-in-laws Grace Cavendish, Edward Talbot, Gilbert Talbot (IDs 8, 63, 82 and 83) and Robert Stapleton (ID 191).

Sending and receiving letters   189

space above their signature included kin and gentlemen servants, to represent politeness, duty and kinship.[117]

We have no existing letters from Bess where she herself used ribbon, floss or decorated paper. We do have an example where she used a neater hand to signal special regard, and she at times used hash strokes around her signature, but she did not use elaborate calligraphy in which she was not trained.[118] There are three examples where Bess used white space for rhetorical effect, once to Burghley in 1578 (ID 121) and two that are similar scribal letters written to Elizabeth I in January 1603, both of which registered deference through widely spaced split subscriptions (one of these is given as Plate 17).[119] Another physical feature used by Bess for communicative and interpersonal purposes was paper size. Most letters from Bess were written on a sheet of paper folded bifolium to create a writing space of around 20 × 30cms; this size was fairly consistent, if we allow for a centimetre or so either way and exclude a few letters on scraps of paper written to her daughters (discussed ahead). However, Bess sent three letters on larger-sized paper. In all three cases, we can observe a high level of vertical or horizontal distance between Bess and her correspondent and a high degree of ranked extremity in the letter content.[120] So Bess (countess of Shrewsbury) in March 1578 wrote to Elizabeth I on paper measuring 23 × 34.5cms and in June c. 1576 to the earl of Leicester on paper measuring 22.5 × 36cms, both letters that expressed profuse thanks; then in October 1585 she wrote to her estranged husband Shrewsbury on paper measuring 22.5 × 34cms, a letter to plead for forgiveness during their marriage crisis.[121] In each case, the extra-large

---

However, it was not invariably used; for example, Anne Talbot did not use significant space when writing to Bess, although she did use neat, calligraphic handwriting.

117 Such as the letters from George Chaworth, John Kniveton, William Kniveton, Sir John Manners and Elizabeth Wingfield; Folger CT, X.d.428 (15, 39, 42, 54, 55, 129 and 131), IDs 14, 33, 35, 44, 45, 96 and 98.

118 For example, Bess's superscription in her own hand, to her husband Shrewsbury during a brief period of reconciliation during their marital dispute, includes attempts at serifs on the <T> of the opening word 'To', [April 1587], ID 186. The letter was also double sealed with an accordion-folded letter-packet.

119 9 January 1603: the first part of the subscription, 'your Ma.ties /', is centred, the second part, 'most humble saruant and / subiect', is right-aligned, and there is white space maintained between the two parts (ID 128). 29 January 1603: the first part of the subscription 'your Ma.ties' is left of centre, the second part, 'most bounden / faythfull saruant / and subiect', is right-aligned, again with white space between the two (ID 129; Plate 17). In both cases the subscription is in an italic scribal hand and is followed by Bess's autograph signature. Both letters concern the troubled relationship between Bess (dowager countess of Shrewsbury) and her granddaughter Arbella Stuart; Bess hoped the queen would arrange for Arbella to be taken off her hands, preferably through marriage.

120 These terms, from politeness theory and historical pragmatics, are discussed in the introduction, p. 6.

121 Bess (countess of Shrewsbury): 17 March 1578, sent, in her own hand, letter to Elizabeth I (ID 120); 27 June c. 1576, sent, in her own hand, letter to the Robert Dudley, earl of Leicester (ID 110); 14 October c. 1585, letter in the hand of Scribe A with signature by

190 *Sending and receiving letters*

paper complemented the letter's deferential linguistic style and substantive content, in which Bess offered effusive expressions of deferential gratitude and loyalty.

The material feature perhaps most revealing among Bess's extant letters involved the dimensions of the folded letter packet, whereby variations in folding correlated with the early modern rhetoric of letter-packet size. As folding has yet to be documented so thoroughly as some other material features, it is worth considering the case of Bess's letters in some detail here.[122] Three types of materials for securing a letter packet are well known to historians and manuscript scholars, which could be used individually or in combination: wax, used either above or below the paper flaps and often pressed down with an embossed seal matrix; paper, used in the form of a tab or band threaded through the packet; and silk, in the form of ribbon or floss tied around the packet. In addition to these Bess gives us a fourth material and method for securing a letter packet, one appropriate to her reputation as a needleworker: thread, sewn through the letter packet using a needle. Of the 181 letters examined for this study, three appear to have been sent unsecured but the remainder can be sorted into an approximate typology of four kinds of letter packets that utilised these four materials: (1) tuck and fold, (2) slit and band, (3) sewn and (4) accordion folded.[123] In common with other contemporary letter collections, most of the letter packets sent to and from Bess were either of the tuck-and-fold or slit-and-band variety.[124] The majority, 121 of the letters, were sent as tuck-and-fold packets; typically, the page was folded three times horizontally and then twice vertically and secured at the back with wax to create a packet of around 9×12cms. Another thirty-eight letters were sent as slit-and-band packets; these tended to be slightly smaller and, typically, the page was folded four times horizontally and in

---

Bess, to Shrewsbury (ID 229). The letter to Shrewsbury is discussed in section 1.3. On the importance of not skimping on paper when writing to one's social superiors see Stewart, *Shakespeare's Letters*, p. 50.

122 The notable exception, from which this study has benefitted, is Burlinson and Zurcher, '"Secretary to the Lord Grey Lord Deputie here"', pp. 50–52. The *Letter-Locking* project, by Jana Dambrogio and Daniel Starza Smith, is currently developing methods and typologies for analysis of letter folding.

123 At least 55 letters are not suitable for analysis because they either were not sent, are now unavailable, are nineteenth-century copies or are letters which have been flattened or re-creased during storage and where it is not possible to discern the original folds. The four-part typology proposed for the remaining letters is, certainly, approximate, as there are numerous small-scale variations within each category.

124 The tuck-and-fold and slit-and-band types are described by Burlingson and Zurcher in relation to Spenser's letters during the time he was secretary to Lord Grey, and they also find these to be the most common way to fold a letter. They make the additional observation that the slit-and-band type is used by Spenser for longer (therefore thicker) letters; '"Secretary to the Lord Grey Lord Deputie here"', p. 63. For other descriptions of the tuck-and-fold method, and further acknowledgement it was most common, see Steen, 'Reading beyond the Words', p. 65, and Preston and Yeandle, *English Handwriting*, p. 60.

Sending and receiving letters 191

half or three times vertically to create a wad of folded paper, which was then slit through with a knife and secured by means of a paper tab or band passed through the cut and stuck down with wax. Both methods were used in the letters Bess sent, whether written in her own hand or copied by a scribe, and when writing to persons across a range of social levels. It would be difficult to argue that the choice between tuck and fold or slit and band correlated with or was determined by any particular factor, such as scribe, location, date, correspondent, bearer, enclosure or type of letter. The other two kinds of letter packets were less common and more restricted in the occasions for their use.

In five cases, sewing was the means of securing the packet and these letters have no traces of wax, paper tabs, silk ribbon or floss. Four of these five sewn letters were sent between Bess and her daughters, Mary (Cavendish) Talbot and Elizabeth (Cavendish) Lennox, and daughter-in-laws Grace (Talbot) Cavendish and Anne (Herbert) Talbot.[125] All four are short notes that do not contain high-security or sensitive information and suggest that sewing was a method of securing that was used *ad hoc* between the female family members. To take the example of the one existing sewn missive sent from Bess herself to her daughter Mary (undated, 1580s), in the hand of Scribe A but signed by Bess, it was not so much a letter as a note jotted on scrap paper.[126] The writing material was a single sheet of paper 15 × 20cms that was folded three times horizontally to create an irregular long and thin packet of 15 × 6cms and then sewn up with a row of stitches running down either short end. Written from Chelsea rather than from one of her or her husband's main bases in Derbyshire or Yorkshire, it may have been that she lacked resources such as writing materials at this location. Certainly, her opening lines complain she had not had any time to send a messenger today: 'since the tyme that I rise this day I haue not had leasur to speake to any boddie to send to you to know how you doe'. Dispatched at six in the evening ('vj of the clocke') and superscribed to 'my Louing daughter the Lady Talbott', Mary must have been staying nearby to Chelsea as Bess expected to receive a reply from her daughter 'this nighte'. For this informal note to her daughter, needle and thread were either the only fastening material available to Bess and Scribe A at Chelsea that evening or the nearest to hand.

While this example of a sewn letter packet is suggestive of the practicalities and informalities of letter-writing, the fourth category of letter packet,

---

125 There is one more letter which can be seen to have been secured only by means of stitch, ID 143, discussed in section 1.1. It is unsigned and with no subscription or superscription, but known to be from Bess (countess of Shrewsbury) in 1573 from the contemporary endorsement. As it is now in the SP, it may perhaps have been to Burghley or Walsingham, or was forwarded to one of them. It was perhaps tucked into another letter or carried on the person of the bearer: it was folded very small, into a letter packet with a vertical height of around only 2.5cm, and its stitching would have kept it tightly secure and flat.

126 ID 181.

192 *Sending and receiving letters*

accordion folded, is suggestive of formal rhetorical intentions. There are seventeen existing letters that were accordion folded, in which the letter was folded somewhere between five and twelve times horizontally, then in half or twice vertically, and then secured at the back with wax to create a narrow letter packet with a horizontal side of 8–11cms and vertical side of 2.5–6cms – around a quarter to half the height of a tuck-and-fold letter packet. The smaller accordion-folded letter packets, then, would have been immediately and markedly distinguishable from run-of-the-mill tuck-and-fold or slit-and-band types. Small enough to fit into a closed hand, they were distinctive for their diminutive size and concertina pattern of creases. Of the seventeen that are now extant, eight were received by Bess and it is no coincidence that four of these were the ones with floss and ribbon discussed earlier.[127] The other four can, likewise, be loosely described as letters of social courtesy from courtiers and kin, rather than more weighty official or business-type letters.[128] The remaining nine were all sent from Bess and eight of these form a distinctive group: they constitute all the existing letters that were sent from Bess during the most troubled period of her life, from August 1584 to November 1590, the period from the collapse of her marriage to the earl of Shrewsbury until his death. Here we have Bess in her darkest days, amid the chaos of her marriage collapse and where she attempted to defend herself against his very serious and often vicious accusations and to secure her own and her children's property. Four were letters to her estranged husband Shrewsbury himself, and the other four were to Burghley and Walsingham; all were written in italic, one in Bess's own hand, the others in the hand of Scribe A, neither of whom used accordion folding apart from here in this sequence.[129] As has been discussed in section 1.3, in these

127 It has not been possible to examine the fold patterns of ID 237 (i.e., the letter from Alethea Talbot on decorated paper with white silk ties, discussed earlier, current location unknown). However, the sale catalogue records an integral address panel on the verso of 7.8 × 2.9cms. Presuming this is accurate, it would mean this letter, too, is likely to have been accordion folded; it also means it is both the most decorative letter and the one folded to the smallest size of letter-packet of all those sent to Bess. The other letters with ribbon have accordion folded letter-packets of the following sizes: 10 × 5cms (ID 41, Plate 12), 8.5 × 4.5cms (ID 168), 9 × 2.7cms (ID 3, Plate 20) and 10 × 3.5cms (ID 4).

128 These are: 10.5 × 5cms, from servant Edward Foxe to his mistress Bess (Lady St Loe), 8 December c. 1565, defending himself against accusations he has been neglecting his duties (ID 28); 10 × 4cms, from Anne (Herbert) Talbot to her mother-in-law Bess (countess of Shrewsbury), 29 March c. 1575, explaining why she has not written more regularly (ID 93); 10 × 4cms, from Robert Devereux, second earl of Essex, to Bess (dowager countess of Shrewsbury), 23 March 1590/1, recommending the bearer, who wishes to enter Bess's service (ID 24); 10.5 × 4.5cms, from Susan (Bertie) Grey, countess of Kent, to Bess (dowager countess of Shrewsbury), 26 January 1592/3, recommending the bearer as a porter (ID 32).

129 These are: 10.5 × 4.6cms, to Shrewsbury, 26 August c. 1584, beseeching him to 'give me liberty to come unto you' (ID 116); 9 × 5.5cms, to Burghley, 6 October 1585, asking for his support as Shrewsbury still will not 'suffer me to come to him' despite his promise to

Sending and receiving letters 193

letters Bess strategically drew on linguistic scripts of humility and deference and cultural ideals of wifehood that emphasised submissiveness. Nowhere else do we find Bess using such scripts when writing to her husband, or casting herself into these roles. However, necessity and circumstances dictated that she did so in these letters and correspondingly the letter packets shrank and the size of the folds contracted. That is to say, there was a direct correlation between the letter's language and the size of the letter packet; spatial and rhetorical forms mirrored one another and both functioned to encode a particular rhetorical stance.

Floss, ribbon, space on the page, paper size and folding patterns were perhaps the most immediately distinctive features of these letters, and the most obvious way of identifying them as particular types of letters. Yet they have typically been overlooked in earlier catalogues and editions. They are features that have a potential role in searching and sorting: to filter for letters by ribbon or accordion folds is immediately to bring together particular strands of the corpus, or to identify particular species of letters – not a failsafe method but a useful first entry point, at least in the case of Bess's correspondence. So there are possible opportunities for information managers here, as well as for editors and for literary and linguistic analysis, which must take account of how the locus meaning was distributed across linguistic, corporeal and material epistolary components. The nature of early modern epistolary culture means, ideally, that catalogues, corpora and editions would be capable of mirroring its material forms and instabilities, and mobile and dynamic multimedia digital environments offer potential opportunities here.[130] Most importantly, it is through careful acknowledgement of the material and pragmatic realities of early modern letter-writing that we are able to describe more accurately its processes. Bess's competency at each stage of the delivery and reception process – from the management of bearers and Carriers, to the selection of enclosures and letter packets – constituted vital facets of her epistolary literacy. As such, Bess's letters convincingly illustrate to us how her competency when it came to harnessing and decoding material features contributed to the success of her engagements with epistolary culture.

---

the queen (ID 152); 11 × 6cms, to Shrewsbury, 14 October c. 1585, assuring him she is a good and faithful wife (ID 229); 9 × 3.6cms, to Walsingham, 2 December 1585, asking for fair treatment (ID 153); 9.5 × 5cms, to Burghley, 13 June 1586, asking for his support during her misery (ID 230); 8.5 × 5.5cms, to Shrewsbury, 4 August 1585, defending herself against his accusations (ID 202); 8.2 × 4.5cms, to Shrewsbury, c. 1587, letter in her own hand in which Bess looks forward to their next meeting (ID 186); 9 × 5cms, to Burghley, 6 October 1587, thanking him for his support during her dispute with Shrewsbury and asking him to act on her behalf again (ID 156). The ninth letter is ID 143, perhaps an enclosure, discussed earlier.

130 These opportunities are presented and discussed in Wiggins, Bryson, Smith, Timmermann and Williams, *Bess of Hardwick's Letters.*

Conclusions

What do we gain from the letters on which this book is based? They are both endlessly fascinating and perpetually frustrating. Fascinating because they offer us a multitude of detail about the realities and perceptions of Bess of Hardwick's life and her interactions with those she encountered. Frustrating because they leave us wanting to know more about the conversations that took place surrounding the letters, as well as the gaps evident in the patterns of her letter-writing. Nonetheless, and despite their limitations, they are the best-documented record of a non-royal English woman's letter-writing from the Tudor period. Furthermore, they document one of the greatest success stories of the age, by either a woman or a man: during her life Bess survived repeated hostilities, lawsuits and treasonous plots against her, ran a large business empire, built two of the most magnificent houses in the country and founded a dynasty that survives to this day. Her story is one of a woman who understood the system and made it work in her favour, and whose route to success involved the judicious use of letters every step along the way. While ultimately the results she achieved were spectacular and remarkable, her use of letters, as has been shown in this book, was consistent with contemporary conventions in general and resembled the practices of other women in many respects. Her letters offer us a lively, expansive and interconnected picture of her epistolary activities and of her remarkably astute understanding of the workings of epistolary culture, its terms and conditions, its material and rhetorical forms, and its interpersonal structures and etiquettes. The letters allow us to review the contours of contemporary epistolary culture in relation to the immediate pressures and demands of one person's lived experience. This opportunity to view letter-writing from, as it were, the inside, from the vantage point of one individual, offers us fresh perspectives upon the wider conclusions of more broad-based studies (invaluable as these are). This perspective has enabled reconstruction, in lucid detail, of patterns of production and reception, and of the evidence for letter-writing as a process. It was a highly collaborative process, one contiguous with other literate activities within the household, and one defined by the uncertainties and irregularities of handwritten culture. It was also a gendered process, in its networks, social roles and subject positions. In broad terms, this characterisation of early modern letter-writing confirms the findings of other recent studies, but Bess's letters offer compelling examples that bring to life the realities and complexities of epistolary culture at a particular historical moment. Furthermore, and well beyond serving as a case study, the arguments presented in this book strongly insist upon the advantages for analysis of three particular methodological imperatives for how we read and interpret early modern letters; these are the communicative function of visual and material features; the value of original language editions; and the advantages offered by digital humanities resources. It is worth saying something about each of these, by way of drawing together some of the threads from this book and to indicate how its findings will impact upon the field and suggest pathways for future research.

The images presented in this book, along with the annotations that accompany transcripts and record material features, are not included for trivial 'decorative' purposes and their interest is not confined to a 'niche' academic sub-discipline. Rather, they are included because material features and contexts are fundamental to the meanings encoded by the letters and to our view of Bess herself. As historians of the book and of reading have shown us, the physical form of the codex can impact upon literary interpretation. Comparably, the physical form of a letter can extend or inflect its meaning: visual and material aspects of early modern letters were designed to communicate meaning or encourage certain kinds of reader-response. A wide range of these features can be found across Bess's letters, and it was through enclosures, bearers, ribbon, space on the page, seals, monograms, calligraphic penmanship, folding patterns and decorated paper that writers registered their politeness or superiority or subordinate relationship to her, or she to them, and through which authority, sincerity and credibility could be conveyed and constructed. The meanings communicated by Bess's letters, then, did not exist separately from their spatial and material forms. They require us to attend carefully to materiality if we are to acknowledge the terms and conditions upon which Bess participated within early modern handwritten culture. Bess's letters were not unusual in this respect; they illustrate many features that were characteristic of contemporary letter-writing practice. As such, the examples discussed in this study suggest how (by building on existing scholarship) we might begin to develop a pragmatics of epistolary materiality, such as would provide an interpretative framework for the management of interpersonal contexts and material features.

The transcriptions presented in this book capture original language and spelling, in semi-diplomatic form and annotated with information about scribes. The debate over modernisation of early modern texts has been

196 *Conclusions*

explored elsewhere.[1] However, from the perspective of this book, what is lost in the process of modernisation is a bank of original-spelling linguistic data. On the one hand, these data are of interest to historical linguists addressing a range of research questions in that field. For example, the scholarly cliché that Tudor women's spelling and handwriting were 'more idiosyncratic' than those of their male contemporaries has been undercut by findings that remind us to be wary of generalisations based on our own preconceptions (or based on unfair comparison between women's writing and printed texts or texts written in the hands of professional scribes).[2] On the other hand, these data are essential for tracking the presence and identity of scribes and collaborators. The scribes, as the discussions in this book have shown, were often more than amanuenses; they were trusted secretaries implicit in the co-creation of the persona performed in each letter. Furthermore, as men and women could act as scribes for one another, and could collaborate together in various ways and to various degrees in the creation of a letter, to track their roles is necessary if we are to trace the gender dynamics of the production and reception process in early modern letters.

In addition to its usefulness as data for historical linguistic analysis, or for detecting signs of collaboration, the retention of original language, spelling and punctuation offers present-day readers the opportunity to hear for themselves the dramatic and revealing switches of tone that can occur between letters from a single sender. Among Bess's correspondence, as has been shown, many of the letters written in her own hand to her husbands and servants were in the conventionalised voice of the authoritative mistress of the household and betrayed a degree of linguistic naivety in their spelling and punctuation. By contrast, the letters she dispatched written in professional secretary-script scribal hands (e.g., in the hands of Scribe D and Timothy Pusey), which dealt with business matters, are stiff with standard legal conventions and openly display the scribe's Latin-based education and legal training. By contrast again, the letters she sent written in a variety of elegant italic-script scribal hands (e.g., in the hands of Scribes A and B) to high-status Court contacts to petition and secure favour are eloquently persuasive and demonstrate a grasp of epistolary diplomacy. These variations in language and tone, which correlate with Bess's use of scribes and co-creators, are fully apparent to the reader only when the letters are encountered in their original spelling, punctuation, vocabulary and syntax, as well as with visual features of the handwriting available. Bess's considered use of different kinds of scribal and holograph writing

---

1 For example, a range of viewpoints that is up to date with current scholarship is presented by Phillips and Williams, *Editing Early Modern Texts*.

2 Relevant findings are presented in section 2.2, which develops and augments some of the findings by Evans, *The Language*, and Sönmez, 'Perceived and Real Differences'.

Conclusions   197

for particular purposes characterised her engagement with scribal culture, and explains part of her extraordinary success as a letter-writer. The co-creation of credibility through these means was a feature of contemporary epistolary literacy, one that Bess was required to manage for the purpose of effective interpersonal communication. It is only by presenting the language of her letters in its original form that we can represent the full range of modes of expression through which Bess constructed her authority and enacted her agency.

These findings, which relate to the interpersonal, scribal and material contexts of letters, and to the processes involved in their production and reception, reveal letters to be challenging sources. For scholars of epistolary culture, the multilayered and fragmentary nature of letters as sources requires robust metadata, both for reliability of referencing and in order to co-ordinate transcripts, visual files and contextual information. That is to say, letters are often scattered across locations, diverse in their type and modes of creation, and resistant to linear ordering or classification by neat groupings (e.g., by date, author, genre, content or context). Therefore, the ability to capture, search and sort different categories of information about text, context, material features and scribes for every letter is necessary if we are to generate readings that combine approaches to language, materiality and palaeography. This study has made extensive use of digital humanities techniques and resources (databases, software tools, markup, searchable library catalogues and high-quality digital images), which underpin traditional skills of textual scholarship and palaeography. The techniques set out here demonstrate the value of methods for converting analogue forms (of which we find a spectrum of variants in handwritten texts) into logical and quantifiable formats. For example, methods for the systematic codification and capture of material features (e.g., the folding patterns of different types of letter packets, or the colour of floss and ribbon) have the potential to be appropriated and adapted by other projects in catalogues, databases and editions. As more of these resources become available there are greater possibilities not only for the kind of 'big data', macro-scale analyses with which digital resources are often associated but also for micro-scale studies which provide their essential complement and counterpart. For scholars of women's history there is a tension between balancing micro-scale projects that attend scrupulously to the details of individual women's lives and the imperative to integrate women's lives into the larger mainstream historical narrative.[3] This tension – between micro- and macro-scale research paradigms – can partially be resolved in the case of Bess's letters through data sharing. The set of letters that are at the core of this book coheres around her life and the analyses attend to the minutiae of their textual, linguistic and bibliographic forms. At the same time, the catalogue

3 This classic tension is discussed, for example, by Bennett, *History Matters*.

198   *Conclusions*

and textual data is being incorporated into other, macro-scale cataloguing and corpus-based projects.[4] As such, and with each of these projects existing in parallel, the materials are simultaneously available to scholars asking questions from different disciplinary perspectives. This ability to repurpose and to incorporate micro- into macro-scale projects is vital for integrating women's history into the wider historical narrative.

---

4 Data from www.bessofhardwich.org is being integrated into WEMLO, EMLO and CEEC: Women's Early Modern Letters Online (WEMLO), Universities of Oxford, Plymouth and Victoria (www.culturesofknowledge.org/?p=2453); Early Modern Letters Online (EMLO), University of Oxford (emlo.bodleian.ox.ac.uk/home); and Corpus of Early English Correspondence (CEEC), University of Helsinki (www.helsinki.fi/varieng/domains/CEEC.html). Studies which incorporate these materials and address research questions from the fields of historical linguistics, history and palaeography include, for example, those by Marcus, 'An Investigation', Maxwell, 'Household Words', and Williams, '"My Evil Favoured Writing"'.

Selected bibliography

Primary sources

Manuscript sources

Arundel Castle

Autograph Letters 1585–1617: Nos 50, 83, 89, 90, 111, 113, 114, 123, 124

Belvoir Castle

Rutland MSS: Letters & Papers XII–XIV

British Library, London

Additional MSS: 24783, 12506, 75372–75387
Cotton MSS: Caligula C. III
Lansdowne MSS: 34, 71

Cambridge University Library

Hengrave Hall MSS: 88/2/81

Chatsworth House, Derbyshire
Devonshire collection:

Hardwick MS 1, 'Account Book of Sir William and Lady Cavendish, 1 November 1551–23 June 1553'
Hardwick MS 5, Account Book for 1579–84, mostly in Bess's hand
Hardwick MS 7, 'Account Book of Money paid by the [Dowager] Countess of Shrewsbury. Kept by Rowland Harrison and totalled by Timothy Pusey. Late 1591 to 1597 includes her visit to London'
Hardwick MS 8, Account Book for 1592–1601, various hands
'Account Book kept by William Cooche for Sir William St Loe, travelling charges when he leaves Chatsworth and attends the Queen at Court, 8th August – 31st December 1560' (bought by the Trustees in 1974)

200 *Selected bibliography*

Hardwick Drawer 143, inventories of Chatsworth, 1550s-80s, receipts and memoranda

Hardwick Drawer 279, copies of will, inventories, codicils and memorandum, schedule of funeral expenses, receipts

Unmarked box 'Bess and Earls Misc. II', documents including an inventory of the contents of Northaw, c. 1540–52

Corpus Christi College, Cambridge

Parker Library: MS 114A, p. 153

Folger Shakespeare Library, Washington DC

Papers of the Bagot family of Blithfield, Staffordshire, 1428–1671 (bulk 1557–1671), Folger MS L.a

Papers of the Cavendish-Talbot family, Folger MS X.d.428, letters and 'Account Book of Sir William and Lady Cavendish of Chatsworth, 1548 Michaelmas-1550'

Folger MS Add 52 6 (V.b.308), 'Edward Whalley's Accompts Steward to Elizabeth Countess of Shrewsbury. 1589–1592'

Hatfield House, Hatfield, Hertfordshire

Cecil Papers: Manuscripts: 3, 9, 10, 32, 80, 84, 86, 91, 92, 99, 135, 202, 213, 250

Huntington Library, San Marino, California

MS HM 803

Keele University Library

Paget Papers: Manuscripts 4, 7, 8, 10

Lambeth Palace Library

Miscellaneous MSS
Shrewsbury MSS
Talbot MSS

Longleat House, Wiltshire

Dudley Papers
Talbot Papers
Thynne Papers

The National Archives, Kew

PROB 10/254, will of Elizabeth, dowager countess of Shrewsbury
PROB 11/111, fols 188–93, will of Elizabeth, dowager countess of Shrewsbury
PROB 11/202, fols 340r-v, will of Timothy Pusey

Selected bibliography 201

SP12, State Papers Domestic, Elizabeth
SP12/207, State Papers Domestic, Elizabeth, Shrewsbury Papers
SP46, State Papers Domestic, Supplementary
13 General Correspondence, 1559–1565
24 General Correspondence, Temp. Elizabeth
SP53, State Papers Scotland, Mary, Queen of Scots

National Library of Scotland, Edinburgh

Manuscripts: 118, 220

Nottingham University Special Collections

Middleton MSS
MS 663, David N. Durant Papers

Pepys Library, Magdalene College, Cambridge

Pepys MS 2403

Sheffield Archives

Bacon Frank MSS MD 6277–79, 6311
Shrewsbury Papers, MD 6311, inventories of jewellery, jewelled clothes and plate, 1567–99

Calendared sources

A Calendar of the Shrewsbury and Talbot Papers in the Lambeth Palace Library and the College of Arms. Volume 1: Shrewsbury MSS in the Lambeth Palace Library (MSS 694–710), ed. by C. Jamison, revised by E.G.W. Bill, Derbyshire Archaeological Society Record Series (HMSO, 1966).
A Calendar of the Shrewsbury and Talbot Papers in the Lambeth Palace Library and the College of Arms. Volume 2: Talbot Papers in the College of Arms, ed. by G.R. Batho (HMSO, 1971).
Calendar of State Papers, Domestic Series, of the Reigns of Edward VI, Mary, Elizabeth, 1547–1580, ed. by R. Lemon, 7 vols (1856–71).
Calendar of State Papers, Domestic Series, of the Reigns of Edward VI, Mary, Elizabeth [and Janes I], 1547–1625, ed. by R. Lemon and M.E.E. Wood, 12 vols (1865–70).
Calendar of State Papers: Foreign Series, of the Reign of Elizabeth, ed. by S.C. Lomas, A.B. Hinds and R.B. Wernham (1914–50).
Calendar of State Papers relating to Scotland and Mary Queen of Scots, 1547–1603, ed. by W.K. Boyd, J.D. Mackie, H.W. Meikle, A.I. Cameron and M.S. Giuseppi, 13 vols (Edinburgh, 1898–1969).
Calendar of State Papers relating to Affairs in the Archives of Venice, 38 vols (HMSO, 1862–1947).

202   *Selected bibliography*

Folger Shakespeare Library Finding Aid: Guide to the Bagot Family Papers, 1428–1671 (bulk 1557–1671), Folger MS L.a. 1–1076.

Folger Shakespeare Library Finding Aid: Guide to the Papers of the Cavendish-Talbot Family, Folger MS X.d.428 (1–203).

HMC, *Calendar of the Manuscripts of the Most Honourable the Marquess of Bath Preserved at Longleat*, Series 58, 5 vols (1904–80).

HMC, *Calendar of the Manuscripts of the Most Honourable the Marquess of Salisbury Preserved at Hatfield House Hertfordshire*, 24 vols (1883–1976).

HMC, *Report on the Manuscripts of His Grace the Duke of Rutland Preserved at Belvoir Castle*, 4 vols (1888).

HMC, *Report on the Pepys Manuscripts Preserved at Magdalene College, Cambridge* (1911).

Printed sources and editions

Akkerman, Nadine (ed.), *The Correspondence of Elizabeth Stuart, Queen of Bohemia*, 3 vols., two published to date (Oxford: Oxford University Press, 2011, 2015).

Allen, Gemma (ed.), *The Letters of Lady Anne Bacon*, vol. 44, Camden Fifth Series (Cambridge: Cambridge University Press, 2014).

Beale, Robert, 'A Treatise of the Office of a Councellor and Principall Secretarie to her Ma[jes]tie', in C. Read (ed.), *Mr Secretary Walsingham and the Policy of Queen Elizabeth*, 3 vols. (Oxford: Clarendon Press, 1925), I, pp. 423–43.

Dawson, Giles, and Laetitia Kennedy-Skipton, *Elizabethan Handwriting, 1500–1650: A Manual* (New York: Norton, 1966).

Day, Angel, *The English Secretorie* (London: John Day, 1578).

Durant, David N., and Philip Riden, *The Building of Hardwick Hall*, Vol. 1: *The Old Hall, 1587–91*, Vol. 2: *The New Hall, 1591–98*, Derbyshire Record Society 4 and 9 (Derby: Blackhall & Partners, 1980; Gloucester: Alan Sutton, 1984).

Erasmus, D., *Collected Works of Erasmus. Volume 25: Literary and Educational Writings 3: De conscribendis epistolis / Formvla / De civilitae*, ed. and trans. by J. K. Sowards (Toronto: Toronto University Press, 1985).

Fairbank, Alfred, and Bethold Wople, *Renaissance Handwriting: An Anthology of Italic Scripts* (London: Faber and Faber, 1960).

Fulwood, William, *The Enimie of Idleness* (London: Leonard Maylard, 1568).

Girouard, Mark, *Robert Smythson and the Elizabethan Country House* (New Haven: Yale University Press, 1983).

Greg, W.W., *English Literary Autographs, 1550–1650*; part I, dramatists; part II, poets (Oxford: Oxford University Press, 1925–1932).

Handover, P.M., *Arbella Stuart: Royal Lady of Hardwick and Cousin to King James* (London: Eyre and Spottiswoode, 1957).

Hannay, Margaret P., Noel J. Kinnamon, and Michael G. Brennan (eds.), *Collected Works of Mary Sidney Herbert, Countess of Pembroke* (Oxford: Clarendon Press, 1998).

———, *Domestic Politics and Family Absence: The Correspondence (1588–1621) of Robert Sidney, First Earl of Leicester, and Barbara Gamage Sidney, Countess of Leicester*, The Early Modern Englishwoman 1500–1750: Contemporary Editions (Aldershot: Ashgate, 2005).

Selected bibliography 203

Harrington, John, *A Tract on the Succession to the Crown 1602*, Roxburghe Club (London: Nicholas and Sons, 1880).

Hoby, Margaret, *Diary of Lady Margaret Hoby, 1599–1605*, Dorothy M. Meads (ed.) (Boston and New York: Houghton Mifflin, 1930).

Hunter, Joseph, *Hallamshire* (London: Printed for the author, by Richard and Arthur Taylor, Shoe-Lane, 1819; second edition, 1869).

Levey, Santina M., and Peter K. Thornton (eds.), *Of Houshold Stuff: The 1601 Inventories of Bess of Hardwick* (London: The National Trust, 2001).

Marcus, Leah S., Janel Mueller, and Mary Beth Rose (eds.), *Elizabeth I: Autograph Compositions and Foreign Language Originals* (Chicago: University of Chicago Press, 2003).

———, *Elizabeth I: Collected Works* (Chicago: Chicago University Press, 2000).

May, Steven W. (ed.), *Queen Elizabeth I: Selected Works* (New York: Washington Square Press, 2004).

Michel Farbenführer (Colour Guide) (Munich: Schwaneberger Verlag, 2000).

Millman, Jill Seal, and Gillian Wright (eds.), *Early Modern Women's Manuscript Poetry* (Manchester and New York: Manchester University Press, 2005).

Ostovich, Helen, and Elizabeth Sauer (eds.), *Reading Early Modern Women: An Anthology of Texts in Manuscript and Print, 1550–1700* (New York: Routledge, 2004).

Ovid, *Heroides*, trans. by Harold Isbell (London: Penguin, 1990).

———, *Metamorphoese*, trans. by David Raeburn (London: Penguin, 2004).

Petti, Anthony G., *English Literary Hands from Chaucer to Dryden* (London: Arnold, 1977).

Preston, Jean F., and Laetitia Yeandle, *English Handwriting, 1400–1650: An Introductory Manual* (Binghamton, NY: Pegasus, 1992).

Pryor, Felix, *Elizabeth I: Her Life in Letters* (London: The British Library, 2003).

Sotheby's sale catalogue, 26 June 1974, item 2840, pp. 12–13; *Catalogue of English Manuscripts and Autograph Letters and Charters From the Celebrated Collection Formed by Sir Thomas Phillipps Bt.*, Wednesday 26 June 1974 at 11am and 3pm.

Steen, Sara Jayne (ed.), *The Letters of Lady Arbella Stuart* (Oxford: Oxford University Press, 1994).

Steer, Francis W. (ed.), *Arundel Castle Archives*, 4 vols. (Chichester: West Sussex County Council, 1968–80).

Strickland, Agnus, *Letters of Mary Queen of Scots and Documents Connected with Her Personal History*, 2 vols. (London: Henry Colburn, 1842).

Taylor, John, *The Carriers Cosmographie* (London: A.G., 1637).

Wall, Alison (ed.), *Two Elizabethan Women: Correspondence of Joan and Maria Thynne 1575–1611*, Wiltshire Record Society 38 (Devizes: Wiltshire Records Society, 1983).

Wiggins, Alison, Alan Bryson, Daniel Starza Smith, Anke Timmermann, and Graham Williams (eds.), *Bess of Hardwick's Letters: The Complete Correspondence, c. 1550–1608*, University of Glasgow, web development by Katherine Rogers, University of Sheffield Humanities Research Institute (University of Glasgow, 2013) [last date of access: February 2016], www.bessofhardwick.org.

Wolfe, Heather (ed.), *Elizabeth Cary Lady Falkland: Life and Letters*, vol. 230, Cambridge Renaissance Texts from Manuscript no. 4 (Tempe: Medieval and Renaissance Texts and Studies, 2001).

204 Selected bibliography

Secondary sources

Selected biographical accounts of Bess of Hardwick

Durant, David N., *Bess of Hardwick: Portrait of an Elizabethan Dynast* (London and Chester Springs: Peter Owen, 1977).

Eisenberg, Elizabeth, *The Captive Queen in Derbyshire* (Derbyshire: Wye Valley Press, 1984).

——, *This Costly Countess – Bess of Hardwick* (Derby: J. H. Hall & Sons, 1985).

Goldring, Elizabeth, 'Talbot, Elizabeth [Bess of Hardwick], Countess of Shrewsbury (1527?–1608)', in *Oxford Dictionary of National Biography* (Oxford University Press, 2004) [last date of access: February 2016] www.oxforddnb.com.

Hogrefe, Pearl, *Women of Action in Tudor England: Nine Biographical Sketches* (Ames, Iowa: Iowa State University Press, 1977), Chapter 3: Bess of Hardwick, Countess of Shrewsbury, 1518?–1608, pp. 59–81.

Hubbard, Kate, *A Material Girl: Bess of Hardwick, 1527–1608* (London: Short Books, 2001).

Lodge, Edmund, *Illustrations of British History, Biography and Manners in the Reigns of Edward VI, Mary, Elizabeth and James I*, 3 vols. (London: G. Nicol, 1791; second edition, London: John Chidley, 1838).

Lovell, Mary S., *Bess of Hardwick, First Lady of Chatsworth* (London: Little Brown, 2005).

Marshall, Rosalind K., *Queen Mary's Women: Female Relatives, Servants, Friends and Enemies of Mary Queen of Scots* (Edinburgh: John Donald, 2006), Chapter 11: Bess of Hardwick and the English Years, pp. 176–91.

Plowden, Alison, *Mistress of Hardwick* (London: BBC Publications, 1972).

Rawson, Maud Stepney, *Bess of Hardwick and Her Circle* (New York: John Lane, 1910).

Riden, Philip, 'Bess of Hardwick and the St Loe Inheritance', in Philip Riden and David Edwards (eds.), *Essays in Derbyshire History Presented to Gladwyn Turbutt* (Chesterfield: Derbyshire Record Society, 2006), pp. 80–106.

Riden, Philip, and Dudley Fowkes, *Hardwick: A Great House and Its Estate* (Chichester: Phillimore in association with the Institute of Historical Research, 2009).

Williams, E.C., *Bess of Hardwick* (London: Longmans, Green, 1959).

Selected historical fiction featuring Bess of Hardwick

Bagwell, Gillian, *Venus in Winter: A Novel of Bess of Hardwick* (New York: Berkley Books, 2013).

Clarke, Susanna, 'Antickes and Frets', in *The Ladies of Grace Adieu and Other Stories* (London: Bloomsbury, 2006), pp. 207–20.

Gregory, Philippa, *The Other Queen* (London: Harper Collins, 2008).

Henley, Virginia, *A Woman of Passion* (New York: Island Books, 1999).

Leslie, Doris, *Wreath for Arabella* (St. Albans: Hutchinson, 1948).

Plaidy, Jean, *The Captive Queen of Scots* (London: Pan Books, 1963).

Westcott, Jan, *The Tower and the Dream* (New York: Bantam, 1975; first printed 1974).

Wilkinson, Linda, *Bloodline: Duty, Dynasty, Death* (unpublished script, 2010).

Selected bibliography   205

Selected secondary sources

Alford, Stephen, *Burghley: William Cecil at the Court of Elizabeth I* (Yale: Yale University Press, 2008).

Ashelford, Jane, *The Art of Dress: Clothes and Society, 1500–1914* (London: The National Trust, 1996).

Auer, Anita, Daniel Schreier, and Richard J. Watts, *Letter Writing and Language Change*, Studies in English Language (Cambridge: Cambridge University Press, 2015).

Beal, Peter, *A Dictionary of Manuscript Terminology, 1450–2000* (Oxford: Oxford University Press, 2008).

———, *In Praise of Scribes: Manuscripts and Their Makers in Seventeenth-Century England* (Oxford: Oxford University Press, 1998).

Beale, Philip, *England's Mail: Two Millennia of Letter Writing* (Stroud: Tempus Publishing, 2005).

———, *A History of the Post in England from the Romans to the Stuarts* (Aldershot: Ashgate, 1998).

Bennett, Judith, *History Matters: Patriarchy and the Challenge of Feminism* (Philadelphia: University of Pennsylvania Press; Manchester: Manchester University Press, 2006).

Benskin, Michael, and Margaret Laing, 'Translations and Mischsprachen in Middle English Manuscripts', in Benskin and Samuels (eds.), *So Meny People*, pp. 55–106.

Benskin, Michael, and M.L. Samuels (eds.), *So Meny People Longages and Tonges: Philological Essays in Scots and Mediaeval English Presented to Angus McIntosh* (Edinburgh: Privately Printed, 1981).

Bergs, Alexander, 'Linguistic Fingerprints of Authors and Scribes', in Auer, Schreier and Watts (eds.), *Letter Writing and Language Change*, pp. 114–32.

Blank, Paula, *Broken English: Dialects and the Politics of Language in Renaissance Writings* (London and New York: Routledge, 1996).

Bloom, J. Harvey, *English Seals* (London: Methuen, 1906).

Bourdieu, Pierre, 'The Economics of Linguistic Exchanges', trans. Richard Nice, *Social Science Information*, 16 (1977): 645–68.

Bowden, Caroline, 'The Library of Mildred Cooke Cecil, Lady Burghley', *The Library*, 6 (2005): 3–29.

———, 'Women as Intermediaries: An Example of the Use of Literacy in the Late Sixteenth and Early Seventeenth Centuries', *History of Education*, 22 (1993): 215–23.

Braudel, Fernand, *Civilization and Capitalism, 15th-18th Century: The Structure of Everyday Life* (Berkley and Los Angeles, CA: University of California Press, 1992).

Braumuller, A.R., 'Accounting for Absence: The Transcription of Space', in W. Speed Hill (ed.), *New Ways of Looking at Old Texts: Papers of the Renaissance English Text Society, 1985–1991*, Medieval and Renaissance Texts and Studies 107 (Binghamton, NY: Renaissance English Text Society, 1993), pp. 47–56.

———, 'Editing Elizabethan Letters', *TEXT*, 1 (1981): 185–97.

Brayshay, Mark, *Land Travel and Communications in Tudor and Stuart England: Achieving a Joined-Up Realm* (Liverpool: Liverpool University Press, 2014).

———, 'Waits, Musicians, Bearwards and Players: The Inter-Urban Road Travel and Performances of Itinerant Entertainers in Sixteenth and Seventeenth Century England', *Journal of Historical Geography*, 31, 3 (2005): 430–58.

206 Selected bibliography

——, 'Royal Post-Horse Routes in England and Wales: The Evolution of the Network in the Late-Sixteenth and Early Seventeenth Century', *Journal of Historical Geography*, 17, 4 (1991): 373–89.

Brayshay, Mark, and Philip Harrison, 'Post Horse Routes, Royal Progresses and Government Communications in the Reign of James I', *Journal of Transport History*, 18 (1997): 116–33.

Brayshay, Mark, Philip Harrison, and Brian Chalkley, 'Knowledge, Nationhood and Governance: The Speed of the Royal Post in Early-Modern England', *Journal of Historical Geography*, 24, 3 (1998): 265–88.

Brown, Elizabeth, '"Companion Me with My Mistress": Cleopatra, Elizabeth I, and Their Waiting Women', in Susan Frye and Karen Robertson (eds.), *Maids and Mistresses, Cousins and Queens: Women's Alliances in Early Modern England* (New York and Oxford: Oxford University Press, 1999), pp. 131–45.

Brown, Penelope, and Stephen C. Levinson, *Politeness: Some Universals in Language Usage*, Studies in Interactional Sociolinguistics no. 4 (Cambridge: Cambridge University Press, 1987).

Brown, Roger, and Albert Gilman, 'Politeness Theory and Shakespeare's Four Major Tragedies', *Language and Society*, 18, 2 (1989): 159–212.

Bruster, Douglas, '"In a Woman's Key": Women's Speech and Women's Language in Renaissance Drama', *Exemplaria*, 4 (1992): 235–66.

Bryson, Ann, *From Courtesy to Civility: Changing Codes of Conduct in Early Modern England* (Oxford: Oxford University Press, 1998).

Burke, Victoria E., 'Let's Get Physical: Bibliography, Codicology and Seventeenth-Century Women's Manuscripts', *Literature Compass*, 4, 6 (2007): 1667–82.

Burke, Victoria E., and Jonathan Gibson (eds.), *Early Modern Women's Manuscript Writing: Selected Papers from the Trinity/Trent Colloquium* (Aldershot and Burlington, VT: Ashgate, 2004).

Burlinson, Christopher, and Andrew Zurcher, '"Secretary to the Lord Grey Lord Deputie here": Edmund Spenser's Irish Papers', *The Library*, 6 (2005): 30–75.

Burnley, J.D., *The History of the English Language: A Source Book* (London and New York: Longman, 1992).

——, 'Curial Prose in England', *Speculum*, 61, 3 (1986): 593–614.

Calabresi, Bianca F.-C., '"You sow, Ile read": Letters and Literacies in Early Modern Samplers', in Heidi Brayman Hackel and Catherine E. Kelly (eds.), *Reading Women: Literacy, Authorship and Culture in the Atlantic World, 1500–1800* (Philadelphia: University of Pennsylvania Press, 2008), pp. 79–104.

Cameron, Deborah, *Feminism and Linguistic Theory*, second edition (Basingstoke: Macmillan, 1992).

Cavallo, Sandra, and Silvia Evangelisti (eds.), *A Cultural History of Childhood and the Family in the Early Modern Age* (Oxford: Berg, 2012).

Cavallo, Sandra, and Lyndan Warner (eds.), *Widowhood in Medieval and Early Modern Europe* (London: Longman, 1999).

Chartier, Roger (ed.), *A History of Private Life, Vol. III: Passions of the Renaissance* (Cambridge, MA: The Belknap Press of Harvard University Press, 1989).

Chartier, R., A. Boureau, and C. Dauphin, *Correspondence: Models of Letter-Writing from the Middle Ages to the Nineteenth Century*, trans. by C. Woodall (Princeton: Princeton University Press, 1997).

Cheney, C.R., *A Handbook of Dates for Students of British History (1945)*, rev. Michael Jones (Cambridge: Cambridge University Press, 2000).

Selected bibliography 207

Clanchy, M.T., *From Memory to Written Record: England 1066–1307* (London: Arnold, 1979).

Clarke, Danielle, 'Nostalgia, Anachronism, and the Editing of Early Modern Women's Texts', *Text*, 15 (2003): 186–209.

———, *The Politics of Early Modern Women's Writing* (London and New York: Routledge, 2001).

———, '"Form'd into Words by Your Divided Lips": Women, Rhetoric and the Ovidian Tradition', in Clarke and Clarke (eds.), *'This Double Voice'*, pp. 61–87.

Clarke, Danielle, and Elizabeth Clarke (eds.), *'This Double Voice': Gendered Writing in Early Modern England* (Basingstoke: Macmillan; New York: St Martin's Press, 2000).

Clarke, Elizabeth, 'Beyond Microhistory: The Use of Women's Manuscripts in a Widening Political Arena', in Daybell (ed.), *Women and Politics*, pp. 211–27.

———, 'Elizabeth Jekyll's Spiritual Diary: Private Manuscript or Political Document?', in Peter Beal and Margaret J. Ezell (eds.), *English Manuscript Studies, 1100–1700*, vol. 9, Writings by Early Modern Women (London: Blackwell, 2000), pp. 218–37.

Collon, Dominique (ed.), *7000 Years of Seals* (London: British Museum Press, 1997).

Crawford, Julie, *Mediatrix: Women, Politics, and Literary Production in Early Modern England* (Oxford: Oxford University Press, 2014).

———, 'Literary Circles and Communities', in Caroline Bicks and Jennifer Summit (eds.), *The History of British Women's Writing, 1500–1610* (Basingstoke and New York: Palgrave Macmillan, 2010), pp. 34–59.

Cressy, David, 'Kinship and Kin Interaction in Early Modern England', *Past and Present*, 113 (1983): 38–69.

———, *Literacy and the Social Order: Reading and Writing in Tudor and Stuart England* (Cambridge: Cambridge University Press, 1980).

Crofts, J., *Packhorse, Waggon and Post: Land Carriage and Communication under the Tudors and Stuarts* (London: Routledge and Kegan Press, 1967).

Culpeper, Jonathan, *Historical Sociopragmatics* (Amsterdam and Philadelphia: John Benjamins, 2011).

Culpeper, Jonathan, and Daniel Kádár (eds.), *Historical (Im)Politeness* (Bern: Peter Lang, 2010).

Culpeper, Jonathan, and Merja Kytö, *Early Modern English Dialogues: Spoken Interaction as Writing* (Cambridge: Cambridge University Press, 2010).

Cusack, Bridget, *Everyday English 1500–1700* (Edinburgh: Edinburgh University Press, 1998).

Cust, Richard, 'News and Politics in Early Seventeenth Century England', *Past and Present*, 112 (1986): 60–90.

Dawson, Mark, *Plenti and Grase: Food and Drink in a Sixteenth Century Household* (Totnes: Prospect, 2009).

Daybell, James, 'Social Negotiations in Correspondence between Mothers and Daughters in Tudor and Early Stuart England', *Women's History Review*, 24, 1 (2015): 1–26.

———, *The Material Letter in Early Modern England: Manuscript Letters and the Culture and Practices of Letter-Writing, 1512–1635*, Early Modern Literature in History (Houndmills and New York: Palgrave Macmillan, 2012).

———, 'Secret Letters in Elizabethan England', in James Daybell and Peter Hinds (eds.), *Material Readings of Early Modern Culture: Texts and Social Practices 1580–1730* (Basingstoke: Palgrave Macmillan, 2010), pp. 47–64.

208 Selected bibliography

————, 'Material Meanings and the Social Signs of Manuscript Letters', *Literature Compass*, 6, 3 (2009): 647–67.

————, 'Women, Politics and Domesticity: The Scribal Publication of Lady Rich's Letter to Elizabeth I', in Hardman and Lawrence-Mathers (eds.), *Women and Writing*, pp. 111–30.

————, 'Scripting a Female Voice: Women's Epistolary Rhetoric in Sixteenth-Century Letters of Petition', *Women's Writing*, 13, 1 (2008): 3–22.

————, 'Women's Letters of Recommendation and the Rhetoric of Friendship in Sixteenth-Century England', in Jennifer Richards and Alison Thorne (eds), *Rhetoric, Women and Politics in Early Modern England* (London and New York: Routledge, 2007), pp. 172–90.

————, *Women Letter-Writers in Tudor England* (Oxford: Oxford University Press, 2006).

————, '"I wold wyshe my doings myght be . . . secret": Privacy and the Social Practices of Reading Women's Letters in Sixteenth-Century England', in Jane Couchman and Ann Crabb (eds.), *Women's Letters across Europe, 1400–1700: Form and Persuasion* (Aldershot and Burlington, VT: Ashgate, 2005), pp. 143–61.

————, '"Suche newes as on the Quenes hye wayes we have mett": The News and Intelligence Networks of Elizabeth Talbot, Countess of Shrewsbury (c. 1527–1608)', in Daybell (ed.), *Women and Politics*, pp. 114–31.

———— (ed.), *Women and Politics in Early Modern England, 1450–1700* (Aldershot and Burlington: Ashgate, 2004).

———— (ed.), *Early Modern Women's Letter Writing, 1450–1700*, Early Modern Literature in History (Basingstoke: Palgrave Macmillan, 2001).

————, '"Ples acsep thes my skrybled lynes": The Construction and Conventions of Women's Letters in England, 1540–1603', *Journal of the Rocky Mountain Medieval and Renaissance Association*, 20 (1999): 207–23.

Dinshaw, Carolyn, and David Wallace (eds.), *The Cambridge Companion to Medieval Women's Writing* (Cambridge: Cambridge University Press, 2003).

Dobranski, Stephen, *Readers and Authorship in Early Modern England* (Cambridge and New York: Cambridge University Press, 2005).

Doran, Susan (ed.), *Elizabeth: The Exhibition at the National Maritime Museum* (London: Chatto and Windus, 2003).

Doty, K., 'Telling Tales: The Role of Scribes in Constructing the Discourse of the Salem Witchcraft Trials', *Journal of Historical Pragmatics*, 8, 1 (2007): 25–41.

Durant, David N., *The Smythson Circle: The Story of Six Great English Houses* (London and Chicago: Peter Owen, 2011).

Erickson, Amy, *Women and Property in Early Modern England* (London: Routledge, 1993).

Evans, Mel, *The Language of Queen Elizabeth I: A Sociolinguistic Perspective on Royal Style and Identity*, Publications of the Philological Society 46 (Chichester: Blackwell, 2013).

Ezell, Margaret, *Writing Women's Literary History* (Baltimore, MD: Johns Hopkins University Press, 1993).

Finlay, Michael, *Western Writing Implements in the Age of the Quill Pen* (Carlisle: Plains, 1990).

Fish, Stanley, 'Is There a Text in This Class?', reproduced in H. Aram Veeser (ed.), *The Stanley Fish Reader* (Malden, MA and Oxford: Blackwell, 1999), pp. 38–54.

Selected bibliography 209

Fitzmaurice, Susan M., *The Familiar Letter in Early Modern English: A Pragmatic Approach*, Pragmatics and Beyond New Series 95 (Amsterdam and Philadelphia: John Benjamins, 2002).

Fitzmaurice, Susan M., and Jeremy J. Smith, 'Evidence for the History of English', in Terttu Nevalainen and Elizabeth Traugott (eds.), *The Oxford Handbook of the History of English* (Oxford: Oxford University Press, 2012), pp. 19–36.

Fitzmaurice, Susan M., and Irma Taavitsainen (eds.), *Methodological Issues in Historical Pragmatics* (Berlin: Mouton de Gruyter, 2007).

Foucault, Michel, 'What Is an Author?', in Paul Rabinow (ed.), *The Foucault Reader* (London: Penguin, 1981), pp. 101–20.

Fox, Adam, 'Rumour, News and Popular Political Opinion in Elizabethan and Early Stuart England', *Historical Journal*, 40, 3 (1997): 597–620.

Fraser, Antonia, *Mary, Queen of Scots* (London: Weidenfeld & Nicolson, 1969).

French, Sara, 'A Widow Building in Elizabethan England: Bess of Hardwick at Hardwick Hall', in Alison Levy (ed.), *Widowhood and Visual Culture in Early Modern Europe* (Aldershot and Burlington: Ashgate, 2003), pp. 161–76.

Friedman, Alice T., 'Hardwick Hall', *History Today*, 45, 1 (1995): 27–32.

———, 'Architecture, Authority, and the Female Gaze: Planning and Representation in the Early Modern Country House', *Assemblage*, 18 (1992): 40–61.

———, '"Portrait of a Marriage": The Willoughby Letters of 1585–1586', *Signs*, 11, 3 (1986): 542–55.

Frye, Susan, *Pens and Needles: Women's Textualities in Early Modern England* (Philadelphia: University of Pennsylvania Press, 2010).

Fumerton, Patricia, *Unsettled: The Culture of Mobility and the Working Poor in Early Modern England* (Chicago: University of Chicago Press, 2006).

Gal, Susan, 'Between Speech and Silence: The Problematics of Research on Language and Gender', *Pragmatics*, 3, 1 (1990): 1–38; reprinted in M. di Leonardo (ed.), *Gender at the Crossroads of Knowledge: Feminist Anthropology in the Postmodern Era* (Berkeley: University of California Press, 1991), pp. 175–203.

Garde-Hansen, Joanne, Andrew Hoskins, and Anna Reading (eds.), *Save as . . . Digital Memories* (Basingstoke: Palgrave Macmillan, 2009).

Gibson, Jonathan, 'The Queen's Two Hands', in Alessandra Petrina and Laura Tosi (eds.), *Representations of Elizabeth I in Early Modern Culture* (New York: Palgrave Macmillan, 2011), pp. 47–65.

———, 'Letters', in Michael Hattaway (ed.), *A Companion to English Renaissance Literature and Culture* (Oxford: Blackwell, 2000), pp. 609–14.

———, 'Significant Space in Manuscript Letters', *The Seventeenth Century*, 12 (1997): 1–9.

Gibson, Jonathan, and Gillian Wright, 'Editing Perdita: Texts, Theories, Reader', in Ann Hollinshead Hurley and Chanita Goodblatt (eds.), *Women Editing/Editing Women: Early Modern Women Writers and the New Textualism* (Newcastle upon Tyne: Cambridge Scholars Publishing, 2009), pp. 155–73.

Girouard, Mark, *Elizabethan Architecture: Its Rise and Fall, 1540–1640* (New Haven and London: Yale University Press, 2009).

———, *Hardwick Hall* (London: The National Trust, 2006).

———, *Robert Smythson and the Elizabethan Country House* (New Haven and London: Yale University Press, 1983).

Goldberg, Jonathan, *Desiring Women Writing: English Renaissance Examples* (Stanford: Stanford University Press, 1997).

210   *Selected bibliography*

———, *Writing Matter: From the Hands of the English Renaissance* (Stanford: Stanford University Press, 1990).

Görlach, Manfred, *Introduction to Early Modern English* (Cambridge: Cambridge University Press, 1978; revised edition, 1991).

Greg, W.W., 'The Bakings of Betsy', *The Library*, 3rd ser., 2 (1911): 225–59.

Guy, John, *My Heart Is My Own: The Life of Mary Queen of Scots* (London: HarperCollins, 2004).

Hamling, Tara, and Catherine Richardson (eds.), *Everyday Objects: Medieval and Early Modern Material Culture and Its Meanings* (Aldershot: Ashgate, 2010).

Hammer, Paul E.J., 'The Earl of Essex, Fulke Greville and the Employment of Scholars', *Studies in Philology*, 91, 2 (1994): 167–80.

———, 'The Uses of Scholarship: The Secretariat of Robert Devereux, Second Earl of Essex, c. 1581–1601', *English Historical Review*, 109 (1994): 26–51.

Hardman, Phillipa, and Anne Lawrence-Mathers (eds.), *Women and Writing, c. 1340–c. 1650: The Domestication of Print Culture* (Suffolk: Boydell and Brewer, 2010).

Harris, Barbara J., *English Aristocratic Women, 1450–1550: Marriage, Family, Property and Careers* (Oxford: Oxford University Press, 2002).

———, 'Women and Politics in Early Tudor England', *Historical Journal*, 33 (1990): 265–67.

Heal, Felicity, 'Food Gifts, the Household and the Politics of Exchange in Early Modern England', *Past and Present*, 199 (2008): 41–70.

Henderson, Judith Rice, 'Humanism and the Humanities: Erasmus's *Opus de conscribendis epistolis* in Sixteenth-Century Schools', in Poster and Mitchell (eds.), *Letter-Writing Manuals*, pp. 141–77.

———, 'On Reading the Rhetoric of the Renaissance Letter', in Heinrich F. Plett (ed.), *Renaissance-Rhetorik / Renaissance Rhetoric* (Berlin and New York: Walter de Gruyter, 1993), pp. 143–62.

———, 'Defining the Genre of the Letter: Juan Luis Vives', *De Conscribendis Epistolis*, *Renaissance and Reformation*, n.s. 7, 19 (1983): 89–105.

———, 'Erasmus on the Art of Letter-Writing', in Murphy (ed.), *Renaissance Eloquence*, pp. 331–55.

Hey, David, *Packmen, Carriers and Packhorse Roads: Trade and Communications in North Derbyshire and South Yorkshire* (Trowbridge and Esher: Leicester University Press, 1980).

Hiltunen, R., and M. Peikola, 'Trial Discourse and Manuscript Context: Scribal Profiles in the Salem Witchcraft Records', *Journal of Historical Pragmatics*, 8, 1 (2007): 43–68.

Hope, Jonathan, *Shakespeare and Language: Reason, Eloquence and Artifice in the Renaissance* (London: Arden, 2010).

———, 'Varieties of Early Modern English', in Haruko Momma and Michael Matto (eds.), *A Companion to the History of The English Language* (Chichester: Blackwell, 2008), pp. 216–24.

Horobin, Simon, 'The Criteria for Scribal Attribution: Dublin, Trinity College MS 244 Reconsidered', *Review of English Studies*, n.s., 60 (2009): 371–81.

Houlbrooke, Ralph A., *The English Family, 1450–1700* (Harlow: Longman, 1984).

Hughes, Rebecca, *English in Speech and Writing* (London: Routledge, 1996).

Selected bibliography 211

Hull, Suzanne W., *Chaste, Silent, and Obedient: English Books for Women, 1475–1640* (San Marino: Huntington Library, 1982; reprinted 1988).

Hunter, Michael, *Editing Early Modern Texts: An Introduction to Principles and Practice* (Basingstoke and New York: Palgrave MacMillan, 2007).

———, 'How to Edit a Seventeenth-Century Manuscript', *The Seventeenth Century*, 10, 2 (1995): 277–310.

Hutson, Lorna (ed.), *Feminism and Renaissance Studies* (Oxford: Oxford University Press, 1999).

———, *The Usurer's Daughter: Male Friendship and Fictions of Women in Sixteenth-Century England* (London: Routledge, 1994).

Immel, Andrea, and Michael Witmore (eds.), *Childhood and Children's Books in Early Modern Europe, 1550–1800*, Children's Literature and Culture (New York and London: Routledge, 2006).

Ioppolo, Grace, '"I Desire to be Held in Your Memory": Reading Penelope Rich through Her Letters', in Dympna Callaghan (ed.), *The Impact of Feminism in English Renaissance Studies* (Basingstoke and New York: Palgrave Macmillan, 2007), pp. 299–325.

Jardine, Lisa, *Erasmus, Man of Letters: The Construction of Charisma in Print* (Princeton: Princeton University Press, 1993).

———, *Still Harping on Daughters: Women and Drama in the Age of Shakespeare* (Sussex, England: Harvester Press; Totowa, NJ: Barnes & Noble, 1983; second edition, New York: Harvester Wheatsheaf, 1989).

Jardine, Lisa, and Anthony Grafton, '"Studied for Action": How Gabriel Harvey Read His Livy', *Past and Present*, 129 (1990): 30–78.

Jucker, Andreas H., and Irma Taavitsainen, *English Historical Pragmatics* (Edinburgh: Edinburgh University Press, 2013).

Justice, George, and Nathan Tinker (eds.), *Women's Writing and the Circulation of Ideas: Manuscript Publication in England, 1550–1800* (Cambridge and New York: Cambridge University Press, 2002).

Kettle, Pamela, *Oldcotes: The Last Mansion Built By Bess of Hardwick* (Frome: Merton Priory Press, 2000).

Kiefer, Frederick, 'Architecture', in Arthur F. Kinney (ed.), *The Oxford Handbook of Shakespeare* (Oxford: Oxford University Press, 2012).

Kilpio, Matti, 'Participal Adjectives with Anaphoric Reference of the Type *The Said, The (A)forementioned* from Old to Early Modern English: The Evidence of the Helsinki Corpus', in Terttu Nevalainen and Leena Kahlas-Tarkka (eds.), *To Explain the Present: Studies in the Changing English Language in Honour of Matti Rissanen*, Mémoires de la Société néo-philologique à Helsingfors 52 (Helsinki: Société Néophilologique, 1997), pp. 77–100.

Kohnen, Thomas, 'Towards a History of English Directives', in A. Fischer, G. Tottie and H.M. Lehmann (eds.), *Text Types and Corpora: Studies in Honour of Udo Fries* (Tubingen: Gunter Narr Verlag, 2000), pp. 165–75.

Lamb, Mary Ellen, 'Constructions of Women Readers', in Susanne Woods and Margaret P. Hannay (eds.), *Teaching Tudor and Stuart Women Writers* (New York: Modern Language Association, 2000), pp. 23–34.

———, 'The Cooke Sisters: Attitudes Towards Learned Women in the Renaissance', in Margaret P. Hannay (ed.), *Silent But For the Word: Tudor Women as Patrons, Translators and Writers of Religious Works* (Kent, OH: The Kent State University Press, 1985), pp. 107–25.

212 Selected bibliography

Lass, Roger (ed.), *The Cambridge History of the English Language Volume 3: 1476–1776* (Cambridge: Cambridge University Press, 1999).

Levey, Santina M., *The Embroideries at Hardwick Hall: A Catalogue* (London: The National Trust, 2007).

———, *An Elizabethan Inheritance: The Hardwick Hall Textiles* (London: The National Trust, 1998).

Levy, F.J., 'How Information Spread among the Gentry, 1550–1640', *Journal of British Studies*, 21 (1982): 11–34.

Love, Harold, *Scribal Publication in Seventeenth-Century England* (Oxford: Clarendon Press, 1993).

Lyall, Roderick, 'The Construction of a Rhetorical Voice in Sixteenth-Century Scottish Letters', *Prose Studies*, 19 (1996): 127–35.

Mack, Peter, *Elizabethan Rhetoric: Theory and Practice* (Cambridge: Cambridge University Press, 2002).

Magnusson, Lynne, 'A Rhetoric of Requests: Genre and Linguistic Scripts in Elizabethan Women's Suitors' Letters', in Daybell (ed.), *Women and Politics*, pp. 51–66.

———, 'Widowhood and Linguistic Capital: The Rhetoric and Reception of Anne Bacon's Epistolary Advice', *English Literary Renaissance*, 31 (2001): 3–33.

———, *Shakespeare and Social Dialogue: Dramatic Language and Elizabethan Letters* (Cambridge: Cambridge University Press, 1999).

Martin, John J., *Myths of Renaissance Individualism* (Basingstoke: Palgrave Macmillan, 2004).

Maxwell, Felicity, 'Enacting Mistress and Steward Roles in a Letter of Household Management: Bess of Hardwick to Francis Whitfield, 14 November 1552', *Lives & Letters: A Journal for Early Modern Archival Research*, 4, 1 (Autumn, 2012): 76–92.

McGann, Jerome, 'The Socialization of Texts', reprinted in David Finkelstein and Alistair McCleery (eds.), *The Book History Reader* (London and New York: Routledge, 2002), pp. 39–46.

McIntosh, Angus, 'A New Approach to Middle English Dialectology', *English Studies*, 44 (1963): 1–11; reprinted in Margaret Laing (ed.), *Middle English Dialectology: Essays On Some Principles and Problems* (Aberdeen: Aberdeen University Press, 1989), pp. 22–31.

McIntosh, Angus, Michael L. Samuels, and Michael Benskin, *A Linguistic Atlas of Late Medieval English*, 4 vols. (Aberdeen: Aberdeen University Press, 1986).

McKitterick, David, 'Women and Their Books in Seventeenth-Century England: The Case of Elizabeth Puckering', *The Library*, 7th ser., 1 (2000): 359–80.

Meres, Natalie, 'Politics in the Elizabethan Privy Chamber: Lady Mary Sidney and Kat Ashley', in Daybell (ed.), *Women and Politics*, pp. 67–82.

———, *Queenship and Political Discourse in the Elizabethan Realms* (Cambridge and New York: Cambridge University Press, 2005).

Meurman-Solin, Anneli, 'Letters as a Source of Data for Reconstructing Early Spoken Scots', Irma Taavitsainen, Gunnel Melchers and Päivi Pahta (eds.), in *Writing in Nonstandard English*, Pragmatics and Beyond 67 (Amsterdam and Philadelphia: John Benjamins, 1999), pp. 305–22.

Milroy, Jim, 'Historical Description and the Ideology of the Standard Language', in L. Wright (ed.), *The Development of Standard English 1300–1800: Theories, Descriptions, Conflicts* (Cambridge: Cambridge University Press, 2000), pp. 11–28.

Selected bibliography 213

Mugglestone, Lynda, *Talking Proper*, revised and extended second edition (Oxford: Clarendon Press, 2003).

Murphy, James J. (ed.), *Renaissance Eloquence: Studies in the Theory and Practice of Renaissance Rhetoric* (Berkley: University of California Press, 1983).

Nevala, Minna, *Address in Early English Correspondence: Its Forms and Socio-Pragmatic Functions* (Helsinki: Société Néophilologique, 2004).

———, 'Inside and Out: Address Forms in 17th- and 18th-Century Letters', *Journal of Historical Pragmatics*, 5, 2 (2004): 273–98.

———, '"By Him That Loves You": Address Forms in Letters Written to 16th-Century Social Aspirers', in Antoinette Renouf (ed.), *Explorations in Corpus Linguistics*, Language and Computers: Studies in Practical Linguistics 23 (Amsterdam and Atlanta: Rodopi, 1988), pp. 147–57.

Nevalainen, Terttu, *An Introduction to Early Modern English* (Edinburgh: Edinburgh University Press, 2006).

———, 'What's in a Royal Letter? Linguistic Variation in the Correspondence of King Henry VIII', in K. Lentz and Ruth Möhlig (eds.), *Of Dyuersitie & Chaunge of Langage: Essays Presented to Manfred Görlach on the Occasion of his 65th Birthday* (Heidelberg: Winter, 2002), pp. 169–79.

———, 'Women's Writings as Evidence for Linguistic Continuity and Change in Early Modern English', in Richard Watts and Peter Trudgill (eds.), *Alternative Histories of English* (London and New York: Routledge, 2002), pp. 191–270.

———, 'Continental Conventions in Early English Correspondence', in H-J. Diller and M. Görlach (eds.), *Towards a History of English as a History of Genres* (Heidelberg: Winter, 2001), pp. 203–24.

Nevalainen, Terttu, and Helena Raumolin-Brunberg (eds.), *Sociolinguistics and Language History: Studies Based on the Corpus of Early English Correspondence*, Language and Computers: Studies in Practical Linguistics 15 (Amsterdam: Rodopi, 1996).

———, 'Constraints on Politeness: The Pragmatics of Address Formulae in Early English Correspondence', in A.H. Jucker (ed.), *Historical Pragmatics* (Amsterdam: John Benjamins, 1995), pp. 541–601.

North, Marcy, L., 'Household Scribes and the Production of Literary Manuscripts in Early Modern England', *Journal of Early Modern Studies*, 4 (2015): 133–57.

Nurmi, Arja, Minna Nevala, and Minna Palander-Collin (eds.), *The Language of Daily Life in England (1400–1800)*, Pragmatics and Beyond New Series 183 (Amsterdam and Philadelphia: John Benjamins, 2009).

Orgel, Stephen, *Impersonations: The Performance of Gender in Shakespeare's England* (Cambridge: Cambridge University Press, 1996).

Orlin, Lena Cowen, 'Empty Vessels', in Tara Hamling and Catherine Richardson (eds.), *Everyday Objects: Medieval and Early Modern Material Culture and Its Meanings* (Aldershot: Ashgate, 2010), pp. 299–308.

Parkes, M.B., *Pause and Effect: An Introduction to the History of Punctuation in the West* (Berkeley: University of California Press, 1993).

Peters, Christine, *Women in Early Modern Britain, 1450–1640*, Social History in Perspective (Basingstoke: Palgrave Macmillan, 2004).

Phillips, Harriet, and Claire Bryony Williams (eds.), *A Handbook of Editing Early Modern Texts*, Material Readings in Early Modern Culture (Abingdon and New York: Routledge, forthcoming).

214 Selected bibliography

Pollock, Linda A., 'The Practice of Kindness in Early Modern Elite Society', *Past and Present*, 211 (2011): 121–58.

——, 'Anger and the Negotiation of Relationships in Early Modern England', *The Historical Journal*, 47, 3 (2004): 567–90.

Poster, Carol, and Linda C. Mitchell (eds.), *Letter-Writing Manuals and Instruction from Antiquity to the Present: Historical and Bibliographic Studies*, Studies in Rhetoric/Communication (South Carolina: The University of South Carolina Press, 2007).

Potter, George R., 'A Note on the Devonshire Papers at Chatsworth House, Derbyshire', *Journal of the Society of Archivists*, 4, 2 (1970): 124–29.

Randall, David, 'Epistolary Rhetoric, the Newspaper and the Public Sphere', *Past and Present*, 198 (2008): 3–32.

Raumolin-Brunberg, Helena, 'Forms of Address in Early English Correspondence', in Nevalainen and Raumolin-Brunberg (eds.), *Sociolinguistics and Language History*, pp. 167–81.

Richardson, Catherine, *Domestic Life and Domestic Tragedy in Early Modern England: The Material Life of the Household* (Manchester and New York: Manchester University Press, 2006).

Richardson, Malcolm, 'The Dictamen and its Influence on Fifteenth-Century English Prose', *Rhetorica*, 2 (1984): 207–26.

Rissanen, Matti, 'Standardisation and the Language of Early Statutes', in Laura Wright (ed.), *The Development of Standard English 1300–1800: Theories, Descriptions, Conflicts* (Cambridge: Cambridge University Press, 2000), pp. 117–30.

Roberts, Sasha, 'Shakespeare "Creeps into the Womans Closets about Bedtime": Women Reading in a Room of Their Own', in Gordon McMullan (ed.), *Renaissance Configurations: Voices/Bodies/Spaces, 1580–1690* (Basingstoke: Macmillan; New York: St Martin's Press, 1998), pp. 30–63.

Robinson, Ian, 'Appendix 1: The History of the Sentence', in *The Establishment of Modern English Prose in the Reformation and the Enlightenment* (Cambridge: Cambridge University Press, 1998), pp. 166–84.

Salmon, Vivian, 'Chapter Two: Orthography and Punctuation', in Lass (ed.), *The Cambridge History of the English Language*, pp. 13–54.

Schneider, Gary, *The Culture of Epistolarity: Vernacular Letters and Letter Writing in Early Modern England, 1500–1700* (Newark: University of Delaware Press, 2005).

——, 'Affecting Correspondences: Body, Behaviour and the Textualisation of Emotion in Early Modern Letters', *Prose Studies*, 23, 3 (2000): 31–62.

Scott-Warren, Jason, 'News, Sociability, and Bookbuying in Early Modern England: The Letters of Sir Thomas Cornwallis', *The Library*, 4 (2000): 382–402.

Slights, William, *The Heart in the Age of Shakespeare* (Cambridge: Cambridge University Press, 2008).

Smith, Jeremy J., 'Punctuation in the Letters of Archibald Campbell, Lord Ilay (1682–1761)', in W. Anderson (ed.), *Language in Scotland: Corpus-Based Studies* (Rodopi: Amsterdam, The Netherlands, 2013), pp. 27–44.

——, *Older Scots: A Linguistic Reader*, Scottish Text Society Fifth Series (Edinburgh and Woodbridge: The Scottish Text Society/Boydell Press, 2012).

——, 'Scots and English in the Letters of John Knox', in Kevin J. McGinley and Nicola Royan (eds.), *The Apparelling of Truth: Literature and Literary Culture in*

Selected bibliography 215

the Reign of James VI: A Festschrift for Roderick J. Lyall (Newcastle upon Tyne: Cambridge Scholars, 2010), pp. 1–10.

————, 'Language, Class and Region in Late Medieval England', *Studies in Medieval English Language and Literature*, 20 (2005): 59–73.

————, *Essentials of Early English* (Abingdon: Routledge, 2005).

————, 'Ideology and Spelling in Sixteenth-Century England', *Il confronto letterario*, 40, Supple. (2004): 11–24.

————, *An Historical Study of English: Form, Function and Change* (London and New York: Routledge, 1996).

————, 'A Linguistic Atlas of Early Middle English: Tradition and Typology', in Matti Rissanen, Ossi Ihalainen, Terttu Nevalainen and Irma Taavitsainen (eds.), *History of Englishes: New Methods and Interpretations in Historical Linguistics* (Berlin and New York: Mouton de Gruyter, 1992), pp. 582–91.

Smith, Jeremy J., and C. Kay, 'The Pragmatics of Punctuation in Older Scots', in Päivi Pahta and Andreas H. Jucker (eds.), *Communicating Early English Manuscripts*, Studies in English Language (Cambridge: Cambridge University Press, 2015), pp. 212–25.

Smith, Jeremy J., and Merja Stenroos, 'Changing Functions: English Spelling Before 1600', in Vivian Cook and Des Ryan (eds.), *The Routledge Handbook of the English Writing System* (London: Routledge, 2016), pp. 125–41.

Sommerville, Margaret R., *Sex and Subjection: Attitudes to Women in Early Modern Society* (London: Arnold, 1995).

Sönmez, Margaret J.-M., 'Perceived and Real Differences Between Men's and Women's Spellings of the Early to Mid-Seventeenth Century', in Dieter Kastovsky and Arthur Mettinger (ed.), *The History of English in A Social Context: A Contribution to Historical Sociolinguistics* Trends in Linguistics Studies and Monographs 129 (Berlin and New York: Mouton de Gruyter, 2000), pp. 405–39.

Stallybrass, Peter, Roger Chartier, John Franklin Mowery and Heather Wolfe, 'Hamlet's Tables and the Technologies of Writing in Renaissance England', *Shakespeare Quarterly*, 55 (2004): 379–419.

Stanbury, Sarah, 'Women's Letters and Private Space in Chaucer', *Exemplaria*, 6 (1994): 271–85.

Steen, Sara Jayne, 'The Cavendish-Talbot Women: Playing a High-Stakes Game', in James Daybell (ed.), *Women and Politics in Early Modern England, 1450–1700* (Aldershot: Ashgate, 2004), pp. 147–63.

————, 'Reading beyond the Words: Material Letters and the Process of Interpretation', *Quidditas*, 22 (2001): 55–69.

————, 'Behind the Arras: Editing Renaissance Women's Letters', in W.S. Hill (ed.), *New Ways of Looking at Old Texts: Papers of the Renaissance English Text Society, 1985–1991* (Binghamton: Medieval and Renaissance Texts and Studies/ Renaissance English Text Society, 1993), pp. 229–38.

————, 'Fashioning an Acceptable Self: Arbella Stuart', *English Literary Renaissance*, 18 (1988): 78–95.

Stewart, Alan, *Shakespeare's Letters* (Oxford: Oxford University Press, 2008).

————, 'The Voices of Anne Cooke, Lady Anne and Lady Bacon', in Clarke and Clarke (eds.), *'This Double Voice'*, pp. 88–102.

————, *Close Readers: Humanism and Sodomy in Early Modern England* (Princeton: Princeton University Press, 1997).

Stewart, Alan, and Heather Wolfe, *Letterwriting in Renaissance England* (Washington, DC: The Folger Shakespeare Library, 2004).

216 Selected bibliography

Strong, Roy, *Gloriana: The Portraits of Queen Elizabeth I* (London: Thames & Hudson, 1987).

Taavitsainen, Irma, and Andreas Jucker, 'Speech Act Verbs and Speech Acts in the History of English', in Susan M. Fitzmaurice and Irma Taavitsainen (eds.), *Methods in Historical Pragmatics* (Berlin and New York: Mouton de Gruyter, 2007), pp. 107–38.

Tanskanen, Sanna-Kaisa, '"Best Patterns for Your Imitation": Early Modern Letter-Writing Instruction and Real Correspondence', in R. Hiltunen and J. Skaffari (eds.), *Discourse Perspectives in English* (Amsterdam and Philadelphia: John Benjamins, 2003), pp. 167–95.

Taylor, Jane, '"Why Do You Tear Me from Myself?" Torture, Truth and the Arts of the Counter-Reformation', in E. van Alphen, M. Bal and C. Smith (eds.), *The Rhetoric of Sincerity* (Stanford, CA: Stanford University Press, 2009), pp. 19–43.

Trigg, Stephanie, 'Speaking with the Dead', in Paul Eggert (ed.), *Editing in Australia* (Canberra: University College ADFA, 1990), pp. 137–49.

Truelove, Alison, 'Commanding Communications: The Fifteenth-Century Letters of the Stonor Women', in Daybell (ed.), *Early Modern Women's Letter Writing*, pp. 42–58.

Vickery, Amanda, 'Golden Age to Separate Spheres? A Review of the Categories and Chronology of English Women's History', *Historical Journal*, 36 (1993): 383–414.

Wakelin, Daniel, *Scribal Correction and Literary Craft: English Manuscripts 1375–1510*, Cambridge Studies in Medieval Literature (Cambridge: Cambridge University Press, 2014).

Walker, Sue, 'The Manners of the Page: Prescription and Practice in the Visual Organisation of Correspondence', *Huntington Library Quarterly*, 66, 3/4, Studies in the Cultural History of Letter Writing (2003): 307–29.

Wall, Alison D., 'Deference and Definance in Women's Letters of the Thynne Family: The Rhetoric of Relationships', in Daybell (ed.), *Women's Letters*, pp. 77–93.

———, 'Elizabethan Precept and Feminine Practice: The Thynne Family of Longleat', *History*, 75 (1990): 23–38.

Wells-Cole, Anthony, *Art and Decoration in Elizabethan and Jacobean England: The Influence of Continental Prints, 1555–1625* (New Haven and London: Yale University Press, 1997).

Whittle, Jane, and Elizabeth Griffiths, *Consumption and Gender in the Early Seventeenth-Century Household: The World of Alice Le Strange* (Oxford: Oxford University Press, 2012).

Whyman, Susan E., *The Pen and the People: English Letter Writers 1660–1800* (Oxford: Oxford University Press, 2009).

———, '"Paper Visits": The Post-Restoration Letter as Seen Through the Verney Family Archive', in Rebecca Erle (ed.), *Epistolary Selves: Letters and Letter-Writers, 1600–1945* (Aldershot: Ashgate, 1999), pp. 15–36.

Wiggins, Alison, 'Digital Editing: The Case of Bess of Hardwick's Letters', in Phillips and Williams (eds.), *Editing Early Modern Texts*, pp. 105–8.

———, 'What Did Renaissance Readers Write in Their Printed Copies of Chaucer?', *The Library*, 9 (2008): 3–36.

———, 'Frances Wolfreston's Chaucer', in Hardman and Lawrence-Mathers (eds.), *Women and Writing*, pp. 77–89.

———, 'Are Auchinleck Manuscript Scribes 1 and 6 the Same Scribe? The Advantages of Whole-Data Analysis and Electronic Texts', *Medium Ævum*, 73 (2004): 10–26.

Selected bibliography 217

Williams, Graham, '"My Evil Favoured Writing": Uglyography, Disease and the Epistolary Networks of George Talbot, Sixth Earl of Shrewsbury', *Huntington Library Quarterly* (forthcoming).

———, *Women's Epistolary Utterance: A Study of the Letters of Joan and Maria Thynne, 1575–1611*, Pragmatics and Beyond New Series 233 (Amsterdam and Philadelphia: John Benjamins, 2013).

———, '"That thought never ytt entered my harte": Rhetoricalities of Sincerity in Early Modern English', *English Studies*, 93, 7 (2012): 809–32.

———, '"Yr Scribe Can Proove No Nessecarye Consiquence for You"?: The Social and Linguistic Implications of Joan Thynne's Using a Scribe in Letters to Her Son, 1607–1611', in Hardman and Lawrence-Mathers (eds.), *Women and Writing*, pp. 131–45.

———, '"I haue trobled wth a tedious discours": Sincerity, Sarcasm and Seriousness in the Letters of Maria Thynne, c. 1601–1610', *Journal of Historical Pragmatics*, 11, 2 (2010): 169–93.

Withington, Phil, and Alexandra Shepard (eds.), *Communities in Early Modern England: Networks, Place, Rhetoric* (Manchester: Manchester University Press, 2000).

Wolfe, Heather, '"Neatly Sealed, with Silk, and Spanish Wax or Otherwise": The Practice of Letter-Locking with Silk Floss in Early Modern England', in S.P. Cerasano and Steven W. May (eds.), *In The Prayse of Writing: Early Modern Manuscript Studies* (London: The British Library, 2012), pp. 169–89.

———, 'Women's Handwriting in Early Modern England', in Laura Knoppers (ed.), *Cambridge Companion to Early Modern Women's Writing* (Cambridge: Cambridge University Press, 2009), pp. 21–39.

Wood, J.L., 'Structures and Expectations: A Systematic Analysis of Margaret Paston's Formulaic and Expressive Language', *Journal of Historical Pragmatics*, 10, 2 (2009): 187–228.

Worsley, Lucy, *Hardwick Old Hall* (London: English Heritage, 1998).

Woudhuysen, H.R., 'The Queen's Own Hand: A Preliminary Account', in Peter Beal and Grace Ioppolo (eds.), *Elizabeth I and the Culture of Writing* (London: British Library, 2007), pp. 1–27.

Wright, Pam, 'A Change in Direction: The Ramifications of Female Household, 1558–1603', in David Starkey (ed.), *The English Court: From the War of the Roses to the Civil War* (New York: Longman, 1987), pp. 147–72.

Wyld, Henry Cecil, *A History of Modern Colloquial English* (Oxford: Blackwell, 1936).

Zemon Davis, Natalie, *The Gift in Sixteenth-Century France* (Oxford: Oxford University Press, 2000).

———, *Fiction in the Archives: Pardon Tales and Their Tellers in Sixteenth-Century France* (Stanford: Polity Press, 1997).

Ziegler, Georgiana, '"More Than Feminine Boldness": The Gift Books of Esther Inglis', in Mary E. Burke, Jane Donawerth, Linda L. Dove and Karen Nelson (eds.), *Women, Writing and the Reproduction of Culture in Tudor and Stuart Britain* (Syracuse: Syracuse University Press, 2000), pp. 24–25.

Unpublished theses

Farber, Elizabeth, 'The Letters of Lady Elizabeth Russell (1540–1609)', PhD thesis, Columbia University (1977).

Harris, Johanna I., 'Lady Brilliana Harley's Letters and the Epistolary Genre in Early Stuart England', PhD thesis, University of Oxford (2008).

218 *Selected bibliography*

Mair, Katherine, 'Anne, Lady Bacon: A Life in Letters', PhD thesis, Queen Mary, University of London (2009).

Marcus, Imogen, 'An Investigation into the Language and Letters of Bess of Hardwick (c. 1527–1608)', PhD thesis, University of Glasgow (2012).

Maxwell, Felicity, 'Household Words: Textualising Social Relations in the Correspondence of Bess of Hardwick's Servants, c. 1550–1590', PhD thesis, University of Glasgow (2014).

Merton, Charlotte, 'The Women Who Served Queen Mary and Queen Elizabeth: Ladies, Gentlewomen and Maids of the Privy Chamber, 1553–1603', PhD thesis, University of Cambridge (1992).

White, Gillian, '"That whyche ys nedefoulle and nesesary": The Nature and Purpose of the Original Furnishing and Decoration of Hardwick Hall, Derbyshire', PhD thesis, 2 vols, University of Warwick (2005).

Index

Account Books 173: Bess and Sir William Cavendish's 98; Bess's attention to 58, 101, 122, 125, 131; examination of Bess's 12, 14, 20, 94–6; payments 23, 143, 162, 172; roles in 144; Scottish Queen's custodianship 154; Sir William St. Loe's 145; Timothy Pusey's role in 133, 136; solicitor Whalley 96–7, 133–4, 147, 155, 159, 166
Alsope, Thomas 145
autograph writing: Bess of Hardwick 30–1, 106–20

Bacon, Lady Anne (Cooke) 22, 29, 83, 104, 147
Baldwin, Thomas 41, 126, 177
Balechouse, John 102
Barlow (Barley), Robert 13, 138
Beal, Philip 143
Bess of Hardwick: autograph writing 30–1, 106–120; biography 13–22; books around her bedchamber 101–6; children of 14; context of letters 2–4; death of 21; husband George Talbot 15–18, 35; husband Robert Barlow (Barley) 13; husband Sir William Cavendish 13–15, 48–9, 98–100, 138, 145; husband Sir William St. Loe 14–15, 100, 138, 145–6; idiolect of 106–20; letter of petition for granddaughter 62–8; letters in curial prose for business and legal matters 54–9; letters of household and estate management to servants 32–9; letters of petition and political friendship 47–54; letters of spousal partnership to

husband (Talbot) 39–47; letter to daughter Mary (Talbot) 80–8; letter to estranged husband (Talbot) during discord 68–80; life and interactions 194–5; life of 11–22; overview of letters 2–4; plain language of 27–61; reputation of 11–22; signature 137–41; understanding of finances 63–4; use of Scribe A 126–31; use of Hardwick Hall secretariat 131–7; use of scribes writing in italic scripts 123–5; use of Sheffield secretariat 125–6
books: Bess's bedchamber 101–6
Boswell (Bosville), Jane (Hardwick) 23
Bradley, E. T. 107
Braumuller, A. R. 3
Brayshay, Mark 143, 159
Bronker, Sir Henry 167
Brooke, Frances (Lady Cobham) 86, 180, 182
Brytten, Elinor 180
Burghley (Lord) *see* Cecil, William (Lord Burghley)
Burlinson, Christopher 135–6
business and legal matters: letters in curial prose 54–9

Caesar, Sir Julius 149
Camden, William 11
Carriers 142, 144–7, 151, 158–9, 183, 193
Cartwright, Mary 92, 93, 130
Cavendish, Charles (son) 14, 18, 71, 83, 85–6, 97, 126, 161–2, 164
Cavendish, Elizabeth (daughter) 14, 17, 50, 59; *see also* Lennox, Elizabeth (Cavendish)

220 Index

Cavendish, Frances (daughter) 14, 87, 103, 187; *see also* Pierrepont, Frances (Cavendish)

Cavendish, Grace (Talbot) 169–72, 191

Cavendish, Henry (son) 14, 83, 156, 167–72, 188

Cavendish, Lucretia (daughter) 14

Cavendish, Mary (daughter) 14, 37, 61, 83, 158; Bess's letter to 80–8; *see also* Talbot, Mary (Cavendish)

Cavendish, Sir William 13–15, 48–9, 98–100, 103, 138, 145, 177, 185

Cavendish, Temperance (daughter) 14, 143

Cavendish, William (son) 14, 17, 18, 21, 71, 86, 92–4, 96–7, 105, 129, 131, 156, 161–3, 166, 168, 170–1, 177

Cavendish arms 100

Cecil, Robert 132, 134, 167

Cecil, Thomas 178

Cecil, William (Lord Burghley) 18, 20, 22, 65–6, 70, 80, 99, 121, 127, 132, 139, 149

Chaworth, George 134

Clifford, George (earl of Cumberland) 148

Cobham, Lady Frances 86, 180, 182; *see also* Brooke, Frances

communications: letters 155–9

composing and scripting letters 4–7; business and legal matters 54–9; epistolary composition and gender dynamics 60–1; household and estate management to servants 32–9; petition and political friendship 47–54; plain language in 27–61; spousal partnership to husband (Talbot) 39–47

Cornwallis, Sir Thomas 129, 161–4

Crompe, James 38, 39, 123, 146, 147

curial prose: business and legal matters 54–9; features of 56

Day, Angel 1–2, 103

Daybell, James 2, 12, 24, 28, 64, 148, 159, 162, 171

Deckenson, William 180

Defoe, Daniel 157

delivery: Carriers 142, 144–7, 151, 158–9, 183, 193; epistolary circulation and 159–60; plot disguising linen sellers 154–5; secret letters 152–3; *see also* sending and receiving letters

Devereux, Robert 150

Digby, Elizabeth 92, 93

Digby, John 130

Dodderidge, John 167

Dudley, Robert (earl of Leicester) 22

Durant, David N. 12–13, 16, 93, 96, 137, 166, 171, 186

Dyckyns 146–7

earl of Leicester: linguistic scripts to 50–4

earl of Shrewsbury *see* Talbot, George (sixth earl of Shrewsbury); Talbot, Gilbert (seventh earl of Shrewsbury)

Elizabeth I (Queen) 12, 14–18, 22, 42, 50, 63, 65, 70, 79–80, 87, 119, 121–2, 125, 134, 140, 152–3, 164, 167, 182, 189

Elizabeth (Princess) 14

enclosures: letters with 173–86

epistolary circulation: delivery dynamics and 159–60

epistolary composition: gender dynamics and 60–1

epistolary literacy 10, 25

epistolary styles: conversational 84–5; feminised 60–1

estate management: letters to servants 32–9

Evans, Mel 109, 122

eye-skip: slip in handwritten texts 45–6

Folger Shakespeare Library 2, 3, 21

formal writing: curial prose in business and legal matters 54–9

Frye, Susan 12

Fulwood, William 103

gender dynamics: letters 60–1

Gerrard, Thomas 132

Gibson, Jonathan 3

Golding, Arthur 101

Grey, Frances 13

Grey, Jane 14, 167

Grey, Susan 131, 150–1

Gunpowder Plot 21

Hacker, John 134

Hammer, Paul 132

handwriting 1, 2, 4, 196; Bess's 14, 106, 108–10, 149; choice of scribe for 121, 123–4, 131; features of 7, 9; of scribe 54, 57, 60; of son Henry 188

Hannam, Christopher 150

Index 221

Hardwick, Bess 13; *see also* Bess of Hardwick
Hardwick, John 13
Hardwick Cross 99–101
Hardwick New Hall 19, 21, 87, 89–90, 93–5, 99, 104–5, 134, 137, 140, 157, 181
Hardwick Old Hall 19, 23, 94, 102, 130
Harrington, Sir John 104
Harrison, Robert 147
Harrison, Roland 133, 136
Hatton, Sir Christopher 177
Hatton, Sir William 95
Herbert, William 180
Hilliard, Nicholas 181
historical narrative 197–8
homoioteleuton: eye-skip 45–6
household management: letters to servants 32–9
Howard, Aletheia (Talbot) 21, 82, 184
Howard, James 184
Howard, Thomas 83
Hunter, Joseph 11

iconography: Bess's signature 137–41
idiolect: Bess 106–20
inventory: Bess's bedchamber 94–7

Jackson, Canon 99
Jenkinson, Sir Henry 97
Johnston, Nathaniel 24

Kitson, Margaret 126, 161, 164
Knightly, Sir Richard 177
Kniveton, Jane (Leach) 36–7, 130–1, 171–2
Knyveton, George 130
Kynnersley, Nicholas 139

Lane, Chancery 74
language 1, 195–7; hierarchical 115–17; political friendship 121–2; scribe's influence in 118–20
Lee, Sir Henry 178
Lennox, Elizabeth (Cavendish) 17, 50, 65, 165–6, 186–7, 191; *see also* Cavendish, Elizabeth (daughter)
letters: accordion-folded 186–93; epistolary styles of 30–2, 35–6, 60–1; gender dynamics 60–1; linguistic scripts and material forms 71–4; materials and methods 22–6; organisation processes 25–6; reading and writing 7–9; scripting

and composing of 4–7; sending and receiving letters 9–11; tools and materials for 97–101
letter writing: definitions 4–11; materials and methods 11–26; research questions for 4–11
Letterwriting in Renaissance England (Stewart and Wolfe) 3
Levey, Santina M. 100
life: Bess of Hardwick 11–22
Life of the Lady Arabella, The (Bradley) 107
Linacre, Marcella 174
linguistics: historical 8–9
literacy: Bess's books showing 101–6
Lodge, Edmund 11, 44–7, 71
Love's Labour's Lost 114

Mack, Peter 103
Magnusson, Lynne 28
Mair, Katy 147, 159
Manners, Edward 150
Manners, Grace 96
Manners, Roger 177
Marchington, William 174
marital correspondence: Bess to husband (earl of Shrewsbury) 39–47; Bess to husband (earl of Shrewsbury) during discord 68–80; deference and respect 71–4; 'good' wife 74–7; linguistic scripts and material forms 71–4; metaphoric language 77–80
marriage: ideal of Odysseus and Penelope 76–7; ideal Renaissance wife 74–7; metaphoric language 77–80
Mary, Queen of Scots 12, 16, 18, 22, 32, 41–2, 45–6, 50, 70, 87, 117, 119, 121–2, 128, 151–4, 175, 181
Metamorphoses (Ovid) 102, 137
metaphoric language 71: marital correspondence 77–80
Mildmay, Sir Walter 177
Montague, James 21

Neale, J. E. 11

Odysseus and Penelope 76–7
Orlando Furioso (Ariosto) 104
Orlin, Lena Cowen 183
Ovid 102, 137

Paget, Lord Thomas 124, 126
Painter, John 102

222   Index

Parry, Blanche 124
PDR (power, distance and ranked extremity) 6, 189
Percy, Mary 87
petition letters: Bess of Hardwick 47–54
Pierrepont, Frances (Cavendish) 87, 183; *see also* Cavendish, Frances (daughter)
politeness 6, 34, 42, 63–6, 171: negative 6, 64–5, 71, 82; positive 6, 52, 63, 66, 82
political friendship: Bess's letters 47–54; language of 121–2
Pollard, A. F. 11
Pollock, Linda 37
postal network 143: delivery 142, 145, 152; sending and receiving letters 142–60
power dynamics 48
punctuation 8–9, 39, 196; Bess's 48, 53, 109–12, 118–19, 123, 126
Pusey, Timothy 60, 93–4, 96–7, 112, 132–6, 147, 166, 171, 185, 196

Queen Elizabeth *see* Elizabeth I (Queen)

Radcliffe, Robert 178
Rawson, Maud Stepney 36, 37, 107
reading and writing letters 7–9; autograph writing and Bess's idiolect 106–20; bedchamber as locus for 89–94; Bess's signature 137–41; books around Bess's bedchamber 101–6; location for 89–106; numeracy, inventories and accounts 94–7; tools and materials for 97–101; writing and idiolect of scribes 120–37
Reason, William 93, 96–7, 133, 136
receiving letters *see* sending and receiving letters

Sadler, Sir Ralph 177
St. Loe, Sir William 14–15, 100, 138, 145–6, 176
Scottish Queen *see* Mary, Queen of Scots
Scribe A 60, 62–4, 67–9, 80, 96, 126–31, 134, 158, 191–2
Scribe B 56, 134–6
Scribe D 55–6, 60, 134–6, 196
scribes 1, 6: Bess's use of 123–5; Bess's use of 'Scribe A' 126–31; Bess's use of Sheffield secretariat 125–6; curial prose in business/legal matters 54–9;

Hardwick Hall secretariat 131–7; influence in drafts 118–20; scribal language 53; writing and idiolect of 120–37
scripting letters *see* composing and scripting letters
sending and receiving letters 9–11; Carriers 142, 144–7, 151, 158–9, 183, 193; communications 155–9; in early postal and delivery networks 142–60; epistolary circulation and delivery 159–60; letters with bearers 161–73; letters with enclosures 173–86; letters with floss and accordion folds 186–93; payments 143–5, 147, 154–5, 162; secret letters 152–3
Sermon Upon the Book of Job (Calvin) 101
servants: letters of household or estate management to 32–9
Seymour, Edward 167
signature: Bess's 137–41
Smyth, Sylvester 97
Smythson, Robert 19, 20
social roles: women's 30, 35, 47, 112, 114–15, 195
Sönmez, Margaret 111, 139
spelling 195–6; Bess's 109–18
Spenser, Edmund 135
Stafford, Lady Dorothy 182
Stanhope, Sir John 134
Steen, Sara Jayne 11, 106–7
Stewart, Alan 2, 144, 159
Stuart, Arbella (granddaughter) 17–19, 27–8, 61, 86, 93–4, 97, 104, 165–6, 176, 182; letter of petition regarding 62–8
Stuart, Charles (first earl of Lennox) 17, 50, 63
Stuart, Elizabeth (Cavendish) 59, 63

Talbot, Anne (Herbert) 191
Talbot, Edward 156, 168–9
Talbot, George (sixth earl of Shrewsbury) 15–18, 52, 100, 138; Bess's letter during marital discord 68–80; Bess's letters of spousal partnership to 39–47
Talbot, Gilbert (seventh earl of Shrewsbury) 18, 42, 75, 83–4, 86, 126, 130, 140, 153, 155–8, 161–6, 173, 178, 180
Talbot, Mary (Cavendish) 37, 61, 127, 140, 158, 178, 183–6, 191; Bess's

letter to daughter 80–8; *see also* Cavendish, Mary (daughter)
Thynne, Sir John 22, 48, 49, 55, 99, 125, 147
Tirrell, Sir Henry 177
transcripts 2, 45–7, 195, 197

visual art: Odysseus and Penelope 76–7

Walpole, Horace 11
Walsingham, Sir Francis 21, 116, 121, 127; letter of petition to 62–8
Whalley, Edward 96–7, 133–4, 147, 155, 159, 166
Whitfield, Francis 32–5, 38, 147

Williams, Ethel Carleton 11, 36, 37, 45
Williams, Graham 109
Willoughby, Henry 149, 151
Wingfield, Anthony 178
Wingfield, Elizabeth (Leach) 16, 88, 178–9, 181–2
Wingfield, Sir John 150
Wingfield household 139–40
Wolfe, Heather 3
Wolly, Hannah 128
Women Letter-Writers in Tudor England (Daybell) 2
Woudhuysen, H. R. 109
writing *see* reading and writing letters

Zurcher, Andrew 135–6